PLURALITY AND QUANTIFICATION

Studies in Linguistics and Philosophy

Volume 69

Managing Editors

GENNARO CHIERCHIA, *University of Milan*
PAULINE JACOBSON, *Brown University*
FRANCIS J. PELLETIER, *University of Alberta*

Editorial Board

JOHAN VAN BENTHEM, *University of Amsterdam*
GREGORY N. CARLSON, *University of Rochester*
DAVID DOWTY, *Ohio State University, Columbus*
GERALD GAZDAR, *University of Sussex, Brighton*
IRENE HEIM, *M.I.T., Cambridge*
EWAN KLEIN, *University of Edinburgh*
BILL LADUSAW, *University of California at Santa Cruz*
TERRENCE PARSONS, *University of California, Irvine*

The titles published in this series are listed at the end of this volume.

PLURALITY AND QUANTIFICATION

edited by

FRITZ HAMM and ERHARD HINRICHS
University of Tübingen, Germany

KLUWER ACADEMIC PUBLISHERS
DORDRECHT / BOSTON / LONDON

A C.I.P. Catalogue record for this book is available from the Library of Congress.

ISBN 0-7923-4841-9

Published by Kluwer Academic Publishers,
P.O. Box 17, 3300 AA Dordrecht, The Netherlands.

Sold and distributed in the U.S.A. and Canada
by Kluwer Academic Publishers,
101 Philip Drive, Norwell, MA 02061, U.S.A.

In all other countries, sold and distributed
by Kluwer Academic Publishers,
P.O. Box 322, 3300 AH Dordrecht, The Netherlands.

Printed on acid-free paper

All Rights Reserved
© 1998 Kluwer Academic Publishers
No part of the material protected by this copyright notice may be reproduced or
utilized in any form or by any means, electronic or mechanical,
including photocopying, recording or by any information storage and
retrieval system, without written permission from the copyright owner

Printed in the Netherlands.

TABLE OF CONTENTS

Introduction	1
Godehard Link / Ten Years of Research on Plurals — Where Do We Stand?	19
Kurt Eberle / The Influence of Plural NPs on Aktionsart in DRT	55
Chris Fox / Mass Terms and Plurals in Property Theory	113
Frans Zwarts / Three Types of Polarity	177
Jaap van der Does / Sums and Quantifiers	239
Henk Verkuyl / Some Issues in the Analysis of Multiple Quantification with Plural NPs	283
Christine Michaux / Reducing the Coordination of Determiners: Some Principles	321
João Peres / Issues on Distributive and Collective Readings	339
Index of Subjects	367
Index of Names	379

FRITZ HAMM/ERHARD HINRICHS

INTRODUCTION

The papers in this volume address central issues in the study of Plurality and Quantification from three different perspectives:

- Algebraic approaches to Plurals and Quantification
- Distributivity and Collectivity: Theoretical Foundations
- Distributivity and Collectivity: Empirical Investigations

Algebraic approaches to the semantics of natural languages were independently introduced for the study of generalized quantification, predication, intensionality, mass terms and plurality. The most prominent modern advocate for an algebraic theory of plurality (and mass terms) is certainly Godehard Link. It is indicative of the *Wirkungsgeschichte* of Link's work that most of the contributions in this volume take the logic of plurals proposed by Godehard Link (Link 1983, 1987) as their foundation or, at the very least, as their point of reference. Link's own paper in this volume provides a concise summary of many of the central research issues that have engaged semanticists during the last decade. Link's paper also contains an extensive bibliography that provides an excellent resource for scholars interested in the semantics of plurals.

Since we can refer readers to Link's paper for an excellent survey of the subject matter of this book, we will limit our attention in this introduction to summarizing the individual contributions in this volume. The book is organized into three main sections; within each section the papers are ordered alphabetically. However, as in much of linguistic theorizing, there is an exception: for reasons pointed out above, Godehard Link's article appears as Chapter 1.

1. ALGEBRAIC APPROACHES TO PLURALS AND QUANTIFICATION

Godehard Link's contribution "Ten Years of Research on Plurals – Where Do We Stand" surveys recent research in the semantics of plurals and goes on to consider three specific questions that have arisen in algebraic approaches to plurality: (i) should groups be included in the ontology for the semantics of noun phrases, (ii) how is the distinction between collectivity and distributivity to be characterized, and (iii) where does this distinction originate – in the semantics of verbal predicates, in the semantics of generalized quantifiers or is it due to the interaction between these two classes of expressions?

The first part of Link's paper gives a short overview of some recent research activities in plural semantics: *typological* studies of distributivity markers which correspond roughly to English *each* or German *je*, the *general* program of an algebraic semantics for natural languages, and Lønning's (1989) work on the metatheory of a *plural logic*. Link's comments on the relationship of *plural theory* to the most prominent approach to anaphora resolution, viz. discourse representation theory, are rooted in the empirical phenomenon of *plural anaphora*. His discussion of how to structure a *formal ontology* of plural terms focuses on the *denotational view* of definite terms like *the men*. Link rejects Barry Schein's (1993) argument that such a view leads to paradox and argues for a *mereological* theory of plural denotations. The first part of his paper concludes with some brief remarks on *AI–related* research on plurals.

The next section examines Landman's (1989) semantic arguments for introducing so–called *groups* into the ontology. The intuitive motivation for assuming the existence of groups, in addition to individual sums (i–sums) and ordinary individuals, derives from examples such as (1)

(1) The boys and the girls had to sleep in different dorms, met in the morning at breakfast, and were then wearing their blue uniforms.

The NP *The boys and the girls* seems at the same time to be interpreted as a uniform i–sum (when considered as argument of *meet*), distribute down to the level of individuals (when considered as argument of *wearing*), and denote something in between these two levels (when considered as argument of *sleep in different dorms*). In order to account for this intermediate–level reading Landman assumes the existence of groups. But he doesn't stop here. Given a domain of discourse M, Landman constructs a cumulative hierarchy of groups over this domain. Link agrees with Landman that the intermediate readings have to be taken seriously[1]; nevertheless he criticizes Landman's approach for two reasons. The first is that the cumulative hierarchy of groups is much too general. Convincing empirical arguments have only been given for *one* intermediate level. The second reason is based on Schwarzschild's (1991) argument against groups. According to this argument, natural language predicates do not differentiate between levels. Schwarzschild suggests instead that it is important to consider the way in which the operative subsums (Schwarzschild's term) are referred to by the NPs in question.

Which sums are, in fact, operative is determined by many factors, including intonation and cross–sentential deixis. Link therefore concludes that Landman's theory of groups is a case of over–representation.

The last section of Godehard Link's contribution is devoted to the topic of *distributivity*. Link introduces Lønning's *standard proposal*, which says that sentences such as (2) have two readings depending on whether the subject NP is interpreted distributively or collectively.[2]

(2) Four men lifted three tables.

Link discusses two arguments which have been leveled against the standard proposal. The first argument says that this approach fails to account for the full range of truth–conditionally relevant readings. This type of criticism is typically based on the by now classical example of Gillon (1987).

(3) Hammerstein, Rodgers and Hart wrote musicals.

Since none of the three composers wrote a musical all by himself, the sentence cannot be read distributively. Furthermore, there is no musical all three wrote together, which shows that the sentence cannot be interpreted collectively. Hence, a third reading seems to be required. Link, however, claims that predicates such as *musical writing* can be true of single individuals as long as they show significant involvement in the composition of a piece, even though no single individual may be the sole author. Regardless of such empirical arguments, Link demonstrates that the algebraic theory of plurals is, in any case, flexible enough to account for the *mixed* reading as well. Link shows that this can be achieved if one incorporates in the algebraic theory "type shifting" operators as suggested by van der Does (1992).[3] Under this strategy the collective and the distributive readings of sentences like (2) turn out to be limiting cases of the mixed reading.

If the distributive and the collective readings are just limiting cases of a third reading, then there should be no ambiguity at all.[4] This observation provides the basis for the second argument against the standard proposal: since the standard approach posits an ambiguity, it fails to capture the generalization inherent in the putative single interpretation. (The argument from a missed generalization). Link rejects this argument as well. For him the empirical boundary between the distributive and the non–distributive domain does give rise to a genuine ambiguity, while the distinction between mixed readings and strictly collective readings is a matter of indeterminacy and not of ambiguity.

The last topic Link discusses concerns the related question of where the distributive/collective distinction originates, in the semantics of noun phrase or of the verb phrase. Link opts for the verb phrase – a position which van der Does (1992)[5] explicitly rejects. Link defends his position by showing that non–monotone increasing determiners, which were shown to be problematic for the VP–strategy by van der Does, can nevertheless be handled by this strategy if additional scope and cardinality requirements are included.

Kurt Eberle's contribution "The Influence of Plural NPs on Aktionsart in DRT" studies characteristic differences among (bare) plural NPs in the way they contribute to the compositional semantics of Aktionsart. It is commonly assumed (cf. Verkuyl (1972) and Dowty (1979) for detailed discussion) that bare plural NPs, when used as arguments of event predicates, lead to an activity reading of the sentence in the terminology of Vendler (1967). However, citing examples from German such as (4) and (5), Eberle notes that the Aktionsarten effect of bare plural NPs is far from uniform.

(4) Beim Stürmer–Training drosch Völler Bälle aufs Tor.
     (At the forward training, Völler kicked balls into the goal)

(5) Sportler brachten die olympische Fackel nach Barcelona.
     (Sportsmen took the olympic torch to Barcelona)

As can easily be verified by applying standard tests for distinguishing the Vendler classes of *activities* from *accomplishments*, events described by sentences such as (4) are *temporally homogeneous*, while events described by sentences such as (5) are *temporally heterogeneous*. Eberle attributes this difference of Aktionart to differences in the availability of distributive readings for plural NPs for a given event description. For event descriptions such as (5), the property of being shot on goal by Völler (temporally) distributes over the members denoted by the plural NP *Bälle*, while such a distributive reading is dispreferred or unavailable for the plural NPs in examples such as (4).

Eberle accounts for the impact of plural NPs on the Aktionsart of a given sentence by significantly modifying and extending the event semantics proposed by Krifka (1987). Eberle formalizes his event semantics in the framework of Discourse Representation Theory (DRT) (Kamp 1981), (Kamp/Reyle (1993)) which is suitably extended to be able to account for plural NPs and Aktionsarten properties of event descriptions. Aktionsarten differences are attributed to the mutually exclusive properties of *temporal discourse–homogeneity* and *temporal discourse–*

heterogeneity. Temporal homogeneity applies to predicates that denote non–punctual, divisible and cumulative events or to predicates that denote iterative events.

Eberle shows that bare plural NPs as arguments of an event predicate describe temporally homogeneous events, only if the bare plural can be interpreted distributively with respect to the event in question. Eberle provides a DRS construction algorithm that compositionally derives the Aktionsarten properties of complex event descriptions. The construction algorithm covers distributive, collective, and cumulative readings of bare plurals and is illustrated by step–by–step derivations of relevant linguistic examples.

The paper "Mass Terms and Plurals in Property Theory" contributed by **Chris Fox** is concerned with three related phenomena.

- The *judge–cleaner*-problem: Why is it that *the judge* and *the cleaner* may well be one and the same person, but have different incomes?

- The *part–whole*-problem: Why can we say that *the dirty water is liquid* and infer that parts of the dirty water are liquid, without inferring that the dirt is liquid?

- The problem of *non–denoting definites*: How can we assign two different semantic values to the definite descriptions *the present king of France* and *the largest prime number* within a classical two–valued theory?

In order to account for the *judge–cleaner*-problem, Landman (1989) introduces a new set of individuals 'individuals under guises or roles' which are made explicit in sentences of the following kind:

(6) a. John, as a judge, earns 20000 £.
    b. John, as a cleaner, earns 2000 £.

Landman's solution to the above problem, therefore, is that the definite description in a sentence like the *The judge earns 20000 £* does not refer to an ordinary individual, but to an intensional individual, an individual in the role of judge, who is different from the individual in the cleaner's role in *The cleaner earns 2000 £*, even if the two individuals in question are the same ordinary individual.

Chris Fox argues for a different approach. Roughly speaking, Fox claims that *roles* are not modifications of individuals, but modifications of predications. This strategy gives rise to modified properties like *earns 20000 £-as-a-judge* or *earns 2000 £-as-a-cleaner* instead of modified individuals such as *John, as a judge* etc. The major advantage of this approach is that only one plural domain is required for the simple reason that the class of individuals is not divided into two parts. Moreover, Fox develops a *general axiomatic* theory of property modification which accounts for the *part–whole*-problem, as well, by providing a method by which to control the distribution of properties to only those parts which are relevant.

While the notion of property modification forms the basis of his analysis to the first two phenomena, Fox does not invoke this idea in his solution to the third issue discussed in the paper. Instead, he pursues a fairly standard solution to the problem of *non–denoting definites* and attributes such cases to the failure of existential presupposition. What is interesting is that his solution is a generalization of Peter Aczel's analysis of Russell's paradox in his paper Frege structures (1980). Consider the class $r = \{x; x \notin x\}$ and the function $f(x) = x \in x$. If one could show that f yields a *proposition* for every value of x and therefore also of r, it would be possible to derive Russell's paradox in the Frege structures. But the predication schema of these structures does not allow such a strong conclusion. It only says that $f(x)$ is a proposition if x is a set. Therefore r cannot be a set because assuming r to be a set leads to a contradiction. The hypothesis that r is a set is analyzed as a kind of category mistake from this perspective.

Fox generalizes this idea by introducing the notion of *denotables*. For example, *The* in *The present king of France* will only yield a denotable if the property to which it applies is not empty. The standard problem with two semantically distinct non–denoting terms arises from the fact that theories of plurals and mass terms often adopt a Boolean Algebra to model part–whole structures. The natural denotation of non–denoting definites is assumed to be the bottom element of the algebra. It follows from the fact that this element is unique that any two non–denoting terms are semantically equated. In his paper, Fox is able to assume that the domain of denotables forms a Boolean Algebra without generalizing this assumption to the domain of non–denotables, and thus avoids the above problem.

Fox adopts an axiomatic approach. The use of this methodological strategy distinguishes his paper from all the others in this volume. Inferences are controlled axiomatically. For example, the axioms allow *Every man dies* to be derived from *The men die* under the assumption that some men exist. The mereological distribution of properties (the *part–whole*-problem) is handled by this method as well.

In an appendix, Fox constructs a model based on Aczel's Frege structures, but enriched with a mereology for his theory, and thereby shows that it is consistent. However, this model should not be understood as the intended model of the theory, but rather as a mere technical device to demonstrate consistency.

Frans Zwarts' paper "Three Types of Polarity" takes as a starting point the Ladusaw–Fauconnier Generalization, which says that the occurrence of negative polarity items like *any* or *ever* are licensed within the argument of a decreasing function, but not within the argument of an increasing function (see e.g. Keenan/Westerståhl (1997)). Zwarts argues that a detailed investigation of the licensing conditions of negative polarity items calls for significant refinements of the Ladusaw–Fauconnier Generalization. He provides evidence from Dutch, German and English which shows that there are at least three types of negative polarity items along with different licensing conditions. For example, the Dutch negative polarity item *er een vinger naar uitsteken (lift a finger)* is licensed by *Niemand (No one)* but not by *Wenigen (Few)*.

(7) a. Niemand heeft er een vinger naar uitgestoken.
        No one   has   it a   finger to stretch out.

    No one lifted a finger

  b. *Wenigen zullen er een vingar naar uitsteken.
        Few   will   it a   finger to stretch out.

    Few people will lift a finger.

The basic idea is that certain polarity items require "stronger" forms of negation than others. The strength of a negation is measured in the following way: Consider first the classical DeMorgan equivalences.

$$\neg(\phi \vee \psi) \leftrightarrow \neg\phi \wedge \neg\psi.$$
$$\neg(\phi \wedge \psi) \leftrightarrow \neg\phi \vee \neg\psi.$$

These laws are valid for the sentential prefix *It is not the case that* or the adverb *not*, but not necessarily for other forms of negation. The conditional in (8-a) is valid, but the one in (8-b) is not.

(8) a. Few trees will blossom or will die $\rightarrow$
        Few trees will blossom and few trees will die
  b. Few trees will blossom and few trees will die $\rightarrow$
        Few trees will blossom or will die

Given that the phrase *Few trees* is considered a negative expression, these and other examples given by Zwarts show that this phrase is governed by only half of the DeMorgan laws. Frans Zwarts therefore considers it a weaker form of negation than *It is not the case that*.

This idea of "measuring" the strength of negation via partial satisfaction of the DeMorgan equivalences leads to three types of negative contexts, which Zwarts calls *subminimal*, *minimal* and *classical*. These three types of negative expressions constitute the licensing contexts for *weak* (example: hoeven (need)), *strong* (e.g. *ook maar iets* (anything (at all))) and *superstrong* (e.g. *mals* (tender)) negative polarity items. This then allows Frans Zwarts to state the following three laws of negative polarity:

Laws of negative polarity

a. Only sentences in which an expression of subminimal negation occurs can contain a negative polarity item of the weak type.
b. Only sentences in which an expression of minimal negation occurs can contain a negative polarity item of the strong type.
c. Only sentences in which an expression of classical negation occurs can contain a negative polarity item of the superstrong type.

Zwarts provides algebraic characterizations of the three different types of negation. For instance, it turns out that *minimal* negation is characterized by *anti–additive* functions. Finally, the laws of negative polarity stated above are expressed in terms of an algebraic description of the hierarchy of negative expressions.

2. DISTRIBUTIVITY AND COLLECTIVITY: THEORETICAL FOUNDATIONS

Jaap van der Does' paper "Sums and Quantifiers" is mainly concerned with the question of how to combine the sum theory of collections with the standard theory of quantification. He starts by investigating the treatment of numerals proposed by Scha and Link. Using Scha's proposal the NP generates the different readings and therefore van der Does calls this strategy the "NP–strategy". Link, on the other hand, assumes that the readings are generated within the VP by means of modification. His strategy is accordingly dubbed the "VP–strategy".

Van der Does assumes that numerals obtain their usual denotation in type $((et)((et)t))$; hence, the following relations between sets.

(9) $\mathbf{n} := \lambda X \lambda Y. |X \cap Y| = n$

INTRODUCTION

He then considers "lifts" of these numerals by transforming them into determiners of type $((et)(((et)t)t))$, i.e. relations between sets and sets of sets. (10) shows the lifted type for the distributive interpretation of the numeral **n**:

(10) $\quad \mathbf{n} := \lambda X \lambda \mathbf{Y}.|\{d \in X : \mathbf{Y}(\{d\})\}| = n$

Here **Y** is a variable of type $((et)t)$. Van der Does also derives collective and neutral lifts and therefore arrives at nine readings for sentences with the structure $[_S[_{NP}Num\ N][_{VP}V[_{NP}Num\ N]]]$. However, in Section 6, he shows that some of these readings cannot be motivated on empirical grounds.

Van der Does also investigates Link's VP–strategy by studying various forms of verb modifiers. The following one, for instance, operates on two–place relations between sets and makes them distributive in the first argument, while leaving the second one unaffected:

(11) $\quad \delta \bullet := \lambda \mathbf{R} \lambda X \lambda Y. \forall x \in X \mathbf{R}(\{x\})(Y)$

Section 4 generalizes the strategy described above in order to give a semantics for arbitrary plural noun phrases. Van der Does does this by seeking systematic and empirically correct ways to relate determiners of type $((et)((et)t))$ to their readings in type $((et)(((et)t)t))$. In Section 4.2, he illustrates this method and shows that it allows for adequate formal descriptions of subtle empirical observations.

Section 5 provides at least a partial answer to a question posed by Godehard Link: "Where exactly does the line of demarcation run between proper readings and mere models realizing a reading?" To answer this question, van der Does introduces the notion of "relative strength" of determiners. Determiner strength is invoked to determine which readings stand in a subsumption relation and can hence be used to reduce ambiguity. Van der Does cites formal results from his Ph.D. thesis (van der Does 1992) which prove that for arbitrary determiners a weakest reading can always be found.

Section 5.2 studies the quantificational force of the lifted determiners. The major result here is that Scha's distributive reading of numerals does generalize to arbitrary determiners, whereas Link's treatment[6] does not. The crucial cases, which show that the NP–strategy is superior to the VP–strategy, are those cases with non–monotone increasing determiners.

The last section is concerned with neutral readings and matters of scope. Van der Does starts this section by considering a problem with neutral reading in sentence (12).

(12) Four men lifted two tables.

Neutral readings occur in situations where the precise number of men lifting tables is important. If the subject has wide scope in example (12), then eight tables at most could be involved in lifting actions. But, unfortunately, the neutral reading, which is equivalent to

(13) $\exists X \subseteq [\![four\ men]\!]\ \exists YcvX\ :\ \mathbf{Y} = [\![lifts\ two\ tables]\!] \cap \wp([\![man]\!])$. $\exists YcvX$ means that there is a $\mathbf{Y}$, which covers X, i.e. $\bigcup \mathbf{Y} = X$.

allows for many more than just eight tables. The number of tables could be anywhere between two and thirty two. This is intuitively incorrect.

Van der Does proposes to solve this problem by considering only covers (denoted by cover*), which satisfy a certain cardinality restriction.

(14) If $\mathbf{Y}$ covers* X, then $|\mathbf{Y}| \leq |X|$

He discusses three such covers, which can be ordered as follows:

(15) partitions $\subseteq$ minimal covers $\subseteq$ pseudo–partitions

Partitions satisfy the strongest restrictions, pseudo–partitions the weakest. Although these restricted covers solve the above mentioned problem, it turns out that partitions and minimal covers are empirically too strict. Pseudo–partitions come close to what is required, but are not satisfactory, either.

Van der Does concludes that the NP of an intransitive sentence and the NP of a transitive sentence with narrow scope may have a neutral reading, but the NP of a transitive sentence which has wide scope may not. The NPs in a transitive sentence can only be neutral if they are scopally independent of each other. This yields the cumulative reading. Disregarding scope, van der Does arrives at the conclusion that three readings have to be distinguished for sentences like (12): roughly, a distributive, a collective and a cumulative one.

Henk Verkuyl's paper "Some Issues in the Analysis of Multiple Quantification with Plural NPs" considers similar issues. Verkuyl addresses three related problems posed by familiar examples such as (16).

(16) Four boys lifted three tables.

The first problem concerns the number of readings that have to be assigned to (16). The answers to this question in the relevant literature range from one to nine (see van der Does, this volume). The second problem that Verkuyl considers is intimately tied to the first: Do plural NPs such as *four boys* and *three tables* give rise to quantifier scope ambiguities? A positive answer to this question would double the number of readings assigned to (16). The last problem concerns cumulative readings for examples such as (16). For such readings Verkuyl focuses on the question whether plural NPs are scopally dependent on one another.

Section 2 of the paper introduces the relationship between sentence aspect and the interpretation of plural NPs. Verkuyl shows that bare plurals and definite plural NPs give rise to two interpretations. They differ as to the cardinality requirements that have to be satisfied with respect to the denotation of the noun and play a crucial role in distinguishing terminative from durative aspect in Verkuyl's terminology. Verkuyl claims that the different cardinality requirements that can be imposed by bare plurals and definite plural also obviate the need for having to distinguish between scopal ambiguities. Whether or not the cardinality requirements in question can be expressed in terms of a single reading is the central topic of the remainder of Verkuyl's paper.

Verkuyl/van der Does' (1991) *one reading hypothesis* is developed in Section 3. The intuitive idea is that sentences like (16) under–inform language users. The interpretation of the subject NP *Four boys*, for instance, varies on a scale from completely collective to completely distributive under this hypothesis. Technically, this is achieved via the notion of partition. The interpretation of (16) under the *one reading hypothesis* basically says[7] that there is a partition of the set of four boys and a partition of the set of three tables such that the "cells" of the respective partitions are elements of the lift–relation.

Verkuyl further shows that the single interpretation assigned under the Verkuyl/van der Does' *one reading hypothesis* to sentences such as (17) is general enough to instantiate the two readings standardly distinguished under a quantifier scoping analysis.

(17)   A medal went to four winners.

Section 4 discusses problems posed by the *one reading hypothesis*. Like van der Does (in this volume), Verkuyl studies various notions of cover, which ranging from no constraint at all to partitions. At the end of this section, Verkuyl agrees with van der Does [8] that three readings (without scope) have to be distinguished for sentences like (16): a distributive, collective and cumulative reading, where scopal dependencies are completely neutralized in the last case.

Section 5 introduces Verkuyl's (1987, 1988) asymmetric approach to multiple quantification, which is motivated by the theory of aspect. He defines a function π, which roughly says that an individual x is at a spatial coordinate p at an index i. This function fixes the way in which individuals (more precisely, members of the external argument) are involved in the respective predication. In Section 6, only two such functions are allowed: the constant function π_c and the injective function π_i. The constant function is used to model some version of Scha's cumulative reading, while the injective function is used to model the distributive interpretation. However, Verkuyl claims that these participancy functions (Verkuyl's term) are much more general tools [9] than the traditional concepts. Verkuyl shows this by clarifying the problems with the *one reading hypothesis*, explained in Section 4, using the illustrated tools and further demonstrates how to integrate the findings of Section 2 into this more general approach.

Section 7 concentrates on the question of whether different notions of *cover* are involved in temporal vs. temporal interpretations. Verkuyl concludes that the constraints on covers not only depend on temporal vs atemporal interpretation but also on other factors like focus etc.

In his last section, Verkuyl reconsiders the question of how many readings must be assigned to (16)? The most severe problem for the *one reading hypothesis* is posed by Scha's cumulative reading, which simply cannot be accounted for under this hypothesis. Verkuyl, however, argues that the very notion of cumulativity is an artificial one, a concept proposed on top of the established notions of distributivity and collectivity. He suggests instead that these notions should apply only on the lexical level. Verkuyl further argues that the participancy functions π_i and π_c may well provide a more adequate understanding of the structural phenomena traditionally covered by the concepts of distributivity, collectivity, and cumulativity.

3. DISTRIBUTIVITY AND COLLECTIVITY: EMPIRICAL INVESTIGATIONS

Christine Michaux's paper "Reducing the Coordination of Determiners: Some Principles" offers an empirical study of conjoined noun phrases in French. Michaux applies a conjunction reduction test to noun phrases conjoined by *et* and *ou* and studies whether the reduction preserves grammaticality and/or semantic interpretation. The relevance of Michaux's study for the topic of this volumes lies in the behavior of collective nouns with respect to the conjunction reduction test. Michaux shows that collective determiners such as *un flopée de* ('a bunch of') and *un tas de* ('a bunch of') preserve semantic interpretation under the reduction test.

(18) une flopée de gosses affamés et une flopée de femmes
(A bunch of famished kids and a bunch of women)
→
une flopée de gosses affamés et de femmes
(A bunch of famished kids and women)

(19) un tas de Belges et un tas de Français
(A bunch of Belgians and a bunch of French)
→
un tas de Belges et de Français
(A bunch of Belgians and French)

By contrast, true collective nouns such as *assemblée* ('assembly') and *tas* ('heap') as well as collectives of measure such as *gorgée* ('sip') change semantic interpretation under the reduction test, as the examples in (20) – (22) show.

(20) une assemblée de fonctionnaires et une assemblée de légionnaires
(An assembly of officials and an assembly of members of the foreign legion)
→
une assemblée de fonctionnaires et de légionnaires
(An assembly of officials and members of the foreign legion)

(21) un tas de feuilles et un tas de sable
(A heap of leaves and a heap of sand)
→
un tas de feuilles et de sable
(A heap of leaves and sand)

(22) une gorgée d'eau et une gorgée de vin
(A sip of water and a sip of wine)
→
une gorgée d'eau et de vin
(A sip of water and wine)[10]

When conjunction reduction does lead to a change in semantic interpretation, Michaux identifies two distinct cases:

a. while the unreduced NP refers to two distinct entities, the reduced NP refers to a single combined entity that is the sum total of the distinct entities denoted by the unreduced NP. This case is exemplfied by (20) – (22).

b. while the unreduced NP refers to two distinct entities with distinct properties, the reduced NP refers to a single entity that has both properties of the referred to by conjuncts in the unreduced NP. This case is exemplified by (23).

(23)   des écrivains et des philosophes
       (Writers and philosophers)
       →
       des écrivains et philosophes
       (Writers who are also philosophers)

Apart from NPs conjoined by *et*, Michaux also considers NPs conjoined by *ou* and points out that there is no difference in semantic interpretation for true collectives when they are conjoined by *ou*, as exemplified in (24).

(24)   un tas de feuilles ou un tas de sable
       (A heap of leaves or a heap of sand)
       →
       un tas de feuilles ou de sable
       (A heap of leaves or sand)

While Michaux does not offer a theoretical explanation for the empirical differences among collectives with respect to the conjunction reduction test, her paper provides an important data collection and a set of descriptive generalizations that any adequate theory of collective nouns in French has to be able to account for.

João Peres' contribution "Issues on Distributive and Collective Readings" raises important empirical issues for the semantic interpretation of plural NPs and plural quantification that arise in the context of algebraic approaches to the semantics of plurals. Drawing on data from English and Portugese and using the logic of plurals LP of Link (1987) as the theoretical point of reference, Peres poses three related questions. The first question concerns the nature of what Link (1987) has dubbed *genuine plural quantification.*

(25)   All competing companies have common interests.

According to Link, an adequate treatment of the semantics of sentences such as (25) requires quantification over plural individuals, i.e. over i–sums. Genuine plural quantification, thus, differs from ordinary distributive and collective readings, exemplified by (26) and (27), respectively.

(26) Some students are falling asleep.

(27) Some students gathered for the party.

For Link (1987) collective readings involve reference to the suprema of the join semilattices denoted by plural nouns, e.g. [[*students*]], while strongly distributive readings involve quantification over sets of atomic individuals in such semilattices. Since the individuals in the denotation of plural nouns form a join semilattice in Link's analysis, Peres entertains the hypothesis that the set of i–sums that are quantified over in cases of genuine plural quantification exhibit such a lattice structure as well. However, according to Peres, this hypothesis is not borne out by examples such as (25); the i–sums that are quantified over need not be closed under the sum–operation with respect to the denotation of the VP *have common interests*.

The second issue that Peres addresses concerns the range of possible readings for so–called *hydras*, i.e. relative clauses with multiple (conjoined) heads, as in (28).

(28) Some of the teams and some of the commissions that had met in secret joined in underground activities after the coup d'etat.

In theory hydra sentence of the form *NP1 and NP2 VP* give rise to a wide range of distributive and collective readings for the conjoined NP and the VP. For example, the set of possible readings for the complex NP in (28) should include a distributive reading such that individual teams and commissions met separately. In addition there seem to be at least two collective readings with the teams and the commissions meeting either as a single group or as two separate groups each consisting of all and only the teams and all and only the commissions. Likewise the property denoted by the VP could either have a distributive reading with teams and commissions acting separately or a collective reading with teams and commissions joining forces. Peres claims that the set of readings that native speakers actually find acceptable among the range of theoretically possible readings is severely constrained by extra–grammatical processing constraints.

The third issue concerns the factors that determine whether an NP receives a distributive reading, a collective reading, or both. Peres adopts the view that the choice of readings is determined by the reference property of the determiner that is contained in the NP in question and by the reference properties that a given predicate has with respect to the argument position that the NP occupies.

The eight papers collected in this volume address three central issues in the study of plurality and quantification in natural languages. The first major theme regards algebraic approaches to plurals and quantification that have emerged as the leading paradigm for the study of these empirical phenomena over the last decade. The second main issue concerns the philosophical and mathematical foundations of concepts such as *distributivity* and *collectivity*. Finally, the authors address a broad range of empirical phenomena in Germanic and Romance languages, including the influence of Aktionsart on plural noun phrases, negative polarity, mass terms, plural quantification, and noun phrase conjunction.

Many of the papers shed new light on the question of how many readings have to be assigned to plural sentences and on the respective consequences for the architecture of the syntax–semantic interface.

NOTES

[1] Moreover Link gives convincing examples from German for the existence of intermediate level readings.

[2] Many papers in the present volume address this problem.

[3] See also van der Does' paper in this volume.

[4] For more explicit argumentation for this position see Verkuyl's paper in this volume.

[5] See also van der Does this volume.

[6] For this point see also Link's paper in this volume.

[7] For a precise statement see Verkuyl's paper.

[8] Van der Does shows that *the one reading hypothesis* makes sentences too adaptive to the situations they describe.

[9] See Verkuyl's paper for a more adequate explanation of the role of these functions.

[10] We owe it to our Swabian colleagues to point out that for certain varieties of German the concept of mixed water and wine has been lexicalized in the compound *Weinschorle*.

ACKNOWLEDGEMENTS

We would like to thank the SLAP series editors, in particular Francis Jeffrey Pelletier, for their advice and the referees for their thorough reviews of the papers contained in this volume. For technical assistance we thank Hans–Peter Kolb, Wolfgang Sternefeld, and especially Stephanie Schwarz who proof–read the entire volume. Our special thanks go to John Griffith whose technical wizardry and tireless effort made all the difference in compiling the name and subject index. Any remaining typos and formatting errors are, of course, our responsibility.

REFERENCES

Aczel, P. (1980): 'Frege structures and the notions of proposition, truth and set'. In Barwise, Keisler, and Kunen (eds.) *The Kleene Symposium*, North Holland Studies in Logic, pages 31 – 59. North Holland.

Dowty, D. (1979): *Word Meaning and Montague Grammar*. Reidel, Dordrecht.

Does, J. van der (1992): *Applied Quantifier Logics: Collectives, Naked Infinitives*. PH.D. dissertation, University of Amsterdam, Amsterdam.

Gillon, B. (1987): 'The Readings of Plural Noun Phrases in English'. *Linguistics and Philosophy* 10, 199 – 219.

Kamp, H. (1981): 'A theory of truth and semantic representation'. In Groenendijk, J. et al. (eds), *Formal Methods in the Study of Language*, Mathematical Centre Tract, Amsterdam.

Kamp, H./Reyle, U. (1993): *From Discourse to Logic*. Kluwer, Dordrecht.

Keenan, E./Westerståhl, D. (1997): 'Generalized Quantifiers in Linguistics and Logic'. In van Benthem, J./ter Meulen, A. (eds.) *Handbook of Logic and Language*, 845 – 847. Elsevier Science Publishers, Amsterdam.

Krifka, M. (1987): *Nominalreferenz und Zeitkonstitution: Zur Semantik von Massentermen, Pluraltermen und Aspektklassen*. Ph.D dissertation, University of Munich. Published by Wilhelm Fink, Munich, 1989.

Landman, F. (1989): 'Groups', Parts I and II. *Linguistics and Philosophy*, 12 559 – 605, 723 – 744.

Link, G. (1983): 'Generalized Quantifiers and Plurals'. In Gärdenfors, P. (ed.), *Generalized Quantifiers. Linguistic and Logical Approaches*, Reidel. Dordrecht.

Link, G. (1987): 'The Logical Analysis of Plural and Mass Terms: a Lattice-theoretical Approach'. In Bäuerle, R., Schwarze, C., von Stechow, A. (eds.) *Meaning, Use, and Interpretation of Language*. Berlin.

Link, G. (1991): 'Plural'. In Wunderlich, D., von Stechow, A. (eds.) *Semantics. An International Handbook of Contemporary Research*. Berlin and New York.

Lønning, J. (1989): *Some Aspects of the Logic of Plural Noun Phrases*. COSMOS–Report 11, Department of Mathematics, University of Oslo.

Scha, R. (1981): 'Distributive, Collective and Cumulative Quantification', In Groenendijk, J. et al. (eds.), *Formal Methods in the Study of Language*. University of Amsterdam, Mathematical Center, Amsterdam. 483 – 512.

Schein, B. (1993): *Plurals and Events*. MIT Press, Cambridge, Massachusetts.

Schwarzschild, R. (1991): *On the Meaning of Definite Plural Noun Phrases*. Ph.D dissertation, University of Massachusetts at Amherst.

Vendler, Z. (1976): *Linguistics in Philosophy*. Cornell University Press, Ithaca, New York.

Verkuyl, H. (1972): *On the Compositional Nature of the Aspects*. Vol 15 of Foundations of Language Suppl. Series. Reidel, Dordrecht.

Verkuyl, H. (1987): 'Nondurative Closure of Events'. In Groenendijk, J. et al. (eds), *Studies in Discourse Representation Theory and the Theory of Generalized Quantifiers. Proceedings of the 5th Amsterdam Colloquium on Formal Semantics 1984*. Foris, Dordrecht, 87–113.

Verkuyl, H. (1988): 'Aspectual Asymmetry and Quantification'. In Ehrich, V., Vater, H. (eds.), *Temporalsemantik. Beiträge zur Linguistik der Zeitreferenz.* Tübingen, 220 – 259.

Verkuyl, H. (1989): 'Aspectual Classes and Aspectual Composition'. *Linguistics and Philosophy* **12**, 39 – 94.

Verkuyl, H./van der Does, J. (1991): 'The Semantics of Plural Noun Phrases'. ILLC–paper.

GODEHARD LINK

TEN YEARS OF RESEARCH ON PLURALS — WHERE DO WE STAND?

1. INTRODUCTION

The ten years mentioned in the title basically refer to the decade of the eighties and the early nineties which witnessed a tremendous amount of research activity on plurals in linguistic semantics and philosophy. This activity grew out of the realization that plurals are all-pervasive in language and hence cannot be regarded as an exotic topic by anyone who wants to give a reasonably complete account of the structure of language.

The pluralic idiom of natural language was typically neglected in the development of formal logic. This discipline evolved out of serious problems in the foundations of mathematics. In the context of mathematics, plural expressions occur only in the informal mathematical *argot*, the metalanguage that the mathematicians use to talk about their subject. It is a technical subdialect of natural language that is used to communicate in an imprecise but very efficient way mathematical ideas that if one were to take the trouble could be written down in the classical formal language of logic which only contains "singular" quantification. Thus a statement like *All non-negative real numbers have real square roots* could be more clumsily rendered as *For every non-negative real number x there is at least one real number y such that the square of y is x.* And in cases where the plural seems more essential to the statement, like in *almost all elements of the sequence lie in this neighborhood*, which means that all but a finite number of elements have the property in question, then this plurality is rephrased in the singular mode by speaking of sets: *with the exception of a finite set of elements of the sequence every member of the sequence lies in this neighborhood.* So it is fair to say that in mathematics, plurals serve no theoretical purpose and can basically be ignored.[1]

Outside the realm of mathematics natural language was not represented in a formal language. It was the philosophers, under the lead of Quine, who took up the Fregean exercises of formalizing natural language as a means for becoming clear about the ontological commitments hidden in linguistic locutions. Now Quine, in his logical regimentation program he prescribed to language (Quine 1960) dealt explicitly with mass terms; but he did not say much about plurals. He did mention, though, certain peculiar plural sentences that proved recalcitrant to a straightforward first-order representation (Quine 1972). So it is perhaps surprising that in spite of a rather long tradition of logical analysis of natural language one of the first philosophical papers explicitly dealing with valid arguments involving plurals is probably (Massey 1976). In linguistic quarters at that time, Montague Grammar was already in full swing, but people there considered the incorporation of plurals into the Montagovian framework just a routine exercise (see e. g., (Bartsch 1973; Hausser 1974; Bennett 1975)).

(Scha 1981) marks the starting point of systematic semantic research on plurals. My paper (Link 1983) tried to bring together the philosophical tradition and the work in linguistic semantics. In it I layed out a different conception of dealing with semantic matters: Instead of set-theoretic modelling I proposed an algebraic approach to the study of plurals and mass terms. The main linguistic motivation was the striking structural analogy between the plural domain and the domain of mass expressions that can best be captured in an algebraic setting. But there was also a rather firm philosophical intuition behind this approach on which I will shortly comment in section 2.

When the study of plurals grew into an independent subject of research it had to situate itself with respect to the leading overall paradigms in linguistic semantics, like Montague Grammar (MG), Generalized Quantifier Theory (GQT), Discourse Representation Theory (DRT), or Situation Theory (ST). There are demands on the systems that go in both directions here: On the one hand, the theory of plurals (PT) has to be flexible enough to meet the formal needs of any one of these systems. One the other hand, such a general framework should not only be able to accommodate plurals in some way or other; it should moreover be structured in such a way as to lend itself to a natural and theoretically coherent incorporation of PT. The kind of plural theory I tried to advance was meant to fit smoothly into any of those frameworks. Among them, DRT has been particularly successful in incorporating plural theory. In fact, some of the basic claims of PT proved to be most valuable in the context of plural anaphora and have led to important developments there (see (Kamp/Reyle 1993)). While I will not comment on ST here, GQT has to be mentioned, which can be considered as a kind of successor framework of MG. The classical paper on GQT, (Barwise/Cooper 1981), remains silent on genuine pluralic issues; they are discussed to a certain degree within the framework in (Link 1987a), with emphasis on their linguistic aspects. A more systematic GQ version of plural theory is used in (Lønning 1989) where also fundamental meta-logical results on PT are arrived at. Finally, van der Does's important study [1992] provides an abstract GQ setting for pluralic determiners and modifiers.

Over the years it has become evident that a typical difficulty in studying plurals is the fact that plural terms are notoriously vague in their reference; in this way they serve the overall efficiency of language in a remarkable way. Formal representations, on the other hand, are typically calibrated for a high degree of precision. The problem here is to come up with representations that are optimally tuned to this empirical level of accuracy. Thus the question is not only how plural phenomena can be represented at all, but also how to avoid overprecision. Let me illustrate this point with a few examples.

(1) The Romans built the aqueduct. They were excellent architects.

(2) [George Bush during the gulf war:] The Germans are awful. They have provided the Iraquis with those horrible chemical weapons, but now they are hiding behind their paychecks.

(3) [A martian:] These earthlings are strange. They build those wonderful structures they call cities only to level them off again every other decade.

Obviously, not all of the Romans built the aqueduct, nor were all of them excellent architects; and presumably, the ones who actually erected the aqueduct were not identical with the architects. Or take the Germans; certain German business men profited from the chemical weapons sale, and certain German politicians hid behind their paychecks, perhaps. But even if they entertain a covert or open relationship these groups can hardly be called identical. The same applies to the various groups of earthlings. Thus the anaphoric plural pronoun can apparently be used (and functions well!) without there being a fixed entity which it refers back to at every occurrence.

Here is another example: Do the sentences under (4) mean that *all* doors were opened, that *all* tools were used at every occasion?

(4) a. The burglars opened the doors with their special tools.

b. The burglars used their special tools to open the doors.

To use the universal quantifier $\forall$ for the representation of all the definite plural noun phrases involved would give their interpretation a degree of precision that is not matched by the empirical semantic facts concerning these data. It is clear then that considerable care has to be exercised to avoid the fallacy of over-representation.

This paper consists of three parts. In the next section I will give a broad overview over some of the current research activities in the field. Among them, four issues are singled out here for special consideration. Section 3. discusses what in my eyes constitutes a prominent case of over-representation. Section 4. finally is concerned with the issue of distributivity. Here I shall mainly comment on recent work by Jaap van der Does and Jan Tore Lønning.

Fixing terminology. Before I start I'd like to settle with some terminology just to give a precise frame for discussion. In general I shall presuppose here some acquaintance with the basic framework of plural logic LP as laid out for instance, in (Link 1983).

A *plural term* is a syntactic expression of natural language (mostly a plural NP) or an expression in the formal representation language (for instance LP). A *plural object* or *plurality* is a semantic entity, the denotation of a plural term. Sometimes a plural term may fail to refer to a plurality: (i) when the plural term is of a purely syntactic nature, like the English word 'scissors'; (ii) when a plural term is used in a spurious way; an example is *all men are mortal* which is totally equivalent to *every man is mortal*; (iii) when a plural term is a *general* NP in the sense that is genuinely quantificational; an example is *most Germans*; (iv) when the plural term is a bare plural in its generic use, e. g. in *dinosaurs are extinct*. In the latter case there is evidence that *dinosaurs* refers to a *natural kind* and not to a concrete collection of entities.[2]

The concept of a *plural character* is a functional notion: a plural character is a plurality that enters a collective relation like *meet* or *share*. It seems that pluralities do not always serve as plural characters; sometimes there are only there to delineate a certain group that is being referred to in a given context of utterance; but the relation they are involved in are purely distributive so that it is only the atomic individuals making up the plurality that have the property in question.

The terms *group* and *collection* will be used in a loose and informal way and often interchangeably; only in Section 3. *group* has a technical meaning. By contrast, technical terms are: *set, class, fusion, individual sum (i-sum)*; in set-theoretic usage a set is a class which is a member of some other class; a class that is not a set is called a proper class; the ordinary usage is such that when a class is known to be a set it is called a set. In philosophical usage, the term *class* is often indiscriminately applied to both sets and classes, in the sense that classes are abstract collections of individuals; he who recognizes classes believes in universals and goes beyond the nominalist position which maintains that there are only particulars/individuals.

2. CURRENT AREAS OF RESEARCH

Cross-linguistic Research. When plurals attracted the attention of the research community in linguistic semantics people soon became curious to learn what kind of cross-linguistic data could possibly be uncovered that have a bearing on the theoretical distinctions to be drawn in the field of semantics. As to the conceptual side intriguing data had already been accumulated in various centers of universal linguistics around the world (see, e. g. (Biermann 1981; Link 1991b; Zaefferer 1991) for relevant information). Here I want to focus on a particular issue, the question of *distributivity*. As it turns out, there is an enormous amount of data in various typologically unrelated languages to the effect that the distributive mode of predication tends to be specifically marked in language. Let us consider a type of sentence where there is a plural subject NP together with a predicate VP which is unspecified with respect to the collective/distributive distinction. In English, for instance, the word *each*, either in a floated quantifier or a postnominal position in the VP, can then be inserted to force the distributive reading of the sentence. A typical example is

(5) a. The men each had a beer.

b. The men had a beer each.

A particle with a similar function is *je* in German, which behaves much like the postnominal *each* (Link 1987a; Link 1987b; Link 1991b). But it is much more flexible and powerful. It can occur repeatedly in a sentence, creating quite intricate quantifier structures (6a), and it can occur even if there is no plural NP that can serve as distributional domain for it (then the missing antecedent has to be constructed from context); see (6b).

(6) a. Die Mütter erzählten je zwei Kindern je ein Märchen.

b. [*The mothers told two children each a fairy tale each.*]

(7) a. Je drei Äpfel waren faul.

b. [*Three apples each were rotten.*]

(Choe 1987a) discovered a similar particle in Korean, and he proposed the fitting term *anti–quantifier* for it. Gil's data on Georgian ((Gil 1988)) as well as long–standing facts about Pashto[3] which can be traced back at least to (Lorimer 1915) show that distributivity can also be marked by reduplication. Thus it appears that language uses a wide range of possibilities to specify the distributive reading of a sentence.

Algebraic Semantics for Natural Language. The lattice–theoretic approach to plurals is to be seen as part of a more general program of an algebraic semantics for natural language. Apart from plurals, considerable headway has been made here in the study of mass terms; see (Bunt 1979; Link 1983; Roeper 1983; Lønning 1987a; Krifka 1987; Krifka 1989a; Landman 1991). Of even greater importance is the semantic research on *events*, including the question whether semantic representations should generally be couched in a language of events. Algebraic work on this subject include (Hinrichs 1985; Bach 1986; Krifka 1987; Link 1987c; Lasersohn 1988; Krifka 1989a; Kamp/Reyle 1993).

Metatheory. In the discussion of plurality the focus has of course been on the problem how the plural semantics is able to account for the linguistic data. On the other hand, there are natural metatheoretical questions that arise in this context. For instance, the logic of plurality LP is couched in a first order language; does that mean that its logical strength is the same as that of pure first order predicate calculus (with identity)? In particular, is there a complete axiomatization for LP? It is these and related questions that are addressed in Lønning's important study (Lønning 1989). Lønning does not discuss the system LP but a similar one, called *plural logic, PL,* that is built on GQ theory. By embedding monadic second order logic into PL and from the fact that already monadic second order logic is incomplete he obtains the result that PL is not complete with respect to classes of semantic structures that display the closure under arbitrary joins (in particular, complete lattices and complete atomic Boolean algebras (CAB)). To delineate the "first–order part" of plural theory, Lønning discusses various subsystems; thus, *Definite Plural Logic* (with definite plural terms like *the boys* and quantification over atoms, but no quantification over proper i–sums) is complete with respect to the class of complete atomic Boolean algebras. Finally, drawing on a classical paper in the study of second order logic ((Orey 1959)), so–called *persistent* formulas are considered; such formulas do not distinguish between full CAB structures and *definably complete* atomic Boolean algebras (DCAB), that is, suitably "thinned–out" structures that admit of a generalized completeness proof in the sense of Henkin's general models. Typically, simple existential sentences with no negated collective predicate in their matrix are persistent. Apart from persistent formulas, a larger class of "standard" formulas is considered which, however, still leaves out general universal quantification over arbitrary sums. The question then is whether the pluralic locutions in language make full use of the expressive power of PL or whether their logical representations can be kept within the class of persistent (or standard) formulas. In (Lønning 1989), this issue is discussed at length. For the status of universal plural quantification in language, see also (Link 1987a). The discussion shows that examples for this quantificational mode are hard to find. In particular, it appears that from a linguistic point of view, the interaction between existential plural quantification and negation is as yet poorly understood.[4] The same holds for the question to which extent the use of pronouns anaphoric to proper sums transcend the realm of "firstorderizable" sentences of English; see the intriguing examples in (Boolos 1984a; Boolos 1984b) and Lønning's discussion of them. Future work will have to pay due attention to these issues.

Plural Anaphora. It can be said that there is a good compatibility between plural theory and DRT. In fact, some of the basic claims of PT proved to be particularly valuable in the context of anaphora. As far as the linguistic aspects of plural anaphora and their semantic representation are concerned, an enormous amount of progress has been made within the framework of DRT; see (Kamp/Reyle 1993). In this work, a wealth of new relevant linguistic data are discussed, and a number of novel techniques of anaphora resolution are developed to account for them. Here is a list of major themes in the study of plural anaphora, together with some of the techniques just mentioned, and typical illustrative sentences.

- Pick–up of suitable antecedents

    - a maximality constraint: no reference to subsums of plural terms

- Construal of antecedents

    - generic use: *Mary killed a wasp. She hates them.*
    - summation: *John took Mary for a ride. They had a lot of fun.*
    - Σ-abstraction: *Every classmate of John's took a girl to Acapulco. They had a lousy time.*

- Dependent plural pronouns

    – λ–abstraction: *Sarah and Mike sent a card to their mother, and Alice did, too.*

- Pluralic donkey sentences: *Few people who own two cars make equal use of them.*

There is a recent critique of the treatment of plural anaphora in DRT by (Krifka 1996). This paper takes a different approach which is based on "paramatrized sum individuals", an idea going back to (Rooth 1987).

Formal Ontology and Philosophy of Mathematics. A basic tenet of plural theory has been a *denotational view* towards definite plural terms like *the men*: such a term denotes a plural object in LP. In linguistic semantics there has been some controversy about the nature of those plural objects. First they were basically assumed to be sets without much of an argument. When it was realized that *mixed predicates* like *lift the piano* subsume individuals and collections alike, and hence that there has to be an extension for them of uniform type, the typical move was to have individual terms denote singleton sets. Thus the denotations of predicates were pushed one level up in the set–theoretic hierarchy. While this is fine from a purely representational point of view, where all that matters is getting the truth conditions right, that practice leaves something to be desired for those who are also concerned with the methodological and philosophical questions arising in this context. As for methodology, my argument has been, as I mentioned above, that set–theoretical modelling in the realm of pluralities misses an important generalization when it comes to incorporating mass terms in one uniform theory of semantics. The philosophical problem is *ontological*: Does the mere fact that people use plural expressions commit them to abstract entities like sets? My answer is of course no, and part of the original motivation for the algebraic approach was to show a way how to avoid that commitment. If you are given a domain of first order individuals then pluralities of those individuals, conceived as mereological fusions, have the same ontological status as the individuals you start with. As (Lewis 1991, p. 81) says: "But given a prior commitment to cats, say, a commitment to cat–fusions is not a *further* commitment. The fusion is nothing over and above the cats that compose it."

Now there are actually two different issues involved here: one concerns the set–theoretic vs algebraic approach, where there might not even be a real philosophical disagreement between the two camps subscribing to those approaches; the linguists that stick to their set–theoretic representations typically show a "don't care" attitude towards philosophical issues like ontological commitment. Both sides, however, embrace the denotational view. On the other hand, the position has also been taken that the denotational view has to be given up; in fact, (Schein 1993) claims that the view is outright paradoxical, and that plural theory is inconsistent. However, this claim is easily disposed of, since, obviously, LP has a model, viz. atomic Boolean algebras minus the zero element; for a more detailed rebuttal, see (Link 1996, chap. 13).

In this context, an interesting line of research has emerged in the philosophy of mathematics that uses the device of plural quantification to give a nominalistic interpretation of (monadic) second order logic which steers clear of any commitment to classes; see (Boolos 1984a; Boolos 1984b; Boolos 1985). The basic linguistic locution that Boolos uses is the relation ... *is one of them* between a first order object and several things ("them"), which he insists are *plurally referred to* and do not form a single set–like collection. Although this relation is a partitive construction and mereology is the theory of parts and wholes, Boolos doesn't give a mereological account; in fact, he never mentions mereology. Such an account, however, is developed in the final chapters of (Link 1996). There it is argued that the distinction that has been made in the philosophy of mathematics between the *logical* and the *iterative* conception of set can be understood in such a way as to equate logical sets with mereological fusions (actually i–sums in LP). That opens up the possibility to develop *within LP* the nominalistic reconstruction of set theory given by (Lewis 1991; Lewis 1993), which is based on a separate mereology of the iterative sets plus Boolos's plural quantification. This is carried out in (Link 1996, chap. 14).

AI–related research. Finally, reference should be made to the growing interest of the NL processing community in plural phenomena. Relevant work includes (Schütze 1989; Allgayer/Reddig–Siekmann 1990; Link/Schütze 1991; Aone 1991) and papers in (Guarino/Poli 1996). This volume also shows how mereology in general, of which plural theory is but a particular instance, can be put to use for both structuring and unifying the "ontologies" of knowledge–based systems.

3. GROUPS AND THE PROBLEM OF OVER-REPRESENTATION

Several authors have felt the need to introduce multi–level plural objects, which have come to be called "groups". That move was prompted by examples like the following ((Landman 1989)).

(8) The boys and the girls had to sleep in different dorms, met in the morning at breakfast, and were then wearing their blue uniforms.

Here the NP *the boys and the girls* has at the same time to stand for a uniform i–sum (to fit the VP 'meet'), to distribute one level down (to fit 'sleep in different dorms'), and to distribute two levels down (for the VP 'wearing'). There are notorious problems for the theory of plurals with such examples since the summing operation obliterates structure: once the sum of the boys and the girls is formed there is no unique way to retrieve the relevant intermediate parts that were used to build that sum; only its atomic parts can always be regained. The question is how to react to this situation. It could be argued, to begin with, that (8) is not representative for the general linguistic phenomenon of conjoining VPs with collective and intermediate level readings, but rather hinges essentially on the word *different* which admits of a special treatment to dispose of Landman's sentence. One reason for trying to avoid the combination of collective and intermediate level readings could be that there is a way to treat the conjunction of two VPs Q and Q' *without* resorting to groups when Q, Q' are of one of the following types: (i) Q, Q' have the same distributivity type; (ii) Q is collective, Q' distributive; (iii) Q is intermediate, Q' distributive (see (Lønning 1989)). The trick is here to combine term conjunction in LP with generalized quantifier conjunction. For example, consider sentence (9), adapted from Lønning, which describes a situation with a mixed double tennis match.

(9) Steffi and Michael and Arantxa and Emilio got $ 10,000 for the match.

Under its distributive reading (9) implies that $ 40,000 were handed out; in the collective case the money totals $ 10,000, but it is also possible that $ 20,000 were paid (intermediate level reading). Now let $\lambda PP(s \oplus m)$ denote the set of all properties applying to the i–sum of Steffi and Michael, $\lambda PP(a \oplus e)$ the set of all properties applying to the i–sum of Arantxa and Emilio. Then $\lambda P[P(s \oplus m) \wedge P(a \oplus e)]$ (the set of all properties that apply to the sum of Steffi and Michael as well as to the sum of Arantxa and Emilio) is an appropriate representation for the subject NP in (9) when the intended reading is the intermediate level one. Now conjoining two VPs Q, Q' poses no problem in the cases (i) – (iii) above: while (i) is obvious, the appropriate term for case (ii) is $\lambda x(Qx \wedge Q'x)(s \oplus m \oplus a \oplus e)$, for case (iii) $\lambda P[P(s \oplus m) \wedge P(a \oplus e)](\lambda x(Qx \wedge$

$Q'x$)). But there is no way to use the same method when a collective and an intermediate level VP are conjoined. This gets the above proposal into trouble empirically since at least in German there are clear cases of such VP conjunctions that do not use the word *different*:

(10) a. Die norwegischen Delegierten und die schwedischen Delegierten trafen sich in der Lobby des Bayerischen Hofs und erhielten je einen Dolmetscher.

b. [*The Norwegian delegates and the Swedish delegates met in the lobby of the "Bayerischer Hof" and were assigned an interpreter each.*]

(11) a. Im Landheim haben die Jungen und die Mädchen je einen Schlafsaal zur Verfügung, können sich aber zu gemeinsamen Aktivitäten im Aufenthaltsraum treffen.

b. [*In summer camp the boys and the girls sleep in a dormitory each, but they are allowed to meet in the hall for common activities.*]

In the face of data like these a number of people, including the present author, have concluded that the introduction of intermediate level entities, called *groups*, is inevitable (see, e.g. (Hoeksema 1983; Link 1984; Landman 1989)). There are two main avenues to proceed here: one is to give some kind of minor modification of the theory just enough to accommodate the data, without touching its core; the other is to give up the theory altogether. While I myself gave, more or less reluctantly, an obvious patch–up to the basic system LP just for that one extra level, Landman thought that this kind of evidence is reason enough to revise the whole of LP in such a way that its mereological character is obliterated. In fact he brings set–theoretic comprehension in again through the back door. Thus, in order to keep the intermediate i–sums in the above NPs separate, the sums (or unions) of atomic individuals are closed off by forming their singletons. For instance, the subject NP in sentence (9) in its intermediate group reading is represented as the set of rank 2,

$$\{\{s,m\},\{a,e\}\}$$

where s stands again for Steffi, m for Michael, a for Arantxa and e for Emilio. Nor does Landman stop at this rank; rather, he basically erects the full cumulative hierarchy of order ω over any given domain of discourse. Thus he defines for a given set A of basic individuals:[5]

$$V_0^A = A$$
$$V_{n+1}^A = 2^{V_n^A} \setminus \{\emptyset\} \quad (n \in \omega)$$
$$V_\omega^A = \bigcup_{n \in \omega} V_n^A$$

Now while the cumulative hierarchy of pure sets has 16 elements of rank 3 Landman's has 127 elements of this rank if A contains just 2 members, and approximately $2^{33\,000}$ if A has 4 elements. Here is an overhead if there ever was one. Set–theoretic modeling has led Landman astray. What's more, there were never, I think, convincing empirical reasons to deal with more than one intermediate level.

What, then, should be done with that remaining level? Recently, intriguing arguments have been advanced to the effect that there is no need to introduce a new kind of entities over and above the mereological i–sums. I shall briefly reproduce the main idea of a paper by Schwarzschild [1990], but see also (Schwarzschild 1991; Krifka 1991c).

Assume that the animals on a farm are just cows and pigs, with young animals and old animals among them. Thus we have the following equality of extensions: || animal || = || cow || ∪ || pig || = || young animal|| ∪ || old animal||. Assume further that the farmer separates the young animals from the old animals. Then the situation can be described by either one of the following five sentences, albeit with varying accuracy:

(12) a. The young animals and the old animals were separated.

b. The animals were separated. ↓

c. The animals were separated by age. ↓

d. The cows and the pigs were separated by age. ↓↑

e. The cows and the pigs were separated. ↓↑

The down and up arrows hint at two generalizations that Schwarzschild abstracts from these data: The *mereological generalization* says that whenever P is true of a group G then P is true of the sum of the entities of level one in the group, denoted by $\downarrow G$; examples for P are *were separated, talked to each other, were given different foods*, etc. According to the the second principle, the *upward closure condition*, when P is true of a sum G of entities of level one P is true of any group $\uparrow G$ formed from G. The claim is then that while natural language predication does not differentiate between levels it is still important which way the i–sum in question is referred to by the plural NP: it determines the *operative subsums* (Schwarzschild) according to which the predicate is to be understood unless there is some other clue that does this job, either in the sentence itself (e.g. an adverbial like *by age*) or in the context of utterance. In (12a), then, the operative subsums are the ones mentioned in the subject NP. (12b) holds because if (12a) is true it is also true that the animals were separated according to some criterion not made explicit here; this is done in (12c) through the adverbial *by age*. Now since according to our assumption the animals are coextensive with the cows and the pigs the NP *the cows and the pigs* can be substituted salva veritate for the NP *the animals* in (12c), whence the truth of (12d). Mereological generalization is applied here, followed by the upward closure condition. Finally, the criterion *by age* is dropped, yielding what might out of context be a misleading way of expressing the situation at hand, but it is nonetheless true. This shows that the NP used to refer to the group under consideration does by no means always contain the information as to what the operative criterion is according to which the group is split up.

Similar observations apply to the *Waterloo* example given in (Hoeksema 1983). When the sentence *Napoleon and Blücher and Wellington fought against each other at Waterloo* is uttered without a pause after *Napoleon* it is hard for a hearer who missed the relevant chapter of history to grasp the intended reading. So it is actually intonation that determines the appropriate operative subsums here. In the last example I'd like to mention, which is again taken from (Schwarzschild 1990), the operative subsums are given by cross-sentential deixis.

(13) a. The pictures that came from Bill's parents and the pictures that came from Sheila's parents were separated.
 b. The books were separated that way, too.

Examples like this undermine the conception that linguistic evidence forces the semanticist to introduce yet another layer of entities (the group level entities) on top of the sum objects of LP theory. It seems that proliferation of entities according to this conception is rather a case of over-representation than a piece of reasonable semantic modeling. Following the suggestions of (Schwarzschild 1990; Krifka 1991c) we conclude that a more careful analysis should put greater emphasis on the interplay between semantics proper and discourse phenomena to be treated in a format like DRT.

4. DISTRIBUTIVITY

Ever since Scha's seminal paper (Scha 1981) there has been a dispute over the question of how many readings there are for a sentence involving (one or more) plural NPs. In my paper (Link 1991a)[6] I expressed my doubts that Scha's fairly complex classification of readings is the right one, and I proposed a rather simple scheme instead which was generated by the basic collective/distributive distinction (C/D distinction, for short). In particular, I came up with seven readings for sentences like (14).

(14) Four men lifted three tables.

Since there are two pluralic argument places, $2 \times 2 = 4$ readings came from the C/D distinction; a possible difference in scope still multiplied the readings by 2 minus 1 (no scope in the double collective case). Now this was a logician's view working in the Montagovian tradition; hence its main goal was to display the various quantifier structures that a plural sentence like the above gives rise to when treated rigorously in a formal framework like LP. Now there were two kinds of critical reactions to this. One was that there is no scope distinction operative here. This objection came from quarters which had for some time taken exception to the Montagovian view that the paradigm sentence *every woman loves a man* has two readings due to scope. While I do appreciate the point made here I will not discuss this issue but rather ignore possible scope distinctions altogether. That leaves us with four readings. For some, even that is too much; thus (Lønning 1991) says that sentence (15a) is not ambiguous contrary to what my scheme predicts.

(15) a. John ate three apples.
 b. John lifted three tables.
 c. John juggled with 6 plates.

In his eyes it is a matter of indeterminacy rather than ambiguity whether those three apples were eaten one by one or swallowed in one fell swoop (pragmatic star). Today, again, I feel sympathetic to his view, although not all questions are answered here. In special contexts the C/D distinction might still matter, witness (15b,c). More importantly, when event variables are introduced into the representation language the question inevitably arises as to what the temporal relations are between the various actions expressed by a plural sentence.

Let us accept the diagnosis of indeterminacy for the sake of exposition. Then the above scheme has been stripped down to two readings only coming from the C/D ambiguity in the pluralic subject NP. This is what Lønning calls the *standard proposal.*[7]

The standard proposal has been objected to in the literature as being too simplistic. Two basic arguments can be distinguished that support this criticism:

- the argument from undergeneration of readings

- the argument from a missed generalization

Simplifying the historical record somewhat, the argument from undergeneration of readings takes up Scha's view that in addition to the collective and the distributive reading we have to admit a *mixed reading* which looks into the subcollections of a given plurality. Over the years a host of intriguing linguistic examples have come up that were designed to substantiate this claim. A "neoclassical" example derives from (Gillon 1987):[8]

(16) a. Hammerstein, Rodgers and Hart wrote musicals.

b. Hammerstein, Rodgers and Hart wrote a musical.

The argument goes like this. None of the three wrote a musical all by himself; so the sentence is not distributive. But also there is no musical that was written by all three of them together; so the sentence cannot be read collectively, either. Rather, there is a certain *cover Y* of the set consisting of the three composers such that every element of Y is a collection satisfying the VP property. (The various accounts differ from one another with respect to the specific nature of those covers: they can be minimal covers, proper partitions or again overlapping "pseudo–partitions"; see (Lønning 1991) for references). In our case, musical history says that, for instance, the collection consisting of the two pair sets {Hammerstein,Rodgers} and {Rodgers,Hart} is a verifying cover for the sentence.

However, I agree with Lønning's analysis that the argument is not as cogent as it might appear. To begin with, the b) sentence cannot have the cover interpretation; it simply doesn't mean that. Either it is read collectively, or the indefinite NP *a musical* is distributed over the subject NP which means that the three individuals each have the property in question. There seems to be no way to get at the intermediate subcollections. Now the a) sentence might invite a mixed interpretation more easily but even here serious doubts remain that have to do with the meaning of bare plural phrases like *writing musicals*. Such properties are *homogeneous* in character and do not imply that a person satisfying them bear the verb relation to a *complete* object falling under the bare plural concept. In the case at hand, each of our three composers can truly be said to have written musicals even if no one wrote a single musical all by himself; their *involvement* in musical writing is sufficient (cf. (Link/Schütze 1991)).

Observe that this is of course an empirical argument pertaining to a certain class of typical examples. Our theory should perhaps be flexible enough to cover the mixed readings, too, just in case future evidence is given to support them. So for the benefit of further discussion let me give representations of them within the algebraic theory of plurals.[9] Even if pluralities are no higher–order objects covers certainly are; so we have to extend the first–order theory LP to include second–order variables ranging over sets of i–sums. For the present purpose it would be pointless to give a rigorous representation in the object language; rather, the notation will be "semantic", i. e. metalinguistic, but with free use of both the suggestive λ–notation and the circled plus to build finite i–sums. Let E be the domain of individuals (i–sums) with variables x, y, z, and $\sqsubseteq$ the i–part relation on E; A is the set of atomic i–sums, with variables u, v, w, and 2^E the set of sets of i–sums with variables X, Y, Z. The principal ideal of an i–sum x is defined by

(17) $x^{\downarrow} := \{y \mid y \sqsubseteq x\}$ the principal ideal of x

When we intersect this set with A we get the set of atoms below x; by the *sup-generation property* of the plural lattice (Lønning 1989; Link 1991c) we have:

(18) $x = \sup(A \cap x^{\downarrow})$

Now let us follow (van der Does 1992) and introduce certain transformations on 2^E, δ for "distributive" and μ for "mixed". Let C stand for the various classes of covers like the ones mentioned above.

(19) $\delta = \lambda X \lambda y . A \cap y^{\downarrow} \subseteq X$

(20) $\mu = \lambda X \lambda y . \exists Y \in C (y = \sup Y \,\&\, Y \subseteq X)$

Let X be the property $[\![wrote.musicals]\!]$ and $oh \oplus rr \oplus lh$ the i–sum consisting of Oscar Hammerstein, Richard Rodgers and Lorenz Hart. Then we have:

(21) $oh \oplus rr \oplus lh \in \delta(\llbracket wrote.musicals \rrbracket) \iff$
$\forall u(u \in A \,\&\, u \sqsubseteq (oh \oplus rr \oplus lh) \Rightarrow u \in \llbracket wrote.musicals \rrbracket) \iff$
$oh \in \llbracket wrote.musicals \rrbracket \,\&\, rr \in \llbracket wrote.musicals \rrbracket \,\&\, lh \in \llbracket wrote.musicals \rrbracket$

Thus this gives the desired distributive reading. By contrast, the μ-operator formalizes the mixed case, as our example illustrates:

(22) $oh \oplus rr \oplus lh \in \mu(\llbracket wrote.musicals \rrbracket)$
$\iff \exists Y \in \mathcal{C}((oh \oplus rr \oplus lh) = \sup Y \,\&\, Y \subseteq \llbracket wrote.musicals \rrbracket)$

With $Y = \{oh \oplus rr, rr \oplus lh\}$ we get the intended meaning:

(23) $oh \oplus rr \in \llbracket wrote.musicals \rrbracket \,\&\, rr \oplus lh \in \llbracket wrote.musicals \rrbracket$

Since $\sup(A \cap x^{\downarrow}) = x$ we see that δ is a special case of μ, in fact the one in which the cover Y is the finest partition of x. Another limiting case is the cover $Y = \{x\}$ which yields the collective reading.

This observation brings us to the second argument against the standard proposal, viz. the argument from a missed generalization. If both the collective and the distributive reading are but special cases of the mixed reading, so the argument goes, then there is no ambiguity there after all. What we have is one representation with two opposite limiting cases. This is what (van der Does 1992) calls the No Ambiguity Strategy (NAS).

While van der Does, in his joint work with Henk Verkuyl (Verkuyl/van der Does 1996), seems to support this strategy he rejects it explicitly in his dissertation. I concur with his later assessment on this topic. Empirical work across languages has established beyond doubt, I think, that the distributive mode of predication is highly marked in language, as already the few data mentioned in section 2. show. The reason seems to be obvious: distributive predication has universal quantificational force and is thus equipped with a precise logical interpretation. By contrast, the collective mode is mostly vague and indeterminate, even when made explicit by means of adverbs like *together*. But predictably, no one has come up yet with a language where there is a special marker for, say, the pseudo–partitional reading.

Thus the empirical line is drawn between the distributive vs the non-distributive (the rest). The rest can be split up in *collective in a narrow sense* (one collective relation with a plural character) or *collective in a broad sense* where the mixed cases are included (lots of collective and/or distributive relations with corresponding plural and/or singular characters). Among the latter, only the *cumulative* case of (Scha 1981) seems to have a special linguistic status in that both the subject NP and the object NP involved in cumulative constructions are *autonomously referring* plural terms. Note, however, that the cumulative "reading" is particularly prominent when both NPs are specified numerically, like in Scha's famous sentence about the Dutch firms and their American computers. Van der Does [1992: p. 55] claims he can also read sentence (24a) cumulatively, where the determiner of the object phrase is no numeral, but pluralic *some*.

(24) a. Hammerstein, Rodgers and Hart wrote some musicals.

b. Some musicals were written by Hammerstein, Rodgers and Hart.

I disagree because that would amount to giving the object phrase a degree of specificity that seems hard to come by. Things look better, however, when the sentence is passivized, as in (24b). Even so, the defender of the standard proposal will always say that it is the indeterminacy in the relation of writing music, and not a linguistic ambiguity, that gives room for the cumulative interpretation here.

In summary, I look at the non–distributive domain as a matter of indeterminacy, not ambiguity (see, again, (Link/Schütze 1991)). Among the non–distributive phenomena only the narrowly understood collective interpretation and the cumulative interpretation stand out as having a fairly context–independent status. By contrast, the basic collective/distributive ambiguity is well–entrenched in language even if mathematically, both the collective and the distributive reading are but special cases of a more general cover interpretation.[10]

A related issue of long standing is the question where exactly the C/D ambiguity arises, in the NP or in the VP. Well, it's the VP, I think, and I have always been convinced of that. So I embrace van der Does's Verb Phrase Strategy (VPS), which he rejects, but which is in my opinion corroborated by ample empirical evidence. Prominent among this evidence are Craige Roberts's arguments from anaphora ((Roberts 1987a)) and sentences involving mixed collective and distributive predicates, like (25a).

(25) a. Four men went to the bar together and each had a beer.

b. $\exists x (x \in [\![4\ men]\!]\ \&\ x \in [\![went.together]\!] \cap \delta([\![had.a.beer]\!]))$

The representation (25b) shows the ease by which such sentences are handled under VPS. Furthermore, data from the German distributivity operator *je* show that the pluralic domain of distribution that *je* operates on is not always unique and can often be only determined by context. For instance, example (7a) above, *Je drei Äpfel waren faul*, doesn't contain a plural NP that could serve as the distributional domain for *je*, but the sentence is perfectly fine in German. It can be felicitously uttered in a situation where there is a fruit stand displaying apples in several baskets each of which contains three rotten apples.[11] It is hard to imagine how a pluralic nominal domain that in some cases has to be reconstructed from context could "know" that it should serve as distributional domain for an anti-quantifier like *je*.

These observations by no means imply, of course, that the NP (the determiner, that is) does not contribute to the meaning of sentences in an essential way. I even suspect that the Determiner Strategy (DETS), which is endorsed by van der Does, is not really that different from the VPS after all. But how could that be in view of van der Does's claim that the DETS in effect supersedes the VPS in that it can handle data on which the latter fails? The crucial case that is adduced in favor of DETS is the behavior of non–MON↑ determiners.

To answer this question, let us start with the basic picture of GQ Theory. The determiner of the subject NP essentially controls the quantificational force of the sentence. No discourse phenomena are taken into account. When the NP contains a numeral, for instance, all that counts is the *number of objects* involved in the relation expressed by the sentence. Thus consider sentence (25a) above. It is true in GQ theory under the usual interpretation of unmodified numerals if the number of men that went to the bar together and had a beer each is at least four. This truth condition is obviously upwardly monotone. However, it doesn't bring out the fact that the plural NP can and in most cases will be used *referentially* when the speaker has a particular group of four men in mind. This i–sum is then the topic of the rest of the discourse, never mind how many men ordered a beer besides that. In DRT there would be a plural reference marker for it. The referential use of indefinite NPs was acknowledged by researchers in the GQ tradition when (Barwise 1987) compromised with discourse theories by distinguishing between *singular* and *general* NPs: indefinite NPs are typically singular in Barwise's sense[12] in that they are open to a referential interpretation. Unlike the original GQ representation, the LP representation given in (26b), which is a simple existential statement, can easily be amended to a quantifier–free discourse format that captures the referential use. That is why I keep the existential quantifier in front. One has to bear in mind, of course, that this entails upward monotonicity.

Van der Does argues that this approach cannot be sustained in the non–MON↑ cases. Those involve determiners like *exactly three* or *at most four*. They are genuinely quantificational in that they give rise to a *general* noun phrase in Barwise's sense: a generalized quantifier which does not provide a reference object for the discourse. DRT typically sets up a duplex condition for them. There is nothing referential involved here. But on the other hand, we do have sentences like the following, in which the subject NP seems to be both referential and quantificational.

(26) At most four men went to the bar together and had a beer each.

Let us consider various possible eye–witness reports:

1. To the best of my recollection, there were no more than 4 men in the room; they went to the bar together and had a beer each, etc.

2. At most 4 men went to the bar together; there were lots of men in the room but it was those men – I am sure they were not more than four – that apparently tried to pick a fight with the stranger at the bar. First they had a beer each etc.

3. The bar keeper: There were at most 4 men that went to the bar together and had a beer each; I can tell it from the number of broken glasses they threw at the stranger: no more than four are missing. etc.

What this shows is that the non–MON↑ determiners are special in that they take scope over the material that follows. The scope does not necessarily extend to the sentence boundary, but can rather vary from context to context. Thus sentences involving such determiners cannot be evaluated *unless the material is specified that goes under their scope*. According to the first report there were no more than four men in the room; the scope is *'men'*. According to the second report there were no more than four men that went to the bar together; here the scope is *'men that went to the bar together'*. And the third report says that there were no more than four men that went to the bar together and had a beer each; here the scope extends over all of *'men that went to the bar together and had a beer each'*. According to this story there might well have been more than four men that went to the bar together; but only a group of no more than four men was such that its members had a beer each.

Now it is plain that it would lead to inadequate results if one were to give representations for the referentially used non–MON↑ determiners, starting with an existential quantifier, *and adding no extra clause* that specifies the scope of the determiner. Since van der Does [1992] does not consider the possibility of adding a scope indicator he thinks that the standard approach is bound to fail here; he concludes from this that the proper representation has to be the one which just applies the cardinality condition to the collection satisfying the property under the scope of the determiner, which he takes to extend to the sentence boundary. That means that the non–MON↑ determiners produce *general NPs*, that is, genuine generalized quantifiers which do not provide a reference object for the discourse. In DRT, this corresponds to a duplex condition without reference marker. But the different context–dependent interpretations of sentence (26) above show clearly that in some way or other an antecedent for later anaphora can nevertheless be created. How can a representation account for this? Well, I think, DR theorists would resort to *antecedent construal by abstraction* (see (Kamp/Reyle 1993)). Informally, for instance, a GQ scheme like *at most n X are Y* would be taken up by the pluralic abstraction term *those X that are Y*. In the first order framework of LP a referential plural NP has to be expressed by an existential quantification. Does that mean that we are bound to produce a MON↑ quantificational force, as (van der Does 1992) seems to suggest? I think not. We do have to add, however, a universally quantified clause to prevent this effect.

Let us consider the *exactly* case first and illustrate it by the following example, which contains the collective predicate *meet*.[13]

(27) a. Exactly five boys met.

b. $\exists x(|x| = 5 \,\&\, x \in [\![boys]\!] \cap [\![met]\!]\,)$

c. $\exists x(|x| = 5 \,\&\, x \in [\![boys]\!] \cap [\![met]\!]$
$\&\, \forall y(|y| = 5 \,\&\, y \in [\![boys]\!] \cap [\![met]\!] \Rightarrow y = x\,))$

d. $\exists x(|x| = 5 \,\&\, x \in [\![boys]\!] \cap [\![met]\!]$
$\&\, \forall y(y \in [\![boys]\!] \cap [\![met]\!] \Rightarrow y = x\,))$

e. $\exists x(|x| = 5 \,\&\, x \in [\![boys]\!] \cap [\![met]\!]$
$\&\, \forall y(y \in [\![boys]\!] \cap [\![met]\!] \Rightarrow y \sqsubseteq x\,))$

Let $\phi[x]$ be the property of being an i–sum x that consists of boys that met. It will certainly not do to interpret sentence (27a) as (27b);

the reason is that (27b) is compatible with all kinds of different i–sums having property ϕ, the cardinalities of which do not even have to equal 5. A fairly natural idea here is to give a representation which is modeled after the uniqueness condition for singular definite descriptions. When we add a universally quantified clause expressing this condition, we still have two options, (27c) and (27d); the difference is whether or not the cardinality condition is included in the uniqueness clause. (27c) says that there is a certain sum of five boys that met, and that this sum is unique among all the other five–atoms sums in having the property ϕ; but there may still be other sums x such that $\phi[x]$ of different cardinality. However, that doesn't give the right meaning. In (27d), the cardinality condition is dropped; but now we are facing a different problem: The current logical form admits of exactly one i–sum x such that $\phi[x]$, and for this x we have $|x| = 5$; if we change the property ϕ into one that is downward persistent (i. e. one that if true of x is also true of all y below x) then this contradicts the uniqueness of x for cardinalities of x greater than one. Downward persistent properties abound; for instance, all starred distributive predicates in plural theory like being a sum of boys[14] are of this kind. Now in the plural domain two concepts for expressing the notion of exactness have to be distinguished that coincide in the singular case: *uniqueness* and *maximality*. While we have to give up the former, we can still postulate the latter: (27e) displays the maximality condition in its extra clause. Thus, exactness does not mean that there is only a single individual in the domain with the property in question, but rather that there is a maximal one among them, and this unique element is picked out.

Note that from this representation we get back the familiar condition of GQ theory for *exactly five* when the predicate *met* is replaced by a distributive predicate, say *laughed*:

(28) a. Exactly five boys laughed.

b. $\exists x(|x| = 5 \ \& \ x \in [\![boys]\!] \cap [\![{}^*laughed]\!]$
$\& \ \forall y(y \in [\![boys]\!] \cap [\![{}^*laughed]\!] \Rightarrow y \sqsubseteq x))$

c. $card([\![boy]\!] \cap [\![laughed]\!]) = 5$

The transition from (28b) to (28c) can be shown as follows.[15] Since $[\![boys]\!] = [\![{}^*boy]\!]$ the formula (28b) yields $x \in [\![{}^*boy]\!] \cap [\![{}^*laughed]\!]$ and $[\![{}^*boy]\!] \cap [\![{}^*laughed]\!] \subseteq x^{\downarrow}$; hence $x = \sup([\![{}^*boy]\!] \cap [\![{}^*laughed]\!])$. Now observe that $[\![{}^*boy]\!] \cap [\![{}^*laughed]\!] = [\![{}^*boy.that.laughed]\!]$, and therefore, by a property of starred predicates (Theorem (T. 4) in (Link 1991c)), $x = \sup([\![{}^*boy.that.laughed]\!]) = \sup([\![boy.that.laughed]\!])$. By sup–generation, we have also $x = \sup(A \cap x^{\downarrow})$. From the injectivity of the sup–operator we get $A \cap x^{\downarrow} = [\![boy.that.laughed]\!] = [\![boy]\!] \cap [\![laughed]\!]$. With $|x| = 5$ and the meaning of $|\cdot|$ we arrive at (28c).

There is further support for the representation of *exactly n* that we have given here. *Exactly n* should mean the same as *at least n and not more than n*, and this equivalence also comes out formally when the latter determiner is regarded as a conjunction of *at least n* and the negation of *more than n* under their natural interpretation. Thus consider (29):

(29) a. At least five and not more than five boys laughed.

b. $\exists x (|x| \geq 5 \ \& \ x \in [\![boys]\!] \cap [\![^*laughed]\!])$
        $\& \ \forall y (y \in [\![boys]\!] \cap [\![^*laughed]\!] \Rightarrow |y| \leq 5)$

c. $\exists x (|x| = 5 \ \& \ x \in [\![boys]\!] \cap [\![^*laughed]\!]$
        $\& \ \forall y (y \in [\![boys]\!] \cap [\![^*laughed]\!] \Rightarrow y \sqsubseteq x))$

The equivalence of (29b) and (29c) is seen as follows. The direction from right to left follows from the isotony of $|\cdot|$. The opposite direction is proved by reductio. Assume that there is a $y \in [\![boys]\!] \cap [\![^*laughed]\!]$ such that $y \not\sqsubseteq x$; then, by the separation property of the plural lattice, there is an atom $u \in A$ such that $u \sqsubseteq y$ and $u \not\sqsubseteq x$. By downward persistence of starred predicates, $u \in [\![boys]\!] \cap [\![^*laughed]\!]$. Define $x' := x \sqcup u$; then $x \sqsubset x'$. But starred predicates are also cumulative, hence $x' \in [\![boys]\!] \cap [\![^*laughed]\!]$. But $|x'| > 5$ which contradicts the second premise in (29b).

Note that the proof fails if genuinely collective predicates are considered; they are in general neither downward persistent nor cumulative. What that means is that it is not enough to restrict the cardinality in the negated determiner *not more than n*; we have to use the $\sqsubseteq$-relation instead. This anticipates a choice that has also to be made when we return to the non–MON↑ determiner scheme *at most n X are Y*. One of the options is to say that there is an i–sum x such that $|x| \leq n$ and $x \in X \cap Y$ while adding the clause that all y with $y \in X \cap Y$ are limited in size by $|y| \leq n$. But that would leave room for the possibility that we are fixing on a discourse referent x with $x \in X \cap Y$, but of smaller size than n, while there are bigger i–sums y around (with $n \geq |y| > |x|$) which also meet the condition $y \in X \cap Y$. To test this option consider (30).

(30) At most four squatters were left in the building. They were dragged out by the police.

I think this two–sentence discourse means that afterwards all squatters are gone. But that is not what our first options predicts; it is compatible with a situation where a group of two squatters was given the treatment by the police while one or two squatters still remain in the house. What is missing here again is the *maximality condition* which garantees that the anaphoric pronoun *they* refers to all of the squatters that are left in the building. This is the second option which can be represented thus.

(31) a. At most four squatters were left.
 b. $\exists x (|x| \leq 4 \ \& \ x \in [\![squatters]\!] \cap [\![{}^*were.left]\!]$
  $\& \ \forall y (y \in [\![squatters]\!] \cap [\![{}^*were.left]\!] \Rightarrow y \sqsubseteq x))$

Since our example involves only distributive predicates this again boils down to the usual GQT condition $\mathrm{card}([\![squatter]\!] \cap [\![were.left]\!]) \leq 4$. The only difference is that the latter condition carries no existential import. In order to arrive at a similar cardinality restriction also in the general case of the existence–free MON↓ determiner *at most n X are Y*, we take the supremum of $X \cap Y$ and put the restriction on the number of its atoms: $\mathrm{card}([\sup(X \cap Y)]^{\downarrow} \cap A) = |\sup(X \cap Y)| \leq n$ (if $X \cap Y = \emptyset$ then $[\sup(X \cap Y)]^{\downarrow}$ is considered to be empty, too).

In summary, then, here is a list of some plural determiners with their semantic interpretation in a GQ framework that incorporates plural theory. Lower case variables run over arbitrary i–sums, upper case variables over sets of i–sums.

Pluralic determiners.

$$[\![some_{pl}]\!] = \lambda X \lambda Y . \exists x (|x| \geq 2 \land x \in X \cap Y) \tag{32}$$

$$[\![n]\!] = \lambda X \lambda Y . \exists x (|x| = n \land x \in X \cap Y) \tag{33}$$

$$[\![at.least\ n]\!] = \lambda X \lambda Y . \exists x (|x| \geq n \land x \in X \cap Y) \tag{34}$$

$$[\![more.than\ n]\!] = \lambda X \lambda Y . \exists x (|x| > n \land x \in X \cap Y) \tag{35}$$

$$[\![not.more.than\ n]\!] = \tag{36}$$
$$\lambda X \lambda Y . \neg \exists x (|x| > n \land x \in X \cap Y) =$$
$$\lambda X \lambda Y . \forall x (x \in X \cap Y \Rightarrow |x| \leq n)$$

$$[\![at.most\ n]\!] = \lambda X \lambda Y . | \sup X \cap Y | \leq n \tag{37}$$

$$\llbracket \text{(some.but) at.most } n \rrbracket = \qquad\qquad (38)$$
$$\lambda X \lambda Y. \exists x \, (\, |x| \leq n \,\wedge\, x \in X \cap Y \,\wedge\, \forall y \, (\, y \in X \cap Y \,\Rightarrow\, y \sqsubseteq x \,))$$

$$\llbracket \text{exactly } n \rrbracket = \qquad\qquad (39)$$
$$\lambda X \lambda Y. \exists x \, (\, |x| = n \,\wedge\, x \in X \cap Y \,\wedge\, \forall y \, (\, y \in X \cap Y \,\Rightarrow\, y \sqsubseteq x \,))$$

As argued above, there are two representations for the non–MON↑ determiner *at most*, one with and one without existential import. The latter gives a pure upward cardinality restriction leaving room for zero, while the former lends itself to anaphora in discourse. Furthermore, in the general case of collective predication, *at most n* is not the same as negated *more than n*; genuine plural determiners just don't work that way (even disregarding the existence question). An old theme is recurring here: universal plural quantification has only a highly restricted role to play in language. That discards Equation 36 as suitable representation in the collective case. Observe finally that due to the maximality condition the determiners in Equations 38 and 39 are not upwardly monotone anymore. So the empirical advantage over the standard proposal that is claimed by van der Does's account for the non–MON↑ cases evaporates.

NOTES

[1] From a linguistic point of view it would be worthwhile to do some systematic field work with mathematicians to find out exactly how they translate their informal talk, which is full of pluralic locutions, into singular mathematical statements.

[2] For a report on the state of the art in the linguistic study of generics see (Carlson/Pelletier 1995).

[3] Thanks to Dietmar Zaefferer for calling my attention to this.

[4] Thus, for instance, while the sentence *Some boys shared a pizza* can be represented by a simple existential plural quantification involving a positively occurring collective predicate (which guarantees its persistence) the negated sentence *Some boys did not share a pizza* doesn't seem to amount to a universal quantification over sums of boys. Rather, under negation proper i–sums tend to "dissolve" and lead to distributive predication. For problems with the role of negation in defining plural determiners, see below.

[5] Landman's definition is slightly different in that he generously throws in another power set operator at the ω level.

[6] This paper was actually written in 1984.

[7] I am following here his lucid exposition in (Lønning 1991).

[8] For the benefit of the uneducated reader (like myself) here are some basic facts about Hammmerstein, Hart and Rodgers: Richard Rodgers and Oscar Hammerstein II together wrote the musical *Oklahoma!* whereas Rodgers and Lorenz Hart wrote *On Your Toes* together, for instance. Again, Rodgers, Hart and Herbert Field wrote

A Connecticut Yankee, Hammerstein and Jerome Kern *Show Boat*, Rodgers, Hammerstein, and Joshua Logan *South Pacific*. But it seems indeed that neither did the three of them write any musical together, nor did any of them write one all by himself. (This is taken from Gorton Carruth, *The Encyclopedia of American Facts and Dates*. Eighth edition, Harper and Row, New York 1987.) Special thanks go to Brandon Gillon for drawing the attention of the community to American culture.

[9] In fact those representations will look pretty much the same as the ones in (van der Does 1992). The reason is that van der Does has as atomic individuals singleton sets over a basic set X, such that set-theoretic union on the power set 2^X models the summing operation. As Lønning [1991] observes, the basic set X serves no purpose whatsoever. This is a typical occasion for a mathematician to abstract away from that artifact of the representation. It is here that the lattices come in.

[10] The analysis given raises an interesting methodological point. Maintaining the ambiguity seems to be at variance with a common methodological principle in science. Galileo, for instance, criticized Aristotle on the grounds that he draws a categorical, in fact metaphysical, dividing line between the state of motion and the state of rest. The failure to view the state of rest as the limiting case of the state of motion at velocity zero constituted a major stumbling block for the progress of science, according to Galileo. Thus Aristotle plainly missed a crucial generalization. Ironically, I find myself siding with empirical linguistics against abstract scientific methodology.

[11] For more on *je* see (Link 1987b).

[12] Including pluralic indefinite NPs! The opposition here is "singular term" vs "general term" in the logical sense; it has nothing to do with the number distinction.

[13] In the following the "cardinality" operator $|\cdot|$ is meant to take individual terms and return the number of atoms in the denotation of that term, that is, $|x| = $ card$(x^\downarrow \cap A)$.

[14] If P is a distributive predicate (i. e. one which is true of atomic individuals only) then $*P$ is true of all i–sums whose atomic parts each have the property P. Nouns like *boy* are distributive; in the text I often use *boys* instead of **boy*.

[15] In this argument formal properties of the plural lattice are used; see (Link 1991c).

REFERENCES

The following bibliography was compiled for a course on the algebraic semantics of plurals and mass terms at the 3rd European Summer School for Logic, Language and Information, Saarbrücken, Germany, 1991, which I taught together with Jan Tore Lønning. While bibliographies can never be complete I hope this one does contain the larger part of the relevant work in the field.

Allan, Keith (1977): 'Classifiers' In *Language* **53**, 285 – 311.

Allan, Keith (1980): 'Nouns and Countability' In *Language* **56**, 541 – 567.

Allgayer, Jürgen and Carola Reddig–Siekmann (1990): 'What KL–ONE lookalikes need to cope with natural language' In (Bläsius/Hedtstück/Rollinger 1990), 240 – 285.

Altham, J.E.J. (1971): *The Logic of Plurality*, Methuen, London.

Aone, Chinatsu (1991): *Treatment of Plurals and Collective-Distributive Ambiguity in Natural Language Understanding.* Ph. D. Dissertation, University of Texas at Austin. MCT Technical Report Number ACT-NL-155-91, Austin, Texas.

Bach, E. (1986): The Algebra of Events. In *Linguistics and Philosophy* **9**, 5 – 16.

Balbes, Raymond and Philip Dwinger (1974): *Distributive Lattices.* University of Missouri Press, Columbia, Missouri.

Bartsch, Renate (1973): The Semantics and Syntax of Number and Numbers. In (Kimball 1973), 51 – 93.

Bartsch, Renate, Johan van Benthem and P. van Emde Boas (eds.) (1989): *Semantics and Contextual Expression.*

Barwise, Jon (1987): 'Noun phrases, generalized quantifiers and anaphora' In [Gärdenfors 1987], 1 – 29.

Barwise, Jon and Robin Cooper (1981): 'Generalized quantifiers and natural language' In *Linguistics and Philosophy* **4**, 159 - 219.

Bäuerle, Rainer, Christoph Schwarze and Arnim von Stechow (eds.) (1983): *Meaning, Use, and Interpretation of Language.* De Gruyter, Berlin.

Bealer, George (1975): 'Predication and matter' In *Synthese* **31**, 493 – 508; also in (Pelletier 1979), 279 – 294.

Bennett, Michael R. (1975): *Some Extensions of a Montague Fragment of English.* Ph. D. Dissertation UCLA, distributed by the Indiana University Linguistics Club.

Bennett, Michael R. (1977): 'Mass nouns and mass terms in Montague grammar' In (Davis/Mithun 1979), 263 – 285.

Bennett, Michael R. (1972): 'Accommodating the plural in Montague's fragment of English' In [Rodman 1972], 25 – 65.

van Benthem, Johan and Alice ter Meulen (ed.) (1984): *Generalized Quantifiers in Natural Language*, Foris, Dordrecht.

van Benthem, Johan and Alice ter Meulen (ed.) (1996): *Handbook of Logic and Language.* Elsevier, Amsterdam.

Biermann, Anna (1981): 'Die grammatische Kategorie Numerus' In (Seiler/Lehmann 1982) , 229 – 243.

Bläsius, Karl H., Ulrich Hedtstück and Claus R. Rollinger (eds.) (1990): *Sorts and Types in Artificial Intelligence.* Springer Lecture Notes in Artificial Intelligence 418, Berlin.

Blau, Ulrich (1978): *Die dreiwertige Logik der Sprache. Ihre Syntax, Semantik und Anwendung in der Sprachanalyse.* de Gruyter, Berlin.

Blau, Ulrich (1981): 'Collective Objects' In *Theoretical Linguistics* **8**, 101–130.

Boolos, George (1984): 'To be is to be a value of a variable (or to be some values of some variables' In *Journal of Philosophy* **81**, 430 – 449.

Boolos, George (1984): 'Nonfirstorderizability again' In *Linguistic Inquiry* **15**, 343.

Boolos, George (1985): 'Nominalist platonism', *Philosophical Review* **94**, 327 – 344.

Brady, M. and R. Berwick (eds.) (1984): *Computational Models of Discourse*. M.I.T. Press, Cambridge, Massachusetts.

Bunt, Harry (1979): 'Ensembles and the formal semantic properties of mass terms' In (Pelletier 1979), 279 – 294.

Bunt, Harry (1981): *The Formal Semantics of Mass Terms*. Doctoral Dissertation, University of Amsterdam.

Bunt, Harry (1985): *Mass Terms and Model–Theoretic Semantics*. Cambridge University Press, Cambridge.

Bunt, Harry (1985): 'The formal representation of (quasi–)continuous concepts' In (Moore/Hobbs 1985), 37 – 70.

Burge, Tyler (1972): 'Truth and mass terms' In *Journal of Philosophy* **69**, 263 – 282.

Burge, Tyler (1975): 'Mass terms, count terms, and change' In *Synthese* **31**, 459 – 478; also in (Pelletier 1979), 199 – 218.

Burge, Tyler (1977): 'A theory of aggregates' In *Noûs* **11**, 97 – 117.

Carlson, Greg and Francis J. Pelletier (eds.) (1995): *The Generic Book*. Chicago University Press.

Carlson, Lauri (1980): *Plural Quantification*. ms., MIT, Cambridge, MA.

Carlson, Lauri (1982): 'Plural quantifiers and informational independence' In *Acta Philosophica Fennica* **35**, 163 – 174.

Cartwright, Helen M. (1963): *Classes, Quantities and Non–singular Reference*. Ph. D. Dissertation, University of Michigan.

Cartwright, Helen M. (1970): 'Quantities' In *Philosophical Analysis* **79**, 25 – 42.

Cartwright, Helen M. (1979): 'Some remarks about mass nouns and plurality', In (Pelletier 1979), 31 – 46.

Chellas, Brian (1975): 'Quantity and quantification' In *Synthese* **31**, 487 – 491; also in (Pelletier 1979), 227 – 231.

Choe, Jae Woong (1987): *Anti–Quantifiers and a Theory of Distributivity*. Ph. D. Dissertation, University of Massachusetts, Amherst.

Choe, Jae Woong (1987): 'A theory of distributivity' In (Groenendijk/Stokhof/Veltman 1987), 21 – 41.

Clarke, Bowman L. (1981): 'A calculus of individuals based on 'connection'' In *Notre Dame Journal of Formal Logic* **22**, 204 – 218.

Clarke, D. S. Jr. (1970): 'Mass terms as subjects' In *Philosophical Studies* **21**, 25 – 29.

Clay, Robert E. (1974): 'Relation of Lesniewski's mereology to Boolean algebra' In *Journal of Symbolic Logic* **39**, 638 – 348.

Cook, Cathleen (1975): 'On the usefulness of quantities' In *Synthese* **31**, 443 – 457; also in (Pelletier 1979), 121 – 135.

Cresswell, Max (1985): 'Review of Landman and Veltman (eds.), *Varieties of Formal Semantics*' In *Linguistics* **23**.

Davey, B. A. and H. A. Priestley (1990): *Introduction to Lattices and Order*. Cambridge University Press, Cambridge.

Davies, Martin (1989): '*Two Examiners Marked Six Scripts*. Interpretations of numerically quantifies sentences' In *Linguistics and Philosophy* 12, 293 – 323.

Davis, Steven and Marianne Mithun (eds.) (1979): *Linguistics, Philosophy, and Montague Grammar*. University of Texas Press, Austin, Texas.

van der Does, Jaap (1991): 'Among Collections' In [van der Does 1991a], 1 – 35.

van der Does, Jaap (ed.) (1991a): *Quantification and Anaphora II*. DYANA deliverable 2.2.b, Edinburgh.

van der Does, Jaap (1992): *Applied Quantifier Logics. Collectives. Naked Infinitives*. Doctoral Dissertation, University of Amsterdam.

van der Does, Jaap (1993): 'Sums and quantifiers' In *Linguistics and Philosophy* 16, 509 – 550.

van der Does, Jaap: (1994): 'On complex plural noun phrases' In [Kanazawa/Piñón 1994], 81 – 115.

van der Does and van Eijck (eds.) (1996): *Quantifiers, Logic, and Language*. Lecture Notes, Vol. 54. Stanford, California: CSLI Publications. Distributed by Cambridge University Press.

Dougherty, Ray C. (1970): 'A grammar of coordinate conjoined structures: I' In *Language* 46, 850 – 898.

Dougherty, Ray C. (1971): 'A grammar of coordinate conjoined structures: II' In *Language* 47, 298 – 339.

Dowty, David (1986): 'A Note on collective predicates, distributive predicates and *All*' In *Proceedings of the Third Eastern States Conference on Linguistics (ESCOL 86)*, Ohio State University, 97 – 115.

Eberle, Rolf A. (1970): *Nominalistic Systems*. Reidel, Dordrecht.

van Eijck, Jan (1983): 'Discourse representation theory and plurality' In (ter Meulen 1983).

Erné, Marcel (1982): *Einführung in die Ordnungstheorie*. Bibliographisches Institut, Mannheim.

Gabbay, Dov and Julius M. E. Moravcsik (1973): 'Sameness and Individuation' In *Journal of Philosophy* 70; also in (Pelletier 1979), 233 – 247.

Gabbay, Dov M. and Franz Guenthner (1989): *Handbook of Philosophical Logic. Volume IV: Topics in the Philosophy of Language*. Reidel, Dordrecht.

Gärdenfors, Peter (ed.) (1987): *Generalized Quantifiers. Linguistic and Logical Approaches*. Reidel, Dordrecht.

Gierz, Gerhard et al. (1980): *A Compendium of Continuous Lattices*. Springer, Berlin-Heidelberg-New York.

Gil, David (1982): *Distributive Numerals*. Ph. D. Dissertation, UCLA, Los Angeles.

Gil, David (1982): 'Quantifier scope, linguistic variation, and natural language semantics' In *Linguistics and Philosophy* 5, 421 – 472.

Gil, David (1988): 'Georgian reduplication and the domain of distributivity' In *Linguistics* **26**, 1039 – 1065.

Gillon, Brendan S. (1987): 'The Readings of Plural Noun Phrases in English' In *Linguistics and Philosophy* **10**, 199 – 219.

Gillon, Brendon S. (1990): 'Plural noun phrases and their readings: A reply to Lasersohn' In *Linguistics and Philosophy* **13**, 477 – 485.

Grätzer, George (1978): *General Lattice Theory*. Birkhäuser, Basel.

Grandy, Richard E. (1975): 'Stuff and things' In *Synthese* **31**, 479 – 485; also in (Pelletier 1979), 219 – 225.

Groenendijk, Jeroen, Theo M. V. Janssen, and Martin Stokhof (eds.) (1981): *Formal Methods in the Study of Language*. Mathematical Centre, Amsterdam.

Groenendijk, Jeroen, Martin Stokhof, and Frank Veltman (eds.) (1987): *Proceedings of the Sixth Amsterdam Colloquium*. ITLI, Amsterdam.

Guarino, Nicola and Roberto Poli (eds.) (1996): 'Special Issue on Formal Ontology in Conceptual Analysis and Knowledge Representation'. In *International Journal of Human and Machine Studies*. Academic Press.

Gupta, Anil (1980): *The Logic of Common Nouns: An Investigation in Quantified Modal Logic*. Yale University Press, New Haven.

Halmos, Paul R. (1963): *Lectures on Boolean Algebras*. Van Nostrand, New York.

Hausser, Roland (1974): 'Syntax and semantics of plural' In *Proceedings of the 10th Regional Meeting of the Chicago Linguistic Society*, 234 – 247.

Heim, Irene, Howard Lasnik and Robert May (1991): 'Reciprocity and Plurality' In *Linguistic Inquiry* **22.1**, 63 – 101.

Hendry, H.E. (1982): 'Complete Extensions of the Calculus of Individuals' In *Noûs* **16**, 453 – 460.

Herzog, Otthein and Claus Rollinger (eds.) (1991): *Text Understanding in LILOG: Integrating Computational Linguistics and Artificial Intelligence*. Springer, Berlin – Heidelberg – New York.

Higginbotham, J. (1980): 'Reciprocal Interpretation' In *Journal of Linguistic Research* **1**, 97 – 117.

Hinrichs, E. (1985): *A Compositional Semantics for Aktionsarten and NP Reference in English*. Ph. D. Dissertation Ohio State University.

Hintikka, Jaakko, Julius M. E. Moravcsik and Patrick Suppes (eds.) (1973): *Approaches to Natural Language*. Reidel, Dordrecht.

Hoeksema, Jack (1983): 'Plurality and Conjunction' In (ter Meulen 1983), 63 – 84.

Hoeksema, Jack (1988): 'The semantics of non–Boolean 'and'' In *Journal of Semantics* **6**, 19 – 40.

Kadmon, Nirit (1987): *On Unique and Non–Unique Reference and Asymmetric Quantification*. Ph. D. Dissertation, University of Massachusetts, Amherst.

Kadmon, Nirit (1989): 'Uniqueness' In *Linguistics and Philosophy* **31**, 273 – 324.

Kamp, Hans and Uwe Reyle (1993): *From Discourse to Logic. An Introduction to Modeltheoretic Semantics of Natural Language, Formal Logic, and Discourse Representation Theory.* Kluwer, Dordrecht.

Kanazawa, Makoto and Christopher J. Piñón (eds.) (1994): *Dynamics, Polarity and Quantification.* CSLI Lecture Notes No. 48, CSLI Publications, Stanford.

Keenan, Edward (1981): 'A Boolean approach to semantics' In (Groenendijk/Janssen/Stokhof 1981).

Keenan, Edward and Leonard Faltz (1985): *Boolean Semantics for Natural Language.* Reidel, Dordrecht.

Keenan, Edward and Yonathan Stavi (1986): 'A semantic characterization of natural language determiners' In *Linguistics and Philosophy* **9**, 253 – 326.

Kimball, John P. (ed.) (1973): *Syntax and Semantics. Vol. 2.* Academic Press, New York.

Krifka, Manfred (1987): 'Nominal reference and temporal constitution: Towards a semantics of quantity' In [Groenendijk/Stokhof/Veltman 1987], 153 – 173.

Krifka, Manfred (1989): *Nominalreferenz und Zeitkonstitution. Zur Semantik von Massentermen, Pluraltermen und Aspektklassen.* Fink, München.

Krifka, Manfred (1989): 'Nominal reference and temporal constitution: Towards a semantics of quantity' In (Bartsch et al. 1989), 75 –115.

Krifka, Manfred (1991): 'Four thousand ships passed through the lock: Object-induced measure functions on events' In *Linguistics and Philosophy* **13**, 487 – 520.

Krifka, Manfred (1991): 'Massenausdrücke.' In [von Stechow/Wunderlich 1991].

Krifka, Manfred (1991): 'How to get rid of groups, using DRT' In *Texas Linguistics Forum* **32**, 71 – 110.

Krifka, Manfred (1996): 'Parametrized sum individuals for plural anaphora' In *Linguistics and Philosophy* **19**.

Landman, Fred (1987): 'Groups, Plural, Individuals and Intensionality' In (Groenendijk/Stokhof/Veltman 1987), 197 – 217.

Landman, Fred (1989): 'Groups', Part I, II. In *Linguistics and Philosophy* **12**, 559 – 605; 723 – 744.

Landman, Fred (1991): *Structures for Semantics.* Kluwer Academic Publishers, Dordrecht.

Landman, Fred and Frank Veltman (1984): *Varieties of Formal Semantics. Proceedings of the Fourth Amsterdam Colloquium.* GRASS Series No.3, Foris, Dordrecht.

Langendoen, Terence D. (1978): 'The Logic of Reciprocity' In *Linguistic Inquiry* **9**, 177 – 197.

Lasersohn, Peter N. (1988): *A Semantics for Groups and Events.* Ph. D. Dissertation, Ohio State University, Columbus.

Lasersohn, Peter N. (1989): 'On the Readings of Plural Noun Phrases' In *Linguistic Inquiry* **20**, 130 – 134.

Lasersohn, Peter N. (1990): 'Group action and spatio–temporal proximity' In *Linguistics and Philosophy* **13**, 179 – 206.

Laycock, Henry (1972): 'Some questions of ontology' In *Philosophical Review* **81**, 3 – 42.

Laycock, Henry (1975): 'Theories of Matter' In *Synthese* 31, 411 – 442; also in (Pelletier 1979), 89 – 120.

Lejewski, Czesław (1958): 'On Leśniewski's ontology' In *Ratio* **1**, 150 – 176.

Lejewski, Czesław (1960/61): 'Studies in the axiomatic foundations of Boolean algebra' In *Notre Dame Journal of Formal Logic* **1** (1960), 23 – 47, 91 – 106; **2** (1961), 79 – 93.

Leonard, Henry and Nelson Goodman (1940): 'The calculus of individuals and its uses' In *Journal of Symbolic Logic* **5**, 45 – 55.

Leśniewski, Stanislaw (1927 – 31): 'O podstawack matematyki' In *Prezeglad Filosoficzny* **30** (1927), 164 – 206; **31** (1928), 261 – 291; **32** (1929), 60 – 101; **33** (1930), 77 – 105; **34** (1931), 142 – 170.

Lewis, David (1991): *Parts of Classes*. With an appendix by John P. Burgess, A. P. Hazen, and David Lewis. Basil Blackwell.

Lewis, David (1993): 'Mathematics is Megethology' In *Philosophia Mathematica* **3**, 3 – 23.

Link, Godehard: 1983, 'The logical analysis of plurals and mass terms: A lattice–theoretical approach', in [Bäuerle/Schwarze/von Stechow 1983], 302 – 323. Reprinted in [Link 1996], chap. 1.

Link, Godehard: 1984, 'Hydras: On the logic of relative constructions with multiple heads', in (Landman/Veltman 1984), 245 – 257. Reprinted in: [Link 1996], chap. 3.

Link, G. (1987): 'Generalized Quantifiers and Plurals' In P. Gärdenfors (ed.) *Generalized Quantifiers, Linguistic and Logic Approaches*. D. Reidel, Dordrecht.

Link, Godehard (1987): '*Je drei Äpfel – three apples each*. Quantification and the German *je*', ms., Stanford In [Link 1996], chap. 5.

Link, Godehard (1987): 'Algebraic semantics of event structures' In [Groenendijk/Stokhof/Veltman 1987], 243 – 262. Reprinted in [Link 1996], chap. 7.

Link, Godehard (1991): 'Plural' In [von Stechow/Wunderlich 1991], 418 – 440. English translation in [Link 1996], chap. 2.

Link, Godehard (1991): 'Quantity and number' In [Zaefferer 1991]. Also in [Link 1996], chap. 9.

Link, Godehard (1991): 'First order axioms for the logic of plurality' Ms., University of Munich. In [Link 1996], chap. 10.

Link, Godehard (1993): 'Algebraic Semantics for Natural Language: Some Philosophy, some Applications' In [Guarino/Poli 1996]. Reprinted in: [Link 1996], chap. 12.

Link, Godehard (1993): 'Ten Years of Research on Plurals. Where do we stand?' Ms., University of Munich. Also in: [Link 1996], chap. 11.

Link, Godehard (1996): *Algebraic Semantics in Language and Philosophy*. CSLI Lecture Notes, CSLI Publications, Stanford.

Link, Godehard and Hinrich Schütze (1991): 'The Treatment of Plurality in L-LILOG' In [Herzog/ Rollinger 1991].

Löbner, Sebastian (1985): 'Definites' In *Journal of Semantics* 4, 279 – 326.

Löbner, Sebastian (1987): 'Natural language and generalized quantifier theory' In [Gärdenfors 1987], 181 – 201.

Lønning, Jan Tore (1987): 'Mass terms and quantification' In *Linguistics and Philosophy* 10, 1 – 52.

Lønning, Jan Tore (1987): 'Collective readings of definite and indefinite noun phrases' In [Gärdenfors 1987], 203 – 235.

Lønning, J. T. (1989): *Some Aspects of the Logic of Plural Noun Phrases*. COSMOS-Report No. 11, Department of Mathematics, University of Oslo.

Lønning, J. T. (1991): 'Among Readings. Some Comments on "Among Collections" ' In: [van der Does 1991a], 37 – 91.

Lønning, J. T. (1996): 'Plurals and collectivity' In [van Benthem/ ter Meulen 1996].

Lorimer, D. L. R. (1915): *Pashtu, Part I*.

Luschei, E. C. (1962): *The Logical Systems of Leśniewski*. North Holland, Amsterdam.

Martin, R. M. (1943): 'A homogeneous system for formal logic' In *Journal of Symbolic Logic* 8, 1 – 23.

Martin, R. M. (1978): *Events, Reference and Logical Form*. Catholic University of America Press, Washington, D. C.

Massey, G. (1976): 'Tom, Dick and Harry, and all the King's men' In *American Philosophical Quarterly* 13, 89 – 107.

Moltmann, Friederike (1996): *Parts and Wholes in Semantics*. Oxford University Press, Oxford.

Montague, Richard (1973): 'Reply to Moravcsik' In [Hintikka/Moravcsik/Suppes 1973], 289 – 294; reprinted as 'The proper treatment of mass terms in English' In [Pelletier 1979], 173 – 178.

Moore, R. and G. Hobbs (eds.) (1985): *Formal Theories of the Common Sense World*.

Moravcsik, Julius M. E. (1973): 'Mass terms in English' In [Hintikka/Moravcsik/Suppes 1973], 263 – 285.

Ojeda, A. E. (1993): *Linguistic Individuals*. CSLI Lecture Notes No. 31. CSLI Publications, Stanford.

Orey, S. (1959): 'Model theory for higher order predicate calculus' In *Transactions from the American Mathematical Society* 92, 72 – 84.

Parsons, Terence (1970): 'An analysis of mass terms and amount terms' In *Foundations of Language* 6, 362 – 388; also in [Pelletier 1979], 137 – 166.

Parsons, Terence (1975): 'Afterthoughts on mass terms' In *Synthese* **31**, 517 – 521; also in [Pelletier 1979], 167 – 171.

Partee, Barbara (1987): 'Noun phrase interpretation and type shifting principles' In [Groenendijk/Janssen/Stokhof 1981], 115 – 143.

Partee, Barbara and Mats Rooth (1983): 'Generalized conjunction and type ambiguity' In [Bäuerle/Schwarze/von Stechow 1983], 361 – 383.

Pelletier, Francis J. (1975): 'Non–singular reference: some preliminaries' In *Philosophia* **5**; also in [Pelletier 1979], 1 – 14.

Pelletier, Francis J. (ed.) (1979): *Mass Terms: Some Philosophical Problems.* Reidel, Dordrecht.

Pelletier, Francis J. (1979): 'A bibliography of recent work on mass terms' In [Pelletier 1979], 295 – 298.

Pelletier, Francis J. and Lenhart K. Schubert (1989): 'Mass expressions' In [Gabbay/Guenthner 1989], 327 – 407.

Pollard, Stephen (1986): 'Plural quantification and the iterative conception of set' In *Philosophy Research Archives* **11**, 579 – 587.

Quine, Willard van Orman (1960): *Word and Object.*, M.I.T. Press, Cambridge, Massachusetts.

Quine, Willard van Orman (1972): *Methods of Logic.*, 3rd edition, Holt, Rinehart and Winston, New York.

Rescher, Nicholas (1962): 'Plurality quantification' In *Journal of Symbolic Logic* **38**, 373 – 374.

Resnik, Michael D. (1988): 'Second–order logic still wild' In *Journal of Philosophy* **85**, 75 – 87.

Roberts, Craige (1987): *Modal Subordination, Anaphora, and Distributivity.* Ph. D. Dissertation, University of Massachusetts at Amherst.

Roberts, Craige (1987): 'Distributivity' In [Groenendijk/Stokhof/Veltman 1987], 291 – 309.

Rodman, R. (ed.) (1972): *Montague Grammar.* ms., UCLA.

Roeper, Peter (1983): 'Semantics for mass terms with quantifiers' In *Noûs* **17**, 251 – 265.

Roeper, Peter (1985): 'Generalization of first–order logic to non–atomic domains' In *Journal of Symbolic Logic* **50**, 815 – 838.

Rooth, Mats (1987): 'Noun phrase interpretation in Montague Grammar, File Change Semantics, and Situation Semantics' In: [Gärdenfors 1987], 237 – 268.

Russell, Bertrand (1903): *The Principles of Mathematics.* Second edition 1937, George Allen & Unwin, London.

Scha, Remko (1981): 'Distributive, Collective and Cumulative Quantification' In [Groenendijk/Janssen/Stokhof 1981], 483 – 512.

Scha, Remko and Stallard, D. (1988): 'Multi–Level Plurals and Distributivity' In *Proceedings of the ACL meeting, June 1988*, 17 – 24.

Schein, Barry (1993): *Plurals and Events.* MIT Press, Cambridge, Massachusetts.

Schütze, Hinrich (1989): *Pluralbehandlung in natürlichsprachlichen Wissensverarbeitungssystemen.* Diplomarbeit, Institut für Informatik, University of Stuttgart.

Schwarzschild, Roger (1990): 'Against groups', in: [Stokhof/Torenvliet 1990], 475 – 493.

Schwarzschild, Roger (1991): *On the Meaning of Definite Plural Noun Phrases.* Ph.D. Dissertation, University of Massachusetts, Amherst.

Schwarzschild, Roger (1992): 'Types of plural individuals' In *Linguistics and Philosophy* **15**, 641 – 675.

Seiler, Hansjakob and Christian Lehmann (eds.) (1982): *Apprehension. Das sprachliche Erfassen von Gegenständen.* Narr, Tübingen.

Shapiro Stewart (1991): *Foundations without Foundationalism. A Case for Second-order Logic.* Clarendon Press, Oxford.

Sharvy, Richard (1978): 'Maybe English has no count nouns: Notes on Chinese Semantics. An Essay in Metaphysics and Linguistics' In *Studies in Language* **2**, 345 – 365.

Sharvy, Richard (1979): 'The indeterminacy of mass predication', in [Pelletier 1979], 47 – 54.

Sharvy, Richard (1980): 'A more general theory of definite desciptions' In *Philosophical Review* **89**, 607 – 624.

Sharvy, Richard (1983): 'Mixtures' In *Journal of Philosophy* **80**, 227 – 239.

Sikorski, Roman (1969): *Boolean Algebras.* 3rd edition. Springer, Berlin.

Simons, Peter M. (1982): 'Plural reference and set theory' In [Smith 1982], 199 – 256.

Simons, Peter M. (1983): 'Class, mass and mereology' In *History and Philosophy of Logic* **4**, 157 – 180.

Simons, Peter M. (1987): *Parts. A Study in Ontology.* Clarendon Press, Oxford.

Smith, Barry (ed.) (1982): *Parts and Moments. Studies in Logic and Formal Ontology.* München.

Smith-Stark, Cedric (1974): 'The plurality split' In *Chicago Linguistics Society Papers* **10**, 657 – 671.

von Stechow, Arnim (1980): 'Modification of noun phrases. A challenge for compositional semantics' In *Theoretical Linguistics* **7**, 57 – 110.

von Stechow, Arnim and Dieter Wunderlich (eds.) (1991): *Semantik / Semantics. Ein internationales Handbuch der zeitgenössischen Forschung / An International Handbook of Contemporary Research.* de Gruyter, Berlin – New York.

Stokhof, Martin and L. Torenvliet (eds.) (1990): *Proceedings of the Seventh Amsterdam Colloquium.* ITLI, Amsterdam.

ter Meulen, Alice (1980): *Substance, Quantities and Individuals: A Study in the Formal Semantics of Mass Terms.* Ph. D. Dissertation, Stanford. Indiana University Linguistics Club, Bloomington.

ter Meulen, Alice (1981): 'An intensional logic for mass terms' In *Philosophical Studies* **40**, 105 – 125.

ter Meulen, Alice (ed.) (1983): *Studies in Model–Theoretic Semantics*, Foris, Dordrecht.

ter Meulen, Alice (1984): 'Events, quantities and individuals' In [van Benthem/ter Meulen 1984], 259 – 279.

Verkuyl, Henk J. (1981): 'Numerals and quantifiers in Xbar–Syntax and their semantic interpretation' In [Groenendijk/Janssen/Stokhof 1981], 567 – 599.

Verkuyl, Henk J. (1991): *NP Structure*. OTS Prepublication Series, Rijksuniversiteit Utrecht.

Verkuyl, Henk J. (1994): 'Distributivity and collectivity: a couple at odds' In [Kanazawa/Piñón 1994], 49 – 80.

Verkuyl, Henk J. and van der Does, J. M. (1996): 'The semantics of plural noun phrases' In [van der Does/van Eijck 1996].

Wald, Jan David (1977): *Stuff and Words: A Semantic and Linguistic Analysis of Non–Singular Reference*. Ph. D. Dissertation, Brandeis University.

Ware, Robert (1975): 'Some bits and pieces' In *Synthese* **31**, 15 – 29.

Webber, Bonnie (1984): 'So what can we talk about now?' In [Brady/Berwick 1984], 331 – 371.

Westerståhl, Dag (1989): 'Quantifiers in formal and natural language' In [Gabbay/Guenthner 1989], 1 – 131.

Zaefferer, Dietmar (ed.) (1991): *Semantic Universals and Universal Semantics*. GRASS Series No 12, Foris, Dordrecht.

Zaefferer, Dietmar (1992): '*And* and *or*: meet and/or join? A problem in the semantics of (non–)propositional connectives' Paper read at the International Congress of Linguistics, Montreal, August 1992.

Zemach, Eddy (1970): 'Four ontologies' In *Journal of Philosophy* **62**, 213 – 247.

KURT EBERLE

THE INFLUENCE OF PLURAL NPs ON AKTIONSART IN DRT

1. INTRODUCTION

Since Vendler's analysis in (Vendler 1967) it is common to distinguish four classes of natural language event descriptions, *states, activities, accomplishments* and *achievements*. In terms of interval semantics these classes are normally characterized as follows:

- *States* are temporally extended and homogeneous. If a state holds at an interval t, it also holds at all subintervals t' of t (even at the time points of t, if the logic considered uses time points). This means that states have the *subinterval property* (cf. (Bennett and Partee 1972)).
  Examples are *Paul speaks French* or *Paul is eating an apple*.

- *Activities* are temporally extended and relatively homogeneous. The subinterval property seems to be restricted to subintervals that pass a *certain limit in size* (cf. (Dowty 1986)).
  An example is *Paul worked in the garden*.

- *Accomplishments* are temporally extended and heterogeneous, i.e. if an accomplishment holds at an interval t, it does not hold at the subintervals of t.
  This is true of *Paul wrote a letter*, for example.

- *Achievements* are punctual: *Paul reached the top*.

Following a linguistic tradition referred to in (Steinitz 1981), we call this classification a classification of the *Aktionsart* of events or event descriptions.[1]

Vendler presents linguistic tests for the determination of the Aktionsart of event descriptions. Activities and states can co-occur with adverbials like *for three hours* but not (at least not without changing the 'normal' meaning of the description) with adverbials like *in three hours*. For accomplishments it is the opposite. The co-occurrence test with *in-* and *for*-adverbials marks a distinction of Aktionsarten that is of decisive importance with respect to a wide range of textual behavior: the distinction between *homogeneous* and *heterogeneous* event descriptions.[2]

It is not the verb alone which decides the Aktionsart of the event introduced by a sentence. The different thematic roles influence the choice. Thus, for instance,

(1) *Peter drank.*

refers to an activity. We can easily say *Peter drank for several hours.* Adding information to (1) about the object consumed can confirm the Aktionsart of (1), as in (2):

(2) *Peter drank beer. / Peter drank cocktails.*

But it can also result in a change of the Aktionsart, as in (3):

(3) *Peter drank a glass of beer.*

Again the in/for–test points up the difference between (2) and (3).

It is often said that bare plurals (and also mass terms) uniformly transform accomplishments and achievements into activities. Calculi that compute the Aktionsart and that treat the influence of bare plural roles in this uniform way using syntactically and/or morphologically motivated feature descriptions of the roles were suggested by (Verkuyl 1972), (Platzack 1979) and (Reyle 1987) among others. We think, however, that, first, the influence of bare plural roles on the Aktionsart is not unique and, second, that this influence must be described in terms of explanatory semantic criteria. We think that this is also true of other role descriptions. However, in this paper we will concentrate on how descriptions of thematic roles that denote sets contribute to the Aktionsart of the entire clause. Here, we will restrict ourselves to German sentences.

(4) a. *Sportler brachten die olympische Fackel nach Barcelona.*
        (SPORTSMEN TOOK THE OLYMPIC TORCH TO BARCELONA.)
    b. *Olympia–Fans fuhren nach Barcelona.*
        (OLYMPICS FANS WENT TO BARCELONA.)
    c. *Beim Stürmer–Training drosch Völler Bälle ins Tor.*
        (AT THE FORWARD TRAINING, VÖLLER KICKED BALLS INTO THE GOAL.)
    d. *Am Mittwoch transportierte ein FIFA–Mitarbeiter Bälle von London nach Rom.*
        (ON WEDNESDAY, A FIFA–EMPLOYEE CARRIED BALLS FROM LONDON TO ROME.)

Provided the reading is chosen that, against the background of world knowledge, is most natural, (4a) and (4d) are accepted in the scope of (pragmatically suitable) in–adverbials, whereas (4b) and (4c) are not. With respect to for–adverbials, we observe the opposite behavior.[3] So the test with in– and for–adverbials corroborates the preferred reading in (4a) and (4d) as an accomplishment, and as an activity in (4b) and (4c). This does not correspond to the outcome of analytic systems such as the ones mentioned above that attribute uniform Aktionsart effect to bare plurals.

Often, the use of a bare plural phrase turns a sentence into a generic statement: For instance, the transition *the car has four wheels* → *cars have four wheels* turns the situation dependent statement about a concrete object *car* into a generic statement about the *kind* CAR. Generic statements, of course, are stative. Clearly, none of the examples of (4) is a generic statement. In this paper, we will not consider the use of bare plurals in generic sentences. We will treat only cases like (4), with situation dependent interpretation and bare plurals that refer to sums or sets of objects, not to kinds (or at least, also to sums or sets and not exclusively to kinds (cf. (Carlson 1980))).

We will try to explain the diverging impact of plural phrases onto the Aktionsart of the correspondingly modified, event descriptions by extending an approach of Krifka's (cf. (Krifka 1987b)). For Krifka, the different Aktionsarten of sentences rely on different structural properties that the extensions of the event predicates of the sentences have in interpreting models. Krifka's approach is an elaborate reformulation of Vendler's point of view within a framework with reified events. We deviate from Krifka's approach in that we also consider event types that describe sets or sums of events (normally introduced via iteration or via summing up the events introduced by quantification over thematic roles). This modification extends, as we think, the fragment with which we can correctly deal with respect to semantic representation and Aktionsart computation. In particular, it allows for a correct, unified account of (4), which, otherwise, to our opinion, can be only fragmentarily evaluated.

Roughly, on this structural basis, we think that in (4a) – (4d) the bare plural phrases uniformly introduce a set or sum of individuals each with identical ontological status, i.e. without a distinction of the type *kind*, *object*. In our opinion, the Aktionsart difference derives from the fact that with *fahren nach Barcelona* in (4b) and *Völler ins Tor dreschen* in (4c) the distribution over the set is preferred (over *Olympia–Fans* in (4b) and over *Bälle* in (4c)), and that with *die olympische Fackel nach Barcelona bringen* and *ein FIFA–Mitarbeiter von London nach Rom fahren* the distribution over the set (*Sportler* in (4a) and *Bälle* in (4d)) is not licensed or, at least, is not preferred. Since, more specifically, we assume in the distributional case some 'distribution in time', the downward heredity, that is typical of activities or states, is guaranteed for (4b) and (4c), provided we make use of a suitable refined notion of homogeneous Aktionsart that includes the evaluation of event types that refer to event sums. (Assuming for (4c) that there is an unknown number of balls hit into the goal one after the other over a certain time t, for subintervals t' of t, we observe the same (specific) property, and accordingly for (4b)).

In order to characterize this conception within a formal theory, we will proceed in the following way. The background of our formalization will be *Discourse Representation Theory* (henceforth DRT, cf. (Kamp 1981)). In the next section we introduce the concepts of this theory that are relevant to our subject. This includes extensions of the DRT–language where needed. On the basis of this, we will motivate and define in section 3 a refined notion of homogeneous and heterogeneous event types that is also applicable to types that refer to sums of events. In section 4 we will sketch a DRS–construction algorithm for collective and distributive readings which comprises an Aktionsart calculus. In section 5 we will extend this algorithm to allow for cumulative readings. This extension gives a means for fine–tuning the construction of the desired representations of (4) and of other plural constructions. In the concluding section 6 we summarize the results of the suggested formal treatment.

The approach described in this paper is a condensed, updated version of some aspects of the broader approach developed in (Eberle 1991).

2. REPRESENTATIONS AND MODEL THEORY

In the framework of Discourse Representation Theory (DRT) (Kamp 1981) a DRS is a pair $<U,K>$ consisting of a set U of discourse referents (DRFs) and a set K of conditions. Since the beginnings of DRT in 1981 several types of conditions have been introduced. (For a recent version of DRT, compare (Kamp and Reyle 1993)). For the purposes of this paper, we will utilize the set of condition types presented below. As in (Eberle 1991) and in (Kamp and Reyle 1993), a semilattice approach has been adopted in order to model plural phenomena of natural language texts. There are several reasons motivating such an approach that we will not, however, go into here.[4] So conditions may take the following forms reflecting the lattice structuring of the domain of models:

1.) $P(a_1,\ldots,a_n)$, where P is an n–ary predicate symbol and the a_i

THE INFLUENCE OF PLURAL NPs ON AKTIONSART IN DRT

are discourse referents. For 2–place relations we will also use infix notation. Among other things the two–place relations used are $\in_i, \leq_i$ and $<_i$, standing in turn for *atomic part, part* and *part proper*.

2.) $P^*(a)$, where P is a one–place predicate symbol, a is a discourse referent and * an operator defined for one–place predicate symbols, the *plural operator*, which, with respect to a particular interpretation, when applied to P, denotes the sums that can be constructed from the objects denoted by P.

3.) $f(a_1, \ldots, a_n) = a$, where f is an n–ary function symbol and $a_1, \ldots, a_n, a$ are discourse referents. Among other things we will use one–place functions for particular thematic roles of events like *agent, theme, object* and the two–place function $\sqcup_i$ which is used to construct the sum of discourse referents. Conditions of the three forms described are also called *atomic* conditions.

4.) $K_1 \, \langle\!\langle\substack{every\\x}\rangle\!\rangle \, K_2$, where K_1, K_2 are DRSs and x is a discourse referent introduced in the universe of K_1. Conditions of this form are also called *duplex* conditions. They reflect universal quantification over the x satisfying the conditions of K_1. K_1 is called the *restrictor* and K_2 the *nuclear scope* of the duplex condition. (There are other duplex conditions, which are of no interest here.)

5.) $z = \Sigma y K$, where K is a DRS, y a DRF of $U(K)$ and z a DRF which stands for – with respect to a particular interpretation I – the sum of those objects o for which K is valid with respect to some I' that develops from I by assigning o to y. We say that we get z via *abstraction* from K.

6.) $(\lambda y K)(z)$, where K is a DRS, y a DRF of $U(K)$, and z a DRF the *defined property* $\lambda y K$ is predicated of.

We require the domain of a model of a DRS to be a complete and complementary join semilattice.

A1 $\forall x,y \ (x \sqcup_i y = y \sqcup_i x)$ commutativity
A2 $\forall x \ (x \sqcup_i x = x)$ idempotence
A3 $\forall x,y,z \ (x \sqcup_i (y \sqcup_i z) = (x \sqcup_i y) \sqcup_i z)$ associativity
A4 $\forall x,y \ \exists^{=1} z \ (x \sqcup_i y = z)$ totally defined function
A5 $\forall x,y \ (x \leq_i y \leftrightarrow x \sqcup_i y = y)$ part
A6 $\forall x,y \ (x <_i y \leftrightarrow x \leq_i y \land \neg x = y)$ proper part
A7 $\forall x,y \ (x \circ_i y \leftrightarrow \exists z(z \leq_i x \land z \leq_i y))$ overlap
A8 $\forall x,y \ (x <_i y \rightarrow \exists^{=1} z(\neg x \circ_i z \land x \sqcup_i z = y))$ complementarity

An important subset of the domain is, of course, the class of atoms.

A9 $\forall x \ (atom(x) \leftrightarrow \neg \exists y(y <_i x))$
A10 $\forall x \exists y \ (y \leq_i x \land atom(y))$

Generalizing $\sqcup_i$ to sup_i which denotes the function that, for any set B of the domain, returns the least upper bound of the elements of B with respect to $\leq_i$, we can characterize the functionality of the operator *:

A11 $\forall B \exists x \ (sup_i(B) = x)$
A12 $\forall P \forall x \ (P^*(x) \leftrightarrow \exists B \ (B \subseteq P \land x = sup_i(B)))$

A8 – A11 (together with the other axioms) guarantee that the lattice structuring reflects the relevant properties of set theory with respect to its use in natural language. The possibility of defining 'elements' emphasizes this:

A13 $\forall x,y(x \in_i y \leftrightarrow x \leq_i y \land atom(x))$

In order to restrict the set of structures suited for the interpretation of DRSs, here, we have used formulae of predicate calculus. This has been done for the sake of brevity only. Of course, using DRSs, we can characterize the same set of suitable interpreting structures. (Therefore, however, we need a condition type, omitted here, which expresses the negation of a statement). Since we want to develop a theory of event descriptions within the framework of DRT, throughout this paper we will consider formulae of predicate calculus as abbreviations of corresponding DRSs.

Now, for K a DRS, and M a model with interpretations for the predicate– and function–symbols, $\hat{f}$ a partial embedding function from

THE INFLUENCE OF PLURAL NPs ON AKTIONSART IN DRT 61

the set of DRFs onto the domain of M, we say that $\hat{f}$ verifies K in M iff $M \models_{\hat{f}} K$, where:

$M \models_{\hat{f}} K$ iff $\hat{f}$ is defined for the DRFs of $U(K)$ and $M \models_{\hat{f}} C(K)$.
$M \models_{\hat{f}} C(K)$ iff for all $c \in C(K)$ $M \models_{\hat{f}} c$.
For $M \models_{\hat{f}} c$, corresponding to the different types of condition, we stipulate that:

I.1) $M \models_{\hat{f}} P(a_1, \ldots, a_n)$ iff $P^M(\hat{f}(a_1), \ldots, \hat{f}(a_n))$

I.2) $M \models_{\hat{f}} P^*(a)$ iff there exists $B \subseteq P^M$ with $sup_i^M(B) = \hat{f}(a)$

I.3) $M \models_{\hat{f}} f(a_1, \ldots, a_n) = a$ iff $f^M(\hat{f}(a_1), \ldots, \hat{f}(a_n)) = \hat{f}(a)$

I.4) $M \models_{\hat{f}} K_1 \langle\text{every}_z\rangle K_2$ iff there exists an extension $\hat{g}$ of $\hat{f}$, DRFs x_1 and x_2 with $x_1, x_2 \notin def(\hat{f})$ such, that from $M \models_{\hat{g}} x_1 = \Sigma x K_1$ and $M \models_{\hat{g}} x_2 = \Sigma x (K_1 \bigcup K_2)$ it follows that $\hat{g}(x_1) = \hat{g}(x_2)$.

I.5) $M \models_{\hat{f}} z = \Sigma y K$ iff $\hat{f}(z) = sup_i^M(A)$,
where $A = \{a \mid \text{there exists } \hat{g} \text{ that extends } \hat{f} \text{ onto } U(K) \text{ with } M \models_{\hat{g}} K \text{ and } a = \hat{g}(y)\}$

I.6) $M \models_{\hat{f}} (\lambda y K)(z)$ iff $\lambda y K$ is a *defined predicate* with respect to the interpretation $<M, \hat{f}>$ and $\hat{f}(z) \in \|\lambda y K\|_{M,\hat{f}}$, where $\lambda y K$ is a *defined predicate* with respect to the interpretation $<M, \hat{f}>$ iff $\hat{f}$ is defined for the *free variables* of K. In this case we stipulate that $\|\lambda y K\|_{M,\hat{f}} = \{a \mid \text{there exists } \hat{g} \text{ that extends } \hat{f} \text{ onto } U(K) \text{ with } M \models_{\hat{g}} K \text{ and } a = \hat{g}(y)\}$.

We call a DRF x a free variable of K iff x is contained in an atomic condition C of $C(K')$, with K' a sub–DRS of K, but is neither element of $U(K')$ nor element of the universe of a sub–DRS of K that contains K'. (Of course, K is a sub–DRS of itself).

It is clear, first, that we will use duplex conditions in order to represent natural language statements like (5)

(5)   *Every farmer owns a donkey.*

(5_{rep})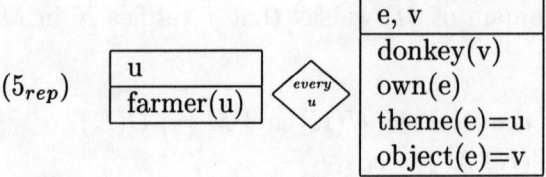

Second, we use abstraction type conditions in order to be able to refer to sums that can be abstracted from conditions like (5_{rep}):

(6)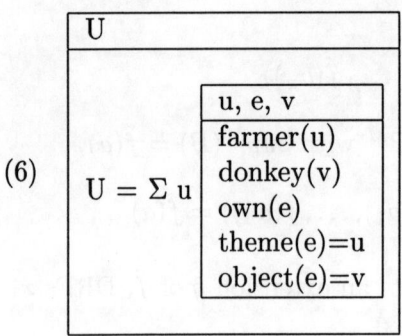

In (6), U stands for the sum of those farmers who own at least one donkey. Exchanging U for V and the u after Σ for v in (6) would provide us with a DRF V referring to the sum of those donkeys that are owned by a farmer.

In (6) we have used the convention that upper case letters are DRFs that denote sums of objects, and that lower case letters are DRFs that denote atomic objects.[5] In addition, in the following, we will use greek letters as DRFs that are underdetermined with respect to their reference to atomic or non–atomic objects. For the abstraction of sums from duplex conditions, we allow for the following abbreviation:

$$\chi_{i_1}, \ldots, \chi_{i_n} :: \boxed{K_1 \;\langle ? \rangle\; K_2}$$

replaces

$$K_1 \;\langle ? \rangle\; K_2$$
$$\chi_{i_1} = \Sigma \chi_{i'_1}(K_1 \bigcup K_2)$$
$$\vdots$$
$$\chi_{i_n} = \Sigma \chi_{i'_n}(K_1 \bigcup K_2)$$

where $\chi_{i'_1}, \ldots, \chi_{i'_n} \in U(K_1) \bigcup U(K_2)$

In order to establish unique reference between the DRF of the sum and the DRF for the objects that make up this sum we use indices: Y_1 sums up y_1, X_7 x_7, χ_3 χ'_3, and so forth. Another notational convenience is the following. We use:

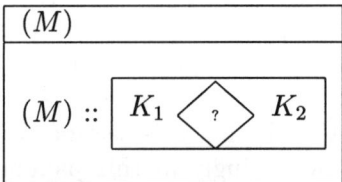

as shorthand for

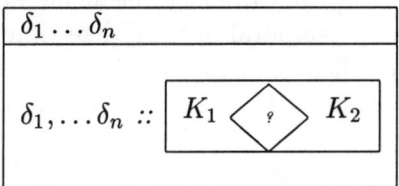

where the set of δ_i, i.e. (M), exhausts the possibilities for abstraction with respect to the corresponding duplex condition. This means that there are $\delta'_1, \ldots, \delta'_n$ the δ_i abstract over in turn such that $\{\delta'_1, \ldots, \delta'_n\} = U(K_1) \bigcup U(K_2)$.

DRT uses a variant of the Davidsonian method of talking about events (Davidson 1967) and treats them as a kind of objects. While we have adopted this, we deviate from the usual DRT-style representation of event descriptions according to which, for instance, the nuclear scope box of (5_{rep}) would be written as follows:

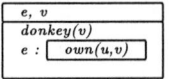

For representing event descriptions, in classical DRT, complex conditions are introduced which are pairs consisting of the DRF for the event, and of a DRS containing the event description in terms of an n-ary event predicate over the DRFs of the thematic roles. Instead of this, (compare the original nuclear scope box of (5_{rep})), we use one-place event predicates and a number of explicit one-place functions corresponding to the thematic roles which allow for relating the values of the thematic roles to the event. (Since we use this alternative notation, above, we have omitted to list the usual condition type of DRT for event descriptions). We abstain from the DRT style in this respect and use one–place event predicates and explicit thematic roles for reasons presented, for instance, in (Bäuerle 1988) and (Krifka 1987b). We will not go into detail with this here. We only mention that the existence of verbs which do not show up any syntactically subcategorized obligatory thematic role (e.g. verbs like *raining, storming* with expletive subject) and the relatively autonomous status of thematic roles (*the agent, the (consumed) object* (of an eating event)) seem to support the choice made. In addition, this notation facilitates linking up with KL–ONE like knowledge representation formalisms.[6] Concluding this section we would like to stress that within DRT (and accordingly in this paper) DRFs introduced by descriptions of events proper and DRFs introduced by state descriptions like the *owning* in (5_{rep}) both refer to elements of the domain of a model that are not purely temporal objects (like time points or time intervals).[7] The defined predicates of the condition type 6.) will be used mainly with regard to event–DRFs. In this case they represent event types.[8]

3. HOMOGENEOUS AND HETEROGENEOUS EVENT TYPES

Our concern is to classify event types by means of structural properties of their extensions in the model. Therefore, we will develop some helpful notions. This will be done mainly by using predicate calculus characterizations. But, as mentioned in the last section, these characterizations can be taken as shorthand for corresponding DRT–statements.

We do not classify events, but event types. Consider the following pair of sentences (and the very similar examples (1) – (3)):

(7)   a.   *Peter trank Wein.*
           (PETER DRANK WINE.)
      b.   *Peter trank ein Glas Wein.*
           (PETER DRANK A GLASS OF WINE.)

(7a) is a homogeneous and (7b) a heterogeneous description, as the test with in– and for–adverbials makes clear. Since, with respect to a specific model, (7a) and (7b) might nevertheless be alternative descriptions of the **same** event, it is clear that the different Aktionsarten cannot be properties of the events themselves, but must be properties of the event types. This is also the standpoint of (Krifka 1987b), (Krifka 1987a). We will postpone discussing Krifka's relevant explication of how the thematic roles compositionally influence the Aktionsart of the entire description in cases like (7a) and (7b) until the end of this section. In the following, for the purpose of investigating suitable notions of homogeneity, we can do with considering the descriptions as not further analyzed predicates. Krifka assumes the domain of a model for a natural language sentence or text to be structured by means of a two–place fusion operation, ⊔, as a semilattice. We stress that Krifka's semilattice structuring has weaker properties than our structuring of the last section. So, for instance, it does not make sense to attribute a numerical value to Krifka's objects which could reflect the cardinality of the set of atoms that such objects subsume, since normally there is no unique partition of an object into atoms. In our modelling, there is. Here the relation $\leq_i$ exclusively reflects the ⊆–relation of set theory, and not the more general part–relation of mereology as Krifka's ≤ does. For this reason, we call Krifka's lattice operation *fusion* and not *sum operation*.

With respect to the dichotomy that the in/for–contrast makes explicit, the relevant distinction for Krifka is the distinction between *cumulative* and *quantized* predicates or, more generally, that between *cumulative* and *non–cumulative* predicates, rather than that between *divisive* and *non–divisive* predicates. Using ⊔ and ≤, cumulativity and divisivity are defined as follows:

A property P is cumulative, $KUM(P)$:
iff
$$\forall x, x' \quad (P(x) \wedge P(x') \rightarrow P(x \sqcup x'))$$

and a property P is divisive, $DIV(P)$:
iff
$$\forall x, x' \quad (P(x) \wedge x' \leq x \rightarrow P(x'))$$

The DIV/nonDIV–distinction would fit better with the more traditional picture of the 'downward looking' subinterval property that we presented in the introduction. Krifka's argument against the latter distinction is the incomplete homogeneity that activities normally show at their lower periphery. *Working*, for example, is understood as divisive though realizations of *working* can contain periods where the activity of working is suspended, and though there is a vague natural temporal threshold such that it does not make sense to call subperiods of a *working* that are below this threshold periods of working. For instance, periods that measure some nanoseconds might show some of the constitutive subactivities that make up walkings, but they never can be called periods of walking. These problems of pauses and perception limits have led Dowty and others to weakening the requirements of homogeneity for activities, what resulted in weak divisivity based definitions of activities, like the one sketched in the beginning of this paper. Such definitions necessarily lack the precision, naturalness and simplicity of the canonical definition of the cumulative reference. Nevertheless we think that divisivity is the decisive feature, or to be more precise, that the definition of homogeneity that classifies the data in a linguistically correct way cannot separate cumulativity from divisivity. In order to motivate this, we will use the test with in- and for-adverbials. The criterion that predicts and structurally explains the combinatory behavior of event descriptions in this respect must play a central role in a structural theory about Aktionsarten. Consider the following critical examples:

(8) a. *Petra arbeitete im Garten.*
     (PETRA WORKED IN THE GARDEN.)
   b. *Die Maschine sendete Licht aus.*
     (THE MACHINE EMITTED LIGHT.)
   c. *Paola streichelte einen Hund.*
     (PAOLA CARESSED A DOG.)
   d. *Paola streichelte (gleichzeitig) zwei Katzen.*
     (PAOLA CARESSED TWO CATS (SIMULTANEOUSLY).)
   e. *In München aß Peter eine Schweinshaxe mit Sauerkraut.*
     (IN MUNICH, HANS ATE A TROTTER WITH SAUERKRAUT.)
   f. *Der Roboter bewegte sich höchstens 50 Meter vorwärts.*
     (THE ROBOT MOVED FORWARD AT MOST 50 METERS.)
   g. *Der Roboter bewegte sich mindestens 50 Meter vorwärts.*
     (THE ROBOT MOVED FORWARD AT LEAST 50 METERS.)
   h. *Die Bombe explodierte.*
     (THE BOMB EXPLODED.)

As the test with in- and for-adverbials shows, (8a) – (8d) are homogeneous event descriptions, whereas (8e) – (8h), with respect to the normal, non-iterative reading, are not. The formal definition of homogeneity to develop must account for this behavior.

All sentences of (8) describe single events. We concentrate on this case first, i.e. on the case of predicates whose extension contains only single events.

Our modelling does not yet contain a structuring of the domain of single events. We introduce the mereological *material part*-relation $\leq_m$ (that corresponds to Krifka's $\leq$):

- $\leq_m$, the *material part* relation structures the domain of a model as a preorder. It extends the subsum relation $\leq_i$, i.e it holds that $\forall x, y \ (x \leq_i y \to x \leq_m y)$, but it does not hold that $\forall x, y \ (x \leq_m y \to x \leq_i y)$.[9]

From $\leq_m$ we define the *material equivalence*:

- $\forall x, y \ (x =_m y \leftrightarrow x \leq_m y \land y \leq_m x)$.

By materially equivalent events we mean events which are identical with respect to some coarse–grained notion of (physically motivated substantial) identity, for instance, in the sense of spatio–temporal regions. Nevertheless, such events may be different with respect to the level we are mainly concerned with here, which is a rather fine–grained ontological level suited for interpretations of natural language texts.[10]

Now, we call e' a *subevent* of e iff $e' \leq_m e$.

Above we have mentioned the problem of pauses and thresholds connected to activities like those described by (8a) and (8c). In order to restrict the test for divisivity to the relevant subevents of an investigated event, we make use of the following concepts:

- *lz* (for *Laufzeit/run time*) applied to an event e of a particular event type (of *working*, for instance), returns the time period (which is not necessarily an interval) at which the active phases of e (the phases of uninterrupted working) occur.

- *limit* applied to an event predicate P returns the threshold value that is specific for P. This value is given in terms of a measure for the substance of events, for instance, it is measured with respect to some spatio–temporal scale.[11]

- *size* applied to an event returns the volume of the event in terms of the scale used for *limit*.[12]

- *max–t–auss* (for **max**imaler **t**emporaler **Auss**schnitt/*maximal temporal segment*) holds for triplets $(\bar{e}, t, e)$, where t is a subinterval of the time at which e occurs and $\bar{e}$ is a maximal subevent of e (in the sense of $\leq_m$) occurring at t, i.e $\bar{e}$ is a maximal temporal segment of e with respect to t.

Now, we call an event predicate P divisive:

(I) DIV(P) iff for each event e of its extension and for each *maximal temporal segment* $\bar{e}$ of e that is temporally located within the *run time* of e and that is voluminous enough in *size* in order to pass the specific *perception limit* for P–events, there exists an event e' that is materially equivalent to $\bar{e}$ and that is a P–event too.

This characterization uses lz in order to obtain cleaned versions, so to speak, of the events of the P–predicate. This fading out of phases that are irrelevant with respect to the event description copies the behavior of the human recipient of a text, as we think, and restricts the application of the divisivity test proper to those phases of the event that are in focus exclusively. In addition, when testing a particular P, the characterization takes into account the P–specific granularity of the P–objects. So, following (I), the event predicate of (8a) will be classified as divisive, though Petra may interrupt her activity now and then for talking to a neighbor or for drinking a glass of beer, and though the remaining active phases are not divisive, when evaluated by means of a threshold value that is suited with respect to *emitting light*–events say, as described in (8b).

Of course, since the realization of the constitutive subactivities takes less time in the case of *emitting light*–events than it takes in the case of *working in the garden*–events, using the threshold value for the *emitting light*–predicate would produce a too fine–grained test for divisivity in the case of (8a).

(8d) explains why the test of (I) makes use of maximal temporal segments instead of the more general subevents. (8d) should be classified as a divisive event description. The event introduced by (8d), e_d, can be analyzed into two events, $e1_d$ and $e2_d$, where $e1_d$ is the caressing of the one of the two cats, and $e2_d$ is the caressing of the other cat. Thus, we obtain $e1_d \sqcup_i e2_d =_m e_d$ and, from this or directly, we obtain the actually relevant conditions $e1_d \leq_m e_d$, $e2_d \leq_m e_d$. $e1_d$ and $e2_d$ are material parts of e_d, i.e. they are subevents of e_d. Provided that e_d is a typical representative of the P–type, besides e_d, $e1_d$ and $e2_d$ will pass the threshold value for P that will be something like the volume of the smallest events of *caressing caused by a human agent*. However, neither $e1_d$ nor $e2_d$ is an event of type P: a caressing of two cats. We notice here that we obtain subevents in different ways as soon as events are understood as objects that are more than purely temporal units like intervals or time points. Material parts, subevents, can be extracted from an event by running along the time axis and segmenting the event into time slices. However, subevents can also be extracted by cutting pieces along the lines of other dimensions or even by mixed cutting procedures. It is reasonable to equip events with qualities that go beyond the scope of pure temporality (for this, compare for instance (Bäuerle 1988)), and it is reasonable to define *subevent* as a not further specified material part of an event. Notice, that, for the e_d-scenario of simultaneously caressing two cats, the definition of *subevent* as time slice, i.e. as temporal segment that exhausts the "spatial breadth" of the event, would rule out the possibility to call $e1_d$ and $e2_d$ *subevents* of e_d. Thus, if we want to dispose of something that is comparable to the subinterval property, that has been formulated within the formally simpler framework of interval semantics, with respect to our more complex event semantics, we need the concept of the maximal temporal segment. Contrasting interval semantics with the event semantics approach with material part relation, the subinterval property corresponds to the divisivity that is restricted to maximal temporal segments. (Of course, within this approach, a *temporal segment* that is not maximal is any subevent whose occurrence time is an interval). Since maximal temporal segments exhaust the "spatial breadth" of the event, both cats play a role in the maximal temporal segments of the cleaned version of a *simultaneously caressing two cats*-event. Thus, for each maximal temporal segment $\bar{e}$ of the cleaned version of a *simultaneously caressing two cats*-event e, there must exist a materially equivalent event e' ($e' =_m \bar{e}$) that is a *simoultaneously caressing two cats*-event too, provided $\bar{e}$ is voluminous enough to allow the perceptibility of such an event type for the equal-sized event e'. The test for divisivity does not require the inheritance of the event type onto $\bar{e}$ itself, since in the presence of ontologically fine-grained text models, as suggested in this paper, materially equivalent events might show divergent behavior with respect to event descriptions. For instance, though materially equivalent, e_d is a single event with

$$e_d \in \lambda e \begin{array}{|l|} \hline e, paola, X \\ \hline cat^*(X) \\ |X|=2 \\ caress(e) \\ agent(e)=paola \\ object(e)=X \\ \hline \end{array}$$

and $e1_d \sqcup_i e2_d$ is an event sum with

$e1_d \sqcup_i e2_d \in \lambda E$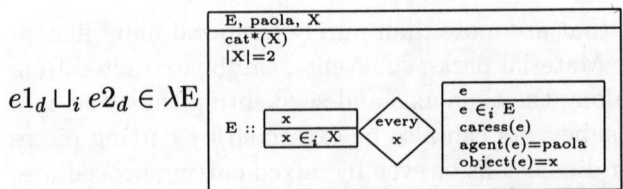

Because of this, there might be some members of a class of materially equivalent, maximal temporal segments that are P-events, and others that are not, and for the latter ones the divisivity test would fail, provided P is the tested event predicate. In order to rule out this false behavior, our definition only requires that there is a representative of each of these classes of critical maximal temporal segments that has the P-quality.

It should be clear by now, that (I) will accept the examples (8a) – (8d), if they come with their natural meaning.

However, (I) will also accept (8f). If the robot moved forward at most 50 meters over the occurrence time of the event of (8f), it moved forward at most 50 meters over the occurrence time of any critical temporal segment of this event.

Nevertheless (8f) is obviously not homogeneous. (8f) is an example that illustrates the necessity of the cumulativity constraint:

(II) We call a predicate P cumulative: CUM(P) iff for all events e, e' of the extension of P that have a *common maximal segment*, there exists an event e'' that is *materially equivalent* to the sum of e and e' ($e \sqcup_i e' =_m e''$) and that is an element of the extension of P too.

The *common maximal segment* is defined as follows:

- For events e, e': e and e' have a common maximal segment, i.e. $e \circ_m^{max} e'$ iff there exists an event $\bar{e}$ and an interval t with max–t–$auss(\bar{e},t,e)$ and max–t–$auss(\bar{e},t,e')$.

With respect to (8f), (II) is not satisfied: there are normally overlapping events of *moving at most 50 meters*–events, that, when amalgamated, are materially equivalent to an event of *moving more than 50 meters*.

In order to preserve homogeneity for (8a) – (8d), we have to show that these examples are cumulative. For the examples (8a) and (8b) this is rather obvious. We concentrate on the examples (8c) and (8d) which are critical in this respect. This allows for explaining the introduction of $\circ_m^{max}$. The amalgamation of two events of *Paola caressing a dog* normally returns an event of *Paola caressing two dogs*. Note, that the event predicate $\lambda e(\exists u(dog(u) \wedge caress(e) \wedge agent(e) = paola \wedge object(e) = u))$, ($= P$), does not require that its elements have the same value of the *object* role. However, if we restrict ourselves to instances e, e' of P that have a common maximal segment for some interval t ($e \circ_m^{max} e'$), we are sure that e and e' refer to the same dog. In this case there exists an event e'' which is materially equivalent to the sum of e and e' and which is an element of P. In this weak sense the P of (8c) is cumulative. We stress that using the relation of temporal overlap instead of $\circ_m^{max}$ in (II) would not be specific enough. It might be that Paola caressed a dog x at t and another dog x' at t' such that for a common time interval t'' she caressed two dogs. The amalgamation of the corresponding events e and e' would result then in an event that is materially equivalent to an event of *Paola caressing two dogs*. A similar reflection which uses the example (8d) of *Paola simultaneously caressing two cats*-events shows that also the simple material overlap is not sufficient: Think of events e, e' of caressing cats a and b, and b and c respectively, that overlap in an event of caressing cat b. e'' ($=_m e \sqcup_i e'$) is a caressing of three cats in this case.

(8f) has shown that divisivity as such is not a sufficient criterion for homogeneity. (8g) shows that cumulativity as such is not a sufficient criterion for homogeneity either.[13] (8g) is cumulative in the sense of (II), but not homogeneous. The threshold value for *moving*-events will be such that for normal events of *moving at least 50 meters* there are maximal temporal segments of enough volume that are materially equivalent to an event of *moving*, but that are not materially equivalent to a *moving at least 50 meters* event respectively. Thus (8g) will not satisfy (I). A similar reflection excludes divisivity for (8e) and, therefore, truly classifies it as non–homogeneous.

It remains to show the non–homogeneity of (8h). The problem of (8h) is that an *exploding*-event is normally understood as punctual, there are no maximal temporal segments that could be temporally shorter than this event, and therefore, the event description has to be understood as trivially fulfilling the divisivity constraint (I). In addition, since the extension of *the bomb exploded* consists of exactly one event, the cumulativity constraint (II) is also trivially satisfied. In order to correctly rule out homogeneity in such cases, we require:

(III) P is homogeneous only if its extension provides at least two events e and e' that have a common maximal segment, without being *material parts* of each other.

(I) – (III) cover the Aktionsart phenomena of the domain of predicates that hold for single events.

We now have to account for the case of homogeneous event descriptions that introduce a sum of events. For an illustrating example, consider the iterative use of *Peter eine Schweinshaxe essen* that develops from (8e), if (8e) is combined with a for–adverbial *for months*:

(9) In München aß Peter monatelang eine Schweinshaxe mit Sauerkraut.
(IN MUNICH, PETER ATE A TROTTER WITH SAUERKRAUT FOR MONTHS.)

Of course, here, even our redefined subinterval property (I) is too restrictive. The threshold of *essen* is smaller than the *size* of the single *eine Schweinshaxe essen*–events. Apparently, in natural language we make use of two different levels of granularity in this respect: The one refers to realizations of the event type that is expressed by the verb. The other, more coarse–grained, refers to periodic realizations of this type. Information from the thematic roles will influence the granularity of the periodicity.[14] We use the operator *ITER* (for *iter*ation) in order to obtain the class of periodic realizations of a particular event type Q. We define *ITER* as an operator for event predicates such that

- for all event sums E and for all event predicates Q:
$ITER(Q)(E)$ iff there exists a set B with $B \subseteq Q$ and $E = sup_i(B)$ and *temp–distr(E)*.

temp–distr is defined as follows.

- Let E be a sum of events, then
temp–distr(E) iff there exists a *grid* T such that for all $e \in_i E$ there exists a $t \in_i T$ with $e \oslash t$ and for all $t, t' \in_i T$ there exist $e, e' \in_i E$ with $temp(e) \neq temp(e'), e \oslash t, e' \oslash t'$.

Here, $\oslash$ stands for the temporal overlap relation, *temp* returns the time of an event. For E with *temp–distr(E)*, we say that E is **temp**orally homogeneously **distr**ibuted.

- For T, a sum of at least two intervals:
T is a grid, i.e. *grid(T)* iff T consists of consecutively ordered atomic

intervals of equal temporal length and meeting each other.

Now, we call a predicate P homogeneous:

(IV) P is homogeneous if there is an event predicate Q such that P is materially equivalent to $ITER(Q)$.

Predicates that satisfy to (IV) are cumulative and divisive, but in a very weak sense. Such predicates P are divisive only in terms of the granularity of the instances of P. I.e., with respect to a particular instance E of P, the downward heredity of P is only required within the limits that are drawn by the segmentation of the grid that corresponds to E into subgrids: Each iterative realization E of *eine Schweinshaxe essen* determines a grid T whose mesh width depends on the frequency of the realization of the single *eine Schweinshaxe essen*–events in E. While these maximal temporal segments of E that are realized at some subgrid of T inherit the quality of being an iterative realization of *eine Schweinshaxe essen* from E, the others do not (necessarily), even if they pass the threshold for *essen*. For instance, subevents of the single *eine Schweinshaxe essen*–events of E may fulfill the threshold–condition for *essen*–events. However, they will never be iterations of *eine Schweinshaxe essen*–events.

Cumulativity is guaranteed for events (or event sums) $\varepsilon, \varepsilon'$ that share a common Q–event, since, in this case, from suited temporally overlapping grids T and T' for $\varepsilon, \varepsilon'$, we obtain a grid T'' for $\varepsilon \sqcup_i \varepsilon'$ by coarsening the more fine–grained grid, T or T', to the granularity of the other, and by taking the sum of these grids: there exists E with $E =_m \varepsilon \sqcup_i \varepsilon'$, with T'' is a grid of E, and $ITER(Q)(E)$.

Among other things that we concentrate on below, these weak requirements on homogeneity seem to be justified, as mentioned, by the iterative use of heterogeneous descriptions like (9) or the following example (10).

(10) *Eine halbe Stunde lang warf sich der Stuntman aus dem Fenster.*
(FOR HALF AN HOUR THE STUNTMAN THREW HIMSELF OUT OF THE WINDOW.)

As (9) and (10) make clear, in the case of for–adverbials plus iteration of a predicate P, the mesh width of the grid that is introduced depends on both the measure introduced by the adverbial, the knowledge about the typical length of P–events, and the knowledge about possible distances between *P*–events. In (9), the grid will consist of intervals that are smaller than months, perhaps weeks. In (10) it will consist of intervals whose length is one or two levels lower than the length *half an hour* with respect to a pragmatic granularity hierarchy of temporal length units. The repetition in (10), then, might follow a five minute rhythm.

Of course, the iterative analysis of examples like (9) and (10) can be expressed in DRT also by universal quantification over the intervals of the grid via a duplex condition, instead of applying the operator *ITER* to the basic event predicate. We will prefer this representation style for iteration readings throughout the rest of this paper.[15]

It is often not clear whether the entities introduced by descriptions that use plural phrases for characterizing thematic roles (as in the following example (11)), or that require iteration, are conceptualized as single events or as event sums.

(11)   *Peter trank fünf Gläser Bier.*
       (PETER DRANK FIVE GLASSES OF BEER.)[16]

Does example (11) introduce one single event of *Peter drinking five glasses of beer* or does it introduce five events of *Peter drinking a glass of beer* (or the corresponding sum respectively)? And does (10) introduce one repetitive event of *the stuntman throwing himself out of the window* or does it introduce an unknown number of *the stuntman throwing himself out of the window*–events (or the corresponding non–atomic sum respectively)? In order to deal correctly with this underdetermination, i.e. in order to treat both cases, in (IV) we have only required that the homogeneous P has to be materially equivalent to some $ITER(Q)$ instead of requiring $P = ITER(Q)$.

Of course, event predicates $P1, P2$ are materially equivalent iff for each element of $P1$ there exists a materially equivalent element of $P2$ and vice versa. We note, that, in accordance with this, (I) – (III) can also deal with this ontological underspecification.

One may suspect that the use of material equivalence in (IV) causes the test described by (I) – (III) to be superfluous, since (IV), with seemingly weaker conditions, besides sum predicates, can test predicates over single events by this means. We stress that one cannot dispense with (I) – (III). Defining homogeneity in terms of iteration ($P =_m ITER(Q)$), in order to deal correctly with thresholds, requires that the defined predicate, P, and the underlying defining predicate, Q, must be materially different. $P =_m ITER(P)$ means, that each instance of P can be infinitely divided into P–instances. For Ps like *Paola working in the garden* this, obviously, is false. However, $P =_m ITER(P)$ seems to be the only possibility of an iterative description of such Ps.

Summarizing we give the following formal characterization of homogeneity.

Definition: Temporal Discourse–Homogeneity

Let P be an event predicate:

$TD--HOM(P)$
$\leftrightarrow$
$([\exists e, e' \; (P(e) \wedge P(e') \wedge e \circ_m^{max} e' \wedge \neg(e \leq_m e' \vee e' \leq_m e))$ \hfill (a)
$\wedge$
$\forall e, e' \; (P(e) \wedge P(e') \wedge e \circ_m^{max} e' \rightarrow \exists e'' \; (e \sqcup_i e' =_m e'' \wedge P(e'')))$ \hfill (b)
$\wedge$
$\forall e, t, \bar{e} \; (P(e) \wedge interval(t) \wedge t \subseteq lz(e) \wedge max\text{--}t\text{--}auss(\bar{e}, t, e) \wedge size(\bar{e}) \geq$
$\qquad \text{limit}(P) \rightarrow \exists e' \; (e' =_m \bar{e} \wedge P(e'))]$ \hfill (c)
$\vee$
$\exists Q \; (P =_m ITER(Q)))$ \hfill (d)

Here, of course, (a), (b), (c) in turn reflect (III), (II), (I). (d) reflects (IV). We call a predicate P satisfying (a) – (c) on the one hand or (d) on the other *temporally discourse*-**hom***ogeneous*, $TD\text{-}HOM(P)$. We call such a predicate P not simply 'temporally homogeneous', or 'homogeneous', in order to point to the fact that P is not necessarily cumulative or distributive with respect to the rigid meaning of these notions, but is cumulative and distributive only with respect to the discourse oriented, pragmatically determined, temporal use of these notions. The usefulness of the presented weak, but interdependent versions of cumulativity and divisivity is confirmed, as we think, by the examples considered this far in this section.

Now we can easily define heterogeneity as the counterpart of homogeneity.

Definition: Temporal Discourse–Heterogeneity

Let P be an event predicate:

$$TD--HET(P) \leftrightarrow \neg TD--HOM(P)$$

The formal means developed until now allow to represent the critical examples (4a) – (4d), according to the analysis sketched in the introduction.

(4) a. *Sportler brachten die olympische Fackel nach Barcelona.*
(SPORTSMEN TOOK THE OLYMPIC TORCH TO BARCELONA.)

($4a_{rep}$)
U, v, e, barcelona
sportsman*(U)
o-torch(v)
take(e)
agent(e)=U
object(e)=v
goal(e)=barcelona

(4) b. *Olympia–Fans fuhren nach Barcelona.*
(OLYMPICS FANS WENT TO BARCELONA.)

($4b_{rep}$)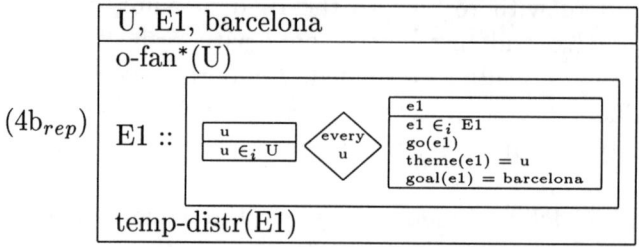

(4) c. *Beim Stürmer–Training drosch Völler Bälle ins Tor.*
(AT THE FORWARD TRAINING, VÖLLER KICKED BALLS INTO THE GOAL.)

THE INFLUENCE OF PLURAL NPs ON AKTIONSART IN DRT   77

(4c$_{rep}$)

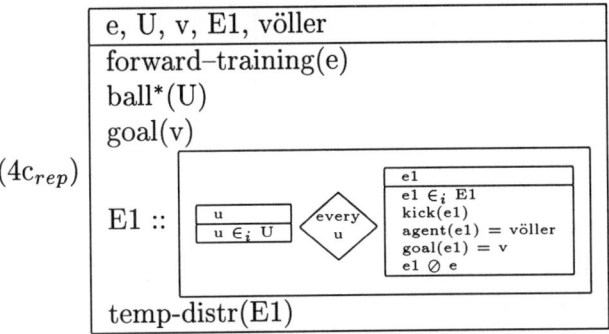

(4) d. *Am Mittwoch transportierte ein FIFA–Mitarbeiter Bälle von London nach Rom.*
(ON WEDNESDAY, A FIFA–EMPLOYEE CARRIED BALLS FROM LONDON TO ROME.)

(4d$_{rep}$)

```
t, u, V, e, london, rome
wednesday(t)
FIFA-employee(u)
ball*(V)
transport(e)
theme(e)=u
object(e)=V
source(e)=london
goal(e)=rome
e ⊆ t
```

In the theoretical framework that we have developed the readings (4b$_{rep}$) and (4c$_{rep}$) of (4b), and of (4c) respectively, are homogeneous event descriptions, because the corresponding event predicates, $P1$ and $P2$, are predicates satisfying the (d)–condition of the *TD–HOM–* definition. $P1$ and $P2$ can be represented as follows:

$P1 = \lambda\ E1$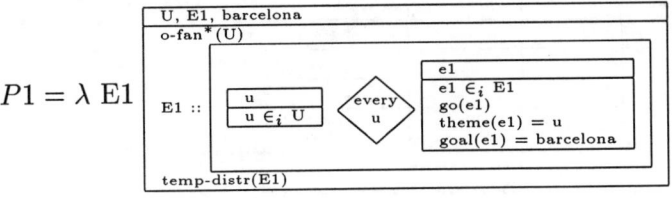

$P2 = \lambda\ E1$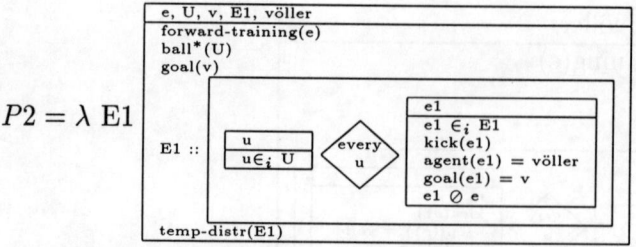

$P1$ and $P2$ satisfy (d), since they are iterations (in the sense of *ITER*) of $Q1$ and $Q2$ respectively, with:

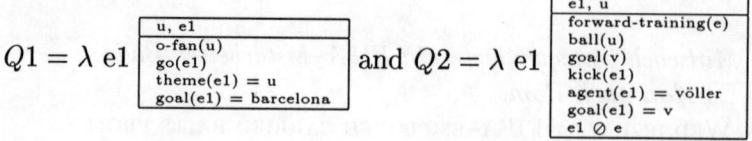

Note that in $Q2$ the DRFs e and v behave like the DRT–constants *barcelona* and *völler*, because they are free variables. With respect to a specific assignment function $\hat{f}$, independently on the interpretation of the DRFs $e1$ and u via extensions of $\hat{f}$, they always denote the same object in the model ($\hat{f}(e)$ and $\hat{f}(v)$ respectively).[17] This possibility for making use of event types, that, so to speak, are *parameterized*, guarantees that defined predicates like $P2$ have indeed an iterative characterization. Without this formal means of free variables we could not make sure that the *forward–training* in $Q2$, and the *goal* respectively, must always be the same. Clearly, with respect to the event type $Q2'$ that develops from $Q2$ by introducing e and v in the universe of the $Q2$–DRS, the extension of $P2$ is a strict subset of the set of iterations of $Q2'$–elements, provided the interpreting model contains several forward trainings and several goals. Thus, the parameterization is indeed needed for the characterization of the $P2$–elements as iterations of events of some other event type.[18] We can graphically render the particular characteristics of (4b) and (4c) as follows:

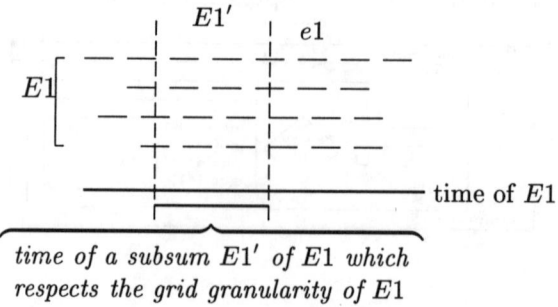

time of a subsum $E1'$ of $E1$ which respects the grid granularity of $E1$

$E1$ consists of an unspecified number of temporally homogeneously distributed atomic events $e1$, each satisfying the same event predicate ($Q1$, or $Q2$ respectively). Because the number of these events is not prescribed by the characterization $P1$ of $E1$, (or by $P2$ respectively), subsums $E1'$ of $E1$ that are distributed over subgrids of the grid of $E1$ can be characterized by the same event type, i.e. by $P1$, (or by $P2$ respectively). This reflects the divisivity of $P1$ and $P2$. Adding $P1$–sums ($P2$–sums) $E2'$ to $E1'$ that share a common $Q1$–event ($Q2$–event) with $E1'$, obviously returns sums $E1' \sqcup_i E2'$ that are $P1$–sums ($P2$–sums). This reflects the cumulativity of $P1$ and $P2$.

We stress that, in contrast to examples like (9), (*Peter eating a trotter for months*), we do not need *type coercion* in order to obtain the homogeneous representations of (4b) and (4c).[19] Analyzing the (simplified) (9), first we obtain the event type

$$R = \lambda\, e\, \begin{array}{|l|} \hline u,\ e \\ \hline \text{trotter}(u) \\ \text{eat}(e) \\ \text{agent}(e) = \text{peter} \\ \text{object}(e) = u \\ \hline \end{array},$$

which is not homogeneous. Since *for months* expects a homogeneous event type, R must undergo a type coercion. Here, this will be effected via iteration. We obtain:

$$R' = ITER(\ \lambda\, e\, \begin{array}{|l|} \hline u,\ e \\ \hline \text{trotter}(u) \\ \text{eat}(e) \\ \text{agent}(e) = \text{peter} \\ \text{object}(e) = u \\ \hline \end{array}\ ),$$

or, spelling out the impact of *ITER*:

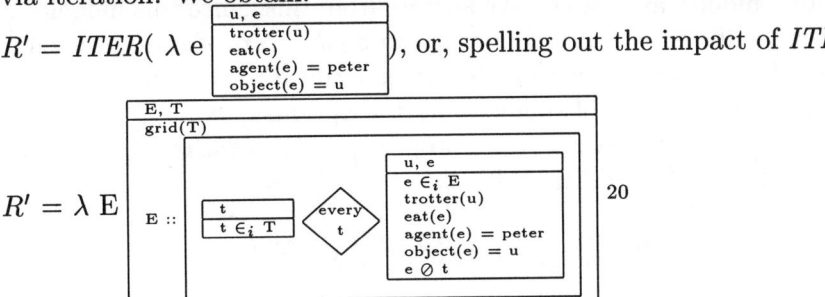

20

Instead of creating another event type with disjoint extension (via iteration), in the case of (4b) and (4c), we have only to strengthen the explicitly given event type by the *temp–distr*–condition.

We have said nothing yet about the condition $e1 \in_i E1$ in the nuclear scope of the duplex condition of $P1$ (and of $P2$ respectively, compare also $e \in_i E$ in R'). Without this condition, the abstraction condition $E1 :: \ldots$ in $P1$ would determine $E1$ to be the maximal sum of $Q1$–events that are related to the u's of U via *theme*. This means that, for each u of U, $E1$ would comprise all the journeys to Barcelona undertaken by u. Clearly, (4b) only refers to a sum $E1$ that accounts for at least one travelling event with respect to each u of the introduced sum of Olympics fans. This sum $E1$ does not necessarily account for all such travelling events.

We easily verify that restricting the abstraction condition $E1 :: \ldots$ by the incorporated condition $e1 \in_i E1$ blocks the inference that $E1$ must be the maximal sum of journeys to Barcelona undertaken by the u's of U. But we stress that this restriction does not alter the property of $E1$ of exhausting the sum U in the sense of providing a travelling to Barcelona for each of the u's of U. This is easily verified too. Of course, the corresponding statement holds for $P2$, and for all the other event types that use the formal means of abstracting event sums from duplex conditions.

($4a_{rep}$) and ($4d_{rep}$) represent heterogeneous event descriptions. However, whereas the theory that we have outlined, in the case of ($4b_{rep}$) and ($4c_{rep}$), really **entails** the Aktionsart, with ($4a_{rep}$) and ($4d_{rep}$), as with the examples of (8), there exists no comparable formal decision yet. It is the knowledge of the language user about the canonical realization of the described event types that requires that the types of (8a) – (8d) satisfy to TD–HOM and that the types of (8e) – (8h), ($4a_{rep}$) and ($4d_{rep}$) do not. In order to constrain the theory in this respect, we can introduce a number of axioms of the type TD–HOM(P) and TD–HET(P) respectively that structure the extensions of the corresponding Ps in interpreting models as desired. We abstain from this, since this modelling would not sufficiently reflect the *compositional nature* of Aktionsarten[21] that we observe not only with regard to quantificational phenomena, but already in the presence of single event descriptions.

Making use of specific role properties like *additivity*, where a (functional) role f is additive iff

$$\forall e, e' \quad (f(e) \sqcup f(e') = f(e \sqcup e'))$$

Krifka explains very convincingly for cases like (7a) and (7b) (*Peter drinking wine* versus *Peter drinking a glass of wine*) how the specific description of thematic roles adds to the basic predicate stemming from the verb and, therefore, how it influences the quality of the entire event description in terms of the structural properties of the corresponding extension in the model. The reasoning that explicates the different Aktionsarten of (7a) and (7b) can be sketched as follows: *wine* is cumulative, because the fusion of two portions of wine is also a portion of wine. In contrast, *one glass of wine* is not cumulative, because the fusion of two glasses of wine is not *one glass of wine*; *drinking* as such is cumulative: two activities of drinking taken together form one (perhaps more complex) drinking activity.

Thus, for $e_1, e_2 \in \lambda e(drink(e) \wedge \exists x(wine(x) \wedge object(e) = x))$, we get that $drink(e_1 \sqcup e_2)$ and $wine(object(e_1) \sqcup object(e_2))$ hold. Since *object* is additive, we get from the latter statement that $wine(object(e_1 \sqcup e_2))$ holds. Therefore, it holds that $e_1 \sqcup e_2 \in \lambda e(drink(e) \wedge \exists x(wine(x) \wedge object(e) = x))$. We easily see that for $P = \lambda e(drink(e) \wedge \exists x(\textit{1-glass-wine}(x) \wedge object(e) = x))$ and $P(e_1), P(e_2)$, it does not hold $P(e_1 \sqcup e_2)$.

Besides the (canonical) adaptation of *additivity* to our structuring using $\sqcup_i, \leq_i, \leq_m$ – we call it *summativity*, the essential properties are the following:

Let P be a predicate symbol that describes single events. Then:

- f is a *constant* role with respect to P, const(f,P)

iff

$\forall e, e', x \ (P(e) \wedge f(e) = x \wedge atom(x) \wedge P(e') \wedge \textit{max-t-auss}(e', temp(e'), e)$
$\rightarrow f(e') =_m x)$

- f is a *gradual* role with respect to P, grad(f,P)

iff

$\forall e, x, x' \ (P(e) \wedge f(e) = x \wedge atom(x) \wedge x' <_m x$
$\rightarrow \exists e' \ (P(e') \wedge \textit{max-t-auss}(e', temp(e'), e) \wedge f(e') =_m x'))$

- f is a *characteristic* role with respect to P, char(f,P)

iff

$\neg grad(f, P) \wedge$
$(const(f, P) \rightarrow (\forall e, e', t(P(e) \wedge P(e') \wedge \textit{max-t-auss}(e', t, e) \rightarrow e' =_m e)))$

Thus, we say that f is a *constant* role with respect to the predicate P, if the maximal P–segments of a P–event e share the f–value with e. Here, we refer to events e with atomic values only, in order to avoid complications with single event conceptualizations of sums that develop from distributions over plural roles. An example of a constant role is the *theme*–role of moving–events. Maximal segments e' of a moving of x that are moving–events are movings of x. In contrast to this, maximal segments of an *eating* x–event that are also eating–events have values of the *object*–role that are material parts of x. We call a role f *gradual* with respect to the predicate P if from the existence of a P–event e with atomic f–value x, we can infer the existence of maximal P–segments e' of e such that for each part x' of x there is a

e' whose f-value is materially equivalent to x'. The *object*-role with respect to consumption predicates like *eating* is a gradual role. We call a role f *characteristic* with respect to the predicate P if f is not gradual with respect to P and if f, in case it is constant, for lack of a rich homogeneous structuring of the P-extension, it is only trivially constant. *Source* and *goal*, for instance, are characteristic with respect to *moving*-events. From a moving to x we cannot infer that all maximal *moving*-segments are movings to x. Nor can we infer the existence of movings to parts to x. Segments of moving events e normally have completely different sources and goals than e.

We can use such role properties in order to compute the Aktionsart of event descriptions that equip the roles with atomic values. The basis is the Aktionsart of the underlying simple event predicate. Of course, the assignment of Aktionsarten to predicate symbols has to be axiomatically given in order that the calculus is sound with respect to interpreting models of the theory. Similarly, the role properties that the calculus uses will be anchored in corresponding axioms of the theory. Constant roles do not change the Aktionsart. Characteristic and gradual roles transpose homogeneous descriptions into heterogeneous descriptions. This can be easily verified. *Going*s and *reading*s are homogeneous, *going of Peter-* and *reading by Peter*-descriptions too, but *going of Peter to France-* and *reading a book by Peter*-descriptions are heterogeneous. We will not go into detail with this type of Aktionsart computation. We also skip presenting the precise theoretical settings for mass terms and measure phrases that allow to infer the correct Aktionsarten for the examples that are relevant in this respect, i.e. (7a), (8f) and (8g). We stress, however, that the role properties must be relativized to the specific predicates, provided that we use identical roles for different predicates. *Object* is gradual with respect to *eating-*, but not with respect to *transporting-* events. There is even a finer distinction. For particular predicates there are roles that can have both a gradual and a constant reading. Paola's *caressing a dog* in (8c) can be a caressing of a level of granularity that does not pay attention to the parts of the dog. With respect to each maximal caressing–segment the dog as a whole is involved. The *object-* role is constant then, but it can also be gradual: Think of the caressing as a task that starts with the caressing of the head and ends with the caressing of the paws. In order to capture the difference, we can introduce a more fine–grained spectrum of roles where the roles can have indices *suk* and *sim* that point to the gradual variant, where the partaking role value is *successively* involved in the event, and to the constant variant, where it is always involved as a whole, i.e. where its parts are involved *simultaneously*. So, in the above discussion about the definition of homogeneity, precisely speaking, we can attribute homogeneous Aktionsart to (8c) only if we refine the *object*–role to $object_{sim}$. The introduction of these indices is inspired by the two–place relations *SUK* and *SIM* that Krifka suggests for plural examples like Paola's caressing of two cats in (8d). As mentioned, Krifka's Aktionsart analysis does not make use of *distributive* readings of plural roles as in ($4b_{rep}$) with respect to the *Olympics–Fans* (travelling to Barcelona) or in ($4c_{rep}$) (the *balls* kicked into the goal). Only *collective* readings are considered, as in ($4a_{rep}$) (the *sportsmen* carrying the olympic torch to Barcelona), or in ($4d_{rep}$) (the *balls* carried to Rome). The suggested Aktionsart analysis completely relies on the transfer of the type of referentiality of the roles to the event description. This transfer proceeds along the lines of role properties like additivity, as discussed with respect to the contrast between (7a) and (7b). The introduction of the roles *SUK* and *SIM* allows to correctly distinguish between the homogeneous and the heterogeneous reading of cases like *Paola caressing two cats* (with *two cats* as filler of *SIM* and of *SUK* respectively).

The problem with an approach that uses exclusively single events is that, for divisivity based notion of homogeneity, we obtain the right result for cases like (4b) (Olympics fans travelling to Barcelona), namely homogeneity (in the sense of point (d) of the TD–HOM–definition, case 'type of single events'), only if the *theme*–role is interpreted as *SUK*, and only if the *goal*–role has the property that event segments corresponding to the successively partaking constituents of the plural role, the Olympics fans in (4b), inherit the value of the *goal* of the entire event. But uniformly requiring this property for *goal* with respect to single moving–events would result in the impossibility of representing the 'Olympics' case of (4a) by a single event, since, under the assumption of this property, each of the sportsmen must run to Barcelona. Of course, this does not truly reflect the 'Olympics' case, where the sportsmen act *successively*, each running a particular section of the way to Barcelona with the torch in hand and handing it to the next sportsman. Actually, only the last of the sportsmen reaches Barcelona with the torch in hand.

Thus, we think that a distributive analysis of cases like (4b) is needed. We render the contrast between simultaneously partaking constituents of a plural role (*SIM*) and successively partaking constituents (*SUK*) by the *temp–sim/temp–distr*–distinction for distributive readings, where *temp–sim* is defined as follows:

- for all event sums E, it holds *temp–sim(E)* iff $\forall e, e' \in_i E(temp(e) = temp(e'))$.

The *suk/sim*–indices are reserved to mark the grad– and const–specification of a role that otherwise would be underspecified in this respect. The assumption is that the lexicon entries provide roles that are specific with respect to the relevant role properties. We stress that with this setting the collective reading of sum values of constant roles is restricted to the case of simultaneity, the collective reading of sum values of gradual roles is not successivity with respect to the partaking atoms, but not further specified gradual affectedness of the sum. The examples that refer to sums whose atoms are successively involved in the event will be represented exclusively by distribution. Thus, we have to correct our analysis of (4a). We represent (4a) as follows:

($4a_{rep}'$)
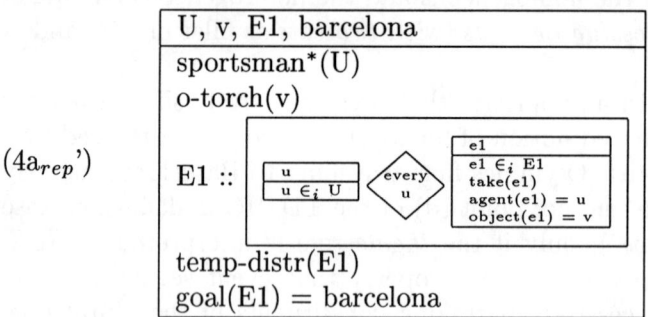

We summarize the essential points of this section. The definition of homogeneity is based on cumulativity and divisivity. It is sensitive to changes of granularity as connected to the transition from non–iterative to iterative event types. It is applicable to types of single events and to types of event sums. The assumption is that there is a set of axioms that determines the Aktionsart of the predicate symbols of the fragment and that there is a set of axioms that, dependent on the specific event predicates, determines the relevant properties of the roles that are used. Here, roles can be summative, constant, gradual or characteristic. From these facts the Aktionsart of event predicates with atomic role values easily can be inferred, if these values are described by count noun–expressions, and, provided a rich axiomatic modelling, also if they are described by mass– and measure–expressions. We skip formally working out this type of Aktionsart calculus and, in the next section, assume lexicon entries of the verbs that already

THE INFLUENCE OF PLURAL NPs ON AKTIONSART IN DRT   85

account for the Aktionsart–influence of the roles introduced by the subcategorized grammatical functions. This lexical account is restricted to the assumption that the roles come with atomic values that are described by predicates that stem from count nouns. The task will be to concentrate on the impact on the Aktionsart in cases where the lexical expectation of atomic role values is contradicted by plural phrases.

4. PARTIAL DRSs FOR DISTRIBUTIVE AND COLLECTIVE READINGS

We develop our DRS–construction algorithm in a Categorial Unification Grammar–like framework, concentrating on the semantic part of the lexical entries and skipping the syntactic part where possible. The relevant parts of the lexical entries for verbs look like follows:

- lesen

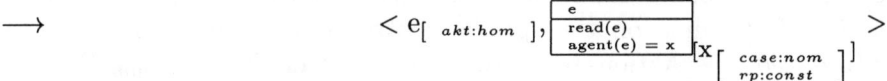

for *s.o. reads*.

- lesen

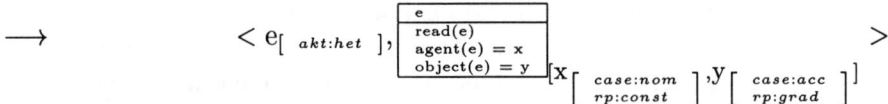

for *s.o. reads s.th.*.

- lieben

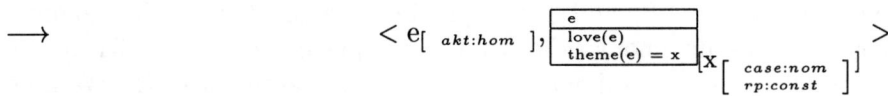

for *s.o. is in love*.

- lieben

$$\longrightarrow \quad < e_{[\ akt:hom\ ]}, \begin{array}{|l|} \hline e \\ \hline love(e) \\ theme(e) = x \\ object(e) = y \\ \hline \end{array} [x \begin{bmatrix} case:nom \\ rp:const \end{bmatrix}, y \begin{bmatrix} case:acc \\ rp:const \end{bmatrix}] >$$

for *s.o. loves a p.*.

Here, German verbs are listed that may or may not occur with direct objects in grammatically correct German sentences. In order to account for this syntactic behavior, we require two lexical entries for *lesen* and *lieben* respectively. The one reflects the case where the verb syntactically is a functor of the type S/NP_{nom}, the other reflects the case where it is a functor of the type $S/NP_{nom}/NP_{acc}$. The assignment of values to the feature *akt* (Aktionsart) in the lexicon is based on the assumption that the DRFs stemming from the subcategorized grammatical functions are atomic objects (introduced by singular NPs using count nouns: *ein Mann, ein Hund, ein Buch*, (*a man, a dog, a book*). Depending on the specific contribution of the thematic roles introduced, the Aktionsart of the event type of the $S/NP_{nom}/NP_{acc}$-entry may be different from the Aktionsart of the event type of the S/NP_{nom}-entry. Adding gradual or characteristic roles with atomic values to homogeneous event types results in heterogeneous event types. In contrast, constant roles with atomic values do not change the Aktionsart. This was mentioned in the previous section. The entries are to be read as follows: The verb introduces a DRS with free variables. These free variables must be bound via lambda conversion by the DRFs introduced by the syntactic arguments of the verb functor. The arguments are the items of the subcategorization list. With respect to the second entry of *lesen* for instance, $[x_{case:nom}, y_{case:acc}]$ is the sketchy representation of the subcategorization list which tells us that *lesen* is a functor with arguments of the type nominal NP and of the type accusative NP, and that applying the functor to the nominal argument results among other things in replacing x by the DRF of the nominal NP and accordingly in the case of the accusative NP. We note that DRSs come with an *index* (i.e. with a DRF directly preceding the DRS). With VPs, it is the event introduced in the universe of the corresponding DRS. With NPs, normally, it is the DRF introduced by the head noun. We use indices because they ease the construction of the semantic representation that parallels the syntactic analysis via functional application (and composition). For instance, in the case of

NPs with relative clauses several DRFs are introduced. Here, the index decides which one must be chosen for binding the corresponding variable of the VP representation.[22] The index and the DRFs of the subcategorization list are annotated by the relevant syntactic and semantic features that describe the structure introducing the corresponding DRF. Thus, $[akt:hom]$ in $< e_{[akt:hom]}, DRS >$ means that $\lambda eDRS$ is a homogeneous event predicate. We note, by the way, that role properties like being a constant role etc. are not part of the information stemming from the corresponding NPs, but are assigned to these NPs by the verb via the subcategorization list and especially via the feature *rp*. Of course, such information represents the axiomatic knowledge mentioned in the last section. Thus, using lexical entries dynamically builds up the data base of our DRT-theory that underlies the evaluation of the constructed DRSs. With respect to nominal phrases, we concentrate on the semantic contribution of indefinite singular and plural noun phrases. In this paper we will say nothing specific about NPs with quantifiers like *many, few, most* etc. However, one easily sees that in the presence of the TD–HOM–definition, such NPs will be treated like indefinite numeral NPs, as far as Aktionsart is concerned. We will say something about definite NPs only in the next section. We omit the construction of the NP representations from the representations of determiners and nouns and render only the schemes of the representations of entire NPs like *a man, three men, men* accounting for the distinction of collective, *temp–sim–* and *temp-distr-*distributive readings that we label in turn by C, D_{tsim} and D_{tdistr}. In the following schemes we abstract from case information. In specific representations this information would be available by means of the case attribute connected to the DRF that the NP determines as the filler of the thematic role corresponding to the NP.

- $\boxed{\text{ein cn}}$, where $cn \in NOUN\begin{bmatrix} num=sg \\ type=count \end{bmatrix}$

$\longrightarrow$

(C) $< \text{x}, \lambda < \varepsilon_{[akt:A]}, \text{DRS}_{[...\text{x}...]} > \left[< \varepsilon_{[akt:A]}, \text{DRS} \cup \boxed{\dfrac{\text{x}}{\text{cn'(x)}}}...] > \right] >$

- $\boxed{\text{n cn}}$, where $n \in DET_{\left[\substack{num=pl \\ quant=ind}\right]}, n \neq \emptyset, cn \in NOUN_{\left[\substack{num=pl \\ type=count}\right]}$

$\longrightarrow$

$(C) \quad < X, \lambda < \varepsilon_{[akt:A]}, \text{DRS}_{[...X...]} > \left[< \varepsilon_{[akt:A]}, \text{DRS} \cup \boxed{\begin{array}{c} X \\ cn'^*(X) \\ |X| = n \end{array}} [...] > \right] >$

$\longrightarrow$

(D_{tsim})

$<x, \lambda < \varepsilon_{1[akt:A]}, \text{DRS}_{[...x...]} >$

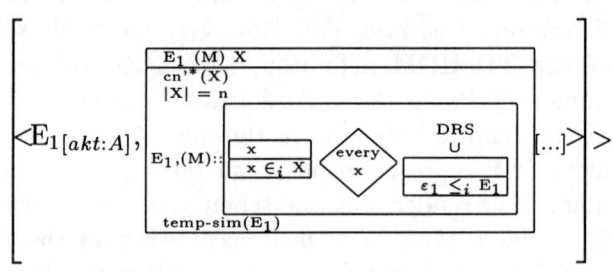

$\longrightarrow$

(D_{tdistr})

$<x, \lambda < \varepsilon_{1[akt:A]}, \text{DRS}_{[...x...]} >$

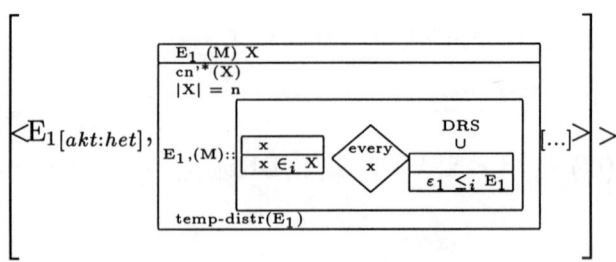

- $\boxed{\emptyset \ cn}$, where $cn \in NOUN_{\begin{bmatrix} num=pl \\ type=count \end{bmatrix}}$

$\longrightarrow$

(C) $\quad < X, \lambda < \varepsilon_{[akt:A]}, DRS_{[...X...]} > \left[< \varepsilon_{[akt:A]}, DRS \cup \boxed{\begin{array}{c} X \\ \hline cn'^*(X) \end{array}}[...] > \right] >$

$\longrightarrow$

(D_{tsim})

$<x, \lambda <\varepsilon_{1[akt:A]}, DRS_{[...x...]}>$

$\left[<E_{1[akt:A]}, \boxed{E_1, (M):: \boxed{\begin{array}{c} x \\ \hline x \in_i X \end{array}} \langle\text{every}\rangle_x \boxed{\begin{array}{c} DRS \cup \\ \hline \varepsilon_1 \leq_i E_1 \end{array}}} [...] > \right] >$

with inner box top: $\boxed{\begin{array}{c} E_1 \ (M) \ X \\ \hline cn'^*(X) \end{array}}$ and bottom: temp-sim(E_1)

$\longrightarrow$

(D_{tdistr})

$<x, \lambda <\varepsilon_{1[akt:A]}, DRS_{[...x...]}>$

$\left[<E_{1[akt:hom]}, \boxed{E_1, (M):: \boxed{\begin{array}{c} x \\ \hline x \in_i X \end{array}} \langle\text{every}\rangle_x \boxed{\begin{array}{c} DRS \cup \\ \hline \varepsilon_1 \leq_i E_1 \end{array}}} [...] > \right] >$

with inner box top: $\boxed{\begin{array}{c} E_1 \ (M) \ X \\ \hline cn'^*(X) \end{array}}$ and bottom: temp-distr(E_1)

The formal description of the NP classes considered should be rather self-explanatory. We represent the cases treated, NPs constructed from the empty determiner or numerals on the one hand and singular or plural count nouns on the other, (and other NPs) by annotated *partial DRSs* that are equipped with indices. Disregarding the annotations, a partial DRS syntactically is a function from DRSs onto DRSs (representing a function from propositions onto propositions).[23] We see that, with respect to the semantic representation, the roles played syntactically by NP and VP are exchanged with each other. Applying the VP–functor to the nominal argument by means of the grammar rules results in applying the semantic representation of the NP, the semantic functor, to the semantic representation of the VP, the semantic argument.[24] Instead of explaining the representation schemes listed, we render constructions of the semantic representations for our examples (4a) and (4d). Therefore, in addition, we need representations of prepositional phrases. Here, we restrict ourselves to the illustrative examples *nach Rom* and *mit Maria*. The first example reflects the case of VP– (or sentence–) modification via a characteristic role (which, here, is *goal*), the second reflects the case of modification via a constant role (which, here, is *commitative*). With respect to our examples (4a) – (4d), the second PP is not needed. We provide its representation only to illustrate that there are PPs that influence the Aktionsart of the sentence differently from source or goal descriptions. We do not give the details of the construction of PPs from prepositions and noun phrases (which, here, are names).

- nach Rom

$$\longrightarrow \ <\text{rome}, \lambda <\varepsilon_{[akt:A]}, \text{DRS}_L> \left[<\varepsilon_{[akt:het]}, \text{DRS} \cup \boxed{\begin{array}{c}\text{rome}\\\hline \text{goal}(\varepsilon)=\text{rome}\end{array}}_L> \right] >$$

- mit Maria

$$\longrightarrow$$
$$<\text{maria}, \lambda <\varepsilon_{[akt:A]}, \text{DRS}_L>$$

$$\left[<\varepsilon_{[akt:A]}, \text{DRS} \cup \boxed{\begin{array}{c}\text{maria}\\\hline \text{commitative}(\varepsilon)=\text{maria}\end{array}}_L> \right]$$

In order to construct the reading ($4a_{rep}'$) of (4a), we must make use of the D_{tdistr} reading of *sportsmen*. Postponing the representation of definite NPs we treat **die** *olympische Fackel* like the corresponding indefinite *eine Fackel*. So the components of ($4a_{rep}'$) are:

($4a_{rep}'$)$_V$: $<e_{1[akt:hom]}, \boxed{\begin{array}{l}e_1\\\text{carry}(e_1)\\\text{agent}(e_1)=x\\\text{object}(e_1)=y\end{array}} [x_{\begin{bmatrix}case:nom\\rp:const\end{bmatrix}}, y_{\begin{bmatrix}case:acc\\rp:const\end{bmatrix}}]>$

THE INFLUENCE OF PLURAL NPs ON AKTIONSART IN DRT 91

$(4a_{rep}')_{NP_{nom}}$:

$<$u, $\lambda <\varepsilon_{1[akt:A]}, DRS_{[...u_{[case:nom]}...]} >$

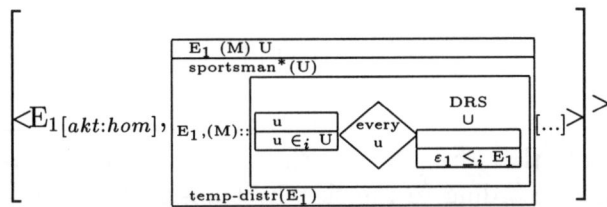

$(4a_{rep}')_{NP_{acc}}$:

$< v, \lambda < \varepsilon_{[akt:A]}, DRS_{[...v_{[case:acc]}...]} >$

$$\left[< \varepsilon_{[akt:A]}, DRS \cup \boxed{\frac{v}{\text{o-torch}(v)}} [...] > \right]$$

$(4a_{rep}')_{PP_{goal}}$:

$<$ barcelona, $\lambda < \varepsilon_{[akt:A]}, DRS_L >$

$$\left[< \varepsilon_{[akt:het]}, DRS \cup \boxed{\frac{\text{barcelona}}{\text{goal}(\varepsilon)=\text{barcelona}}} L > \right]$$

Now, we first apply the verb to the nominative NP, i.e., semantically we apply the representation of the nominative NP, $(4a_{rep}')_{NP_{nom}}$, to the representation of the verb, $(4a_{rep}')_V$. This means that the verb representation is unified with the indexed and annotated DRS-variable that the lambda abstraction of $(4a_{rep}')_{NP_{nom}}$ refers to, ($< \varepsilon_{1[akt:A]}, DRS_{[...u_{[case:nom]}...]} >$). Here, the case information guarantees that x unifies with u and that u is indeed the filler of the agent role. Also ε_1 unifies with e_1 and A with hom. The result of the application is the bracketed indexed and annotated DRS to the right of the NP representation after unification. So, from applying the verb to the nominative NP, the following representation results:

$(4a_{rep'})_{NP_{nom},V}$:

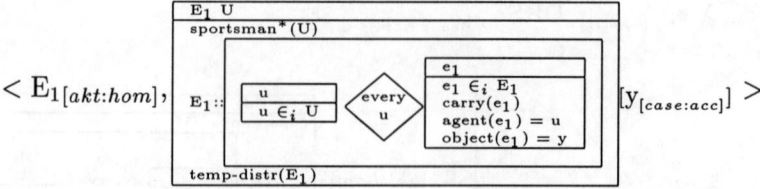

Note that the [*case: nom*]-item is removed from the subcategorization list according to the sketchy transition from [...x...] to [...,...] that we have used in the NP–representation schemes. Notice further that the application of the D_{tdistr}–reading of bare plural NPs always results in homogeneous event descriptions. The next step consists of applying the representation of the accusative NP, $(4a_{rep'})_{NP_{acc}}$ to what we have constructed so far. Here, unifying y with v, ε with E_1, A with *hom*, DRS with the DRS of $(4a_{rep'})_{NP_{nom},V}$, we obtain:

$(4a_{rep'})_{NP_{acc},NP_{nom},V}$:

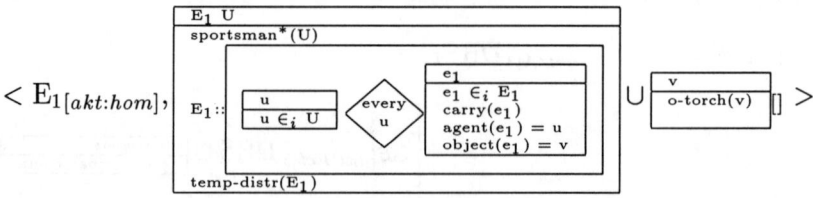

This is equivalent to:

$(4a_{rep'})_{NP_{acc},NP_{nom},V}$:

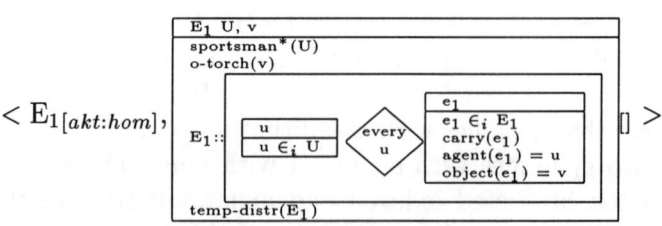

Here, we notice that indefinite singular NPs do not change the Aktionsart of the incoming event description. They confirm the expectation underlying the lexical entry of the verb. It is easy to show that, on the basis of our definitions of homogeneity and heterogeneity and with respect to these notions, the collective and the *tsim*–distribution reading of (subcategorized) plural NPs behave in accordance with this. In the final step we apply $(4a_{rep'})_{PP_{goal}}$ to $(4a_{rep'})_{NP_{acc},NP_{nom},V}$. This yields:

$(4a_{rep}')_{PP_{goal},NP_{acc},NP_{nom},V}$:

$< E_{1[akt:het]},$ 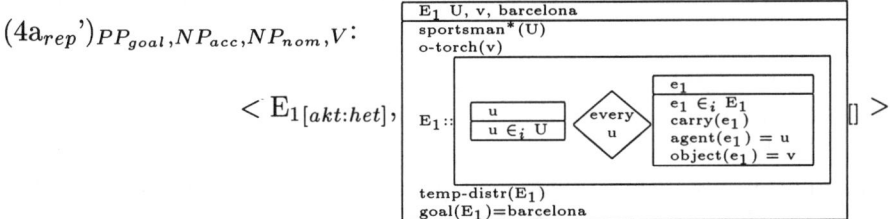 $>$

Here, we have skipped the step of carrying out the union of incoming DRS and role–DRS that we have made explicit in the preceding application step. We see that PPs leave the subcategorization list unchanged. Since in $(4a_{rep}')_{PP_{goal},NP_{acc},NP_{nom},V}$, this list is empty, we can remove it without consequences. The result is the indexed $(4a_{rep}')$ with the Aktionsart *het(erogenous)* annotated. Of course, we obtain *het*, since subevents do not (necessarily) inherit the *goal* of the entire event. This is different with respect to constant PP–roles like *commitative* or *instrument*. In order to keep track of the construction steps of a sentence reading, we introduce list–expressions where the items describe the role–readings using the labels of the representation schemes and the role name, and where the order of the list items reflects the order of the application steps. For instance, we write $[C^{goal}, C^{object}, D^{agent}_{tdistr}]$ for the above construction of the representation $(4a_{rep}')$. We think that, with respect to the construction of the representation $(4d_{rep})$ of the *carrying balls from London to Rome*–example, we can do without explicitly rendering the construction steps. This would be more or less a repetition of the "unifying in" described above. So, we just mention that we can construct $(4d_{rep})$ via $[C^{goal}, C^{source}, C^{agent}, C^{object}]$. For this construction, the incorporated Aktionsart calculus computes in turn the values *hom, hom, hom, het, het*, where the first value comes from the lexical entry of the verb and the last evaluates the sentence representation. The other values are assigned to the intermediate event descriptions.

Representing names as follows

- Paola
  $\longrightarrow$

$< \text{paola}, \lambda < \varepsilon_{[akt:A]}, \text{DRS}_{[...\text{paola}...]} >$

$$\left[\langle \mathcal{E}_{[akt:A]}, \mathrm{DRS} \cup \boxed{\begin{array}{c}\text{paola}\\ \text{[...]}\end{array}} \rangle \right]>$$

we construct the different readings of the *Paola caressing two cats*–example (8d) discussed in the last section, i.e. ($8d_{rep}$) and ($8d_{rep}'$) via [C^{agent}, C^{object}] and [$C^{agent}, D^{object}_{tdistr}$] respectively. The Aktionsart calculus entails *hom* in the first case and *het* in the second. The transition from any given Aktionsart to *het* in the case of temporally distributed numeral–NPs is justified by the fact that the number of objects that partake as fillers of the NP–role in the introduced event sum E is definite such that subsums of E and also sums that contain E, of course, normally show another number of partaking objects and, therefore, cannot be described by the same event type. In particular, this type cannot be of the form ITER(Q).

As it stands, our construction algorithm runs into problems with respect to the preferred homogeneous readings of examples like (4b) and (4c), ($4b_{rep}$) and ($4c_{rep}$), or with respect to the following heterogeneous (12).

(12) *Drei Akrobaten sprangen auf ein schönes, junges Pony.*
(THREE ACROBATS JUMPED ONTO A BEAUTIFUL YOUNG PONY.)

A natural reading of (12) is that there is one pony onto which the three acrobats jumped in turn:

($12_{rep_{tdistr}}$)

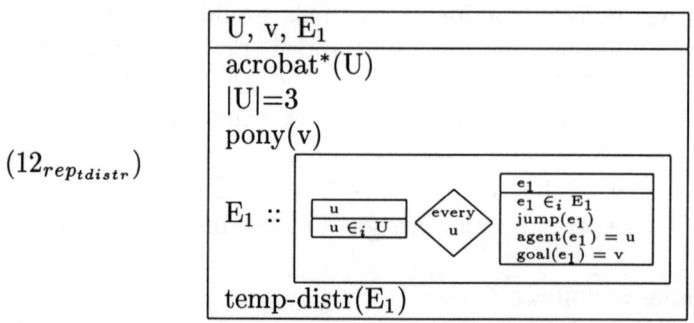

So, in all three cases, (4b), (4c), (12), there is a reading that distributes over some role. In (4b) this is the *theme*–role, in (12) it is the *agent*–role, in (4c) it is the *object*–role. All of (4b), (4c), (12) introduce a specific goal (Barcelona, the football goal and the pony respectively). The wide scope reading of the goal, which assigns the goal to the sum $E1$, is not sufficient to render the fact that all of the single events $e1$ have the same goal. But the narrow scope reading (with the DRF of the role introduced in the nuclear–scope box) does not render this either, at least not in the case of (12), since here, in contrast to (4b), the goal is not a DRT–constant like *barcelona*, and in contrast to (4c), it is not introduced via a definite description, so that it could be linked to a wide scope antecedent. Note, that DRT claims that DRFs from definite descriptions must be *accessible* from the outside of the sentence DRS, i.e. they must be introduced in the universe of this DRS or they must be linked to an antecedent that is introduced in this position (Kamp and Reyle 1993). This is different in the case of indefinites however. With the narrow scope reading of (12), we cannot be sure that the goal–DRFs introduced for the $e1$–events refer to the same object in the model. The problem can be solved, as is often done, by attributing the status of a subcategorized role to *goal*. In this case, the *goal*–equation, $goal(e)=x$, is part of the DRS introduced by the lexical verb–entry. Then giving the subcategorized *goal-PP* wide scope ensures that the representation of the goal description is part of the main DRS and, in particular, that the goal–DRF is an element of the universe of the main DRS, (though the *goal-equation* is part of an embedded DRS). We will not revise our approach in this respect because there are other roles (source, path, direction) that show similar effects and that, therefore, all had to be subcategorized. There are also other phenomena that suggest searching for a general solution to the problem of protecting (parts of) a role description from being located inside the nuclear scope of a duplex condition that is introduced by the later application of a distributive role. These are the phenomena connected to the cumulative reading.

5. PARTIAL DRSs FOR CUMULATIVE READINGS

We first turn to the *cumulative reading* as such[25], and to its technical prerequisites. From this, at the end of this section, we obtain solutions for the specific problem of the examples (4b), (4c), (12).

(13) *Zwölf bekannte Maler porträtierten die zwölf EG–
       Außenminister.*
       (TWELVE WELL-KNOWN PAINTERS PAINTED THE TWELVE EC-
       FOREIGN SECRETARIES.)

The most natural reading of (13) certainly is the one that says that each of the twelve Foreign Secretaries is painted by one or more painters (probably by one) and that each of the painters paints one or more Secretaries (probably one). This is the cumulative reading. Often, the cumulative reading is treated as a specific interpretation of a fairly underdetermined collective reading that, for (13), would only say that there exists an event of painting where twelve painters partake as agents and the twelve Secretaries partake as objects. In the approach suggested in this paper, we cannot treat the cumulative reading as a specific interpretation of an underdetermined collective reading, since our collective reading is rather specific: It entails that the atoms of the role fillers that are sums partake simultaneously in the event. So, our collective reading would only allow for cumulative interpretations that are very specific with respect to the temporal order of the single events that the complex event of the cumulative reading is composed of. However, we think that we do not have to modify our collective reading, because it seems to us that there are reasons for assigning a representation in its own right to the cumulative reading.

(14)   *Die zwölf EG–Außenminister wurden von zwölf bekannten Malern porträtiert, in jeweils einer Woche.*
(THE TWELVE EC–FOREIGN SECRETARIES WERE PAINTED BY TWELVE WELL–KNOWN PAINTERS IN ONE WEEK EACH TIME.)

We think that the cumulative reading that we have spelled out with respect to (13) is also the natural reading of (14): Each of the twelve Foreign Secretaries is painted by one or more painters (probably by one) and each of the painters paints one or more Secretaries (probably one). However, (14) is more informative than (13). Here, in addition, there is an in–adverbial that comes with the *floating quantifier jeweils*. The impact of floating quantifiers is to call for the distributive reading of a thematic role $TR1$ that is different from the one that introduces the floating quantifier, $TR2$, such that $TR1$ has wide scope over $TR2$ (cf. (Link 1987), (Krifka 1987b)). Thus, *jeweils* calls for the distributive reading of *zwölf bekannte Maler* or of *die zwölf EG–Außenminister*, resulting – in the cumulative perspective – in an analysis that says that for each Secretary (or for each painter) there exists a painting event that took at most one week, and that the sum of painters amount to twelve, (as well as the sum of Secretaries).[26] Provided that the presented cumulative analysis is a natural reading of (14), it is clear that this reading can never be subsumed by a collective reading, independent of how liberally we define collective readings, because in (14) we are forced by the floating quantifier to distribute over at least one of the role descriptions. In order to understand the peculiarity of the general cumulative reading, compare the following representations:

$(13_{rep:[D^u(object),D^l(agent)]})$:

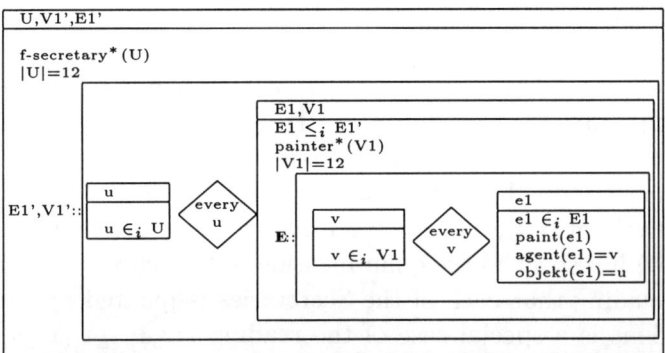

$(13_{rep:[D^u(object),D^u(agent)]})$:

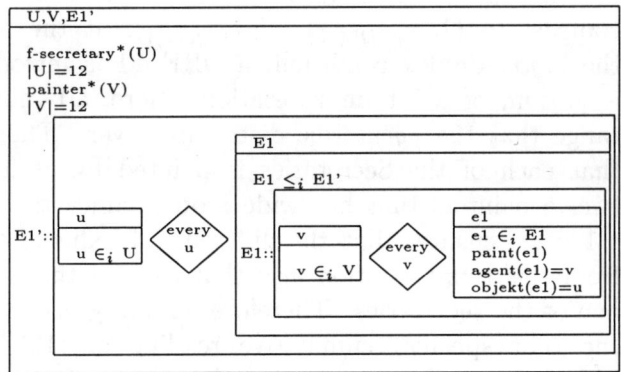

$(13_{rep:[D^u(object),D^{ul}(agent)]})$:

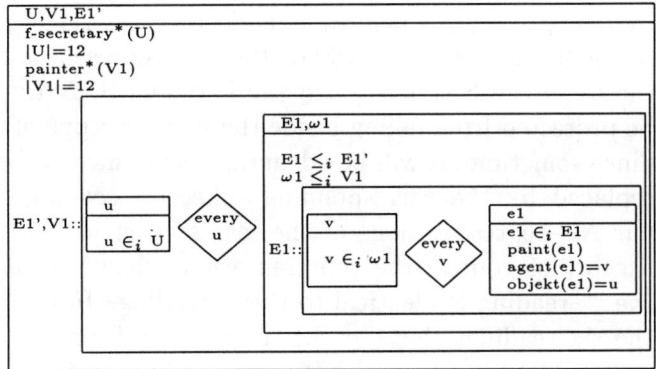

$(13_{rep:[D^u(object),D^l(agent)]})$ is the fully distributive reading of (13). This reading can be constructed by means of our algorithm developed in the last section. Here, the introduction and the sortal description of the sum–DRF of the *agent*–role,

$$\boxed{\begin{array}{c} , V1 \\ \hline painter^*(V1) \\ |V1|=12 \end{array}},$$

is part of the nuclear scope of the duplex condition introduced by the *object*–role. This *agent*–DRS is not introduced at the level of the sentence–DRS (we call this level the *upper* level) but is introduced at a *lower* level. In contrast to this, in the case of $(13_{rep:[D^u(object),D^u(agent)]})$ the same DRS is introduced at the upper level. Its DRF has wide scope with respect to the quantification of the *object*–role. Here, we obtain the reading that each of the Secretaries is painted by each of the painters. This is a special case of the reading $(13_{rep:[D^u(object),D^{ul}(agent)]})$ which is the desired non–specific cumulative reading. Here, the DRS that introduces the sum–DRF $V1$ of the *agent* and that renders the sortal description of $V1$ is also introduced at the upper level. But, in contrast to $(13_{rep:[D^u(object),D^u(agent)]})$, at the nuclear scope level of the *object*–duplex condition, a DRF $\omega 1$ is introduced that stands for a subsum of a $V1$–interpretation. Here, $\omega 1$, not $V1$, determines the range that the *agent*–role distributes over. Thus, we get the reading that each of the Secretaries is painted by at least one of a sum of twelve painters that has wide scope. Since the abstraction condition $V1 :: \ldots$ ensures that the different $\omega 1$ exhaust the sum $V1$, we infer from this representation also that each of the painters paints at least one of the secretaries. Therefore, $(13_{rep:[D^u(object),D^{ul}(agent)]})$ is indeed the (non–specific) cumulative reading of (13).[27] The superscripts by which we have annotated the labels of the readings of the roles indicate how we will modify the DRS–construction algorithm of the last section in order to account for the two cumulative schemes reflected by $(13_{rep:[D^u(object),D^u(agent)]})$ and $(13_{rep:[D^u(object),D^{ul}(agent)]})$. We will segment each of the DRSs of the NP–representations into two DRSs, the upper DRS, DRS^u, and the lower DRS, DRS^l. Upper DRSs will be protected from falling inside the nuclear scope of a duplex condition. Since sometimes it will be advantageous to have a D^u– or a D^{ul}–reading replaced by the corresponding collective reading, we split up all of our NP–representations of the last section in $^u-, ^l-$ and ^{ul}–readings, except, of course, the representation scheme of singular NPs, where the ^{ul}–reading is identical to the ^{u}–reading. In the following we render the six readings that we obtain this way from the D_{tdistr}–readings of numeral and bare plural NPs. We use '|' in order to separate the upper and the lower DRS of the resulting representation. $DRS^{u,l}$ designates the pair of DRSs $< D^u, D^l >$ of the semantic argument.

THE INFLUENCE OF PLURAL NPs ON AKTIONSART IN DRT

- $\boxed{\text{n cn}}$, where $n \in DET_{\left[\begin{smallmatrix} num=pl \\ quant=ind \end{smallmatrix}\right]}, n \neq \emptyset, cn \in NOUN_{\left[\begin{smallmatrix} num=pl \\ type=count \end{smallmatrix}\right]}$

$\longrightarrow$

(D^u_{tdistr})

$\langle x, \lambda \langle \varepsilon_1 {}_{\left[\begin{smallmatrix} akt:A \\ quant:B \end{smallmatrix}\right]}, DRS^{u,l}_{[...x...]} \rangle$

$$\left[\langle E_1 {}_{\left[\begin{smallmatrix} akt:het \\ quant:B \end{smallmatrix}\right]}, \begin{array}{|c|} \hline DRS^u \\ \cup \\ \hline \begin{array}{|c|} \hline X \\ \hline cn'^*(X) \\ |X|=n \\ \hline \end{array} \\ \hline \end{array} \; \Bigg| \; \begin{array}{|l|} \hline E_1(M) \\ \hline E_1,(M)::\begin{array}{|c|}\hline x \\ \hline x \in_i X \\ \hline\end{array} \; \text{every}_x \; \begin{array}{|c|}\hline DRS^l \\ \cup \\ \hline \varepsilon_1 \leq_i E_1 \\ \hline\end{array} \\ \text{temp-distr}(E_1) \\ \hline \end{array} \; [...] \rangle \right]$$

$\longrightarrow$

(D^l_{tdistr})

$\langle x, \lambda \langle \varepsilon_1 {}_{\left[\begin{smallmatrix} akt:A \\ quant:B \end{smallmatrix}\right]}, DRS^{u,l}_{[...x...]} \rangle$

$$\left[\langle E_1 {}_{\left[\begin{smallmatrix} akt:het \\ quant:B \end{smallmatrix}\right]}, DRS^u \; \Bigg| \; \begin{array}{|l|} \hline E_1(M) \; X \\ \hline cn'^*(X) \\ |X|=n \\ \hline E_1,(M)::\begin{array}{|c|}\hline x \\ \hline x \in_i X \\ \hline\end{array} \; \text{every}_x \; \begin{array}{|c|}\hline DRS^l \\ \cup \\ \hline \varepsilon_1 \leq_i E_1 \\ \hline\end{array} \\ \text{temp-distr}(E_1) \\ \hline \end{array} \; [...] \rangle \right]$$

$\longrightarrow$

(D^{ul}_{tdistr})

$\langle x, \lambda \langle \varepsilon_1 {}_{\left[\begin{smallmatrix} akt:A \\ quant:B \end{smallmatrix}\right]}, DRS^{u,l}_{[...x...]} \rangle$

$$\left[\langle \varepsilon_{1'} {}_{\left[\begin{smallmatrix} akt:het \\ quant:+ \end{smallmatrix}\right]}, \begin{array}{|c|} \hline DRS^u \\ \cup \\ \hline \begin{array}{|c|} \hline X_2 \\ \hline cn'^*(X_2) \\ |X_2|=n \\ \hline \end{array} \\ \hline \end{array} \; \Bigg| \; \begin{array}{|l|} \hline \varepsilon_{1'}(M) \; x_2 \\ \hline x_2 \leq_i X_2 \\ \hline \varepsilon_{1'},(M)::\begin{array}{|c|}\hline x \\ \hline x \in_i x_2 \\ \hline\end{array} \; \text{every}_x \; \begin{array}{|c|}\hline DRS^l \\ \cup \\ \hline \varepsilon_1 \leq_i \varepsilon_{1'} \\ \hline\end{array} \\ \text{temp-distr}(\varepsilon_{1'}) \\ \hline \end{array} \; [...] \rangle \right]$$

- $\boxed{\emptyset \text{ cn}}$, where $cn \in NOUN_{\left[\begin{smallmatrix} num=pl \\ type=count \end{smallmatrix}\right]}$

$\longrightarrow$

(D^u_{tdistr})

$\langle x, \lambda \langle \varepsilon_1 {\scriptsize \begin{bmatrix} akt:A \\ guant:B \end{bmatrix}}, \text{DRS}^{u,l}_{[...x...]} \rangle$

$$\left[\langle E_1 {\scriptsize \begin{bmatrix} akt:A1 \\ guant:B \end{bmatrix}}, \begin{array}{c} \text{DRS}^u \\ \cup \\ \hline X \\ \hline cn'^*(X) \end{array} \mid \begin{array}{|l|} \hline E_1 \text{ (M)} \\ E_1,(M)::\boxed{\begin{array}{c} x \\ x \in_i X \end{array}} \langle \text{every} \atop x \rangle \begin{array}{c} \text{DRS}^l \\ \cup \\ \hline \varepsilon_1 \leq_i E_1 \end{array} \\ \hline temp\text{-}distr(E_1) \\ \hline \end{array} [...] \rangle \right] \rangle$$

$\longrightarrow$

(D^l_{tdistr})

$\langle x, \lambda \langle \varepsilon_1 {\scriptsize \begin{bmatrix} akt:A \\ guant:B \end{bmatrix}}, \text{DRS}^{u,l}_{[...x...]} \rangle$

$$\left[\langle E_1 {\scriptsize \begin{bmatrix} akt:A1 \\ guant:B \end{bmatrix}}, \text{DRS}^u \mid \begin{array}{|l|} \hline E_1 \text{ (M) X} \\ cn'^*(X) \\ E_1,(M)::\boxed{\begin{array}{c} x \\ x \in_i X \end{array}} \langle \text{every} \atop x \rangle \begin{array}{c} \text{DRS}^l \\ \cup \\ \hline \varepsilon_1 \leq_i E_1 \end{array} \\ \hline temp\text{-}distr(E_1) \\ \hline \end{array} [...] \rangle \right] \rangle$$

$\longrightarrow$

(D^{ul}_{tdistr})

$\langle x, \lambda \langle \varepsilon_1 {\scriptsize \begin{bmatrix} akt:A \\ guant:B \end{bmatrix}}, \text{DRS}^{u,l}_{[...x...]} \rangle$

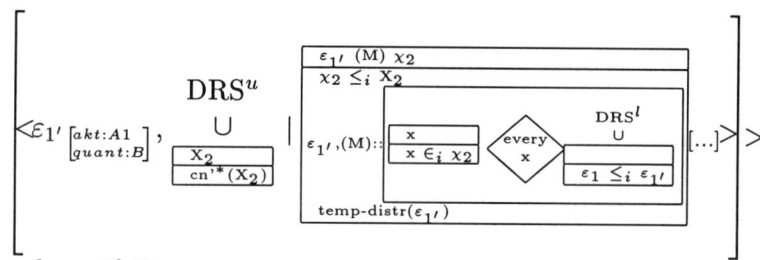

where $A1 = hom$, if $B = -$
and $\quad A1 = het$, if $B = +$

Considering the further above mentioned linking constraints of definite descriptions, it suffices to assign $^u-$, $^{ul}-$representations to definite NPs. Also it is clear, that we require that the entry for the verb puts the verb representation into the lower DRS. Thus, the upper DRS of the verb entry is empty. We will not offer examples of the intermediate steps of the construction of a sentence representation. This would be similar to the illustrative construction of the last section in particular with respect to the unifications made. Instead of this, we concentrate on the final step of constructing $(13_{rep:[D^{ul}(object), D^{ul}(agent)]})$ in the more specific version that uses the *tdistr*-readings. Generally, the constructions $[D^u(object), D^{ul}(agent)]$, $[D^l(object), D^{ul}(agent)]$ and $[D^{ul}(object), D^{ul}(agent)]$ should result in the same representation. The differences between these constructions should affect the reading only if there is an additional role that could exploit the different behavior of the upper and the lower DRS via a new duplex condition. So, what must we do, for instance, in order to turn the result of $[D^{ul}(object), D^{ul}(agent)]$ into the representation $(13_{rep:[D^u(object), D^{ul}(agent)]})$ that we have depicted further above?

$([D^{ul}_{tdistr}(object), D^{ul}_{tdistr}(agent)])$:

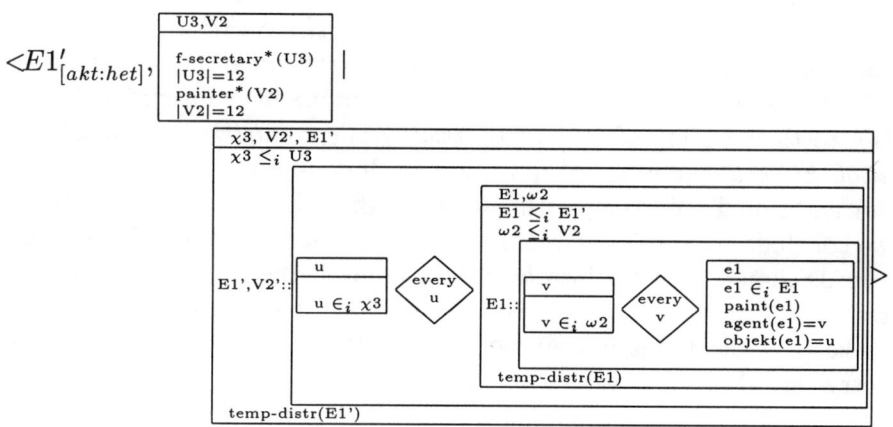

Obviously, the last construction step consists of unifying the DRFs that are annotated by the same number ($\chi 3$ with $U3$, $V2'$ with $V2$) and by carrying out the DRS–union with respect to the upper and the lower DRS. With respect to the Aktionsart, some minor reflections make clear that the splitting up into $^u-, ^l-$ and ^{ul}–readings of the NPs should have no effect. The final construction step shows that this is so, at least with respect to the role that is applied last.[28] However, this does not entail that, with respect to the Aktionsart, constructions using the new representations behave like constructions using exclusively the ones of the last section. Consider the following example:

(15) *Reporter sprachen mit den zwölf EG–Außenministern.*
      (REPORTERS TALKED TO THE TWELVE EC–FOREIGN SECRETARIES.)

Here, the construction via $[D_{tdistr}(agent), D^u_{tdistr}(object)]$ should entail the Aktionsart–value *hom* for the corresponding reading, because a homogeneously distributed sum E of events that we can describe by *a reporter talks to the twelve Foreign Secretaries* is introduced. Thus, subsums of E that are admissible with respect to a suited grid of E, summing up such events, also are *reporters talking to the twelve Secretaries*–events. In contrast, the construction via $[D_{tdistr}(agent), D^{ul}_{tdistr}(object)]$ should entail the value *het*, because, here, the homogeneously distributed sum E consists of events that we can describe by *a reporter talks to some of the twelve Foreign Secretaries*. This means that admissible subsums of E are not necessarily *reporters talking to the* **twelve** *Secretaries*–sums. Omitting for a moment the definite description of the twelve Secretaries, we see that in the case of $D_{tdistr}(agent), D^l_{tdistr}(object)]$, as in the first case, the construction should entail *hom*, because, here, E consists of events that we can describe by *a reporter talks to twelve Secretaries*, as admissible subsums of E do. For E, as well as for subsums, the total number of secretaries is unknown and, therefore, admissible subsums of E satisfy to this reading of (15) (with *zwölf Außenministern* instead of *den zwölf EG–Außenministern*), just as E itself does. Passing over some minor additional reflections with respect to the other NP–representations, we conclude from this, first, that the *tdistr*–distributive reading of bare plurals should turn *het* into *hom* if and only if the event type P of the resulting E does not make use of a ^{ul}–reading of a numeral NP. In order to keep track of this information we use the feature *quant*. The verb entry introduces the value "-" for this feature. This value is changed only by ^{ul}–readings of numeral NPs as rendered in the representations above. We easily see that the value of this feature is relevant only with respect to the *tdistr*–readings of bare plural NPs. For (15), we obtain the Aktionsart–value *hom* also, for instance, with respect to the readings constructed via $[D_{tdistr}(agent), C^u(object)]$ or $[C(agent), C^u(object)]$. We get the value *het*, for instance, with respect to the readings constructed via $[C(agent), D^{ul}_{tdistr}(object)]$ or $[D_{tsim}(agent), D^{ul}_{tdistr}(object)]$.

Summarizing, we notice that the application of *tdistr*–distributively read numeral–NPs entail the *akt*–value *het*, that the application of *tdistr*–distributively read bare plural–NPs entail the *akt*–value *hom*, provided that the actual *quant*–value is "-", and that all the other readings, including the *tdistr*–version of bare plurals in the case of *quant*=+, do not change the incoming *akt*–value.

Considering the constructions of (15), we note that we encounter technical problems with respect to our definition of the *temp–sim/temp–distr*–predicates. Obviously, when stating that the entire event of the description, E, must be temporally distributed, *temp–distr(E)*, we do not want to refer to the single events that the sum E is composed of, as we do, but we want to refer to **those** subsums that we obtain from the event description of **that** embedded DRS that is next to the E–describing DRS with respect to the recursive definition of DRSs. The same is true in the case of *temp–sim(E)*. We can remedy this shortcoming by restricting the *temp–distr/temp–sim*–requirements introduced by a particular role f with respect to a sum E to those subsums of E that are described by the event type that we obtain from the nuclear scope of the duplex condition introduced by the role f. We skip formally spelling out this correction.

Splitting up PP–representations according to the splitting up of the NP–representations presented, with the role equation (or role relation) put into the lower DRS, we arrive at our homogeneous representations ($4b_{rep}$) and ($4c_{rep}$) of the examples (4b), *Olympics fans going to Barcelona*, and (4c), *at the forward–training Völler hitting balls into the goal*, for instance, via $[D^l_{tdistr}(theme), C^u(goal)]$ in the first case and via $[C^u(agent), D^{ul}_{tdistr}(object), C^u(\oslash)C^u(goal)]$ in the second. Via $[D^l_{tdistr}(agent), C^u(goal)]$, we also obtain the heterogeneous ($12_{rep_{tdistr}}$).

We add two more refinements, aiming at the lexicon, that further adjust the applicability of the algorithm. The cumulative reading that we can construct show a certain asymmetry. We cannot truly represent the reading (*) of (16) that, as (Scha 1981) points out, is the most natural reading of (16).

(16)   *600 Dutch firms own 5000 American computers.*

(*) *There is a number of collections of Dutch firms such that each collection owns a collection of American computers, and such that the total of the Dutch firms amounts to 600 and the total of the computers amounts to 5000.*

We can represent readings, where in the nuclear scope of the duplex condition of the distribution a collection is introduced, but not readings where in the restrictor of the duplex condition a collection is introduced also, as needed in (*). In order to cope with cases like (*), we stipulate:

• for all sums X, for all sets P: $cover(P,X) \leftrightarrow sup_i(P) = X$

We skip the obvious generalization of the distributive reading of roles that we obtain from this, and immediately render the satisfying result of applying this to (16):

(16_{rep})

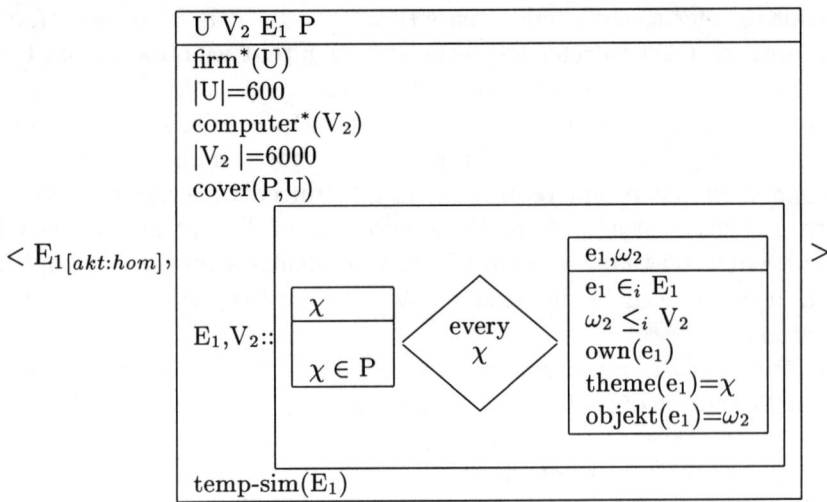

In section 3, using the example of for–adverbials, we discussed how the cooperative behavior of the recipient of the utterance can turn one event description into another via *type coercion*. With respect to those contexts where this change in the event type seems to be fairly regular, it appears to be good policy to incorporate corresponding constraints into the representation of those contexts. For illustration, we consider the context that is provided by for–adverbials.

THE INFLUENCE OF PLURAL NPs ON AKTIONSART IN DRT

- $\boxed{\text{3 Stunden lang}}$

$\longrightarrow$

$(D^l_{tdistr}(duration))$:

$<,\lambda <\varepsilon_1 \begin{bmatrix}akt:het\\quant=B\end{bmatrix}, \text{DRS}^{u,l}{}_L>$

$$\left[<E_1 \begin{bmatrix}akt:het\\quant:B\end{bmatrix}, \text{DRS}^u \mid \begin{array}{|l|} \hline T, E_1, (M) \\ \text{grid}(T) \\ \text{hour}(E_1)=3 \\ \hline (M), E_1 :: \boxed{t \in_i T} \overset{\text{every}}{\diamondsuit} t \begin{array}{|l|} \hline \text{DRS}^l \\ U \\ \hline \varepsilon_1 \leq_i E_1 \\ \varepsilon_1 \oslash t \\ \hline \end{array} \\ \hline \end{array} \right]$$

We have skipped to represent the normal case where the incoming Aktionsart-value is *hom*, $(C^l(duration))$. In this case, the incoming event description is changed only by adding the duration statement. Doing this, of course, determines the Aktionsart-value of the outgoing event description to be *het*. In contrast, in case the incoming event description is *het*, it must be modified. Normally, this is effected by iteration. It is this kind of type coercion that we have rendered. Another possibility could be the progressivization of the event description. We presented the ^{l}-reading only, since it is the most/only acceptable reading of a duration statement of the type *for XX TIME-MEASURE* with or without type coercion. We stress, that applying iteration to an event type P is different from restricting P by means of a *temp-distr*-condition. With respect to the extension of P in the model, we obtain in the second case a subset of the extension of P, in the first case we do not.

The refinements of this section contribute to further increase the number of readings. For efficient text understanding this poses a problem. Psychologically, in most contexts, it seems justifiable to analyze event types at a level that abstracts from the *temp-distr/temp-sim*-distinction. In this psychological perspective of the recipient of the text, the *temp-distr/temp-sim*-alternatives can be seen as specifications of a given type that one gets aware of only if the context focuses on disambiguating constraints. Taking this point of view one step further, investigations on text understanding will comprise relating the means for a detailed analysis of situations that we have developed in this paper to suggestions of underspecified representations like (Reyle 1993) and to spell out the conditions that necessitate a precise determination of a particular situation considered. But this is outside the scope of this paper.

6. CONCLUSION

In this paper we have outlined a DRS–construction algorithm that copes with different readings of plural NPs. This algorithm comprises an Aktionsart calculus that parallels the construction of the semantic representation. We have presented a definition of temporally discourse–homogeneous and temporally discourse–heterogeneous event types. Here, we have used the formal analysis of some sample sentences that make use of plural NPs and that are critical with respect to the Aktionsart in order to spell out a definition of these notions that is also applicable to the case of event types that refer to event sums. Based on this definition, that can deal with different levels of granularity, the main result was, that, for non–generic sentences, event roles that are described by bare plurals turn heterogeneous event descriptions into homogeneous descriptions only if, first, they are interpreted in a reading that we have called the temporally distributive reading, and, second, if there exists no other event role that suspends the effect of homogeneity that comes with this specific distributive reading of bare plurals. Only quantized NPs in the so called ^{ul}–readings can suspend this effect. In contrast to this, the temporally distributive, and, from this, also the non further specified distributive reading of quantized NPs turn homogeneous event descriptions into heterogeneous descriptions. Thus, our approach presents a rather differentiated account of the Aktionsart phenomena connected to plural phrases.

NOTES

[1] A distinction is often drawn between the Aktionsart and (morphological) *aspect*, where the latter stands for things expressed by the *imparfait* :: *passé simple*-opposition in French or the difference between *simple past* and *past progressive* in English. Notwithstanding such definitions, for the sake of simplicity, we will not distinguish between *aspect* and *Aktionsart* in this paper.

[2] Since achievements combine more easily and with less deformation of the initial 'normal' meaning with in–adverbials than with for–adverbials, we have classified them as heterogeneous descriptions. This is also justified by the similarity to accomplishments in the presence of a number of other Aktionsart sensitive phenomena.

[3] Of course, specific additional contextual information might alter this outcome. For instance, (4a) is easily accepted in the scope of a for–adverbial, if the peculiarity of the Olympics tradition with several sportsmen partaking in one event of taking the

torch from Athens to the place of the games is suspended in favor of a reading where the torch is taken to Barcelona several times, each time by a different sportsman.

[4] For a discussion see in particular (Link 1983), also (Schütze 1989), (Link and Schütze 1991), (Krifka 1987b), (Krifka 1987a), (Kamp and Reyle 1993) but, for a controversal debate, also (Landman 1989a), (Landman 1989b).

[5] Thus, $\boxed{\begin{array}{c} u \\ \vdots \end{array}}$ is an abreviation for $\boxed{\begin{array}{c} u \\ \hline \text{atom}(u) \\ \vdots \end{array}}$ and $\boxed{\begin{array}{c} U \\ \vdots \end{array}}$ is an abreviation for $\boxed{\begin{array}{c} U \\ \hline \neg \boxed{\text{atom}(U)} \\ \vdots \end{array}}$.

[6] Compare for instance (Eberle 1991), where, on the basis of the *feature logic with subsorts* presented in (Smolka 1988), a language for sort expressions (including the *-operator) is developed which is used to attribute rather fine–grained sortal information to the DRFs of DRSs, thus allowing for specific and efficient inference procedures for text representations.

[7] To this point, again, compare (Eberle 1991). For alternative approaches see also (Galton 1984), (Galton 1987), (Löbner 1988).

[8] For simplicity, we will use the term *event* not just for events proper (accomplishments and achievements), but also for states and activities and sums of events, activities or states. The intended meaning should be clear from the context. Also, we mention that, properly speaking, in this approach the terms *accomplishment, achievement, activity* and *state* refer to event types, not to the events themselves. So, more precisely, the term *event* can refer to single objects that are instances of predicates that are instances of some Aktionsart class, and it can refer to sums of such objects.

[9] For instance, a branch b of a tree t is a material part of this tree ($b \leq_m t$): the substance of b is contained in the substance of t. However, it does not hold $b \leq_i t$, since t lacks the internal structure that determines t as a sum that could subsume b as an atom.

The structuring using both $\leq_m$ and $\leq_i$ developed in (Eberle 1991) and used here, is based on the work of Link about objects and portions of matter ((Link 1983), (Link 1984), (Link 1991)).

For an exhaustive description of the formal means that are introduced in the following, as mentioned, compare the more detailed study in (Eberle 1991).

[10] We do not want to deeply motivate different ontological levels for events here. For clarification, think of the well–known example that Bach has used in order to distinguish between materially identical, but otherwise different events:

(17)   Jones poured poison into the water main$_{e_1}$.
        versus
        Jones poisoned the populace$_{e_2}$.   (Bach 1986)

In Bach's scenario the events e_1 and e_2 refer to the same physical entity, but they function as different events. In order to model such scenarios, we can use interpreting models (text–worlds) that are structured by means of distinguishing criteria that go beyond the level of the pure physical appearance, that include, for instance, intentionality and elements of agent centered action theory. With respect to such models, event descriptions like those of (17) might refer to different events, even if these events are physically equivalent in one way or the other. With the notion of *material part* and the relation of material equivalence that is defined from this notion, we reach the level of such fine-grained interpreting models and can state, for instance, that in (17) it holds $e_1 =_m e_2$ and $e_1 \neq e_2$.

[11] Of course, the threshold value of a complex event predicate should be computed from the value of the underlying simple event predicate that stems from the representation of the verb used in the corresponding natural language description. Normally, we obtain $limit(\lambda e P(e)) = limit(\lambda e (\exists x (P(e) \wedge R(e) = x)))$. To a certain extent, however, the computation should take into account the granularity changing influence of particular thematic roles. (Compare *running of an ant*–events to *running of an elephant*–events in this respect.)

[12] The threshold value for an event predicate refers to the 'volume' of events rather than to the occurrence time, since, as it seems, the perceptibility of the realization of a particular event type depends not only on the temporal dimension but also on some non-temporal criteria. For instance, consider the type *working*. An action that shows a lot of movements on the part of the agent per time unit probably fulfills the decisive features of *working* in shorter time than a less intense instance of the same type, that shows less movements per time unit. This difference in 'spatiality' should have an impact on the definition of the *size*–function.

[13] The contrast (8f) – (8g) has also been used in the ontological considerations of (Shoham 1987).

[14] For degrees of granularity, compare also (Hobbs 1985).

[15] Suggestions for a quantificational analysis of duration adverbials can be found, for instance, in (Dowty 1979), (Hoepelman 1979), (Reyle 1987). But, for a critical position, compare also (Krifka 1987b).

[16] In (Ogihara 1990), (Kamp 1990), (Caenepeel and Moens 1991), data are discussed that seem to suggest that the possibility of conceptualizing a described situation as a single event is closely related to the (semantic) acceptability of applying progressivization to the corresponding natural language description.

[17] Compare section 2, point 6 of the truth conditions.

[18] The definite descriptions *beim Stürmertraining* and *ins Tor* indicate that for a more precise rendering of the event type referred to in (4c), we should also make use of this formal means, the parameterization, with respect to $P2$. We omit this.

[19] We use *type coercion* as introduced in (Moens and Steedman 1988), but applied to event types, not to events.

[20] Having a closer look to the definition of $ITER$, we see that the second representation does not completely correspond to the first one: for simplicity, here, we have omitted to make sure that for different intervals t, t' we obtain different overlapping events e, e' ($t \oslash e$ and $t' \oslash e'$).

[21] Cf. (Verkuyl 1972) for the notion.

[22] Compare (Reyle 1985), (Reyle 1987), or (Zeevat et al. 1987) to a more detailed motivation of indices.

[23] For partial DRSs, compare also (Reyle 1987), (Eberle 1991), (Kamp and Reyle 1993).

[24] This inversion is often advocated in the literature on unification-based grammar formalisms. For an example of an application compare, for instance, (Bouma 1989).

[25] Compare, for instance, the detailed studies (Scha 1981), (Scha and Stallard 1981) on this subject. We stress that the cumulative reading of a sentence must not be confused with the cumulative extension of a predicate in the model. Until now we have used the notion only in the second sense.

[26] Properly speaking, we think that in the case of (14) it might be that we have to quantify over the situations introduced by the entire event rather than to quantify

over the atoms of the sum introduced by the description *zwölf bekannte Maler* or by the description *die zwölf EG-Außenminister* respectively, since the meaning of the adverbial seems to be that each of the single events that compose the entire event of (14) took at most one week. But this formal analysis indirectly requires the distribution over at least one of the role descriptions and corresponds to the outlined analysis in substance.

[27] As in sections 3 and 4, the conditions of the type $e1 \in_i E1$ and $E1 \leq_i E1'$ in the above representations guarantee that $E1, E2$ are not necessarily maximal sums with respect to the event types that characterize them.

[28] It is true that, in the D_{tdistr}^{ul}-case of numeral NPs and in the D_{tdistr}^{u}-case of bare plural–NPs, the event type corresponding to the representation of the lower DRS developed at the particular intermediate construction step of applying the respective role entails the "wrong" Aktionsart value. But we think that the human recipient of the sentence does not evaluate these event types as such, but augments them according to the information presented by the actual upper DRS. This means that he interprets the result of the actual role application more or less like the result of a last role application. This can be modelled formally in order to prove the correctness of the algorithm suggested in this section.

REFERENCES

Bach, E. (1986): The algebra of events. *Linguistics and Philosophy* **9**, 5–16.

Bäuerle, R. (1988): Ereignisse und Repräsentationen. *LILOG Report 43*. IBM Deutschland, WT LILOG. Stuttgart.

Bennett, M. and Partee, B. (1972): Toward the logic of tense and aspect In English. *Technical report*. System Development Corporation. Santa Monica, California.

Bouma, G. (1989): Lilog prototype 1 – grammar documentation: Semantics. (ms.) IMS, Universität Stuttgart.

Caenepeel, M. and Moens, M. (1991): Progressives, perfects and the temporal structure of discourse. In H. Kamp (ed.), *Tense and Aspect in English*. Centre for Cognitive Science. Edinburgh. 4–40. DYANA Deliverable R2.3.A.

Carlson, G. (1980): Reference to kinds in English. In J. Hankamer (ed.), *Outstanding Dissertations in Linguistics*. Harvard University. Harvard.

Davidson, D. (1967): The logical form of action sentences. *Essays on Actions and Events*. Clarendon Press. Oxford. 105–121.

Dowty, D. R. (1986): The effects of aspectual class on the temporal structure of discourse: Semantics or pragmatics?. *Linguistics and Philosophy* **9**, 37–62.

Dowty, D. R. (1979): *Word Meaning and Montague Grammar*. Reidel. Dordrecht.

Eberle, K. (1991): Ereignisse: Ihre Logik und Ontologie aus textsemantischer Sicht. *IWBS Report 192*. IBM Deutschland, WT LILOG. Stuttgart.

Galton, A. (1984): *The Logic of Aspect. An Axiomatic Approach*. Clarendon Press. Oxford.

Galton, A. (1987): The logic of occurrence. In A. Galton (ed.), *Temporal Logics and their Applications*. Academic Press. London. 169–196.

Hobbs, J. (1985): Granularity. *Proceedings of the Ninth International Joint Conference on Artificial Intelligence.*

Hoepelman, J. (1979): *Verb Classification and the Russian Verbal Aspect. A Formal Treatment.* Narr. Tübingen.

Kamp, H. (1981): A theory of truth and semantic representation. In J. Groenendijk, T. Janssen and M. Stokhof (eds.), *Formal Methods in the Study of Language.* Mathematical Centre Tract. Amsterdam.

Kamp, H. (ed.) (1990): *Tense and Aspect in English.* Centre for Cognitive Science. Edinburgh. chapter 1 Introduction, 1–3. DYANA Deliverable R2.3.A.

Kamp, H. and Reyle, U. (1993): *From Discourse to Logic.* Kluwer Academic Publishers. Dordrecht.

Krifka, M. (1987a): Nominal reference and temporal constitution: Towards a semantics of quantity. *FNS–Bericht 17.* Forschungsstelle für natürlich–sprachliche Systeme, Universität Tübingen.

Krifka, M. (1987b): *Nominalreferenz und Zeitkonstitution. Zur Semantik von Massentermen, Pluraltermen und Aspektklassen.* Dissertation. Universität München.

Landman, F. (1989a): Groups i. *Linguistics and Philosophy* **12**(5), 559–606.

Landman, F. (1989b): Groups ii. *Linguistics and Philosophy* **12**(6), 723–744.

Link, G. (1983): The logical analysis of plurals and mass terms: A lattice–theoretical approach. In R. Bäuerle, R. Schwarze and A. von Stechow (eds.), *Meaning, Use and Interpretation of Language.* de Gruyter. Berlin. 302–323.

Link, G. (1984): Plural. In D. Wunderlich and A. von Stechow (eds.), *Semantik. Ein internationales Handbuch der zeitgenössischen Forschung.* De Gruyter. Berlin.

Link, G. (1987): Generalized quantifiers and plurals. In P. Gärdenfors (ed.), *Generalized Quantifiers. Linguistic and Logical Approaches.* Reidel. Dordrecht.

Link, G. (1991): First order axioms for the logic of plurality. In J. Allgayer (ed.), *Processing Plurals and Quantification.* (= CSLI Lecture Notes). Stanford.

Link, G. and Schütze, H. (1991): The treatment of plurality in L_{LILOG}. In O. Herzog and C.-R. Rollinger (eds.), *Text Understanding in LILOG: Integrating Computational Linguistics and Artificial Intelligence.* Springer. Berlin, Heidelberg. 342–352.

Löbner, S. (1988): Ansätze zu einer integralen semantischen Theorie von Tempus, Aspekt und Aktionsarten. In V. Ehrich and H. Vater (eds.), *Temporalsemantik. Beiträge zur Linguistik der Zeitreferenz.* Niemeyer. Tübingen. 163–191.

Moens, M. and Steedman, M. (1988): Temporal ontology and temporal reference. *Computational Linguistics* **14.2 (Special Issue on Tense and Aspect)**, 15–28.

Ogihara, T. (1990): The semantics of the progressive and the perfect in English. In H. Kamp (ed.), *Tense and Aspect in English.* Centre for Cognitive Science. Edinburgh. 3–38. DYANA Deliverable R2.3.A.

Platzack, C. (1979): *The Semantic Interpretation of Aspect and Aktionsarten. A Study of Internal Time Reference in Swedish.* Foris. Dordrecht.

Reyle, U. (1985): Grammatical functions, discourse referents and quantification. *Proceedings of the Ninth International Joint Conference on Artificial Intelligence.* Los Angeles.

Reyle, U. (1987): Zeit und Aspekt bei der Verarbeitung natürlicher Sprachen. *LILOG Report 9.* IBM Deutschland, WT LILOG. Stuttgart.

Reyle, U. (1993): Dealing with ambiguities by underspecification: Construction, representation, and deduction. *Journal of Semantics* **10**(2), 123–179.

Scha, R. J. (1981): Distributive, collective and cumulative quantification. In J. Groenendijk, T. Janssen and M. Stokhof (eds.), *Formal Methods in the Study of Language.* Mathematical Centre Tract. Amsterdam. 483–512. Part 2.

Scha, R. J. and Stallard, D. (1981): Multi–level plurals and distributivity.

Schütze, H. (1989): Pluralbehandlung in natürlichsprachlichen Wissensverarbeitungssystemen. *IWBS Report 73.* IBM Deutschland, WT LILOG. Stuttgart.

Shoham, Y. (1987): Temporal logics in AI: Semantical and ontological considerations. *Artificial Intelligence* **33**, 89–104.

Smolka, G. (1988): A feature logic with subsorts. *LILOG Report 33.* IBM Deutschland, WT LILOG. Stuttgart.

Steinitz, R. (1981): Der Status der Kategorie "Aktionsart" in der Grammatik (oder: Gibt es Aktionsarten im Deutschen?). *Linguistische Studien, Reihe a: Arbeitsberichte.* Akademie der Wissenschaften, Zentralinstitut für Sprachwissenschaft. Berlin.

Vendler, Z. (1967): *Linguistics in Philosophy.* Cornell University Press. Ithaca, New York.

Verkuyl, H. J. (1972): *On the Compositional Nature of the Aspects.* Vol. 15 of *Foundations of Language Suppl. Series.* Reidel. Dordrecht.

Zeevat, H., Calder, J. and Klein, E. (1987): Unification categorial grammar. In N. Haddock, E. Klein and G. Morrill (eds.), *Categorial Grammar, Unification Grammar and Parsing.* Centre for Cognitive Science, Edinburgh.

CHRIS FOX

MASS TERMS AND PLURALS IN PROPERTY THEORY

1. INTRODUCTION

In essence, this paper presents a semantic theory which:

(i) Allows apparently coreferring terms to corefer whilst permitting different, possibly contradictory predicates to apply to those terms without resulting in inconsistency. For example, "the cleaner" and "the judge" may have different incomes, even though both positions may be taken by one person;

(ii) Allows the distribution of properties into *mereological* (part–whole) terms without distributing to inappropriate parts. We might say "the dirty water is liquid", and infer that parts of the dirty water are liquid, without inferring that the dirt is liquid;

(iii) Gives a treatment of so–called 'non–denoting' definites within a classical, two–valued theory which does not require that non–denoting terms be equated, so that "the present king of France", and "the largest prime number" can be distinguished in the semantics.

Points (i) and (ii) are intimately related. They stem from an attempt to devise a semantic theory of plurals and mass terms with a minimum of ontological commitments.

It is always possible both to block inappropriate distributive inferences, and to allow different properties to hold of apparently coreferring terms by adopting a highly intensional ontology. In such an ontology, dirt is not (in a formal sense) a part of dirty water, and a judge (who is John) is represented by some term distinct from the individual denoted by "John". However, part of the motivation behind this paper is to see just how far we can go in preventing inappropriate inferences of these kinds without presupposing such an ontology.

This is not to say that in devising a semantic theory we should never make ontological commitments. However, we should be cautious in asserting that certain commitments are *necessary* to explain the empirical data, when they might only be required by a particular analysis, perhaps to make up for some undesirable artifact of the chosen formalisation.

It is in this sense that point (iii) is related to (i) and (ii). It is concerned with constraining inferences without requiring a special element in the domain for 'non–denoting' definite descriptors, or a three–valued theory.

All three themes are concerned with intensionality of subject noun phrases. They involve the issue of distinguishing uses of noun phrases that appear to corefer on an unsophisticated extensional account.

1.1. Intensional Subjects

The intensionality of subject position noun phrases is apparent with sentences involving collective nouns such as "committee". For example, we might have two different committees with the same members. We can predicate different properties of these two committees without fear of contradiction; if one of the committees is having a meeting it does not mean that the other committee with the same members is also having a meeting (Bennett, 1977; Link, 1984).

As Landman points out, similar issues arise with singular nouns. For example, if we have a judge and the cleaner, we appear to be able to say:

> The judge earns £20000.
> The cleaner earns £2000.

without contradiction, even if one individual, John, is both judge and cleaner (Landman, 1989). Landman argues that the definite noun phrases cannot be taken to simply denote the relevant individual which then has the property denoted by the verb phrase applied to it.

These arguments parallel those exemplified by the Evening Star–Morning Star problem. The Morning Star and the Evening Star both refer to the planet Venus. On an unsophisticated account these definite descriptions might then be equivalent. However, we can say:

> The Morning Star and the Evening Star were once thought
> to be different.

without meaning that the Morning Star was once thought to be different from itself. This sentence differs from the judge–cleaner example in that it involves a propositional attitude.

Landman suggests that the individuals referred to in these sentences are really individuals under certain roles. An individual may have different properties under different roles. The properties an individual has under one role may contradict those it has under another role. This may be made explicit in English by such sentences as:

> John, as a judge, earns £20000.
> John, as a cleaner, earns £2000.

He proposes a new, distinct ontology for the denotations of individuals acting under different *guises* or *roles*. Landman effectively predicates "earns £20000" of *John-as-a-judge*, and "earns £2000" of *John-as-a-cleaner*, where *i-as-a-p* is a new kind of intensional individual.

Landman adopts a strongly typed theory where the individuals acting under guises cannot be taken to be new individuals themselves.[1] As a consequence, when dealing with plurals, Landman requires not only a lattice–theoretic structure over the domain of individuals, following Link for example (Link, 1983; Link, 1984; Link, 1987; Link, 1991b), but also a similar, but separate structure over the intensional individuals.

Landman suggests that it might be fruitful to consider a theory where his 'individuals under guises' are considered to be individuals themselves[2], and also to use a more weakly typed theory such as Ray Turner's axiomatisation (Turner, 1987; Turner, 1990; Turner, 1992) of Aczel's Frege Structures (Aczel, 1980). These options, together with the property modifier treatment, are explored in more detail elsewhere (Fox, 1993; Fox, 1994c).

Given the sentence:

The judge is strict.

where John is the judge, it might seem more natural to say "John is a strict judge" than "John, as a judge, is strict". The sentence "the judge is strict" could well be taken to be elliptic for "the judge is a strict judge". Even when the "as a ..." construction is natural, the use of commas, when it is adjacent to the nominal, suggests some *movement* has occurred:

John, as a judge, earns £20000.
John earns £20000 as a judge.

This, perhaps, gives some support to the policy of treating roles as property modification (or, in this presentation, as properties modified by the verb phrase) rather than modification of the individual, although syntactic arguments like this are potentially hazardous.

Following this, the judge–cleaner example can be treated by assuming the predication is modified, rather than the individual. So we would have the properties "(earns £20000)-as-a-judge" and "(earns £2000)-as-a-cleaner". The property modifiers will correspond, in some sense, to the *subsective adjectives* (Kamp, 1975) even though in the final theory they may be derived from the translation of natural language verbs.[3] The term they modify shall usually be derived from the subject nominal, so we would have, in effect:

> John is a £20000 earning judge.
> John is a £2000 earning cleaner.

This approach means that only one plural domain is required as there are no new 'individuals under guises'.

Landman argues in favour of 'intensional individuals', over some form of modification to the predication, on the basis of examples involving comparatives, such as:

> The judge and the cleaner have different incomes.

where, again, John might be both judge and cleaner.

Presumably he sees this as a problematic example for a property modifier approach as there only appears to be one property—"have different incomes"—yet there would be two property modifiers. That is, on a property modifier approach, the interpretation of the verb would have to provide for as many modifiers as there are constituent noun phrases in the subject. If roles modify the interpretation of the noun phrases, then, trivially, there are always the same number of objects to be modified as there are modifiers. However, the appearance of only one verb phrase in the natural language sentence does not preclude there being more than one appropriate property in the semantic representation of the sentence. Landman's objection must rest on the assumption that "have different incomes" is represented by some single, irreducible property in the semantics. In particular, his objection must assume that there can be no useful reduction of the phrase modified by the adverb "different". If, in the truth conditions of the sentence, we can provide a property to be modified for each noun phrase, then an interpretation can be given to the sentence using property modifiers. We could paraphrase the comparative sentence as:

> The income *from cleaning* earned by the person who is the cleaner is different to the income *from judging* earned by the person who is the judge.

with the outcome that:

> John's income as a judge is different to his income as a cleaner.

if John is both judge and cleaner.

So, it does seem that Landman's problematic example *can* be treated by way of a more complex predication, provided care is taken with the analysis of the comparative itself (Fox, 1994c; Fox, 1993), as indicated in Section 4. As a consequence, the examples involving the intensionality of subject position noun phrases can be treated without complicating the ontology. Apparently coreferring items can be allowed to corefer whilst possessing different properties.

This can also be used to treat examples involving reference to an object and the material of which it is made. Thus, given a ring made from gold it is possible to say:

> The gold is old.
> The ring is new.

without contradiction, as "the gold" in effect refers to an object under the guise of being gold, and "the ring" may refer to the same object under the guise of being a ring.[4]

In the final theory, property modifiers are used to control inferences exemplified by distribution, whilst allowing (though not requiring) an inhomogeneous ontology; dirt and water may be parts of dirty water, for example. Inferences involving distributive properties can cause problems with such ontologies, because we want to distribute to the correct parts. Landman's insights enable us to embellish the application of a property to a term so that we can recover these parts. This is elaborated in Section 1.2.

In general, how do we know under which aspect the application of a property to a term should be restricted? That is, in Landman's terminology, where do *roles* come from? With sentences where the subject is not a proper name, one possibility suggests itself: if we take "the man is tall", then the subject noun phrase can provide the information that enables us to interpret this as "the man is a tall man". However, a sentence may be ambiguous as to whether such a device is appropriate:

> The cleaners are badly paid.

may mean either that the cleaners are badly paid cleaners, or that the cleaners are badly paid people. If we take the latter reading, where does the aspect of being a person come from? Perhaps a theory of context and salience could provide the answer. I see several possibilities:

(i) take "badly paid" as ambiguous between being *badly paid as an X* where the subject fills in the X and just plain *badly paid (as a person)*;

(ii) take "The cleaners" as ambiguous between *the cleaners as cleaners*, and *the cleaners as individuals*;

(iii) have some sortal hierarchy, which says *a cleaner is a person*, and allow individuating terms, optionally, to be generalised;

(iv) some other, more general, theory of context and salience.

It should be noted that, under whichever role we treat the cleaners, we can obtain the correct individuation. It is not, however, possible to take the sentence as ambiguous between providing a role and not, since we must know how to obtain the appropriate nice parts.

Considering sentences involving proper names, when we say that "John is tall" and "Everest is tall", it should be clear that we are not asserting that John and Everest are both in the class of tall objects. Presumably, we mean "John is a tall person" and "Everest is a tall mountain". These could then be taken as forms of ellipsis. But what information do we use to complete the interpretation? The translation of proper nouns can include the role under which they are to be considered, so we could have, in some sense, *the person John* and *the mountain Everest* as our representations of these names. These considerations are the same as those that arise in the interpretation of adjectives (Kamp, 1975; Montague, 1974). The final theory (Section 4.) is only concerned with sentences involving quantified noun phrases. Their semantic representation gives rise to some appropriately modified predication in the truth conditions.[5]

If guises are added to the theory, either with the aid of property modifiers, or new terms, then presumably these can be inherited by anaphoric reference. For example:

> There is [a judge]$_i$.
> [He]$_i$ is strict.

should give rise to:

> There is a strict judge.

This would seem easier to formalise if Landman's restricted individuals are used, rather than property modifiers, as this would be a simple extension of existing discourse theories (for example (Kamp, 1981; Heim, 1982; Kamp and Reyle, 1993)). However, the property modifiers need only arise in the truth conditions. If the resolution of the anaphora occurs before this stage, then there may be no call for additional complexity.

1.2. Mass Terms and Distribution

Sentences containing mass terms provide another class of examples where it seems that we might wish to allow nominals to corefer, whilst requiring that different properties hold of them. This becomes apparent with distributive inferences. If we apply a property to a term, the property is said to be distributive if it holds of the parts of that term. With count nouns we know that we should only distribute at most as far as the individuals. With mass terms, consideration of natural language alone does not always make it obvious when to stop performing distributive inferences. If we have some water, and we say it is liquid, then we would like to infer that parts of it are also liquid. Clearly, we only want those parts of it that are water to be considered liquid, rather than individual molecules or fragments of such. The problem is that in the conventional compositional analysis, we cannot gain access to the property that indicates the appropriate parts ("water" in this case) unless we put constraints on the denotation of "water".

The problem can be demonstrated without appeal to the atoms of physics. If we have some dirty water, we can say that "the dirty water is liquid" and expect to be able to infer that parts of the dirty water are liquid, without inferring that some dirt is liquid. Here, however, limits on the appropriate inferences are discernible from our intuitions about language. We are interested only in distributing properties to the 'nice' parts of terms, where the nice parts of some cats, for example, are cats, rather than bits of cats (Lewis, 1991).[6]

We can avoid distributing properties to the wrong parts if we constrain the ontology so that parts of water are water and parts of dirty water are dirty water. This is an homogeneous ontology, which is intended to be argued for, in part, by Bunt's *homogeneous reference hypothesis*:

> "A mass noun refers in such a way that no particular articulation of the referent into parts is presupposed, nor the existence of minimal parts." (Bunt, 1985)

If we were pedantic, we might argue that an homogeneous ontology *does* presuppose a particular articulation of the referents into parts. We shall look at the question of minimal parts below in Section 1.3.

Although an homogeneous ontology avoids distributing to inappropriate parts (as there are no inappropriate parts) it should not be taken as a conclusive argument in favour of such an ontology. The reason we might consider inappropriate parts in an inhomogeneous ontology is that in the representation, the property used to denote the term in question is present only by way of its extension (or the supremum of its extension). If the suprema, or fusions, of the extensions of two distinct properties are equal, then distributing into one will be equivalent to distributing into the other, even though the two properties may hold of different parts. If we allow the suprema to be equal, and we wish to control distributive inferences, then we need some way of keeping track of the property whose suprema we are distributing into.

There is a sense in which theories that give homogeneous extensions to mass terms have effectively encoded the property used to denote a mass term in the extension. However, Landman's 'individuals under guises' provide an alternative, explicit way of associating the property that has been used to denote with the denotation. This property can then be used to control distributive inferences with mass terms. If we implement Landman's intensional individuals using property modifiers, then we can control distributive inferences with mass terms using an ontology of plain individuals, and some Boolean algebra–like structure that need not be homogeneous. As an example, we might interpret the sentence "all water is liquid", as predicating "liquid–water" of the mereological sum of all water. That predicate can then distribute to those parts that are water (as opposed to arbitrary parts of the sum).

There is a potential problem with this, depending upon our view of the meaning of "liquid". For this treatment of distribution to work, it must be assumed that the smallest denotables that have the property of being "water" must still be large enough to possess any distributive properties. This treatment of distribution would fail if we consider a molecule of water to be water, yet only allow a more substantial body of water to be liquid. Further, if we consider "being liquid" to be a property of a collection of molecules that are a physically continuous body, then this account would fail if denotable water could consist of the fusion of discontinuous fragments of water, each fragment being too small to be attributed the property of being liquid.[7] Such criticisms seem to assume a reductive account of the extension of mass terms to notions in modern physics. We can maintain that the denotables that we can refer to by a term like "water" are precisely those terms to which we can attribute properties such as "being liquid". We could view an attempt to ascertain the smallest such denotable in terms of physical molecules as rather like trying to give a reductive account of the meaning of "a table" in terms of a physical arrangement of components.

We might look more closely at the notion of smallest part in modern physics. It tells us that the smallest element of water is a water molecule, precisely because a water molecule is the smallest physical component of water that possesses the properties that distinguish it as water for the purposes of theories in physical science. If we accept that the property of "being liquid" cannot be attributed to molecules in isolation, then for the purposes of this theory of semantics, the smallest component of water that counts as water will have to be something more than a molecule. This does not prevent reference to *molecules of water*, as this sentence demonstrates. According to this theory, we might then say "the water is liquid" without entailing that "the molecules of water are liquid".

Notice that we can use the same machinery to control distribution with plurals.

In order to stop distribution at an appropriate point, it is not necessary to use the full intensionality of the property modifier regime: all that is required is for the property which is modified to provide the correct individuation. Any additional intensionality can, in principle, be thrown away. Thus we can always consider cleaners as cleaners, and John as John. However, Landman provides sufficient indication as to why we might not want to do this.[8]

Even if we can constrain the distribution of simple properties to appropriate 'nice' parts, there are added complications with disjunctive properties, as noted by Roeper (Roeper, 1983). For example, with the sentence:

> All phosphorus is red or white.

it is not sufficient to be able to pick out the nice parts of phosphorus and say of them that they are red, or that they are white, because there may be some bits of phosphorus that are both red and white. There are also similar complications with negation (Lønning, 1987). Clearly, care must be taken when giving the truth conditions of such examples. These problems would also affect a treatment with homogeneous extensions.

It could be argued that if we were to adopt an homogeneous ontology then there would be no identification of, for example, "the gold" and "the ring" in "the gold ring", as they have different parts. Indeed the ring has no proper parts that constitute a complete ring. This is an argument originally intended to be against the identification of substances (the denotation of mass terms) and physical matter, attributed to Quine by Parsons:

> "even if all and only furniture was composed of wood, it would not follow that wood = furniture, since parts of the

chairs might be wood without being furniture." (Parsons, 1970).

It can be taken as an argument against the need to keep track of the property used to refer, and in favour of a particular ontology for the denotations of noun phrases.

Bunt disputes the wood–furniture example, suggesting that the problem lies in taking "furniture" to be a mass term with minimal parts. He cites the same example, replacing the individuating term "furniture" with "sawdust", so that all the wood in the world is made into sawdust. He then says that "wood" and "sawdust" can legitimately be equated, in non–intensional contexts (Bunt, 1985). However, this cannot be the case, as we might truthfully say "this *sawdust* was made yesterday", without commitment to "this *wood* was made yesterday".[9]

It might still be argued that the sawdust and wood are distinguishable because they have different nice parts: there are parts of the sawdust that are not sawdust, but are wood. However, it is conceivable that some sawdust might be sufficiently finely ground for its minimal nice parts to constitute the minimal nice parts of wood, but we would still want to be able to predicate different things of the sawdust and wood. So, even if an ontology is adopted where terms are equated only if they have the same minimal parts, there is still some motivation for using Landman's intensional individuals, or property modifiers.

As stated before, in the final analysis it might turn out that we really do need an highly intensional ontology where apparently coreferring terms do not corefer. However, the notion of a term being considered under a guise does permit such coreference. Again, if terms under guises are represented using modified predications, then constraints on appropriate distributive inferences can be guaranteed without additional ontological commitments other than some part–whole structure in the domain.

There have been previous attempts to provide a formalisation of part–whole structures that do not assume an homogeneous ontology. Moravcsik gives two theories that seek to do just this (Moravcsik, 1973).

He represents predication with the part–of relation. In the first theory, "x is water" is represented by:

$$x \leq \text{water}'_{sp}$$

where water'_{sp} consists of the objects not too small to count as water. This explicitly creates an homogeneous term from a potentially inhomogeneous one. Unfortunately, representing predication in this way means that all mass terms must be homogeneous (Fox, 1993) on pain of inconsistency (Bunt, 1985), as the representation of the sentence "water is water" (water' $\leq$ water'$_{sp}$, where water' is the potentially inhomogeneous mereological sum of "water") requires that all unconstrained parts of water are not too small to count as water.

In his second theory, Moravcsik seeks to constrain the part–of relation to make it homogeneous in character. The expression:

$$x \leq_{sp(m)} m$$

is used to indicate that x must be a part of m not too small to count as m. Or, to express it more generally, it must be either a *nice* part of m, or a sum of *nice* parts. As it stands, this account does not deal with all the data. If we have:

The puddle is water.
Water is wet.

then we should be able to prove that the puddle is wet. If predication is modelled by the part–of relation, then in this case we require transitivity across the different kinds of part–of relations (Bunt, 1985). Moravcsik does not elaborate on the relationships between the different orderings.

The arguments in this paper are concerned only with the ontology of things that are the denotations of natural language, rather than with some reductive ontology of the physical world. For example, I will take it that a cat can be the same cat even if it looses a whisker, following the familiar arguments of Aristotle (Burge, 1975), and that part–whole structures in the denotation of natural language can survive physical mereological change (Cartwright, 1965), thus some water can be the same water even after some of it evaporates. Also, if there is some dirty water, it may remain the same dirty water even if the dirt is in dynamic equilibrium with some sludge at the bottom of the water.

This paper does not attempt to address the general problem of identification of substances and objects. There may be good arguments for not identifying a gold ring with the gold that it is made from. On the other hand, there are examples where different descriptors surely do denote the same object, such as "the Evening Star" and "the Morning Star".

The final theory presented in this paper will allow extensions to be equated, and terms to be part of other terms, without equating definite descriptors or allowing unmotivated distributive inferences. By using property modifiers, some aspects of a highly intensional homogeneous ontology can be obtained in a more extensional one.

1.3. *Atomicity*

For mass terms, an additional issue is whether the part–whole structure in the domain should be *atomic*. If we are only dealing with count terms, then there seem to be good arguments for an atomic domain, in particular, we can refer to minimal parts with singular count nouns.

With mass terms, the answer it is not so clear. Although modern physics tells us that everyday substances are atomic, this need not be reflected in the ontology required for natural language semantics. Indeed, as non–linguistic research was required to demonstrate the atomicity of physical substance, it would be strange then to argue that atomicity can be derived solely from the semantics of natural language. Further, there are abstract things that we refer to by way of non–count terms which might not be atomic, such as space and time.

It seems that natural language semantics is consistent regardless of whether the denotations of mass terms are taken to be atomic or not. This suggests that a formal theory of mass terms should be incomplete in this respect: we should neither be able to prove that mass terms are atomic nor that they are atomless.

The theory presented in this paper strives to show that we can obtain a consistent theory of mass terms, and plurals, which works whether or not the domain is taken to be homogeneous or atomic. There may be issues that force us to decide between these ontologies, but we seem to be able to go quite a long way without making such choices.

1.4. *Axiomatic Semantics*

It might be argued that some position has to be adopted on the point of atomicity, for example, because the rigours of model–theoretic semantics demand it. If we view the formal semantics programme as consisting of natural language data and its model, then this might be correct.

When examining new phenomena in natural language, the model–theoretic approach is to look for some mathematical structure, or system, which appears to display the appropriate behaviour. This structure is then used as a model for the formal semantics of natural language. The representation language is made to adopt the behaviour of this model by asserting that all the entailments of the model are legitimate inferences in the representation (completeness), and all inferences in the representation are supported by the model (soundness).

By insisting that the entailments of the representation are precisely those of the model, there is a danger that artifacts of the model may lead to too strong a logic. For example, if the model employs a type hierarchy to avoid self application paradoxes, as in Montague semantics, then the constraints of the strongly typed regime are inherited by the semantic representation, even if not justified by (or even counter to) considerations of natural language itself. Demanding completeness requires all issues to be decided one way or another, even when our intuitions provide no useful insight.

On this view, any intermediate representation language is considered merely as a formal aid in expressing generalisations (Lønning, 1987). We can demonstrate that this intermediate language is redundant by showing there is a compositional mapping between it and the model, and that the language is sound and complete with respect to the model. Typically, a model for the semantics of mass terms will either be atomic or not. Completeness for the intermediate language will then mean that the representation must favour a particular ontology.

This suggests that, in model–theoretic semantics, we are forced to decide upon the ontology; we cannot leave such questions open in the semantic representation without making it incomplete with respect to a given model.

However, formally we need not demand that the intermediate representation language is complete with respect to any given model. The behaviour of the intermediate language—the inferences which it licenses—can be governed by axioms expressed in that language, rather than by adopting the inferences permitted in the model via completeness. We can give axioms that are too weak to make inferences about the ontology, such as whether it is atomic or homogeneous.

With this axiomatic methodology, we first establish the empirically accepted behaviour of natural language—in this case, natural language plurals and mass terms—and then axiomatise this in a suitable framework. Together with a suitable inference rule in the logic, such as *modus ponens*, these axioms allow proofs to be performed directly in the representation language. A model that satisfies these axioms can be found later. With this approach, the purpose of a model is merely to show that the theory is consistent.

Such axiomatic theories have already been proposed for the semantics of natural language. An example is the basic theory used in this paper: Turner's axiomatisation of Aczel's Frege Structures (PT). In PT, the notion of *proposition* is defined axiomatically (rather than syntactically). The axioms are too weak to prove that the logical paradoxes, such as the Liar, are represented by propositions. Only propositions may have their truth conditions considered. In this way, the theory allows self predication without being inconsistent. The theory is highly intensional: propositions are distinct from truth values (or sets of possible worlds); and properties are distinct from sets (or functions from individuals to sets of possible worlds).

The theory can be strengthened with axioms that satisfy our intuitions, as required. Only those aspects of behaviour of which we are certain need be axiomatised. Any term whose status is in doubt can be left unanalysed.

It is because of the fine–grained intensionality of PT that Landman suggests it might be a useful vehicle for formalising intensional individuals. PT seems a most suitable framework in which to express the semantic theory, as we require both some means of representing terms under guises, and also an axiomatic theory in order to avoid some of the commitments that might be required with model–theoretic semantics.

1.5. Definites

The motivation for the treatment of definite noun phrases given in this paper is related to issues of subject position intensionality. Theories of plurals and of mass terms often adopt something like a Boolean algebra to model part–whole relations. By definition, such algebras have a bottom element. As usually defined, this is the 'natural' denotation of 'non–denoting' definites. However, this has the undesirable consequence that all non–denoting terms are equated (Parsons, 1970; Parsons, 1975). For example, on such an account "the present king of France" and "the largest prime number" would be the same even though their use indicates different existential presuppositions. Also, the theory must address the question of the nature of sentences containing such definites. In Russellian theories, predication of this bottom element is taken to result in a false proposition. Alternatively, a logic with either truth–value gaps or some 'unknown' truth value is used, in which case predication of the bottom element has either an indeterminate truth value, or some third unknown value (Blau, 1981).

A *free logic* treatment would allow us to say that such descriptors denote elsewhere (van Fraassen, 1966; Link, 1991a). The result of predication of such terms is undefined. Predication of non–denoting terms can be viewed as a variety of category mistake.

The property theory I shall use has been axiomatised to address much more awkward examples of category mistakes, namely the logical paradoxes that result from unconstrained self predication. As mentioned above, PT avoids the paradoxes by having axioms too weak to prove propositionhood of such sentences. Only those things which are propositions may have truth values (PT rejects bivalence). A similar position is open to us with non–denoting terms. We may have a class of denotable objects over which natural language quantifiers range. If a definite descriptor is represented as a supremum of denotables, then we can require (in the axioms) that the supremum is itself denotable only if the extension of the corresponding property is not empty. This achieves the effect of 'denoting elsewhere' in free logic. The undefinedness of predication of such terms can be obtained by requiring that all natural language derived properties are properties of denotables, and can only provably form propositions with terms that are provably denotable. We cannot prove that properties of denotables form propositions with non–denoting terms, and so we cannot consider their truth conditions. For example, the sentence "the present king of France is bald" will not provably be a proposition, and so it has no truth conditions.

We can also avoid equating non–denoting definite descriptors. Essentially, we can adopt the axioms of a Boolean algebra, but guard those axioms so that they only apply to 'denoting' terms. The axioms will then be too weak to prove that non–denoting terms are equal.[10] The representation of quantified noun phrases will contain quantifiers that are restricted to range over denotable terms.

Adopting the various views advocated models the effect of a free logic, without raising the question of what it means not to denote within a theory. Natural language predication of non–denoting definite descriptors is consigned to the same dustbin as other unhelpful constructions, such as the Liar sentence. It just becomes another case of a sortal category mistake.

In summary, axiomatic property theory avoids the paradoxes by having axioms that are too weak to prove that they are propositions. It is possible to adopt the same weak approach to both: (i) the nature of the denotation of so–called non–denoting definite descriptors; and (ii) the nature of the result of applying a property of denotables to such definite descriptors.

This is currently a static theory: non–denoting definite descriptors within a sentence will prevent a proof of propositionhood, no matter how deeply embedded.[11]

1.6. Other Issues

The theory developed here is not concerned with representing the various possible *intermediate* distributive readings, where properties are only distributed as far as certain sub-collections. In an intermediate distributive reading of the sentence:

The boys and the girls met.

the verb "met" might be taken to distribute to the subcollections consisting of "the boys" and "the girls". Similarly with reciprocals:

The boys and the girls hate each other.

we might wish to make explicit the relevant groups that hate each other. I only elaborate upon the fully distributive, and the fully collective readings. The collective readings are assumed to subsume any intermediate distributive readings.

One way in which these intermediate distributive readings have been tackled is by using *structured groups*, where the appropriate groups of a term are distinguished in some way, such as by non–associative brackets, or distinct kinds of summation, for example (Hoeksema, 1983; Hoeksema, 1987; Higginbotham, 1981; Link, 1984; Roberts, 1987; Landman, 1989). However, I find Schwarzschild's arguments against structured–group representations to be convincing (Schwarzschild, 1990; Schwarzschild, 1992). He argues, as does Gillon, that structuring the representation of the noun phrase using brackets, or non–associative conjunction does not give the correct interpretation in general, as some sentences require us to consider *minimal covers* rather than *partitions* of the extension of the noun phrase (Gillon, 1992). Also, he shows that the correct structuring can depend upon properties used in the preceding discourse, and that obtaining this structure should not be thought of as the resolution of an ambiguity in the representations of noun phrases. This echoes some elements of the formal theory presented here, although the connection will not be explored.

In the theory presented, the operator that models conjunction is associative, and the operator that models the definite determiner also does not add structure to the representation of nominal terms. For simplicity, I do not adopt Schwarzschild's proposed context sensitive distribution operator that produces appropriate intermediate interpretations, nor do I offer a reductive interpretation of reciprocals.

The arguments for committee–like objects to be intensional, and distinct from their members is strong. To account for the different interpretation of sentences with these terms, it would be fairly straightforward to add ideas from Barker's theory (Barker, 1992).

The theory that I shall use for representing the semantics of natural language is essentially first–order. This means that considerations of how the scoping of accepted readings of sentences affects the logical power of English (Lønning, 1989) cannot be considered within this theory. The problem of undecidable semantics arises when the semantic theory allows arbitrary fusions of (potentially infinite) collections which cannot be denoted by natural language nominals. In the theory to be adopted, only those collections that are in the extension of a denotable property may be considered. Thus, the issue of undecidability does not arise. This has consequences for the representation of mathematical statements: the statements of arithmetic cannot be expressed in this theory.

1.7. Outline of Paper

After presenting the property–theoretic framework (Section 2.), I initially axiomatise a part–whole structure (Section 3.) which does not make any assumptions about atomicity (minimal parts). It also characterises a notion of 'natural language denotable' that does not force non–denoting terms to be equated, nor force propositions involving non–denoting definites to be true or false, even though PT has a two–valued base logic. A model for this theory is given in the appendix.

This is the bare essentials for a part–whole structure in PT. It could be turned into a treatment of plurals by adding atomicity, or a treatment of mass terms by adopting an homogeneous ontology. I shall use this as a basis for the extensions of nominal expressions in the final theory (Section 4.), which adds notions of singular and plural, and allows a unified treatment of mass terms and plurals.[12] The final theory also adds axioms for generalised conjunction.

A treatment of some of the puzzles in the literature is given, namely:

(i) simple distributive inferences with plurals;
(ii) the argument "all water is wet, the puddle is water, therefore the puddle is wet" (Bunt, 1985);
(iii) the sentence "all water is water" (Bunt, 1985);
(iv) the disjunction "all phosphorus is red or white" (Roeper, 1983);
(v) the comparative "the cleaner and the judge earn different incomes" (Landman, 1989) which, according to Landman, cannot be treated by a theory that uses property modifiers in place of individuals under guises.

This theory does not cover distributive inferences into conjoined noun phrases in order to avoid some combinatorial complexity in the presentation.

2. PROPOSITIONS, PROPERTIES, AND TRUTH

In this section, I present a theory of propositions, properties and truth (PT) due to Turner and Aczel (Turner, 1990; Turner, 1992; Aczel, 1980). Before giving the general framework and the formal details of PT, I shall try and motivate why such a theory is useful for the semantics of natural language.

Many workers in this field use an extensional logic as a basis for their representations ((Link, 1991a; Lønning, 1989) for example). In general, such extensional representations are inadequate for the semantics of natural language (Chierchia, 1982; Chierchia, 1984; Chierchia and Turner, 1988). Intensionality is apparent in the case of opaque predication. The notion of possible worlds is often introduced into the representation language in order to account for this phenomenon. In such approaches, a proposition is a set of possible worlds, and a property is a function from individuals to propositions. Possible worlds can be used to analyse modal notions such as possibility and necessity. Given an accessibility relation, *possibly p* is the set of worlds that have an accessible world in p. The possible worlds analysis has been extended to model knowledge and belief (Hintikka, 1962; Kripke, 1963). This set–theoretic account fails on certain instances of propositional attitudes: an agent may know a certain proposition p, and there may be some proposition q, denoting the same set of possible worlds, yet we might not want to conclude that the agent knows q. The possible worlds account of knowledge and belief forces us to this unwanted conclusion. Such propositions are typified by those involving mathematical truths.

A further problem with possible worlds models is that they are typically strongly typed. Properties and relations can only hold of objects of a specific type. To generalise semantic notions across different types, type lifting, or type shifting has to be employed (Partee and Rooth, 1983). The strong typing bars self predication and so avoids the paradoxes involving self–reference, such as the Liar: "this sentence is false". However, the strong typing also disallows unproblematic cases of self predication, such as "this sentence is six words long", and prevents the expression of universal properties.

These problems can be overcome if we treat propositions and properties as primitives. A property like "red" is not the set of red things, it is just itself, the property of being red. Similarly, the proposition, "$2 + 2 = 4$" is not merely a truth value, or a set of possible worlds, but it is a basic object, different from "$e^{i\pi} + 1 = 0$", even though, from the laws of mathematics, these propositions must always be true together.

PT exemplifies such a language: it has a highly intensional notion of properties and propositions which avoids the paradoxes without banning self predication through strong typing.

2.1. General Framework

Conceptually, PT can be split into two components, or levels. The first is a language of terms which consists of the untyped λ-calculus embellished with logical constants. A restricted class of these terms will correspond to *propositions*. When combined appropriately using the logical constants, other propositions result. As an example, given the propositions t, s, the conjunction of these, $t \wedge s$, is also a proposition, where $\wedge$ is a logical constant.

Some of the propositions will, further, be *true* propositions. When combining propositions with the logical constants, the truth of the resultant proposition will depend upon the truth of the constituent propositions. Considering the previous example, if t, s are both propositions that are true, then $t \wedge s$ will also be a true proposition.

There may be terms that form propositions when applied to another term. These terms are the properties. The act of predication is modelled by λ-application.

The essential point to note is that this is a highly intensional theory as the notion of equality is that of the λ-calculus: propositions are not to be equated just because they are always true together; similarly, properties are not to be equated just because they hold of the same terms (i.e., form true propositions with the same terms).

There are problems with the theory so far: the logical constants have no proof theory; and the notions of being a proposition, or a true proposition, cannot be expressed within this language of terms. That is, although we can consider terms as propositions, or true propositions, and comprehend how the propositionhood and truth of a term depends upon the propositionhood and truth of its constituent terms, we cannot express these notions formally *within* the language of terms: some *metalanguage* is required. This is the purpose of the second component of PT: the language of *well formed formulae* (wff). This is a first-order language where the terms (the objects which can be quantified over) are those of the λ-calculus extended with logical constants, as discussed above. The language of wff has two predicates, P for "is a proposition", and T for "is a true proposition". Clearly, this gives the formal means for axiomatising the behaviour of propositions and true propositions. For example, the informal discussion concerning the behaviour of the logical constant $\wedge$ can be formalised as follows:

"given the propositions t, s, the conjunction of these, $t \wedge s$, is also a proposition":

$$P(t) \& P(s) \to P(t \wedge s)$$

"if t, s are propositions that are true, then $t \wedge s$ will also be a true proposition":

$$P(t) \& P(s) \to (T(t \wedge s) \leftrightarrow (T(t) \& T(s)))$$

Axioms for T must always be restricted so that only terms that are propositions are considered.

The distinction between wff and terms can be taken to be akin to that between extension and intension in Montague semantics (Montague, 1974; Dowty et al., 1981). In that theory, however, intensions are derived from extensions.[13] As a consequence, the equality of intensions is that of the extensions, so propositions will be equated if they are always true together, and properties will be equated if they hold of the same objects. This is in contrast to PT, where the intensions are basic. Propositions in the language of terms may have the same truth conditions when T is applied, but this does not force them to be the same proposition, so we might have:

$$T(s) \leftrightarrow T(t)$$

but that does not mean that the terms are equal:

$$s = t$$

Similarly, in the language of wff, properties may hold of the same terms, yet they may be distinct. The λ-equality of terms is thus weaker than the notion of logical equivalence obtained when considering truth conditions in the meta–language.

A useful parallel can be drawn between PT and Frege's notions of *sense* and *reference*. We can take a proposition in the language of terms as corresponding to the *sense* of a statement. The *referents* of statements can be thought of as truth values, or truth conditions, which are obtained in the language of wff by applying T to the proposition.

It is possible to give a proof theory for the language of terms without recourse to a formal meta–theory like the language of wff (Hindley and Seldin, 1986). This might not be so useful for the semantics of natural language, as the resultant theory would not explicitly capture the extensional level.

2.2. Formal Theory

The following presents a formalisation of the languages of terms and wff, together with the axioms that provide the closure conditions for P and T.

Language of terms

Basic Vocabulary:

> Individual variables: $x, y, z, \ldots$
> Individual constants: $c, d, e, \ldots$
> Logical constants: $\vee, \wedge, \neg, \Rightarrow, \Xi, \Theta, \approx$

Inductive Definition of Terms:

(i) Every variable or constant is a term.
(ii) If t is a term and x is a variable then $\lambda x.t$ is a term.
(iii) If t and t' are terms then $t(t')$ is a term.

The theory is governed by the following axioms:

Axioms of the $\lambda\beta$–Calculus

$$\begin{aligned} \lambda x.t &= \lambda y.t[y/x] \text{ } y \text{ not free in } t \\ (\lambda x.t)t' &= t[t'/x] \end{aligned}$$

This defines the equivalence of terms.

All variables and constants, including the logical constants, are terms. Composition of terms allows us to build all those expressions of interest, and all those that are not. We need the meta–language, the language of wff, to classify those terms of interest and to give their logical behaviour.

The Language of Wff

Inductive Definition of Wff:

(i) If t and s are terms then $s = t, \mathrm{P}(t), \mathrm{T}(t)$ are atomic wff.
(ii) If φ and φ' are wff then $\varphi \,\&\, \varphi', \varphi \vee \varphi', \varphi \to \varphi', \sim\!\varphi$ are wff.
(iii) If φ is a wff and x a variable then $\exists x \varphi$ and $\forall x \varphi$ are wff.

The closure conditions for propositionhood are given by the following axioms:

Axioms of Propositions

(i) $\quad \mathrm{P}(t) \,\&\, \mathrm{P}(s) \to \mathrm{P}(t \wedge s)$
(ii) $\quad \mathrm{P}(t) \,\&\, \mathrm{P}(s) \to \mathrm{P}(t \vee s)$
(iii) $\quad \mathrm{P}(t) \,\&\, \mathrm{P}(s) \to \mathrm{P}(t \Rightarrow s)$
(iv) $\quad \mathrm{P}(t) \to \mathrm{P}(\neg t)$
(v) $\quad \forall x \mathrm{P}(t) \to \mathrm{P}(\Theta \lambda x.t)$
(vi) $\quad \forall x \mathrm{P}(t) \to \mathrm{P}(\Xi \lambda x.t)$
(vii) $\quad \mathrm{P}(s \approx t)$

Truth conditions can be given for those terms that are propositions:

Axioms of Truth

(i) $\quad \mathrm{P}(t) \,\&\, \mathrm{P}(s) \to (\mathrm{T}(t \wedge s) \leftrightarrow \mathrm{T}(t) \,\&\, \mathrm{T}(s))$
(ii) $\quad \mathrm{P}(t) \,\&\, \mathrm{P}(s) \to (\mathrm{T}(t \vee s) \leftrightarrow \mathrm{T}(t) \vee \mathrm{T}(s))$
(iii) $\quad \mathrm{P}(t) \,\&\, \mathrm{P}(s) \to (\mathrm{T}(t \Rightarrow s) \leftrightarrow \mathrm{T}(t) \to \mathrm{T}(s))$
(iv) $\quad \mathrm{P}(t) \to (\mathrm{T}(\neg t) \leftrightarrow \sim\!\mathrm{T}(t))$
(v) $\quad \forall x \mathrm{P}(t) \to (\mathrm{T}(\Theta \lambda x.t) \leftrightarrow \forall x \mathrm{T}(t))$
(vi) $\quad \forall x \mathrm{P}(t) \to (\mathrm{T}(\Xi \lambda x.t) \leftrightarrow \exists x \mathrm{T}(t))$
(vii) $\quad \mathrm{T}(t \approx s) \leftrightarrow t = s$
(viii) $\quad \mathrm{T}(t) \to \mathrm{P}(t)$

The last axiom states that only propositions may have truth conditions.

Note that the quantified propositions $\Theta \lambda x.t, \Xi \lambda x.t$ can be written as $\Theta x(t), \Xi x(t)$, where the λ-abstraction is implicit.

The notions of n-place relations can be defined recursively:

(i) $\quad Rel_0(t) \leftrightarrow \mathrm{P}(t)$
(ii) $\quad Rel_n(\lambda x.t) \leftrightarrow Rel_{n-1}(t)$

We can write $Rel_1(t)$ as $Pty(t)$.

As an illustration of how this theory addresses the paradoxes that can arise when self-reference is permitted, consider a predicate R whose extension is those predicates that do not apply to themselves. If such a predicate exists, then we can derive the paradoxical proposition:

$$RR \leftrightarrow \sim\!RR$$

In PT we can define a term corresponding to R as follows:

$$R =_{\text{def}} \lambda p. \neg pp$$

From the definition of Pty and the Axiom of Propositions (iv) we can trivially prove that if we have a property p, then Rp is a proposition, that is:

$$\text{Pty}(p) \to \text{P}(Rp)$$

Thus, the Axioms of Truth can be applied to Rp if p is a property. The paradoxical proposition originally arose when considering RR. For it to occur in PT, the Axioms of Truth must apply to this term. For these axioms to apply, we must show RR is a proposition. This in turn requires that R is a property. This cannot be proven, as R does not form a proposition with arbitrary terms, only with properties. Thus the paradoxical proposition does not arise. This exemplifies how PT allows unproblematic instances of self predication, whilst avoiding the category mistake that gives rise to paradoxical propositions.

After giving some examples of how we might use PT for natural language semantics, I shall embody a part–whole structure within the language of terms, following the essence of Link's theory (Link, 1991a).

2.3. Natural Language Examples

As an example of how PT can be used in the semantics of natural language, the sentence:

> Every boy laughed.

could be represented by the term:

$$\Theta x(\text{boy}'x \Rightarrow \text{laughed}'x)$$

This object is independent of any truth conditions. To find the truth conditions of the sentence, we must first show that the term representing it is a proposition, that is:

$$\text{P}(\Theta x(\text{boy}'x \Rightarrow \text{laughed}'x))$$

This is an expression in the language of wff. According to the axioms for P, this will hold if:

$$\forall x(\text{P}(\text{boy}'x) \,\&\, \text{P}(\text{laughed}'x))$$

If the sentence is a proposition, then its truth conditions are given by:

$$T(\Theta x(\text{boy}'x \Rightarrow \text{laughed}'x))$$

According to the axioms, this holds if and only if:

$$\forall x(T(\text{boy}'x) \to T(\text{laughed}'x))$$

Not all sentences will express propositions. As an example, the axioms should not allow the representation of:

This sentence is false.

to be a proposition, otherwise the theory would fall foul of the paradoxes.

Not all logical constants in the representations of sentences will be interpreted as logical connectives in the truth conditions. The sentence:

Mary believes that every boy laughed.

might be represented with the term:

$$\text{believe}'(\Theta x(\text{boy}'x \Rightarrow \text{laughed}'x))(\text{mary}')$$

If this is a proposition, then in its truth conditions T will not apply to "every boy laughed":

$$T(\text{believe}'(\Theta x(\text{boy}'x \Rightarrow \text{laughed}'x))(\text{mary}'))$$

This corresponds to the idea that the object of a believe is an intensional proposition, not a truth value, or set of possible worlds.

3. MEREOLOGY IN PT

This section is concerned with axiomatising a mereological (part–whole) structure over the natural language denotable terms. It is intended to give a general treatment of part–whole relations which seems to be required for treatments of both mass terms and plurals. It is not necessarily a physical mereology, counter to the nominalistic bent of earlier presentations of mereology (Leonard and Goodman, 1940). A model for this theory is given in the appendix.

To represent sentences involving mass terms and plurals in PT, we can add terms and axioms for a summation, a supremum operator, and a part-of relation. The axioms will resemble those of a Boolean algebra over a subclass of terms. In this formalisation, the axioms will be too weak to prove that the suprema of empty properties are equated. This will allow non-denoting definite descriptors to be distinguished.

Although there is no restriction on term formation in PT, it does seem appropriate to have such a structure only amongst those terms which can be referred to by natural language definite descriptors. This can be achieved by restricting the scope of the relevant axioms. To have a Boolean structure on all terms is an unmotivated and unnecessary strengthening of the theory.[14]

Lønning, in his consideration of the logical complexity of a representation with plural terms, notes that there may be some objects which cannot be denoted by natural language nominals, yet which cannot be excluded by consideration of the representation language in isolation. A formal theory of nominals (plurals or mass terms) can be said to be *complete* (in the lattice-theoretic sense) if any arbitrary collection of terms has a supremum (as opposed to just any finitely *denotable* collection having a supremum). This gives rise to a second-order logic which cannot be given a general model (Orey, 1959; Lønning, 1989). However, it is not clear whether natural language allows or requires quantification over arbitrary sums that cannot be referred to directly by natural language.

Link only allows those sets that are the extensions of natural language derived properties to have suprema. This is called *definable completeness* (Lønning, 1989; Link, 1991a). Lønning examines other options. In the theory presented in this section, set-like objects are represented by properties. Quantification over 'sets' is then taken to be quantification over the properties in the representation language. These properties are by their nature definable. Therefore, you cannot quantify over arbitrary sets within PT. This automatically leads to definable completeness of the language of representation with respect to its model. Further, to make sense of the semantics of nominals in this theory, the quantifiers contained in the representation of natural language sentences are constrained to range over only those terms which represent natural language nominals.

In summary, the following theory axiomatises a mereology as a Boolean algebraic-like structure, which will not be provably atomic, and will not provably contain a bottom element. The theory is intended to capture the structure that appears to underlie the referents of natural language nominal expressions.

Language of mereological terms

To the basic vocabulary of terms is added:

Predicative constant: δ
Operative constants: $\oplus, \otimes, \sigma$

It is intended that δ will hold of natural language denotable terms. The term σ is the supremum operator, and the term $\oplus$ is the summation operator. Within the domain of denotables, $\otimes$ will be its dual.

The language of wff remains unchanged from basic PT. The theory is governed by the axioms of the $\lambda\beta$–calculus as before, together with the previous axioms for propositions P and truth T.

Further Axioms For a Mereology in PT

The term $\oplus$ acts as a summation operator. The order in which the terms are combined is irrelevant, so the operator is both symmetric and associative:

Axiom 3.1. *Symmetry.*
$$a \oplus b = b \oplus a$$

Axiom 3.2. *Associativity.*
$$a \oplus (b \oplus c) = (a \oplus b) \oplus c$$

Combining a term with itself will result in nothing new:

Axiom 3.3. *Idempotence.*
$$a \oplus a = a$$

An ordering can be defined in terms of $\oplus$. This simplifies the expression of some of the axioms:

Definition 3.1. *Definable ordering.*
$$t \leq s =_{\text{def}} t \oplus s = s$$

An internal form of the ordering can also be defined:

Definition 3.2. *Internal ordering.*
$$t \ll s =_{\text{def}} t \oplus s \approx s$$

The first ordering is an expression in the language of wff, as such it is a proposition. The second, internal ordering is an expression in the language of terms. As such, it can be used directly in the semantic representation of sentences.

The terms that are of interest are those which correspond to the extensions of referring descriptions. The predicative constant δ is a property which holds of any such natural language denotable term:

Axiom 3.4. *Internal notion of denotable.*

$$P(\delta t)$$

As syntactic sugar, the predicate Δ can be defined in the language of wff which holds of natural language denotables:

Definition 3.3. *A term is denotable, as an external wff, iff it is true that it is denotable as an internal proposition.*

$$\Delta t =_{\text{def}} T(\delta t)$$

The sum of two denotables will itself be denotable:

Axiom 3.5. *The sum of denotables is a denotable.*

$$\Delta a \,\&\, \Delta b \to \Delta(a \oplus b)$$

We want to be able to form the suprema of classes of denotables. The term σ is intended to do this. It is not restricted to forming suprema of denotables, although we are only interested in its behaviour with denotables. The following axiom is indifferent to whether there is a bottom element, and to whether such an element is a denotable. It is also indifferent as to what a 'non–denoting' definite descriptor denotes: the axiom is deliberately too weak to justify saying that a 'non–denoting' definite descriptor is a denotable. If a property has a mixed extension, this axiom remains silent as to whether the supremum of such a property is a denotable. In effect, σ is a generalisation of $\oplus$.

Axiom 3.6. *If some property has an extension, and it is contained in the domain of denotables, then its supremum is also in the domain of denotables.*

$$\forall p((\text{Pty}(p) \,\&\, \forall x(T(px) \to \Delta(x)) \,\&\, \exists x(Tpx)) \to \Delta(\sigma x p x))$$

This corresponds to a notion of completeness in the domain of denotables. As PT naturally has a Fregean interpretation of a set as a collection of objects that form the extension of some property, then this completeness is only of the *definable* sets: this axiom thus expresses the notion of definable completeness with bounded quantification.

My approach to the so–called 'non–denoting' definite descriptors is to deliberately adopt weak axioms that do not indicate their behaviour. In particular, the result of attributing a natural language property to a 'non–existent' term should not be a statement that is true, or false, it should be a term that cannot be proven to have either truth value. As propositions have truth values, this suggests that the result of such an attribution should not be a proposition. This effect can be achieved by having the denotation of 'properties' that arise in the representation of natural language restricted to a class of terms that only form propositions when attributed to terms that are provably denotable. I shall adopt a weaker view which defines a class of terms that cannot be *proven* to produce propositions when attributed to 'non–denoting' terms (or rather, terms that are not provably in the class of denotables):

Definition 3.4. *A property of denotables produces a proposition, given some denotable.*

$$\text{Pty}_\Delta(p) =_{\text{def}} \forall x(\Delta(x) \rightarrow \text{P}(px))$$

We can define forms of the quantifiers that are restricted to denotable terms:

Definition 3.5.

$$\forall_\Delta x\varphi =_{\text{def}} \forall x(\Delta x \rightarrow \varphi)$$

Definition 3.6.

$$\exists_\Delta x\varphi =_{\text{def}} \exists x(\Delta x \,\&\, \varphi)$$

Restricting ourselves to these quantifiers, we achieve the effect of a free logic, where free variables range over all terms, and quantified variables range over denoting terms. As before, these quantifiers can be given internal analogues, and a supremum operator which is restricted to denotables can also be defined:

Definition 3.7.

$$\Theta_\delta x(t) =_{\text{def}} \Theta x(\delta x \Rightarrow t)$$

Definition 3.8.

$$\Xi_\delta x(t) =_{\text{def}} \Xi x(\delta x \wedge t)$$

Definition 3.9.

$$\sigma_\delta x(px) =_{\text{def}} \sigma x(\delta x \wedge px)$$

If two denotables are not equal, then there is a denotable that is part of one, but not part of the other. The antecedent should be strengthened, as two denotables may be unequal, yet one be wholly contained in the other:

Axiom 3.7. *Different denotables have different parts.*

$$\forall_\Delta xy(x \not\leq y \to \exists_\Delta u(u \leq x \,\&\, u \not\leq y))$$

The term $\sigma_\delta xpx$ is intended to form the fusion of all denotables having the property p. Any denotable with the property p should be part of this term:

Axiom 3.8. *All denotables having a particular property must be a part of the supremum of denotables having that property.*

$$\forall p \forall_\Delta y((\text{Pty}_\Delta(p) \,\&\, \text{T}(py)) \to y \leq \sigma_\delta xpx)$$

I shall illustrate the need for the following axiom by way of example. If we consider the denotable substance "cold mud", any bit of cold mud will be part of the fusion of mud. If we take the fusion of bits of cold mud, it will also be part of the fusion of mud:

Axiom 3.9. *If all denotables having property p are part of some other denotable y, then the supremum of denotables having p must also be a part of y.*

$$\forall p \forall_\Delta y((\text{Pty}_\Delta(p) \,\&\, \forall_\Delta x(\text{T}(px) \to x \leq y)) \to \sigma_\delta xpx \leq y)$$

The intuition behind the next axiom is that different collections have different suprema. There is a complication, as there is no reference to atoms in this theory: (i) we cannot consider a unique way of dividing a denotable into its minimal parts; (ii) different collections of denotables may have the same supremum if they *cover* the same denotables; further, (iii) we cannot guarantee to pick denotables that are part of a denotable with the required property. However, in this final case, the denotable will have a part which has the required property:

Axiom 3.10. *Different portions of denotables have different suprema: something that is part of the supremum of a property must be part of something with that property, or have a part with that property.*

$$\forall p \forall_\Delta u((\text{Pty}_\Delta(p) \,\&\, u \leq \sigma_\delta xpx) \to (\exists_\Delta z(pz \,\&\, u \leq z) \vee \exists_\Delta z(pz \,\&\, z \leq u)))$$

Obviously, this is not much use if we have uncountable parts, but that would always cause problems.

It is possible to define an operator * which turns a property into a cumulative property (Lønning, 1989; Link, 1991a):

Definition 3.10.

$$* =_{\text{def}} \lambda p \lambda t(t \approx \sigma x(px \wedge x \ll t))$$

There is no obvious role for a distributive operator (Lønning, 1989; Link, 1991a) in this theory as it stands, as there are no atoms to distribute to. I will indicate how distributive behaviour can be regained in Section 4.

The denotable of which all other denotables are a part (top) can be given by:

Definition 3.11. *The top element $\top$ of the denotables is the supremum of all denotable terms.*

$$\top =_{\text{def}} \sigma_\delta x(x \approx x)$$

Complement can also be defined:

Definition 3.12. *The complement $\overline{s}$ of the supremum s of denotables having property p is the supremum of denotables not having property p.*

$$\overline{\sigma_\delta x \varphi} =_{\text{def}} \sigma_\delta x(\neg \varphi)$$

A bottom element $\bot$ can be defined as $\overline{\top}$, but it can not be proven that $\Delta \bot$.

Amongst the denotables, $\otimes$ is the dual of $\oplus$. This will be used in the final theory to model disjunction:

Axiom 3.11. *Within the domain of denotables, $\otimes$ is the dual of $\oplus$.*

$$\Delta a \,\&\, \Delta b \to \overline{a \oplus b} = \overline{a} \otimes \overline{b}$$

I give the duality by way of an axiom, although it is possible to make both $\otimes$ and $\oplus$ definitional using the following equalities:

$$\begin{aligned} \sigma_\delta xpx \oplus \sigma_\delta xqx &= \sigma_\delta x(px \vee qx) \\ \sigma_\delta xpx \otimes \sigma_\delta xqx &= \sigma_\delta x(px \wedge qx) \end{aligned}$$

noting that any denotable a can be given as the supremum $\sigma_\delta x(x \approx a)$. These equalities are a consequence of the axioms given. If they are taken as definitional, then the axioms governing $\oplus$ (and $\otimes$) are satisfied.

To implement the formal semantics of natural language in a Montague style using PT, we can define types for the representations of syntactic categories. This follows an existing account (Turner, 1990; Turner, 1992), where types are predicates in the language of wff, except that the types here use properties of denotables in place of plain properties:

Definition 3.13.

$$Det_\Delta(f) =_{\text{def}} \forall x(\text{Pty}_\Delta(x) \rightarrow Quant_\Delta(fx))$$

Definition 3.14.

$$Quant_\Delta(f) =_{\text{def}} \forall x(\text{Pty}_\Delta(x) \rightarrow P(fx))$$

These correspond to the syntactic categories of determiner and quantifier.

The function space types can be defined with:

Definition 3.15.

$$(P \Longrightarrow Q)(f) =_{\text{def}} \forall x(P(x) \rightarrow Q(fx))$$

To have a conventional lattice–theoretic treatment of plurals would just require the addition that the denotable terms are founded on atoms. However, it is possible to treat count terms without recourse to atoms. For example, we could say that a singular property—corresponding to a singular count term—can hold of a term only if it does not hold of any proper part of that term. A plural property—corresponding to a plural count term—would then be the collective form of a singular property.

These axioms are no stronger than those for an atomic theory of plurals in PT (Fox, 1993). As this is the case, a model of PT extended with an atomic Boolean algebra can also be used to show consistency of this potentially atomless theory.

In the next section, I show how these roles can be used to obtain the correct distributive behaviour for mass terms without assuming homogeneous extensions, and for plurals without assuming atomicity.

4. THE FINAL THEORY

We now have most of the formal machinery in place to develop the semantic theory proper. Just to recap, this theory is intended to: (i) allow apparently coreferring items to corefer; (ii) control the distribution of properties into inhomogeneous terms; and, (iii) treat non–denoting descriptors as giving rise to a category mistake.

I will only examine sentences with intransitive verbs and unconjoined quantified noun phrases in detail. Coverage of transitive and ditransitive verbs would require some additional effort not least in empirically determining the acceptable readings. This theory produces only non-generic interpretations of natural language sentences.

First, the representations of natural language sentences used in this section are introduced. For clarity, these representations use determiners such as "all" and "every" that are not part of the formal theory so far.[15]

This is followed by rules that type these representations so that, if appropriate, they can be proven to be propositions, and hence carriers of truth values. Axioms are then presented which give the truth conditions of sentences.

The rest of the section is concerned with strengthening the theory in order to control distributive inferences using property modifiers, and to obtain other appropriate entailment patterns.

I shall not examine conjoined nouns and noun phrases in this semantic theory. This is not because it is impossible to do so, but because it avoids further combinatorial complexity, which would make central aspects of the theory harder to grasp.

I shall assume that we do not want to rule out the possibility that objects may be equated with a fusion of substance(s), or that 'different' objects, and substances—objects referred to by the suprema of different properties—may have the same extension, in particular, that compound substances like "muddy water" may have the same extension as their constituent substances, "mud and water".

4.1. Representations of Sentences

This paper assumes that sentences like:

> The man dies.

are represented by terms of the form:

$$the'(man')(dies')$$

where the' is a generalised quantifier that requires two properties.

Adjectives take the noun they modify as an argument, so:

> The tall man dies.

is represented by:

$$the'(tall'man')(dies')$$

Adjectives and nouns appearing after the copula are treated in the same manner as verbs:

> The bull is black.
> The puddle is water.

being represented by:

> the'(bull')(black')
> the'(puddle')(water')

respectively.

As mentioned, this theory does not treat conjoined (and disjoined) nouns and noun phrases directly. However, one of the later examples does involve a disjunction of adjectives. Conjunction (disjunction) can be represented by $\hat{\oplus}$ ($\hat{\otimes}$, respectively), regardless of the conjoined (disjoined, respectively) categories. These operators are new terms in the language. Clearly, $\hat{\oplus}, \hat{\otimes}$ can be axiomatised much as $\oplus, \otimes$. The difference being that $\hat{\oplus}, \hat{\otimes}$ are atomic, and only conjoin finite sets of terms.[16] It is intended that they represent generalised conjunction (disjunction) between arbitrary categories.

Assuming that there is no ellipsis, the sentences:

> The drunk and alcoholic died.
> The blue and red bike disappeared.
> All phosphorus is red or white.

can have readings represented by:

> the'(drunk' $\oplus$ alcoholic')(died')
> the'((blue' $\oplus$ red')bike'))(disappeared')
> all'(phosphorus')(red' $\otimes$ white')

For completeness, closure conditions for arbitrary conjoined and disjoined semantic categories are presented.

As we are interested in the truth conditions of the terms representing sentences, we should first be able to prove that they are terms which are capable of having truth values. That is, we should be able to prove that they are propositions. To do this, we need to type the semantics of the categories. The simplicity of the semantics proposed requires terms to belong to more than one type. This is possible in PT as it is only weakly typed.

4.2. Types

In principle, we could give arbitrary types to terms representing the objects from the various syntactic categories, as long as the representations of well formed sentences were propositions. However, for clarity, types will be used that closely mirror Montague style semantics, as in (Turner, 1990; Turner, 1992). Thus, although the proposal above is to represent nouns with terms that do not have any arguments, when the truth conditions are given, they will behave as predicate–like objects, as is usual in a Montague–style treatment:

Lemma 4.1. *The denotations of nouns are of the type* Pty_Δ.

Using the same motivation, the type corresponding to the category of the determiners will be akin to that used in more conventional representations (restricted to the denotables). This will result in noun phrase being represented by quantifiers (of denotables). However, the definite descriptor "the" must be given a more complex type, compatible with the proposed treatment of non–denoting terms:

Lemma 4.2. *Except for the definite descriptor, the interpretations of determiners are of the type* Det_Δ.

The type of the definite descriptor "the" should be restricted so that it conforms to the goal of not being able to prove propositionhood of a sentence when it contains a definite descriptor which "fails to denote". Thus the denotation of "the" should only form a quantifier with a property of denotables which has an extension in the denotable terms:

Lemma 4.3. *The interpretation of the definite descriptor is of the type:*

$$\forall p((\text{Pty}_\Delta(p) \,\&\, \exists_\Delta x(\text{T}(px))) \to Quant_\Delta(\text{the}'p))$$

If we put aside the use of property modifiers for the moment, verb phrases will be properties of denotables. This typing ignores Strawson's and Lasersohn's observations on felicitous use of non–denoting noun phrases (Strawson, 1964; Lasersohn, 1993). Besides copula phrases, the only verb phrases I shall consider are intransitive verbs. These will be represented by terms of the same type as verb phrases. This means that the syntactic rule which allows an intransitive verb to be considered as a verb phrase has no effect on the semantic type.

Lemma 4.4. *Intransitive verbs are of the type* Pty_Δ.

MASS TERMS AND PLURALS IN PROPERTY THEORY 147

Adjectives can modify nouns. In the semantics, an adjective should take a property (of denotables) and produce a new property (of denotables):

Lemma 4.5. *Adjectives are in the type* $\text{Pty}_\Delta \implies \text{Pty}_\Delta$.

In the proposed representation, adjectives can also behave like a verb phrase, when they appear after the copula, so they can also be of the same type as intransitive verbs:

Lemma 4.6. *Adjectives are of type* Pty_Δ.

The two types that adjectives belong to correspond with the the conventional typing for predicative and subsective uses of adjectives (Kamp, 1975). A more linguistically principled theory might give the copula the explicit function of modifying the type of adjectives and nouns to that of verb phrases.

This is sufficient to prove propositionhood of the representations of felicitous sentences without conjunction or disjunction. Other axioms are required to type the sums and products of terms. These will strengthen the closure conditions of types. The motivation is to mirror the syntactic closure conditions for conjoined and disjoined categories in a grammar. When we conjoin or disjoin two nouns, the result is a noun. As the representation of a noun, at some level, corresponds to a property of denotables, then if we form the sum or product of two properties of denotables, then the result will be a new property of denotables. This is expressed in the following two axioms:

Axiom 4.1. *The sum of two properties of denotables, is a property of denotables.*

$$(\text{Pty}_\Delta(r) \,\&\, \text{Pty}_\Delta(w)) \to \text{Pty}_\Delta(r \hat{\oplus} w)$$

Axiom 4.2. *The product of two properties of denotables, is a property of denotables.*

$$(\text{Pty}_\Delta(r) \,\&\, \text{Pty}_\Delta(w)) \to \text{Pty}_\Delta(r \hat{\otimes} w)$$

It will be useful to indicate how to derive the truth conditions of complex properties of denotables, applied to denotables. The extension of a conjunction (disjunction) of properties of denotables is the intersection (union, respectively) of the extensions of the conjoined (disjoined, respectively) properties:

Axiom 4.3. *The sum of properties of denotables, applied to a denotable, is true if the conjunction of those properties, applied to that denotable, is true.*

$$(\mathrm{Pty}_\Delta(r) \,\&\, \mathrm{Pty}_\Delta(w) \,\&\, \Delta(x)) \to (\mathrm{T}(r\hat{\oplus}w)x \leftrightarrow \mathrm{T}(rx) \,\&\, \mathrm{T}(wx))$$

Axiom 4.4. *The product of properties of denotables, applied to a denotable, is true if the disjunction of those properties, applied to that denotable, is true.*

$$(\mathrm{Pty}_\Delta(r) \,\&\, \mathrm{Pty}_\Delta(w) \,\&\, \Delta(x)) \to (\mathrm{T}(r\hat{\otimes}w)x \leftrightarrow \mathrm{T}(rx) \,\mathrm{v}\, \mathrm{T}(wx))$$

The closure conditions for the conjunction and disjunction of terms of the type $Quant_\Delta$ are given next:

Axiom 4.5. *The sum of two quantifiers of denotables is a quantifier of denotables.*

$$(Quant_\Delta(f) \,\&\, Quant_\Delta(g)) \to Quant_\Delta(f\hat{\oplus}g)$$

Axiom 4.6. *The product of two quantifiers of denotables is a quantifier of denotables.*

$$(Quant_\Delta(f) \,\&\, Quant_\Delta(g)) \to Quant_\Delta(f\hat{\otimes}g)$$

Finally, the closure conditions on propositions are:

Axiom 4.7. *The sum of two propositions is a proposition.*

$$(\mathrm{P}(p) \,\&\, \mathrm{P}(q)) \to \mathrm{P}(p\hat{\oplus}q)$$

Axiom 4.8. *The product of two propositions is a proposition.*

$$(\mathrm{P}(p) \,\&\, \mathrm{P}(q)) \to \mathrm{P}(p\hat{\otimes}q)$$

The sums and products of propositions will correspond to the conjunctions and disjunctions of sentences. Sentential conjunction and disjunction will have the standard interpretations. This can be enforced with:

Axiom 4.9. *The sum of two propositions is a true proposition if both propositions are true.*[17]

$$(\mathrm{P}(p) \,\&\, \mathrm{P}(q)) \to (\mathrm{T}(p) \,\&\, \mathrm{T}(q) \leftrightarrow \mathrm{T}(p\hat{\oplus}q))$$

Axiom 4.10. *The product of two propositions is a true proposition if one of the factor propositions is true.*

$$(\mathrm{P}(p) \,\&\, \mathrm{P}(q)) \to ((\mathrm{T}(p) \,\mathrm{v}\, \mathrm{T}(q)) \leftrightarrow \mathrm{T}(p\hat{\otimes}q))$$

4.3. Truth Conditions

Were we not using property modifiers, plurals and mass terms, then the truth conditions of the representations of simple sentences—for example, of the form "every $p\ q$" and "some $p\ q$"—could reflect the more conventional interpretations of the quantifiers (Turner, 1990; Turner, 1992). Thus we would have, for example:

$$P(\text{every}'(p)(q)) \to (T(\text{every}'(p)(q)) \leftrightarrow T(\Theta_\delta x(px \Rightarrow qx)))$$
$$P(\text{some}'(p)(q)) \to (T(\text{some}'(p)(q)) \leftrightarrow T(\Xi_\delta x(px \wedge qx)))$$

As we are using property modifiers, the truth conditions must be complicated somewhat. The conditions can be stated with the axioms that follow.

The determiner "every" gives rise to universal quantification over the denotable terms:

Axiom 4.11.

$$P(\text{every}'(p)(q)) \to (T(\text{every}'(p)(q)) \leftrightarrow T(\Theta_\delta x(px \Rightarrow qpx)))$$

Notice that the verb phrase and noun combine to form a modified property qp. The types of the terms will have to be fixed if the right hand side of the internal biconditional is to form a proposition independently of these axioms.

The determiner "some" in a sentence should give rise to quantification over collections in the truth conditions:

Axiom 4.12.

$$P(\text{some}'(p)(q)) \to (T(\text{some}'(p)(q)) \leftrightarrow T(\Xi_\delta x(px \wedge qpx)))$$

These truth conditions implicitly require the notion of atomicity (or singularity), that is, q only ranges over singular individuals, not mass terms or plurals. This could be guaranteed by a semantic restriction in the truth conditions. Indeed, I define a semantic notion of singularity later. Here, however, I shall assume that any grammar used to obtain the representations has syntactically restricted the use of "every" to semantically singular terms.

The determiner "all" is more problematic: in the truth conditions of a sentence it should not give rise to universal quantification over collections, as this always forces a distributive reading. It must thus be treated more akin to the definite descriptor. I shall allow sentences like "all $p\ q$" to be true even if the extension of the property p is empty:

Axiom 4.13.

$$P(\text{all}'(p)(q)) \to (T(\text{all}'(p)(q)) \leftrightarrow (\Delta(\sigma_\delta xpx) \to T(qp(\sigma_\delta xpx))))$$

The definite descriptor gives rise to predication of the supremum:

Axiom 4.14.

$$P(\text{the}'(p)(q)) \to (T(\text{the}'(p)(q)) \leftrightarrow T(qp(\sigma_\delta xpx)))$$

In order to make the right–hand sides of the biconditionals in these axioms provably propositions, independently, then the verbs must be able to act as property modifiers:

Lemma 4.7. *The denotations of verbs are in the type* $\text{Pty}_\Delta \Longrightarrow \text{Pty}_\Delta$

As nouns can also act as verb–like terms when appearing after the copula, they can also be in this type:

Lemma 4.8. *The denotations of nouns are in the type* $\text{Pty}_\Delta \Longrightarrow \text{Pty}_\Delta$

Adjectives are already of this type, so no additional lemma is required to type them for occurrences after the copula.

If verb phrases had been typed independently of intransitive verbs, and the type changing function of the copula was made explicit, then this last lemma would become redundant.

4.4. Property Modifiers

Considering terms of the form $\text{died}'\text{men}'x$, as mentioned before, I shall take died' here to be the semantic equivalent of a subsective adjective. Although I use the word "adjective", I am referring to a semantic category that need not be limited to the representation of natural language adjectives. This is not new. For example, Hoepelman has suggested that nouns may, in the semantics, be treated as a special case of adjective (Hoepelman, 1983).

It is fruitful to look at the kinds of behaviours defined in work on the semantics of adjectives, as it transpires that these behaviours are also useful in explaining how to obtain intuitively useful inferences in a semantic theory which uses property modifiers to represent Landman's notion of roles. Later in this section, property modifiers are given behaviours which might seem rather *ad hoc* in isolation. However, the suggested inferences have independent motivation from considerations of the semantics of natural language modifiers, and would already be required in a comprehensive semantics of natural language.

As PT is weakly typed, to some extent we can avoid deciding whether adjectives should be exclusively property modifiers, or properties.[18] There is no need for formal devices to change the type of a subsective adjective (and general property modifiers), such as operators or dummy predicates.

I shall assume that properties introduced in the representation of natural language are typically properties of denotables, and that property modifiers are properties of denotables that can also modify other properties to produce new properties.[19]

To motivate the formal definition of a property modifier: if we take "red" to be a property modifier, then it may produce a proposition when applied to some natural language denotable term. Given some other property, like "book", a new property is created, that of being a red book. The proposition will be true if that denotable is red. Unless extra conditions are added, a red book need not be red, but it is a book.

Definition 4.1. *A property modifier r is a property of denotables which, given a property of denotables p, forms a new property of denotables rp, and if that new property holds of some denotables, then the original property of denotables p also holds of it.*

$$\mathcal{PM}(r) =_{\text{def}} \text{Pty}_\Delta(r) \;\&\; \forall p(\text{Pty}_\Delta(p) \to (\text{Pty}_\Delta(rp) \;\&\; \forall_\Delta x(\text{T}(rpx) \to \text{T}(px))))$$

As modifiers (both semantic and syntactic) can be conjoined and disjoined, it is necessary to add typing rules to make $\mathcal{PM}$ closed under $\hat{\oplus}$ and $\hat{\otimes}$.

Axiom 4.15. *The sum of two property modifiers is a property modifier.*

$$(\mathcal{PM}(r) \;\&\; \mathcal{PM}(w)) \to \mathcal{PM}(r\hat{\oplus}w)$$

Axiom 4.16. *The product of two property modifiers is a property modifier.*

$$(\mathcal{PM}(r) \;\&\; \mathcal{PM}(w)) \to \mathcal{PM}(r\hat{\otimes}w)$$

I will not show how these conjoined and disjoined modifiers effect the truth conditions of propositions until Example 4.4., towards the end of this section.

Following the suggestion that some of the behaviours of adjectives are desirable for property modifiers, we can define Bunt's notions of distributive, collective, and homogeneous adjectives (Bunt, 1979)[20]:

Definition 4.2. *A term r is* cumulative *(a cumulative modifier) iff it is a property modifier, and when restricting a property (of denotables) p, if it holds of denotables x, y, it also holds of the sum $x \oplus y$.*

$$\mathcal{C}_{\mathcal{PM}}(r) =_{\text{def}}$$
$$\mathcal{PM}(r) \,\&\, \forall p \forall_\Delta xy((\text{Pty}_\Delta(p) \,\&\, \text{T}(rpx) \,\&\, \text{T}(rpy)) \to \text{T}rp(x \oplus y))$$

This can be generalised to arbitrary (definable) suprema:

Definition 4.2.'

$$\mathcal{C}_{\mathcal{PM}}(r) =_{\text{def}} \quad \mathcal{PM}(r) \,\&\, \forall pq((\text{Pty}_\Delta(p) \,\&\, \text{Pty}_\Delta(q) \,\&\,$$
$$\forall_\Delta x(\text{T}(qx) \to \text{T}(rpx))) \to \text{T}(rp(\sigma_\delta xqx)))$$

The following notion of distributive property modifiers is central to this theory's treatment of distributive inferences into denotable terms. Essentially, distribution must be restricted to the appropriate nice parts of a term. If r is distributive property modifier and p is a property, then if we predicate rp of a denotable x the appropriate nice parts of x to distribute to are those that have the property p. In general, we must not assume that r itself distributes to these parts, but allow rp to distribute (although for some pairs r, p, if rp holds, then we may infer r holds).

Definition 4.3. *A term r is* distributive *(a distributive modifier) iff it is a property modifier, and when restricting any property (of denotables) p, if it holds of denotables x, it also holds of any part y of the denotables x, which is also in the extension of p.*

$$\mathcal{D}_{\mathcal{PM}}(r) =_{\text{def}}$$
$$\mathcal{PM}(r) \,\&\, \forall p \forall_\Delta xy((\text{Pty}_\Delta(p) \,\&\, \text{T}(rpx) \,\&\, \text{T}(py) \,\&\, y \leq x) \to \text{T}rp(y))$$

If we say "the water is liquid", and take the truth conditions of this to be interpreted as:

$$\text{T}(\text{liquid}'\text{water}'(\sigma x \text{water}' x))$$

then, assuming that liquid' is distributive, any part of $\sigma x\text{water}'x$ that is water will be liquid water.

An homogeneous modifier is one that is both cumulative and distributive[21]:

Definition 4.4. *A term r is* homogeneous *(an homogeneous modifier) iff it is cumulative and distributive.*

$$\mathcal{H}_{\mathcal{PM}}(r) =_{\text{def}} \mathcal{C}_{\mathcal{PM}}(r) \,\&\, \mathcal{D}_{\mathcal{PM}}(r)$$

It seems to be the case that whenever the representation of a word is a cumulative property modifier, as defined above, it is typically a cumulative property of denotables, in the following sense:

Definition 4.5. *A* strongly cumulative term *is a cumulative property of denotables.*

$$\mathcal{C}_S(s) =_{\text{def}} \text{Pty}_\Delta(s) \,\&\, \forall_\Delta t(\text{T}(st) \leftrightarrow t = \sigma_\delta x(sx \wedge x \ll t))$$

Typically, those words that are considered to be homogeneous will be homogeneous modifiers, and cumulative properties:

Definition 4.6. *A* strongly homogeneous term *is an homogeneous modifier, and a strongly cumulative property.*

$$\mathcal{H}_S(S) =_{\text{def}} \mathcal{H}_{\mathcal{PM}}(s) \,\&\, \mathcal{C}_S(s)$$

4.5. Singulars and Plurals

In the domain of count nouns, plurals are typically strongly homogeneous. We may wish to relate the interpretation of a plural to that of its syntactic singular. A singular term is not homogeneous. This result can be achieved as follows:

Definition 4.7. *A* singular *is a property of denotables which, if it holds of a denotable, does not hold of any of its parts.*

$$Sing(s) =_{\text{def}} \text{Pty}_\Delta(s) \,\&\, \forall_\Delta x(\text{T}(px) \to \sim\exists y(y \leq x \,\&\, \text{T}(py) \,\&\, y \neq x))$$

If s is a singular property, we can represent its (improper) plural form with $^\pi s$.[22] The intention of the next axiom is to state that any supremum of terms that have the singular property s will have the plural property $^\pi s$:

Axiom 4.17. *If some denotables each have the singular property p, then the supremum of those denotables has the plural property $^\pi p$.*

$$\forall p(Sing(p) \to \forall q(\text{Pty}_\Delta(q) \,\&\, \forall_\Delta x(\text{T}(qx) \to \text{T}(px)) \to \text{T}(^\pi p(\sigma xqx))))$$

This is a generalisation of the intuition that the sum of two terms with the singular property s have the plural property $^\pi s$:

$$\forall p(Sing(p) \& \mathrm{T}(pa) \& \mathrm{T}(pb) \to \mathrm{T}(^\pi p(a \oplus b)))$$

There must also be a means of relating terms in the extension of a pluralised property with those in the extension of the singular property:

Axiom 4.18. *A term in the extension of a pluralised property must be founded on terms that are in the extension of the singular property.*

$$\forall p(Sing(p) \to \forall_\Delta u(\mathrm{T}(^\pi pu) \to \exists q(\mathrm{Pty}_\Delta q \& \forall x(\mathrm{T}(qx) \to \mathrm{T}(px)) \& u =$$

$$\sigma_\delta xqx)))$$

This is effectively the converse of the previous axiom. Taking these two axioms together, a plural property holds of a term if and only if that term is the fusion of terms having the singular property.

The equivalence:

$$\sigma xpx = \sigma x^\pi px$$

can be proved.

If a plural property holds of a term, but does not hold of any proper part of that term, then it must be the case that the underlying singular property also holds of the term:

Axiom 4.19. *If a denotable has the property $^\pi p$, (where p is a singular property) and no proper part of it does, then it also has the property p.*

$$\forall p \forall_\Delta x((Sing(p) \& \mathrm{T}(^\pi px) \& \sim\exists_\Delta y(y \leq x \& y \neq x \& \mathrm{T}(py))) \to \mathrm{T}(px))$$

In this formal theory, we also wish to be able to have plural forms of property modifiers:

Axiom 4.20. *Property modifiers have plural forms.*

$$\forall p((\mathcal{PM}(p) \& Sing(p)) \to \mathcal{PM}(^\pi p))$$

Typically, when a plural property modifier is modifying a singular property, and the resultant property holds of a term, then the singular property modified by the singular property modifier also holds of that term. This is formalised in the following axiom:

Axiom 4.21. *If x is in the extension of $^\pi pq$ and q is singular, then x is also in the extension of pq.*

$$\forall pq \forall_\Delta x((\mathcal{PM}(p) \& Sing(p) \& \mathrm{Pty}_\Delta(q) \& Sing(q) \& \mathrm{T}(^\pi pqx)) \to \mathrm{T}(pqx))$$

MASS TERMS AND PLURALS IN PROPERTY THEORY

This results in a useful inference, allowing the representation of "the men die" to entail the representation of "every man dies" (assuming there are some men). This will be elaborated in Example 4.1., below.

4.6. Examples and Further Axioms

Example 4.1. I shall demonstrate the use of these notions with the sentence "the men die". If there are some men (so that the sentence forms a proposition), from the application of T to its representation:

$$T(die'men'(\sigma_\delta x men' x))$$

we can derive the truth conditions for "every man dies":

$$\forall_\Delta x (T(man'x) \to T(dies'man'x))$$

I will take the two terms, men' and die' to be strongly homogeneous property modifiers. Further, I will take it that men' = $^\pi$man', and die' = $^\pi$dies'. From the assumption that die' is a property modifier, we can infer:

$$T(die'men'(\sigma_\delta x men'x)) \to$$
$$\forall_\Delta y (T(men'y) \& y \leq (\sigma_\delta x men'x) \to T(die'men'y))$$

Given the homogeneous behaviour of men, and its relation to its singular, we can show:

$$T(die'men'(\sigma_\delta x man'x)) \to$$
$$\forall_\Delta y (T(man'y) \& y \leq (\sigma_\delta x man'x) \to T(die'man'y))$$

From the axioms for σ, this gives:

$$T(die'men'(\sigma_\delta x man'x)) \to \forall_\Delta y (T(man'y) \to T(die'man'y))$$

From the fact that die' is the plural of dies', Axiom 4.21. allows us to infer that the internal consequent implies:

$$T(dies'man'y)$$

Thus:

$$T(die'men'(\sigma_\delta x men'x)) \to \forall_\Delta y (T(man'y) \to T(dies'man'y))$$

This example shows that even with a semantic theory intended to cover some awkward examples, our intuitions concerning simpler cases are supported, if rather indirectly. •

It is possible to define notions corresponding to transparent, or predicative adjectives, like those presented by Bunt and Roeper (Bunt, 1985; Roeper, 1983). The behaviour defined is required to cope with Bunt's "wet puddle" argument, which is formalised in the next example.

Definition 4.8. *A term r is transparent (a transparent modifier) with respect to a property (of denotables) p, iff it is a property modifier, and when restricting p, if it holds of denotables x, it also holds of x by itself. Further, if r and p hold of x, by themselves, then rp holds of x.*

$$\mathcal{T}_p(r) =_{\text{def}} \mathcal{PM}(r) \,\&\, \text{Pty}_\Delta(p) \,\&\, \forall_\Delta x(\text{T}rpx \leftrightarrow (\text{T}rx \,\&\, \text{T}px))$$

This is rather like Hoepelman's notion of *strongly predicative adjectives*, except that here transparency is indexed to *particular* properties of denotables, whereas strongly predicative adjectives are transparent with respect to *all* properties (of denotables). His notion of weakly predicative adjectives cannot be expressed in this theory as it stands, as there is no formal notion of polar opposites (tall v. short, for example).[23] We may wish to maintain that all property modifiers are transparent with respect to themselves, echoing one of Landman's axioms, which can be paraphrased as "John as a judge is a judge" (Landman, 1989):

$$\forall p(\mathcal{PM}(p) \to \mathcal{T}_p(p))$$

This does not cause the collapse of compound property modifiers, which might be useful in a theory of adjectives: Hoepelman, for example, would use tall'tall'man'x to indicate a man who is tall for a tall man. If, however, we take chessplayer' to be a transparent property modifier, it would cause the collapse of chessplayer'chessplayer'x to just chessplayer'x. Hoepelman would prefer to use this to indicate chessplayers who are relatively good at chess, in a body of other chessplayers (Hoepelman, 1983).

We are now in a position to consider some more examples. The next two show how the theory can address Bunt's *desiderata* for a theory of mass terms (Bunt, 1985).

Example 4.2. Considering the argument:

>All water is wet
>The puddle is water
>∴The puddle is wet

MASS TERMS AND PLURALS IN PROPERTY THEORY   157

Assuming that there is a puddle, the truth conditions of the three sentences are given by:

$$T(\Theta_\delta x(\text{water}'x \Rightarrow \text{wet}'\text{water}'x))$$
$$T(\text{water}'\text{puddle}'(\sigma_\delta x\text{puddle}'x))$$
$$T(\text{wet}'\text{puddle}'(\sigma_\delta x\text{puddle}'x))$$

After applying the axioms of truth, the argument becomes:

$$\forall_\Delta x(T(\text{water}'x) \to T(\text{wet}'\text{water}'x))$$
$$\underline{T(\text{water}'\text{puddle}'(\sigma_\delta x\text{puddle}'x))}$$
$$\therefore T(\text{wet}'\text{puddle}'(\sigma_\delta x\text{puddle}'x))$$

The terms wet' and water' can be taken to be transparent, with respect to each other and puddle'.[24] From the transparency of water' with puddle', and the second premise, we have:

$$T(\text{water}'(\sigma_\delta x\text{puddle}'x))$$

and thus, from the first premise, we obtain:

$$T(\text{wet}'\text{water}'(\sigma_\delta x\text{puddle}'x))$$

From this and the transparency of wet' with water', we have:

$$T(\text{wet}'(\sigma_\delta x\text{puddle}'x))$$

and from the transparency of wet' with puddle':

$$T(\text{wet}'\text{puddle}'(\sigma_\delta x\text{puddle}'x))$$

which is what was wanted.   •

Example 4.3. Taking the sentence "all water is water", the truth conditions of its representation are given by:

$$\Delta(\sigma x\text{water}'x) \to T(\text{water}'\text{water}'(\sigma x\text{water}'x))$$

Assuming that there is some water, the truth conditions of the sentence are dependent upon:

$$T(\text{water}'\text{water}'(\sigma x\text{water}'x))$$

From the transparency of water', with respect to itself[25], and our assumption that it can also be treated as a property modifier, we have:

$$\forall_\Delta x(T(\text{water}'x) \leftrightarrow T(\text{water}'\text{water}'x))$$

From the homogeneity of water′, and axioms for the supremum operator (assuming that there is some water), we can infer that:

$$T(\text{water}'(\sigma x \text{water}'x))$$

Taking these two results together, we can infer:

$$T(\text{water}'\text{water}'(\sigma x \text{water}'x))$$

on the assumption that there is some water, thus we obtain the desired result (cancelling the assumption):

$$\Delta(\sigma x \text{water}'x) \to T(\text{water}'\text{water}'(\sigma x \text{water}'x))$$

Thus "All water is water" is true.

So the results that Bunt considers to be essential for a theory of mass terms are obtained.

Next, it is shown that the theory can cope with Roeper's "phosphorus" example, provided that the theory is strengthened to indicate how the disjunction (product) of property modifiers affects the truth conditions. Following this, I strengthen the behaviour of conjoined (summed) property modifiers.

Example 4.4. In the theory as it stands, the truth conditions of the sentence "all phosphorus is red or white" (Roeper, 1983):

$$T(\Theta_\delta x(\text{phosphorus}'x \Rightarrow (\text{red}'\hat{\otimes}\text{white}')\text{phosphorus}'x))$$

cannot be unpacked as far as we might like. To give a full elaboration of the truth conditions requires an additional axiom for the product of subsective adjectives.

Axiom 4.22. *A property of denotables p modified by the product of two property modifiers r, w holds of a denotable x, iff either (1) the property of denotables, modified by either property modifier, holds of that denotable; or (2) that denotable can be divided in two u, v, such that the property of denotables holds of one part u, when modified by the first property modifier, r, and the other part v, when modified by the second, w.*

$$\forall rwp \forall_\Delta x(\mathcal{PM}(r) \,\&\, \mathcal{PM}(w) \,\&\, \text{Pty}_\Delta p \to$$
$$(T((r \otimes w)px) \leftrightarrow (\; T(rpx) \lor$$
$$T(wpx) \lor$$
$$\exists_\Delta uv(x = u \oplus v \,\&\, T(rpu) \,\&\, T(wpv))))$$

Thus, "all phosphorus is red or white" is true, on this narrow scope reading of the disjunction, if it is the case that any fusion of phosphorus is red; or it is white; or if it has two parts that are phosphorus, and one part is white, and the other is red. Note that this narrow scope reading subsumes the wide scope reading of the disjunction ("all phosphorus is red, or all phosphorus is white").

An apparent inadequacy of this axiom is that if there is some gold making up a ring and the gold is half white gold and half yellow gold, then, from axiom above we can infer:

The gold is white or yellow.

It should be noted that this conclusion does not subsume the wide scope reading:

The gold is white or the gold is yellow.

Even so, it might seem a slightly odd conclusion. We can argue that the narrow scope disjunction is fine, as it might be paraphrased:

The quantities of gold that make up the ring are white or yellow.

The reason we do not usually utter the disjunction is that, as a sentence (rather than a paraphrase of a conclusion), it is ambiguous since it subsumes the representation of the sentence:

The gold is white or the gold is yellow.

We can then appeal to pragmatic considerations that suggest we strive to be maximally informative, and hence are more likely to use the sentence:

The gold is white and yellow.

rather than:

The gold is white or yellow.

It can seem unsatisfactory when an appeal to pragmatics is made to gloss over some difficulties in an essentially formal theory. However, in this case some comfort can be drawn from the other uses of disjunction. In a Montague–style analysis, from:

Mary laughed and John talked.

we can infer:

> Mary laughed or John talked.

even though we would be unlikely to utter the disjunction in place of the conjunction should it be the case that we know Mary laughed and John talked.

I think that we can say little about the case of conjoined property modifiers. If something is black and white, it may be acceptable to say that there are parts of it that are black, and parts that are white. However, in dissecting the object, these attributions of colour may be invalid.[26]

If we take the sentence:

> John is an angry and hateful person.

it is not easy to contemplate the idea that there are necessarily parts of John which are angry, and other parts which are hateful. We could account for this sentence by assuming movement has occurred (in the syntax) from "John is an angry person and John is a hateful person". However, we may then posit movement in cases of exclusive properties, black and white, for example. These readings could be ruled–out by semantic considerations. In which case, we might also want the constraint that $(r\hat{\oplus}w)px$ can only be a proposition if rp, wp are exclusive properties.

With or without this constraint, I am fairly certain that we can have the following:

Axiom 4.23. *If a property of denotables p, modified by a property modifier r, holds of a denotable u, and modified by another property modifier w, holds of another denotable v, then the property of denotables, modified by the sum of the property modifiers $r\hat{\oplus}w$, holds of the (denotable) sum of denotables $u\hat{\oplus}v$.*[27]

$$\forall rwp \forall_\Delta uv((\mathcal{PM}(r) \,\&\, \mathcal{PM}(w) \,\&\, \text{Pty}_\Delta p \,\&\,) \to$$
$$((\text{T}(rpu) \,\&\, \text{T}(wpv)) \to \text{T}((r\hat{\oplus}w)p(u \oplus v))))$$

In the case when rp, wp are exclusive properties, we may also have the converse of this.

Axiom 4.24. *If two property modifiers w, r are exclusive, when modifying a property of denotables p, then if the sum $w \oplus r$ modifying p holds of a denotable x, then x is the sum of denotables u, v, where wp holds of u and rp holds of v.*[28]

$$\forall wrp(\mathcal{PM}w \,\&\, \mathcal{PM}r \,\&\, \text{Pty}_\Delta p \,\&\, \sim\exists_\Delta x(\text{T}(wpx) \,\&\, \text{T}(rpx)) \to$$
$$\forall_\Delta x(\text{T}((w\hat{\oplus}r)px) \to \exists_\Delta uv(x = u \oplus v \,\&\, \text{T}(wpu) \,\&\, \text{T}(rpu))))$$

MASS TERMS AND PLURALS IN PROPERTY THEORY 161

The next example shows how the theory allows contradictory properties to be attributed to objects, even when their extensions are equated. Although with the example chosen, we might prefer not to equate the extensions for philosophical reasons, it will serve as an illustration.

Example 4.5. The well–worn sentences:

> The gold ring is new.
> The gold is old.

become:
$$\text{the}'(\text{gold}'\text{ring}')(\text{new}')$$
$$\text{the}'(\text{gold}')(\text{old}')$$

Assuming there is some gold and a gold ring, the truth conditions of these terms are given by:

$$T(\text{new}'(\text{gold}'\text{ring}')(\sigma_\delta x(\text{gold}'\text{ring}')x))$$
$$T(\text{old}'\text{gold}'(\sigma_\delta x\text{gold}'x))$$

Even if the gold is realised by the gold ring:

$$\sigma_\delta x(\text{gold}'\text{ring}')x = \sigma_\delta x\text{gold}'x$$

there is no intrinsic contradiction in the truth conditions of these sentences. •

The final example shows how the theory copes with the comparative sentences which Landman uses to argue against a property modifier treatment of roles (Landman, 1989).

Example 4.6. Take the comparative sentence:

> The judge and the cleaner earn different incomes.

Essentially, its treatment in the theory rides on the meaning of "earn different incomes". In a strongly typed logic, it may be hard to see how "earn different incomes" can be expressed. Weakly typed logics like PT make it easier, the expression is just $\text{earn}'(\text{different}'\text{incomes}')$. We can represent the sentence as:

$$((\text{the}'\text{judge}')\hat{\oplus}(\text{the}'\text{cleaner}'))(\text{earn}'(\text{different}'\text{incomes}'))$$

where:

$$T(((\text{the}'\text{judge}')\widehat{\oplus}(\text{the}'\text{cleaner}'))(\text{earn}'(\text{different}'\text{incomes}'))) \leftrightarrow$$
$$T(\Xi_\delta ab(\ \text{income}'a \wedge \text{income}'b \wedge$$
$$\text{the}'(\text{judge}')(\text{earn}'a) \wedge \text{the}'(\text{cleaner}')(\text{earn}'b) \wedge$$
$$\text{different}'(^\pi\text{income}')(a \oplus b)))$$

This meaning postulate should be generalised to cope with arbitrary noun phrases.

We can give a weak meaning postulate for "different incomes", along the lines:

$$\forall_\Delta u(T(^\pi\text{income}'u) \rightarrow$$
$$(\exists_\Delta ab(T(\text{income}'a) \,\&\, T(\text{income}'b) \,\&\, a \leq u \,\&\, b \leq u \,\&\, a \neq b) \rightarrow$$
$$T(\text{different}'(^\pi\text{income})u)))$$

so that "different incomes" hold of something if it is a collection of incomes, and two of the incomes are not equal.

The treatment of some of the examples is perhaps rather indirect and involved. However, the main reason for giving the details is to show that the ideas developed can be used in compositional semantics. Clearly some additional effort must be expended to extend the coverage of this theory to transitive and ditransitive verbs, and to incorporate a dynamic component to produce an analysis of intermediate distribution and reciprocals as suggested by Schwarzschild (Schwarzschild, 1990; Schwarzschild, 1992).

No treatment of committee–like objects, or proper names is offered here. It should be a simple matter to add Barker's account of collective nouns (Barker, 1992).

5. CONCLUSIONS

If there are lessons to be learnt from this paper, they are that (i) care should be taken in assuming a particular ontology is empirically motivated just because it helps to cope with problems in some particular formal theory of natural language semantics. By way of illustration, a formal treatment for some plural and mass term phenomena can be provided without having to come to decisions on what perhaps are essentially philosophical, rather than semantic issues (Parsons, 1975) concerning homogeneity and atomicity. Similarly, (ii) care should be taken in assuming that certain empirical phenomena, such as non–denoting definites, necessitate a move away from classical two–valued logic in the truth–conditional semantics of natural language.

The theory has a rather limited coverage. However, the manner in which the issues are addressed exemplifies an axiomatic approach to semantics. In essence, the methodology of devising formal semantics theories is not seen as providing some compositional mapping between language and a mathematical model. Rather, the central goal is seen as obtaining appropriate inferences within a tractable theory. If we seek to do this by way of model–theoretic semantics, then there is the constant risk of building a theory that is too strong (it might sanction undesirable, or unmotivated inferences) or two powerful (where there may be no tractable proof theory). In this axiomatic treatment, we are free to choose axioms for the representation language that sanction only those inferences which conform to our intuitions. The theory can remain incomplete with respect to issues for which we have no clear, theory independent intuitions.

The weak typing of PT helps simplify the task of producing a semantic theory, as terms can belong to more than one type. For example, one term may appear as both a property, and a property modifier. There is no strong hierarchy of types, which might require various type–lifting strategies over semantic terms.[29]

Strong typing is often used in natural language semantic theories to avoid the self–predication paradoxes, whereas PT avoids these paradoxes axiomatically, making the theory too weak to prove that paradoxes of self–predication are propositions. Incomplete axioms can also be used to address the category mistake apparent in predication of non–denoting terms and to proofs of the existence of atomic mass terms. The latter satisfies our intuitions that mass terms can be used regardless of one's theory of substances and matter. Further, this allows the effects of different ontological choices on the semantics of nominals to be explored within the one theory: the final theory neither forces nor prevents the formal equality of certain terms, like "the mud and the water" with "the muddy water".

If we use a first–order theory, such as PT, then we can guarantee that we have a semi–decidable proof theory. This means that it lends itself to implementation. As the behaviour of natural language representations are described directly as axioms in PT, rather than as restrictions on a model of the representation, a system that uses this theory for semantic representation can perform useful inferences. This is surely a desirable objective for formal semantics: not just to provide a symbolic representation of sentences, but to indicate how intuitively acceptable inferences can be performed, preferably in a computationally tractable framework.

The weak treatment of non–denoting terms is compatible with a proof–theoretic implementation of a natural language system. As an example, the failure to ascribe a truth value to the sentence "the present king of France is bald" can be mechanically demonstrated to be due to the non–existence of "the present king of France". Thus, in an implementation of a question answering system, the helpful answer:

> There is no present king of France.

could be generated automatically, in response to the question:

> Is the present king of France bald?

Clearly, such an implementation would be dependent upon a suitable formal theory of questions and answers.

The treatment of existence presuppositions could be examined further, and may prove to be extendible to cover other examples of presupposition.

The paper does not address the contextual, dynamic effects that seem to affect intermediate distributive readings and reciprocals (Schwarzschild, 1990; Schwarzschild, 1992). A strengthened PT can be used to embody Martin–Löf's type theory (Martin-Löf, 1982; Martin-Löf, 1984) (Turner, 1990, Chapter 5). This can, in turn, be used to model some of the dynamic aspects of natural language semantics (Sundholm, 1989; Ranta, 1991; Davila-Perez, 1994). It then seems that there is scope for further work directed at treating dynamic effects in PT, using ideas from Martin–Löf's type theory (Fox, 1994b; Fox, 1994a), which might be used to account for the contextual effects required to obtain a reductive analysis of intermediate distributive readings and reciprocals. A property modifier could indicate the relevant parts, where that property modifier is obtained anaphorically following Schwarzschild's suggestion. This would extend the application of property modifiers in the domain of plurals.

A A Model of PT with Boolean Terms

We can show that property theory with mereological terms (PT+Δ) is consistent if we can provide a model which verifies all of its axioms.

First of all we need a model for the λ-calculus. This can be used to build a model of PT. We then require the model of PT to be strengthened to satisfy the axioms for denotable terms. Link and Lønning have both effectively shown that their axioms, with atomicity, are satisfiable if the denotable domain is a (definably) complete atomic Boolean algebra (Link, 1991a; Lønning, 1989). As my axioms for denotables are essentially a weaker version of Link's axioms in (Link, 1991a) then a Boolean algebra should verify them also.

We thus need a model of PT, where the natural language denotable terms belong to a complete Boolean algebra. The model presented for PT shall 'naturally' satisfy full completeness, as opposed to definable completeness. However, as we are only interested in showing that PT+Δ is consistent, then the model can be stronger than this theory: if we only need definable completeness, then it does not matter if we actually have full completeness in the model, nor does it matter that the Boolean algebra is atomic.

A1. A Model of the λ-Calculus with Summed Terms

Following an existing approach (Scott, 1973), we shall build a model of the λ-calculus from *domains* consisting of *complete lattices*. In the limit we have a domain D_∞ isomorphic to its own continuous function space, so $D_\infty \cong [D_\infty \longrightarrow D_\infty]$. We can define mappings $\Phi : D \longrightarrow [D \longrightarrow D]$ and $\Psi : [D \longrightarrow D] \longrightarrow D$.

Definition 1.1. *A Scott Model is a triple* $\mathcal{D} = \langle D, \Phi, \Psi \rangle$ *with D a domain and* Φ, Ψ *as above.*

The terms of λ-calculus can be interpreted in such a structure relative to an assignment function g which assigns elements of D to variables, and interpretation function i which assigns elements of D to constants. The function $g[d/x]$ is the function g except that d is bound to x. Reference to $\mathcal{D}$ is dropped in the following. i is assumed to be fixed.

$$\begin{aligned}
\mathcal{I}[x]_g &= g(x) \\
\mathcal{I}[c]_g &= i(c) \\
\mathcal{I}[\lambda x t]_g &= \Psi(\lambda d. \mathcal{I}[t]_{g[d/x]}) \\
\mathcal{I}[t(t')]_g &= \Phi(\mathcal{I}[t]_g)(\mathcal{I}[t']_g)
\end{aligned}$$

We want to be able to give a model of the λ-calculus extended with sums and products of terms. We can do this with:

$$\begin{aligned}
\mathcal{I}[t \oplus t']_g &= \bigsqcup \{\mathcal{I}[t]_g, \mathcal{I}[t']_g\} \\
\mathcal{I}[t \otimes t']_g &= \bigsqcap \{\mathcal{I}[t]_g, \mathcal{I}[t']_g\}
\end{aligned}$$

A2. A Model of PT+Δ

Following (Aczel, 1980):

Definition 1.2. *A model for PT shall be taken to be a Frege structure $\mathcal{M} = \langle \mathcal{D}, T, P \rangle$ where $\mathcal{D}$ is a model of the Lambda Calculus and*

$$T : P \longrightarrow \{0, 1\}$$
$$P : D \longrightarrow \{0, 1\}$$

Where T and P satisfy the structural requirements in (Aczel, 1980).

The characteristic functions T and P provide the extensions of the truth predicate and the proposition predicate, respectively. The structural requirements they conform to verify the appropriate axioms of PT. For example, the function T characterises a subset of P. Thus the terms have a subclass consisting of terms that correspond to propositions. This subclass, in turn, has a subclass of terms corresponding to the true propositions.

The language of wff can now be given truth conditions.

$$\begin{array}{lll}
\mathcal{M} \models_g s = t & \text{iff} & \mathcal{I}[t]_g = \mathcal{I}[s]_g \\
\mathcal{M} \models_g \mathrm{T}(t) & \text{iff} & T(\mathcal{I}[t]_g) = 1 \\
\mathcal{M} \models_g \mathrm{P}(t) & \text{iff} & P(\mathcal{I}[t]_g) = 1 \\
\mathcal{M} \models_g \varphi \& \psi & \text{iff} & \mathcal{M} \models_g \varphi \text{ and } \mathcal{M} \models_g \psi \\
\mathcal{M} \models_g \varphi \vee \psi & \text{iff} & \mathcal{M} \models_g \varphi \text{ or } \mathcal{M} \models_g \psi \\
\mathcal{M} \models_g \varphi \rightarrow \psi & \text{iff} & \mathcal{M} \models_g \varphi \text{ implies } \mathcal{M} \models_g \psi \\
\mathcal{M} \models_g \sim \varphi & \text{iff} & \mathcal{M} \models_g \text{ not } \varphi \\
\mathcal{M} \models_g \forall x \varphi & \text{iff} & \text{for all } d \in D \ \mathcal{M} \models_{g[d/x]} \varphi \\
\mathcal{M} \models_g \forall x \varphi & \text{iff} & \text{for some } d \in D \ \mathcal{M} \models_{g[d/x]} \varphi
\end{array}$$

A wff φ of PT is valid in a model $\mathcal{M}$ iff $\mathcal{M} \models_g \varphi$ for all assignment functions g.

For a model of PT+Δ we need a stronger base model than $\mathcal{M}$. We require those terms representing denotables to form a complete (atomic) Boolean algebra. Models of the λ–calculus, in general, do not possess these properties. This problem can be addressed by giving a substructure of $\mathcal{M}$ the desired properties, and letting the natural language denotable terms denote appropriate objects in this structure. Thus, denotable objects will form a sub–domain.

A Complete Atomic Boolean Algebra

A Complete Atomic Boolean Algebra B is given by the following axioms, adapted from (Hughes and Cresswell, 1973):

(i) B contains at least 2 elements.
(ii) If $a, b \in B$ then $a' \in B$ and $a \sqcup b \in B$.
(iii) If $a, b \in B$ then $a \sqcup b = b \sqcup a$.
(iv) If $a, b, c \in B$ then $a \sqcup (b \sqcup c) = (a \sqcup b) \sqcup c$.
(v) For all $a, b \in B$, if there is some $c \in B$ such that $a \sqcup b' = c \sqcup c'$ then $a \sqcup b = a$.
(vi) For all $a, b, c \in B$ if $a \sqcup b = a$ then $a \sqcup b' = c \sqcup c'$.
(vii) For all $a \neq (c \sqcup c') \in B$ there exists $u \in B$, such that $u \sqcup a = q$ and for all $i \in B$ such that $i \sqcup u = u$ either $i = (c \sqcup c')$ or $i = u$.
(viii) Any (non–empty) set $E \subseteq A$ has a least upper bound, $\sqcup E \in A$.

The axioms (i)–(vi) give a Boolean algebra. Axiom (vii) makes the algebra atomic. Axiom (viii) makes it complete. The notions *bottom* 0; *top* 1; $a \sqcap b$; and $a - b$ can be defined:

$$1 =_{\text{def}} a \sqcup a'$$
$$1' =_{\text{def}} 0$$
$$a \sqcap b =_{\text{def}} (a' \sqcup b')'$$
$$a - b =_{\text{def}} a \sqcap b'$$

There is one well–known theorem that will be of use later:

Lemma 1.1. *In an atomic Boolean algebra, every element is the supremum of the atoms it dominates (each element of B is defined by the atoms it dominates).*

Proof: From (Halmos, 1963): each element $p \in B$ is an upper-bound of the set of atoms $E \subseteq B$ that it dominates. We must demonstrate that if r is an arbitrary bound of E, then $p \sqsubseteq r$. Assume otherwise, that $p - r \not\sqsubseteq 0$. From atomicity it follows there is a $q \in B$ where $q \sqsubseteq p - r$. As $p - r \sqsubseteq p$, the atom $q \in E$. But since $(q \sqcap r) \sqsubseteq ((p - r) \sqcap r)$ this contradicts that r is an upper-bound of E. □

We can draw two corollaries from this result:

Corollary 1.1. *Different collections of atoms have different suprema.*

Corollary 1.2. *Different suprema dominate different atoms.*

Definition 1.3. *Let* $\mathcal{M}_\Delta = \langle \mathcal{D}, T, P, B \rangle$ *be a model of* PT+Δ. *Where* $B : D \longrightarrow \{0, 1\}$ *characterises those elements of D that are in a complete atomic Boolean sub–domain of D, with the same ordering and join operator.*

We can now express the conditions for $\delta t, t \leq t'$:

$$\mathcal{M}_\Delta \models_g \mathrm{T}(\delta(t)) \quad \text{iff} \quad B(\mathcal{I}[t]_g) = 1$$
$$\mathcal{M}_\Delta \models_g t \leq t' \quad \text{iff} \quad \mathcal{I}[t]_g \sqsubseteq \mathcal{I}[t']_g$$

Thus, natural language denotable terms denote items in the complete atomic Boolean algebra.

As it does not matter what 'non–denoting' definite descriptors denote, the definite descriptor $\sigma x \varphi$ can be given an interpretation:

$$\mathcal{I}[\sigma x \varphi]_g = \bigsqcup \{a | T(\mathcal{I}[\varphi]_{g[a/x]}) = 1\}$$

It can be demonstrated that the model satisfies the axioms given for denotable terms.

Theorem 1.1. *The summation operator $\oplus$ is symmetric, idempotent and associative (Axioms 3.1.; 3.2.; 3.3.):*

Proof: Trivial: the summation operator is modelled by the lattice theoretic join $\sqcup$ which is also symmetric, idempotent and associative. □

Theorem 1.2. *The domain of denotables is closed (Axiom 3.5.).*

$$\Delta a \,\&\, \Delta b \rightarrow \Delta(a \oplus b)$$

Proof: From the axioms of the Boolean algebra: if $a, b \in B$, then $a \sqcup b \in B$. □

Theorem 1.3. *The domain of denotables is (definably) complete (Axiom 3.6.).*

$$\forall p((\mathrm{Pty}(p) \,\&\, \forall x(\mathrm{T}(px) \rightarrow \Delta(x)) \,\&\, \exists x(\mathrm{T}(px))) \rightarrow \Delta(\sigma x p x))$$

Proof: From the completeness of the Boolean algebra: if $X \subseteq B$, then $\sqcup X \in B$. The axiom is weaker, as it requires that there is a denotable in the extension of the property. □

Theorem 1.4. *Different denotables have different parts (Axiom 3.7.).*

$$\forall_\Delta xy(x \not\leq y \rightarrow \exists_\Delta u(u \leq x \,\&\, u \not\leq y))$$

Proof: From Corollary 1.2., we can prove that for all denotable x, y, if $x \not\leq y$ then there is a denotable u that is part of x but not part of y, and that denotable is atomic in the model. This supports Axiom 3.7., which has a weaker consequent: it does not require u to be atomic. □

Theorem 1.5. *Denotables within the extension of a property (of denotables) must have an upper–bound (Axiom 3.8.).*

$$\forall p \forall_\Delta y ((\text{Pty}_\Delta(p) \,\&\, \text{T}(py)) \to y \leq \sigma_\delta xpx)$$

Proof: The axioms of the Boolean algebra define $\sqcup X$ as an upper-bound on the members of the set $X \subseteq B$. The supremum operator σ is modelled by $\sqcup$. Further, all PT definable properties of denotables will have their extension in B. □

Theorem 1.6. *The supremum of the extension of a property of denotables is the smallest denotable that dominates all the terms in the extension (Axiom 3.9.).*

$$\forall p \forall_\Delta y ((\text{Pty}_\Delta(p) \,\&\, \forall_\Delta x (\text{T}(px) \to x \leq y)) \to \sigma_\delta xpx \leq y)$$

Proof: From the axioms of the Boolean algebra: $\sqcup X$ is the *least* upper-bound of X, where $X \subseteq B$. □

Theorem 1.7. *Different portions of denotables have different suprema (Axiom 3.10.).*

$$\forall p \forall_\Delta u ((\text{Pty}_\Delta(p) \,\&\, u \leq \sigma_\delta xpx) \to (\exists_\Delta z(pz \,\&\, u \leq z) \vee \exists_\Delta z(pz \,\&\, z \leq u)))$$

Proof: From Corollary 1.1. we can prove that for all p, u, where p is a property of denotables and u is a denotable, if u is atomic in the model, and it is part of the supremum of the denotables that are p, then u is part of some denotable z in the extension of p. However, the theory is not atomic. If there is no mention of atomicity in the antecedent, then the model will support the axiom if the consequent is weakened to also allow u to be part of some term in the extension of p. □

ACKNOWLEDGEMENTS

Thanks to Ray Turner, Gennaro Chierchia, Hans Kamp, Richard Ball, Camilla Beswick and two anonymous reviewers for their comments on previous versions of this work.

Some of the work presented in here was researched with the aid of a Science and Engineering Research Council Studentship. A version of the ideas presented in this paper is also contained in (Fox, 1993).

NOTES

[1] If individuals are of type e and properties are of type p, then Landman's new individuals–under–guises are taken to be of the same type as quantifiers, $\langle\langle e,p\rangle,p\rangle$, rather than of type e.

[2] That is, individuals–under–guises are taken to be of type e.

[3] Subsective adjectives have also been called *restrictive* or *affirmative* adjectives (Hoepelman, 1983).

[4] It might seem that the gold and the ring can be distinguished because "the ring" individuates, and "the gold" does not. However, in general it is not clear that there is always a means to distinguish such terms, as with the Morning Star–Evening Star. Also, see the later argument on wood–furniture and food–potatoes in Section 1.2.

Landman also applies this treatment of intensionality to the 'committee' example. For him, the two committees are represented by the same object (the collection of members) under different guises. Although there should be some systematic connection between the committees and their members, it seems counter–intuitive to make the collection of members a constituent part of the term representing the committees: if the members change then the committees are no longer the same, and we have an identification problem. Barker's treatment of collectives seems more appropriate (Barker, 1992). He has some function that returns the members of a committee, but the terms representing committees themselves are independent of their members. Here is one case where linguistic examples require a particular ontology.

[5] The sentence "a cleaner strikes" could be represented as something like:

$$\exists x(\text{cleaner}'\, x \land (\text{strikes}'(\text{cleaner}'))x)$$

This is true should there be a cleaner who is a striking cleaner (or alternatively, who is striking, as a cleaner).

[6] This observation was also made by Quine. He says that we only want to distribute to those parts that are not "too small" to count as the appropriate sort of term (Quine, 1960). Roeper makes a related point concerning the distribution of disjunctive properties (Roeper, 1983), as discussed below. Lønning also addresses the issue of inappropriate parts as they arise in sentences involving negation (Lønning, 1987).

[7] These criticisms were suggested to me by Hans Kamp.

[8] It may be noted that theories of individuals under different roles may allow descriptors with no extension in the denotable terms to denote the bottom element $\perp$. The bottom element could then be considered under different guises, preventing different 'non–denoting' terms being equated.

[9] If this is ruled inadmissible in an extensional theory, as it is some 'intensional context', then we might question what a '*non*-intensional context' could be.

In whatever way we arrange the example, wood and sawdust definitely do seem to be different. If property modifiers, or Landman's roles, are not used, then an intensional ontology may be required. However, the theory presented in this paper is weak enough to allow the extensions of these expressions to be equated.

Two definite descriptions (brought to my attention by an anonymous referee) where there might not be such an obvious distinction as there is between "wood" and "sawdust", are "the food" and "the potatoes", where the potatoes (read as a mass term) exclusively constitutes the food. If there is necessarily no example which distinguishes between these expressions, then meaning postulates would have to be added to that effect.

[10] The model for the theory may well contain a proper Boolean algebra, with a bottom element, but the theory itself will say nothing about it.

[11] As has been indicated by Strawson, there are sentences involving non-denoting terms, to which some find it acceptable to ascribe a truth value. This is typified by passive constructions such as "The exhibition was visited by the present king of France" which some take to be a false proposition, unlike "The present king of France visited the exhibition" (Strawson, 1964). One argument is that the existence presupposition only occurs for definite descriptors which are in the foreground, or active, in some sense. The theory presented does not preclude a strengthening of the axioms to allow propositionhood to be proved in such cases, should a suitable formal theory of the foreground/background distinction be forthcoming. A simple-minded response could be to give a Russellian, quantificational representation of passive definite descriptors, or to allow the passive form of "visit" to form propositions with terms that are not provably denotable. Lasersohn gives some other examples in which he claims the use of non-denoting terms is felicitous (Lasersohn, 1993). A tentative treatment is offered for some of these examples is given elsewhere (Fox, 1993).

The treatment of existential presuppositions with definites given in this paper can be extended to missing antecedents for anaphoric expressions (Fox, 1994c).

[12] Unified in the sense that the extensions of mass terms and plurals can be part of the same part–whole structure, and axioms governing distributive inferences, for example, can apply to both.

[13] In Montague's intensional logic IL, an intension is given by applying the operator $^\wedge$ to an extension.

[14] An additional reason for having only a subclass of terms in a Boolean structure becomes apparent when considering the model theory of PT. A model of PT can be constructed using a lattice theoretic model for the λ–terms (Turner, 1990). It is convenient to use the ordering and join in this lattice to model the summation and supremum operators. If, however, we give a Boolean structure to all terms, it is not possible to do this: no model of the λ–calculus could then be constructed.

[15] It would be fairly trivial to either add them to the theory, or to use logical determiners where appropriate.

[16] They form an atomic Boolean algebra, rather than a complete Boolean algebra. The additions required to the model given in the appendix are fairly trivial.

[17] It might be thought that this axiom, together with Axiom 4.3. will allow us to show "some man walked and talked" if "some man walked and some man talked". However, this would require an improper existential elimination.

[18] For a comparison of these two approaches (considering 'predicates' rather than 'properties') see (Kamp, 1975).

[19] It might be fruitful to formalise a version of this theory where the property modifiers are constructed from properties using some operator. This has been suggested to me by Gennaro Chierchia. In such a theory, rather than represent "John is a strict judge" with something like (strict'judge'j'), where strict' is both a property of denotables, and a property modifier, we would use (as'judge'strict'j'), where judge' is only a property of denotable, and as' is a function that turns such a property into a property modifier. I suspect that this would simplify some aspects of the theory, though perhaps at the cost of a unification with a treatment of natural language modifiers.

[20] Obviously, I assume the adjectives in question are subsective, and that they act as property modifiers.

[21] Note that these distributive and cumulative notions are different from those

given by $*$ and ^{D} (Link, 1991a; Lønning, 1989), which produce collective and distributive properties respectively.

[22] The improper plural form subsumes the singular form: $^\pi p$ will hold of one or more ps, as opposed to the two or more with English plurals.

[23] Hoepelman suggests we might take "red" to be weakly predicative: a red tomato may be red compared to the existent tomatoes, but we might not wish to class it as unadorned "red". It is weakly predicative as a red tomato is definitely not "unred", the polar opposite of "red", (green, blue, black, etc.), and a tomato that is truly red is a red tomato.

[24] Note that if we additionally take wet$'$ to be distributive, it does not mean that "wet" distributes to all parts. The distribution is only motivated when the distributive 'property' appears as a property modifier, so it can still only distribute to relevant parts.

[25] We cannot claim that it is transparent, period, as there is a counter example: a water meadow is not water.

[26] Confusion is increased with the uses of "black and white", for example, in "black and white television".

[27] It might be thought that from something like "some ball is a red ball and some ball is a white ball" we are able to infer "some ball is a red and white ball". However, this would be to assume that "some ball" is itself a denotable term, rather than something which gives rise to quantification over denotable terms.

[28] As it stands this axiom is too strong for plurals. From "the red and white ball p" we might infer that there is a red ball and there is a white ball". If we made explicit the analysis of distribution into syntactically conjoined terms, then this problem could be avoided.

[29] Perhaps to be distinguished from type–lifting as used in categorial grammars to account for ellipsis (Dowty, 1988).

REFERENCES

Aczel, P. (1980). Frege structures and the notions of proposition, truth and set. In Barwise, Keisler, and Keenan (eds.), *The Kleene Symposium*, North Holland Studies in Logic, 31–39. North Holland.

Barker, C. (1992). Group terms in English: Representing groups as atoms. *Journal of Semantics* **9**, 69–93.

Bennett, M. (1977). Mass nouns and mass terms in Montague grammar. In Davis, S. and Mithun, M., editors, *Linguistics, Philosophy, and Montague Grammar*, 263–285. University of Texas Press, Austin.

Blau, U. (1981). Collective objects. *Theoretical Linguistics*, 8:101–130.

Bunt, H. (1979). Ensembles and the formal semantic properties of mass terms. In Pelletier, F., editor, *Mass Terms*, 249–277. D. Reidel, Dordrecht.

Bunt, H. (1985). *Mass Terms and Model Theoretic Semantics*. Cambridge University Press.

Burge, T. (1975). Mass terms, count nouns, and change. *Synthese*, 31:459–478.

Cartwright, H. M. (1965). Heraclitus and the bath water. *Philosophical Review*, 74:466–485.

Chierchia, G. (1982). Nominalisation and Montague grammar: a semantics without types for natural languages. *Linguistics and Philosophy*, 5:303–354.

Chierchia, G. (1984). *Topics in the Semantics of Infinitives and Gerunds*. PhD thesis, University of Massachusetts, Amherst.

Chierchia, G. and Turner, R. (1988). Semantics and property theory. *Linguistics and Philosophy*, 11:261–302.

Davila-Perez, R. (1994). Constructive type theory and natural language. Computer Science Memorandum 206, University of Essex.

Dowty, D. (1988). Type raising, functional composition, and non-constituent conjunction. In Oehrle, R. T., Bach, E., and Wheeler, D. (eds.), *Categorial Grammars and Natural Language Structures*, 153–197. D. Reidel, Dordrecht.

Dowty, D., Wall, R., and Peters, S. (1981). *Introduction to Montague Semantics*. Reidel, Dordrecht.

Fox, C. (1993). *Plurals and Mass Terms in Property Theory*. PhD thesis, University of Essex, Colchester, U.K.

Fox, C. (1994a). Discourse representation, type theory and property theory. In Bunt, H., Muskens, R., and Rentier, G.(eds.), *Proceedings of the International Workshop on Computational Semantics*, 71–80, ITK, Tilburg.

Fox, C. (1994b). Existence presuppositions and category mistakes. Presented at the Fifth Hungarian Symposium in Logic and Language, Noszvaj. University of Essex. m.s.

Fox, C. (1994c). Individuals and their guises: A property-theoretic analysis. In *Proceedings of the Ninth Amsterdam Colloquium, December 1993*, volume II, pages 301–312.

Gillon, B. S. (1992). Towards a common semantics for English count and mass nouns. *Linguistics and Philosophy*, 15:597–639.

Halmos, P. R. (1963). *Lectures on Boolean Algebras*. D. Van Nostrand, Princeton, New Jersey.

Heim, I. (1982). *The Semantics of Definite and Indefinite Noun Phrases*. PhD thesis, University of Massachusetts, Amherst. Thesis Distributed by Graduate Linguistics Student Association.

Higginbotham, J. (1981). Reciprocal interpretation. *Linguistic Research*, 3:97–117.

Hindley, R. and Seldin, J. (1986). *Introduction to Combinators and the Lambda Calculus*. London Mathematical Society Student Texts 1. Cambridge University Press.

Hintikka, J. (1962). *Knowledge and Belief: an Introduction to the Two Notions*. Cornell University Press.

Hoeksema, J. (1983). Plurality and conjunction. In ter Meulen, A. (ed.), *Studies in Modeltheoretic Semantics*, 63–83. Foris, Dordrecht.

Hoeksema, J. (1987). The semantics of non-boolean "and". Paper presented at the LSA/ASL meeting, Stanford.

Hoepelman, J. (1983). Adjectives and nouns : a new calculus. In Rainer, Bäuerle, Schwartze, C., and von Stechow, A. (eds.), *Meaning, Use, and Interpretation of Language*, 190–220. Walter de Gruyer, Berlin.

Hughes, G. and Cresswell, M. (1973). *An Introduction to Modal Logic*. Methuen, London.

Kamp, H. (1975). Two theories of adjectives. In Keenan, E. (ed.), *Formal Semantics of Natural Language*, 123–155. Cambridge University Press.

Kamp, H. (1981). Theory of truth and semantic representation. In Groenendijk, J., Janssen, T., and Stokhof, M. (eds.), *Formal Methods in the Study of Language*, Mathematical Centre Tracts 135, 277–322. Amsterdam.

Kamp, H. and Reyle, U. (1993). *From Discourse to Logic*. Kluwer, Dordrecht.

Kripke, S. (1963). Semantical considerations on modal logic. *Acta Philosophica Fennica*, 16:83–89.

Landman, F. (1989). 'Groups', Parts I and II. *Linguistics and Philosophy*, 12:559–605, 723–744.

Lasersohn, P. (1993). Existence presuppositions and background knowledge. *Journal of Semantics*, 10:113–122.

Leonard, H. and Goodman, N. (1940). The calculus of individuals and its uses. *Journal of Symbolic Logic*, 5:45–55.

Lewis, D. (1991). *Parts of Classes*. Blackwell, Oxford.

Link, G. (1983). The logical analysis of plurals and mass terms: A lattice theoretic approach. In Bäuerle, R., Schwarze, C., and von Stechow, A., editors, *Meaning, Use and Interpretation of Language*, pages 302–323. Walter de Gruyer, Berlin.

Link, G. (1984). Hydras: On the logic of relative constructions with multiple heads. In Landman, F. and Veltman, F., editors, *Varieties of Formal Semantics*, pages 245–257. Foris, Dordrecht.

Link, G. (1987). Generalised quantifiers and plurals. In Gärdenfors, P., editor, *Generalised Quantifiers. Linguistic Approaches*, pages 151–180. Reidel, Dordrecht.

Link, G. (1991a). First order axioms for the logic of plurality. University of Munich. m.s.

Link, G. (1991b). Plurals. In von Stechow, A. and Wunderlich, D., editors, *Handbuch der Semantik*. de Gruyter, Berlin.

Lønning, J. (1987). Mass terms and quantification. *Linguistics and Philosophy*, 10:1–52.

Lønning, J. (1989). Some aspects of the logic of plural noun phrases. University of Oslo. Cosmos Report Number 11.

Martin-Löf, P. (1982). Constructive mathematics and computer programming. In Cohen, Los, Pfeiffer, and Podewski, editors, *Logic, Methodology and Philosophy of Science VI*, pages 153–179. North Holland.

Martin-Löf, P. (1984). *Studies in Proof Theory (Lecture Notes)*. Bibliopolis, Napoli.

Montague, R. (1974). *Formal Philosophy: Selected Papers of Richard Montague*. Yale University Press, New Haven/London. Edited with an introduction by R.H. Thomason.

Moravcsik, J. (1973). Mass terms in English. In Hintikka, K., Moravcsik, J., and Suppes, P. (eds.), *Approaches to Natural Language*, 263–285. D. Reidel, Dordrecht. Synthese Library.

Orey, S. (1959). Model theory for higher order predicate calculus. *Transactions from the American Mathematical Society*, 92:72–84.

Parsons, T. (1970). An analysis of mass terms and amount terms. *Foundation of Language*, VI(3):362–388.

Parsons, T. (1975). Afterthoughts on mass terms. *Synthese*, 31:517–21.

Partee, B. and Rooth, M. (1983). Generalised conjunction and type ambiguity. In Bäuerle, C., Schwartze, and von Stechow, A.(eds.), *Meaning, Use and Interpretation of Language*, 361–383. Walter de Gruyter, Berlin.

Quine, W. (1960). *Word and Object*. MIT Press, Cambridge, Mass.

Ranta, A. (1991). Intuitionistic categorial grammar. *Linguistics and Philosophy*, 14:203–239.

Roberts, C. (1987). *Modal Subordination, Anaphora, and Distributivity*. PhD thesis, University of Massaschusetts.

Roeper, P. (1983). Semantics for mass terms with quantifiers. *Noûs*, 17:251–265.

Schwarzschild, R. (1990). *On the Meaning of Plural Noun Phrases*. PhD thesis. Draft.

Schwarzschild, R. (1992). Types of plural individual. *Linguistics and Philosophy*, 15:641–675.

Scott, D. (1973). Models for various type-free calculii. In P. Suppes et al. (eds.), *Logic, Methodology and Philosophy of Science IV*, North Holland Studies in Logic and the Foundations of Mathematics, 157–187. North Holland.

Strawson, P. (1964). Identifying reference and truth-values. *Theoria*, 3:96–118.

Sundholm, G. (1989). Constructive generalised quantifiers. *Synthese*, 79:1–12.

Turner, R. (1987). A theory of properties. *Journal of Symbolic Logic*, 52(2):455–472.

Turner, R. (1990). *Truth and Modality for Knowledge Representation*. Pitman.

Turner, R. (1992). Properties, propositions and semantic theory. In Rosner, M. and Johnson, R. (eds.), *Computational Linguistics and Formal Semantics*, Studies in Natural Language Processing, 159–180. Cambridge University Press, Cambridge.

van Fraassen, B. C. (1966). Singular terms and truth value gaps. *The Journal of Philosophy*, LXIII:481–495.

FRANS ZWARTS

THREE TYPES OF POLARITY

1. INTRODUCTION

There can be no doubt that the phenomenon of polarity, though usually the subject of syntactic and semantic study, is essentially of a purely lexical nature.[1] This is evident to anyone who is familiar with the distribution of so-called negative polarity items. The fact that expressions such as *hoeven* and *ook maar iets* in Dutch, *brauchen* and *auch nur irgendetwas* in German, or the English cognates *need* and *anything (at all)* require the presence of a negative element somewhere in the sentence, is a property which is intrinsic to the items in question and must therefore be accounted for in the lexicon. If there is any doubt as to the lexical nature of this phenomenon, it is completely eradicated by the distinction between negative polarity items of the weak and those of the strong type. In order to get a clear view of the content of this distinction, one does well to take the following Dutch examples into consideration.

(1) a At most one child will himself need to justify *Hoogstens verantwoorden.*

  één kind zal zich hoeven te

  'At most one child need justify himself.'

  b *Niemand zal zulk een beproeving hoeven te doorstaan.*
    No one will such an ordeal need to go through
    'No one need go through such an ordeal.'

  c *Weinig handelsreizigers blijken hem te kunnen velen.*
    Few salesmen appear him to can abide
    'It appears that few salesmen can abide him.'

  d *Geen van de leerlingen schijnt haar te kunnen velen.*
    None of the students seems her to can abide
    'It seems that none of the students can abide her.'

(2) a **Hoogstens zes kinderen hebben ook maar iets/bemerkt.*
    At most six children have anything noticed
    'At most six children noticed anything.'

  b *Niemand heeft van de regenbui ook maar iets bemerkt.*
    No one has of the rain anything noticed
    'No one noticed anything of the rain.'

    c   *Weinig ouders hebben bijster veel brieven ontvangen.
        Few parents have very many letters received
        'Few parents received very many letters.'

    d   *Geen van de kooplieden toonde zich bijster tevreden.*
        None of the merchants showed himself very content
        'None of the merchants showed himself very content.'

The contrast between (1) and (2) makes it clear that expressions such as *ook maar iets* and *bijster* place stronger restrictions on their environments than the negative polarity items *hoeven* and *kunnen velen*.[2] We must not suppose that this is a peculiar feature of Dutch, for precisely the same pattern can be found in German, as shown by the sentences in (3) and (4).[3]

(3) a   At most one woman will herself to justify need *Höchstens eine*
                                                           brauchen.
       Frau wird sich zu verantworten

       'At most one woman need justify herself.'

    b   No one will such an ordeal to go through need *Keiner wird*
                                                                 brauchen.
       solch eine Prüfung durchzustehen

       'No one need go through such an ordeal.'

    c   *Nur wenige Kaufleute scheinen dich ausstehen zu können.*
        Only a few merchants seem you stand to can
        'It seems that only a few merchants can stand you.'

    d   None of the deputies seems her stand to can *Keine der*
                                                            können.
       Abgeordneten scheint sie ausstehen zu

       'It seems that none of the deputies can stand her.'

(4) a   noticed*Höchstens zehn Kinder haben auch nur*flirgendetwas
            At most ten children have anything
       bemerkt.

       'At most ten children noticed anything.'

b *Keiner von diesen Leuten hat auch nur irgendetwas bemerkt.*
None of these people has anything noticed
'None of these people noticed anything.'

c Only a few merchants have very content been*Nur wenige gewesen.
Kaufleute sind sonderlich zufrieden

'Only a few merchants have been very content.'

d *Kein einziger Lehrer ist sonderlich freundlich gewesen.*
Not one teacher has very friendly been
'Not one teacher has been very friendly.'

Other examples illustrating this remarkable division within the class of negative polarity items include idiomatic expressions such as *lift a finger* (G: *einen Finger rühren*, D: *er een vinger naar uitsteken*), *utter a sound* (G: *einen Muckser von sich geben*, D: *een kik geven*), and *bat an eyelash* (G: *mit der Wimper zucken*, D: *een spier vertrekken*). As the sentences in (5) indicate, such phrases are not satisfied with the presence of a negative constituent of the form *at most n N*. Instead, they require a more prominent negation such as *none of the N* or *none of the n N*.

(5) a None of the fifteen students lifted a finger.

b *At most eighteen porters will lift a finger.

c None of the sixteen children uttered a sound.

d *At most five representatives uttered a sound.

e None of the seven children batted an eyelash.

f *At most eighteen children batted an eyelash.

In German and Dutch, similar patterns can be attested. Parallel to the examples in (5), we find the contrasting sentences in (6) and (7).

(6) a *Keiner der Athleten hat einen Finger gerührt.*
None of the athletes has a finger moved
'None of the athletes lifted a finger.'

b At most one woman has a finger moved*Höchstens eine Frau gerührt.
hat einen Finger

'At most one woman lifted a finger'.

c   *Kein Junge hat einen Muckser von sich gegeben.*
No boy has a sound of himself given
'No boy uttered a sound.'

d   Only few may a sound of themselves give*Nur wenige mögen
geben.
einen Muckser von sich*

'Only a few may utter a sound.'

e   *Keiner der Männer hat mit der Wimper gezuckt.*
None of the men has with the eyelash drawn
'None of the men batted an eyelash.'

f   **Wenige Athleten haben mit der Wimper gezuckt.*
Few athletes have with the eyelash batted
'Few athletes batted an eyelash.'

(7) a   *Niemand heeft er een vinger naar uitgestoken.*
No one has it a finger to stretch out
'No one lifted a finger.'

b   **Weinigen zullen er een vinger naar uitsteken.*
Few will it a finger to stretch out
'Few people will lift a finger.'

c   *Geen van de aanwezigen heeft een kik gegeven.*
None of the present has a sound given
'None of those present uttered a sound.'

d   **Hoogstens zes bedienden zullen een kik geven.*
At most six servants will a sound give
'At most six servants will utter a sound.'

e   *Geen van de ukken heeft een spier vertrokken.*
None of the toddlers has a muscle moved
'None of the toddlers batted an eyelash.'

f   **Slechts zes ukken mogen een spier vertrekken.*
Only six toddlers may a muscle move
'Only six toddlers may bat an eyelash.'

This state of affairs immediately raises the question as to how such differences should be accounted for. In what follows, I will show that we need to make a distinction between subminimal and minimal negation. Although this difference may not at first seem clear, it finds its origins in the indisputable fact that noun phrases of the forms *no one* and *none of the merchants* embody a stronger type of negation than those of the forms *at most six children* and *few parents*. This becomes apparent when we compare the logical behavior of the expressions in question with that of the sentential prefix *it is not the case that*. By way of illustration we consider two examples.

(8) a   It is not the case that Jack ate or Jill ran   ↔
        It is not the case that Jack ate and it is not the case that Jill ran

   b   It is not the case that Jack ate and Jill ran   ↔
        It is not the case that Jack ate or it is not the case that Jill ran

One sees immediately that the biconditionals in (8) must both be accepted as valid – a state of affairs which admits no other explanation than that the operation in question is governed by the laws of De Morgan.[4] This observation is important because it has frequently been argued that the logical patterns in (8) characterize the use of negation. Although such a conclusion is correct with respect to the sentential prefix *it is not the case that* and the negative adverb *not*[5], it must be regarded as misleading when it comes to other forms of negation. Not only does natural language contain a variety of negative expressions, their logical behavior is also not the same. In order to convince ourselves of this simple fact, we consider the conditionals in (9).

(9) a   Few trees will blossom or will die   →
        Few trees will blossom and few trees will die

   b   Few trees will blossom and few trees will die   ↛
        Few trees will blossom or will die

   c   Few trees will blossom and will die   ↛
        Few trees will blossom or few trees will die

   d   Few trees will blossom or few trees will die   →
        Few trees will blossom and will die

From these examples it is clear that the phrase *few trees*, considered as a negative expression, differs substantially from the sentential prefix *it is not the case that*. Of the four conditionals presented in (9), only two are valid: the one in (9a) and the one in (9d). In other words, the logical behavior of noun phrases of the form *few N* is governed by one half of the first law of De Morgan and one half of the second law of De Morgan. In this regard, they are by no means alone, for it requires little reflection to realize that noun phrases of the forms *at most n N*, *not all N*, *only a few N* and *no more than n N* behave in much the same way. What this suggests is that the expressions in question embody a weak form of negation. For that reason they will henceforth be referred to as expressions of subminimal negation – a name which is borrowed from that part of the classical propositional calculus known as subminimal logic.[6]

It turns out that there exists, in fact, a whole hierarchy of negative expressions. For not only do we have phrases of the forms *few N* and *at most n N*, but we also find cases such as *no N*, *none of the N* and *no one*. The latter category differs from the former in that it expresses a stronger form of negation. The following conditionals provide an illustration.

(10) a No man escaped or got killed →
        No man escaped and no man got killed

    b No man escaped and no man got killed →
        No man escaped or got killed

    c No man escaped and got killed ↛
        No man escaped or no man got killed

    d No man escaped or no man got killed →
        No man escaped and got killed

From these examples we may conclude that the noun phrase *no man*, regarded as a negative expression, differs considerably from *few trees*. Of the four conditionals presented in (10), no less than three must be accounted valid: the one in (10a), the one in (10b), and the one in (10d). What this means is that the logical behavior of noun phrases of the form *no N* is determined by the first law of De Morgan as a whole and one half of the second law of De Morgan. We must not suppose that this is a mere accident, for it is easy to see that the property in question also holds of noun phrases of the forms *none of the N*, *neither N* and *no one*. The conclusion must therefore be that expressions of this type embody a stronger form of negation than phrases like *few N* and *at most n N*. For that reason they will henceforth be referred to as expressions of minimal negation.[7]

In order to complete the hierarchy of negation, we must return to the biconditionals in (8). The validity of these examples makes it clear that the sentential prefix *it is not the case that* is governed by both the first and the second law of De Morgan. In the same way, the negative adverb *not* can also be shown to obey the two laws of De Morgan. What this means is that such elements express an even stronger form of negation than noun phrases like *no N* and *none of the N*. As a matter of fact, they will henceforth be referred to as expressions of classical negation.

With this apparatus at our command, we can explain the patterns in (1) through (7). For it is easily established that the distinction between weak and strong forms of negative polarity can be reduced to that between subminimal and minimal forms of negation. By way of illustration we give here a formulation of the laws which govern the occurrence of negative polarity items.

(11) **Laws of negative polarity**

    a Only sentences in which an expression of subminimal negation occurs, can contain a negative polarity item of the weak type.

    b Only sentences in which an expression of minimal negation occurs, can contain a negative polarity item of the strong type.

According to the first law, the presence of a subminimal negation is a necessary condition for the appearance of negative polarity items of the weak type. On the other hand, the second law stipulates that negative polarity items of the strong type require the presence of a minimal negation. To forestall any misunderstanding, we note that every expression of minimal negation is also an expression of subminimal negation.[8] In order to get a clear view of the domain of application of both laws, one does well to take the following examples into consideration.

(12) a *Niemand schijnt ook maar iets te hebben ondernomen.*
        No one   seems anything   to have   undertaken
        'No one seems to have undertaken anything.'

     b At most eight arrows have anything hit*Hoogstens acht
                                                      geraakt.
       pijlen hebben ook maar iets

       'At most eight arrows hit anything.'

     c *Geen van de geleerden toonde zich   bijster tevreden.*
        None of   the scientists showed himself very   content

'None of the scientist showed himself very content.'

d *Weinig ouders hebben bijster veel giften ontvangen.
    Few   parents have   very   many gifts received

'Few parents received very many gifts.'

The contrast between (12a) and (12c), on the one hand, and (12b) and (12d), on the other, proves that the presence of a subminimal negation is not sufficient to justify the occurrence of the negative polarity items *ook maar iets* and *bijster*. Apparently, it is only expressions such as *niemand* and *geen van de geleerden* that are capable of licensing the polarity items in question. That this is by no means a coincidence, is shown by the German sentences in (13).

(13) a None of the merchants has anything undertaken
        Keiner   der Kaufleute hat auch nur irgendetwas unternommen.

   'None of the merchants undertook anything.'

   b noticed*Höchstens sechs Eltern haben auch nurflirgendetwas
             At most six   parents have anything
      bemerkt.

   'At most six parents noticed anything.'

Again, we see that the presence of the subminimal negation *höchstens sechs Eltern* is not sufficient to legitimize the occurrence of *auch nur irgendetwas*. In the same way, the examples in (14) and (15) clearly show that the Dutch negative polarity item *noemenswaardig* and its German counterpart *nennenswert* are incompatible with the weak negations *hoogstens zes ouders* ('at most six parents') and *höchstens sieben Athleten* ('at most seven athletes'). Instead they require the presence of a stronger form of negation – *geen van de wezen* ('none of the orphans') in (14a) and *keiner der anderen Athleten* ('none of the other athletes') in (15a).[9]

(14) a Geen van de wezen   heeft noemenswaardige verliezen
        None of the orphans has   appreciable   losses
        geleden.
        suffered

   'None of the orphans has suffered any appreciable loss.'

b At most six parents obtain an appreciable result *Hoogstens
resultaat.
zes ouders behalen een noemenswaardig

'At most six parents will obtain any appreciable result.'

(15) a None of the other athletes was him appreciably better
*Keiner der anderen Athleten war ihm nennenswert
überlegen.*
'None of the other athletes was appreciably better than him.'

b At most seven athletes were him appreciably better
**Höchstens sieben Athleten waren ihm nennenswert
überlegen.*
'At most seven athletes were appreciably better than him.'

Similarly, the contrast between the Dutch examples in (16a) and (16b) makes it clear that, of the negative phrases *niet één rechercheur* ('not one detective') and *niet alle kruiers* ('not all porters'), only the first can act as a licencing expression for *ook maar iets*.

(16) a Not one detective will anything accomplish *Niet
bewerkstelligen.
één rechercheur zal ook maar iets*

'Not one detective will accomplish anything.'

b Not all porters will anything accomplish **Niet
bewerkstelligen.
alle kruiers zullen ook maar iets*

'Not all porters will accomplish anything.'

As a final illustration of the difference between weak and strong negation, we consider the sentences in (17).

(17) a *Niet één leerling toonde zich bijster tevreden.*
Not one student showed himself very content
'Not one student showed himself very content.'

b Only one mother shows herself very content **Slechts één
tevreden.
moeder toont zich bijster*

'Only one mother shows herself very content.'

The fact that the occurrence of *bijster* in (17b) leads to an unacceptable result entails that the negative expression *slechts één moeder* does not possess the same properties as *niet één leerling*.

Although these patterns may well seem perplexing at first, in the light of the distinction between subminimal and minimal negation they admit only one explanation: the class of expressions which are capable of licensing the occurrence of the negative polarity items *ook maar iets* and *bijster* is coextensive with the class of minimal negations. This conclusion is corroborated in a surprising manner by the findings of Hoppenbrouwers (1983: 128). From his study of the different uses of negative polarity items in Dutch, it appears that expressions such as *een snars* ('a thing'), *een zier* ('one bit') and *in de verste verte* ('in the slightest') display more or less the same characteristics as *ook maar iets* and *bijster*. As an illustration we consider the following sentences.

(18) a *Geen van de leerlingen heeft er een snars van begrepen.*
         None of the students has it a thing of understood
         'None of the students understood a thing.'

   b At most eight parents have it a thing of understood
      *Hoogstens acht ouders hebben er een snars van begrepen.
      'At most eight parents understood a thing.'

   c Not one representative will it a bit for feel *Niet één vertegenwoordiger zal er een zier voor voelen.*
      'Not one representative will at all be interested.'

   d Only four merchants will it a bit for feel **Slechts vier kooplieden zullen er een zier voor voelen.*
      'Only four merchants will at all be interested.'

   e *Niemand heeft de kinderen in de verste verte overtuigd.*
      No one has the children in the slightest convinced
      'No one has convinced the children in the slightest.'

   f Not every speech has him in the slightest convinced
      *Niet elk betoog heeft hem in de verste verte overtuigd.

'Not every speech has convinced him in the slightest.'

Despite the fact that in each of these sentences a negative subject occurs, it is only the minimal negations *geen van de leerlingen, niet één vertegenwoordiger* and *niemand* that lead to an acceptable result. In view of the lawlike character of this pattern, it is reasonable to equate the class of licencing expressions for *een snars, een zier* and *in de verste verte* with the class of minimal negations.

This state of affairs forces us to make an absolute distinction between negative polarity items of the weak type and those of the strong type. The difference finds its origin in the fact that phrases like *hoeven* and *kunnen velen* place no other restriction on the licencing expression than that it belong to the class of subminimal negations. Negative polarity items which exhibit such behavior will invariably be regarded as weak.

That this class has more members than the expressions *hoeven* and *kunnen velen* alone, is obvious from the work of Hoppenbrouwers (1983). On the basis of his findings, we must conclude that the different uses of phrases as *kunnen schelen* ('care'), *kunnen luchten of zien* ('can stand') and *laten gezeggen* ('be gainsaid') show remarkable similarities with those of *hoeven* and *kunnen velen*. In this regard, the next nine sentences speak for themselves.

(19) a   *Het kan geen van de leerlingen iets schelen.*
It   can none of   the students anything care
'None of the students cares a bit.'

b   *Weinig leerlingen kan het echt iets schelen.*
Few   students can it really anything care
'Few students really care a bit.'

c   **Het kan de meeste onderwijzers iets schelen.*
It   can most   teachers   anything care
'Most teachers care a bit.'

d   *Niet één echtgenoot kan hem luchten of zien.*
Not one spouse   can him abide
'Not one spouse can abide him.'

e   *Slechts één docente kan hem luchten of zien.*
Only   one teacher can him abide
'Only one teacher can abide him.'

f   **Sommige atleten kunnnen hem luchten of zien.*
Some   athletes can   him abide
'Some athletes can abide him.'

g *Geen van de vrouwen laat zich iets gezeggen.*
   None of the women let herself be gainsaid
   'None of the women will be gainsaid.'

h *Niet alle rechters laten zich iets gezeggen.*
   Not all judges let themselves be gainsaid
   'Not all judges will be gainsaid.'

i **De meeste kinderen laten zich iets gezeggen.*
   Most children let themselves be gainsaid
   'Most children will be gainsaid.'

From this collection of examples we may deduce that in principle every subminimal negation is capable of acting as a licencing expression for verbs such as *kunnen schelen, kunnen luchten of zien* and *laten gezeggen*. Consequently, these phrases must be regarded as negative polarity items of the weak type. In that regard, they clearly differ from expressions like *een snars, een zier* and *in de verste verte,* for these can only appear if somewhere in the sentence a minimal negation is present. This means that such constituents place significantly stronger demands on the licencing expression, which is the reason why they will henceforth be referred to as negative polarity items of the strong type.

In order to prevent losing track of these patterns, the available information has been collected in table 1. Although the stock of polarity items surely comprises more than the eighteen expressions mentioned there, it is indisputable that the distinction between weak and strong forms of negative polarity bears a lawlike character. Expressions of the first category are content with a subminimal negation as licencing element, those of the second category require the presence of a minimal negation somewhere in the sentence. It is this opposition that forms the foundation of the laws stated in (11).

Table 1: Eighteen negative polarity items in Dutch, with occasional counterparts in German or English

Weak

hoeven
(**G**: brauchen,
E: need)

kunnen velen (**E**: can abide)

kunnen uitstaan
(**E**: can stand,
G: ausstehen können)

kunnen schelen (**E**: care)

kunnen luchten of zien
(**G**: ausstehen können,
E: can stand)

laten gezeggen
(**G**: sagen lassen, **E**: be gainsaid)

een oog dichtdoen
(**G**: ein Auge zumachen,
E: sleep a wink)

een vlieg kwaad doen
(**E**: hurt a fly)

er veel mee op hebben
(**G**: viel davon halten)

Strong

ook maar iets
(**G**: auch nur irgendetwas,
E: anything (at all))

bijster (**G**: sonderlich)

een snars
(**E**: a thing)

een zier (**E**: one bit)

in de verste verte
(**G**: im entferntesten,
E: in the slightest)

noemenswaardig
(**G**: nennenswert)

een spier vertrekken
(**G**: mit der Wimper zucken,
E: bat an eyelash)

een kik geven
(**E**: utter a sound,
G: einen Mucks von sich geben)

er een vinger naar uitsteken
(**G**: einen Finger rühren,
E: lift a finger)

We must not suppose that our description exhausts the matter. The distinction between weak and strong forms of negative polarity is, as we have seen, a peculiarity which is intrinsic to the expressions in question and must therefore be accounted for in the lexicon. In particular, this entails that phrases such as *kunnen velen* and *kunnen uitstaan* are to be regarded as lexical items with respect to polarity. In that regard, they are by no means alone, for on precisely the same grounds expressions like *kunnen schelen* and *kunnen luchten of zien* must also be considered genuine lexical units. This view of the matter is, indeed, corroborated by the fact that the final verb cluster in Dutch has become petrified in a number of cases. For it is well known that verbs such as *welgevallen* ('befall'), *gezeggen* ('gainsay') and *velen* ('abide') can only occur in the infinitival form, as shown by the examples in (20).

(20) a *U   stelt dat sommigen anderen niet kunnen velen.*
        You state that some   others   not can   abide
        'You state that some cannot abide others.'

   b *Zij   ontkennen dat hij zich   niets laat gezeggen.*
      They   deny   that he himself not   let be gainsaid
      'They deny that he will not be gainsaid.'

   c *U   zegt dat Ot zich   het vonnis liet welgevallen.*
      You say that Ot himself the verdict let befall
      'You say that Ot let the verdict befall to him.'

Not only are such sentences incompatible with the notion of V-Raising, originally defended in Evers (1975), but they also show that the behavior of the Dutch verb cluster is in many cases purely lexically determined. It turns out that this is an important observation, among other things, because it suggests a lexicalist solution to the problem of the Dutch verb cluster – a possibility which is also mentioned in Pullum and Gazdar (1982: 501).[10]

Besides the two types of negative polarity discussed so far, there exists a third type which we will refer to as *superstrong* polarity. Elements belonging to this class include the English expression *one bit* and the Dutch adjective *mals* 'tender'. As the ungrammatical examples in (21) and (22) show, such phrases are not content with a subminimal or minimal negation. Instead, they require the presence of the negative adverb *not* (**D**: *niet*) somewhere in the sentence.[11]

(21) a *Few people were one bit happy about these facts.

   b *No linguist was one bit happy about these facts.

   c The men weren't one bit happy about these facts.

(22) a **Weinig van zijn oordelen waren mals.*
        Few   of   his opinions were   tender
        'Few of his opinions were soft.'

   b **Niet één van zijn oordelen was mals.*
      Not one of his opinions was tender
      'Not one of his opinions was soft.'

c *Zijn oordelen waren vaak niet mals.*
   His opinions were often not tender
   'His opinions often weren't soft.'

In terms of the hierarchy of negation expressions, the restrictions on the occurrence of phrases like *one bit* may be described as showing that superstrong polarity items require the presence of an expression of classical negation. Consequently, the laws which govern the occurrence of negative polarity items should be modified as follows.

(23) **Laws of negative polarity**

a Only sentences in which an expression of subminimal negation occurs, can contain a negative polarity item of the weak type.

b Only sentences in which an expression of minimal negation occurs, can contain a negative polarity item of the strong type.

c Only sentences in which an expression of classical negation occurs, can contain a negative polarity item of the superstrong type.

According to the third law, the presence of a classical negation is a necessary condition for the appearance of superstrong polarity items. To forestall any misunderstanding, we note that every expression of classical negation is also an expression of minimal negation.

The remainder of this article can be summarized as follows. In sections 2, 3, 4 and 5, we expound the distinction between subminimal, minimal and classical negation, using the algebraic notions of a monotonic quantifier, a quasi-filter, a quasi-ideal, an ultrafilter and a prime ideal. Section 6 introduces the corresponding functional perspective and discusses in these terms the notion of a monotonic function. Anti-additive and antimorphic functions are discussed in section 7. Finally, in section 8, the laws governing the use of negative polarity items are formulated.

2. TWO TYPES OF MONOTONICITY

In order to get a clear view of the distinction between subminimal and minimal negation, one does well to take the following example into consideration.

(24) At most one villager sang.

At most one villager sang loudly.

Provided that the predicate *sang loudly* applies only to what the predicate *sang* also applies to, the conditional in (24) must be regarded as true. To put it another way, if the state of affairs in the universe is such that the class of individuals who sang loudly is a subset of the class of individuals who sang, then we may legitimately pass from the proposition *At most one villager sang* to *At most one villager sang loudly*. Clearly, this raises the question of how to account for such inferences.

We assume that each verb phrase will receive a subset of some universe U as its semantic value. Such a way of portraying the matter entails that the universe of possible denotations of verb phrases may henceforth be equated with $P(U)$ – that is, the first power set of U. Since the collection $P(U)$ with the usual set-theoretical operations of union, intersection, and complementation can be regarded as a Boolean algebra, we shall from now on speak of the **algebra of verb phrases**.[12] We assume as well that each noun phrase receives a collection of subsets of U as its semantic value. This implies that the universe of possible denotations of noun phrases may be equated with $P(P(U))$ – that is to say, the second power set of U. Since this set also displays the characteristic features of a Boolean algebra, it is said to be the **algebra of noun phrases**.

The algebraic nature of the categories NP and VP enables us to give a precise formulation of a notion which is frequently used in the linguistic literature – to wit, that of a quantifier. Henceforth, what is meant by **a quantifier on a Boolean algebra B** is simply a subset of B. Such a definition immediately explains why it is natural to regard noun phrases as quantifiers. For if these expressions receive a collection of subsets of U as their semantic value, they can semantically be equated with a subset of $P(U)$ – that is to say, with a subset of the algebra of verb phrases. However, this entails that noun phrases could just as well be regarded as quantifiers on the algebra of verb phrases.

It is now possible to say how the interpretation of an expression like *at most one villager* differs from that of other noun phrases. For it is easily seen that each set which contains at most one villager, is a member of the quantifier associated with the expression *at most one villager*. This turns out to be important because it entails that the quantifier in question has the property that the conditions $X \in Q$ and $Y \subseteq X \subseteq U$ imply $Y \in Q$. Such quantifiers are commonly referred to as **monotone decreasing quantifiers**.[13] For the sake of clarity we record this in the form of a definition.

(25) **Definition**

Let B be a Boolean algebra. A quantifier Q on B is said to be **monotone decreasing** iff for each two elements X and Y of the algebra B:

if $X \in Q$ and $Y \subseteq X$, then $Y \in Q$.

Noun phrases which invariably receive a monotone decreasing quantifier on the VP-algebra as their semantic value will henceforth be called monotone decreasing noun phrases.

From the fact that the conditional in (24) is valid when the predicate *sang* is true of whatever the predicate *sang loudly* is true of, it follows immediately that noun phrases of the form *at most n N* are monotone decreasing. Similarly, one easily proves that expressions of the forms *not every N*, *no N*, *neither N* and *none of the n N* also have the property of downward monotonicity. For if the predicate *ate fish* only applies to what the predicate *ate* also applies to, then the conditionals in (26) are all valid.

(26) a   Not every clergymen ate   →   Not every clergymen ate fish
     b   No federal attorney ate   →   No federal attorney ate fish
     c   Neither connoisseur ate   →   Neither connoisseur ate fish
     d   None of the six men ate   →   None of the six men ate fish

Meanwhile, the suspicion arises that noun phrases of the monotone decreasing type have a counterpart. It turns out that this is indeed the case. To pave the way, we begin by considering an example.

(27) At least one villager sang loudly   →   At least one villager sang

Provided that the predicate *sang* applies to whatever the predicate *sang loudly* applies to, the conditional in (27) must be accounted true. In other words, if the state of affairs in the universe is such that the class of individuals who sang loudly is a subset of the class of individuals who sang, then we may legitimately pass from the proposition *At least one villager sang loudly* to *At least one villager sang*. What this means, is that the quantifier associated with the expression *at least one villager* has the property of being closed under extension: if $X \in Q$ and $X \subseteq Y \subseteq U$, then $Y \in Q$. Such quantifiers are usually called **monotone increasing quantifiers**. For the sake of clarity we give the following definition.

(28) **Definition**

Let B be a Boolean algebra. A quantifier Q on B is said to be **monotone increasing** iff for each two elements X and Y of the algebra B:

if $X \in Q$ and $X \subseteq Y$, then $Y \in Q$.

Noun phrases which invariably receive a monotone increasing quantifier as their semantic value, will accordingly be referred to as monotone increasing noun phrases.

From the fact that the conditional in (27) is valid when the predicate *sang loudly* applies only to what the predicate *sang* also applies to, it follows immediately that noun phrases of the form *at least n N* are monotone increasing. In an analogous manner, one easily proves that expressions of the forms *some N, all N, the n N* and *both N* are also endowed with the property of upward monotonicity. For if the predicate *ate* is true of whatever the predicate *ate fish* is true of, then the entailments in (29) are all valid.

(29)   a Some porters ate fish → Some porters ate
     b All children ate fish → All children ate
     c The six nuns ate fish → The six nuns ate
     d Both lawyers ate fish → Both lawyers ate

On the basis of such tests, one can usually arrive at rather trustworthy judgments concerning the presence of monotonicity properties. For the sake of clarity, the outcomes of these tests have been collected in table 2. The forty-four classes of noun phrases mentioned there must all be regarded as being either upward or downward monotonic. Do not suppose that this exhausts the matter, for a more accurate analysis shows that there are several alternative ways to determine whether a given noun phrase possesses the property of downward monotonicity. This turns out to be a consequence of the fact that monotone decreasing quantifiers can be given a number of equivalent characterizations. The next theorem provides the details.

Table 2: Forty-four monotonic noun phrases, with their Dutch counterparts

Monotone increasing

every N (**D**: ieder(e) N)
all N (**D**: alle N)
each N (**D**: elk(e) N)
some N (**D**: sommige N)
sm N (**D**: enkele N)[14]
nearly all N (**D**: vrijwel alle N)
both N (**D**: beide N)
at least n N (**D**: minstens n N)
many N (**D**: veel N)
several N (**D**: verscheidene N)
more than n N
(**D**: meer dan n N)
the n N
(**D**: de n N)
the more than n N
(**D**: de meer dan n N)
the N [pl]
(**D**: de N [pl])
the N [sg]
(**D**: de N [sg])
most N (**D**: de meeste N)
everything (**D**: alles)
something (**D**: iets)
everyone (**D**: iedereen)
someone (**D**: iemand)
not only NP (**D**: niet alleen NP)
proper names

Monotone decreasing

not every N (**D**: niet ieder(e) N)
not all N (**D**: niet alle N)
not each N (**D**: niet elk(e) N)
no N (**D**: geen N)
only a few N (**D**: slechts enkele N)
almost no N (**D**: vrijwel geen N)
neither N (**D**: geen van beide N)
at most n N (**D**: hoogstens n N)
few N (**D**: weinig N)
only n N (**D**: slechts n N)
no more than n N
(**D**: niet meer dan n N)
none of the n N
(**D**: geen van de n N)
none of the more than n N
(**D**: geen van de meer dan n N)
none of the N
(**D**: geen van de N)
not a single N
(**D**: geen enkel(e) N)
not one N (**D**: niet één N)
not everything (**D**: niet alles)
nothing (**D**: niets)
not everyone (**D**: niet iedereen)
no one (**D**: niemand)
only NP (**D**: alleen NP)
negated proper names

(30) **Theorem**

Let B be a Boolean algebra. The following three statements about a quantifier Q on B are equivalent:

(a) Q is monotone decreasing;
(b) if $X \cup Y \in Q$ then $X \in Q$ and $Y \in Q$;
(c) if $X \in Q$ or $Y \in Q$, then $X \cap Y \in Q$.

With the aid of this result, one can give a precise account of the conditions which have to be fulfilled, if an expression is to be counted as belonging to the class of monotone decreasing noun phrases. The corollary below provides us with the relevant information.

(31) **Corollary**

A noun phrase is monotone decreasing iff the following schemata are logically valid:

(a) NP (VP$_1$ or VP$_2$) → (NP VP$_1$ and NP VP$_2$);
(b) (NP VP$_1$ or NP VP$_2$) → NP (VP$_1$ and VP$_2$).

The significance of these two schemata lies in the fact that each of them gives us both a positive and a negative test for downward monotonicity. Put differently, if one of the two schemata is valid, then the other is valid as well and, therefore, the noun phrase in question must be regarded as being monotone decreasing. If, however, one of the two schemata is invalid, then the other is invalid as well and, consequently, the relevant noun phrase does not possess the property of downward monotonicity. By way of illustration we consider some examples. It is clear, for instance, that the conditionals in (32) and (33) are both valid – a state of affairs which admits no other explanation than that expressions of the forms *few N* and *only NP* belong to the class of monotone decreasing noun phrases.

(32) Few hangmen complained or resisted →

Few hangmen complained and few hangmen resisted

(33) Only judges resign or only judges get strangled →

Only judges resign and get strangled

However, if we consider the conditionals in (34) and (35), then it is immediately clear that neither can be accepted as valid.

(34) More than nine nuns prayed or knelt $\not\to$
More than nine nuns prayed and more than nine nuns knelt

(35) More men than women escaped or died $\not\to$
More men than women escaped and more men than women died

For even though there may be more than nine nuns who prayed, there need not be any who knelt, in which case the antecedent of the conditional in (34) is true, but its consequent false. In an analogous manner, it is easily shown that the conditional in (35) is invalid. For if two man escaped and one woman died, then the antecedent is true, but the consequent false. We must therefore conclude that noun phrases of the forms *more than n N* and *more N_1 than N_2* are not monotone decreasing.

It should be pointed out in this connection that the class of monotone increasing quantifiers can be characterized in several alternative ways. In order to convince ourselves of this fact, we consider the following theorem.

(36) **Theorem**

Let B be a Boolean algebra. The following three statements about a quantifier Q on B are equivalent:

(a) Q is monotone increasing;
(b) if $X \cap Y \in Q$, then $X \in Q$ and $Y \in Q$;
(c) if $X \in Q$ or $Y \in Q$, then $X \cup Y \in Q$.

In this case, too, we can give a precise specification of the conditions which have to be fulfilled, if an expression is to be regarded as a monotone increasing noun phrase. The next corollary provides the necessary details.

(37) **Corollary**

A noun phrase is monotone increasing iff the following schemata are logically valid:

(a) NP (VP_1 and VP_2) $\to$ (NP VP_1 and NP VP_2);
(b) (NP VP_1 or NP VP_2) $\to$ NP (VP_1 or VP_2).

It is easy to see that each of the two schemata gives us both a positive and a negative test for upward monotonicity. As an illustration we note that the conditionals in (38) and (39) are both valid – a circumstance which, in view of the above result, admits of no other explanation than that proper names and definite descriptions are both monotone increasing.

(38) Jonathan called and begged →
Jonathan called and Jonathan begged

(39) The girl sighed or the girl coughed →
The girl sighed or coughed

On the other hand, if we take the conditionals in (40) and (41) into consideration, then it is immediately clear that neither can be regarded as valid.

(40) No fireman said good-bye and left ↛
No fireman said good-bye and no fireman left

(41) Only women got whipped or only women starved ↛
Only women got whipped or starved

For if there are precisely two firemen, one of whom said good-bye without leaving and one of whom left without saying goodbye, then the antecedent of the conditional in (40) is true, but its consequent false. In an analogous manner, one easily proves that the conditional in (41) is invalid as well. For if those who got whipped can all be regarded as being women, whereas those who starved not only include women, but also men, then the antecedent is true and the consequent false. This state of affairs leads to the conclusion that noun phrases of the forms *no N* and *only NP* are not monotone increasing.

3. QUASI-IDEALS AND QUASI-FILTERS

It would be wrong to suppose that a logical analysis of some depth can confine itself to the distinction between upward and downward monotonic noun phrases. A more accurate inspection shows that the members of each of these two classes exhibit substantial differences. In order to convince ourselves of this, we consider two examples.

(42) No flower will dry up or will fade →
No flower will dry up and no flower will fade

(43) No flower will dry up and no flower will fade →
No flower will dry up or will fade

It is clear that the validity of the conditional in (42) is a consequence of the monotone decreasing nature of the expression *no flower*. This explanation does not hold, however, for the reverse proposition in (43). The fact that we have again a valid implication, must instead be attributed to the circumstance that the monotone decreasing quantifier which is associated with *no flower*, is in addition closed under (finite) unions. Such quantifiers will henceforth be called quasi-ideals.[15] More precisely:

(44) **Definition**

Let B be a Boolean algebra. A quantifier Q on B is said to be a **quasi-ideal** iff for each two elements X and Y of the algebra B:

(a) if $X \cup Y \in Q$, then $X \in Q$ and $Y \in Q$;

(b) if $X \in Q$ and $Y \in Q$, then $X \cup Y \in Q$.

Noun phrases which invariably receive a quasi-ideal on the VP-algebra as their semantic value, will accordingly be referred to as quasi-ideals.

From the fact that the conditionals in (42) and (43) are both valid, it follows immediately that expressions of the form *no N* must be regarded as quasi-ideals. This is not to say that the property in question cannot be expressed in a different way. For it is well known that two conditionals, one of which is the reverse of the other, may be replaced equivalently by a biconditional – a state of affairs which entails that, as a proof of *no flower*'s being a quasi-ideal, we may as well point to the validity of the proposition in (45).

(45) No flower will dry up or will fade ↔

No flower will dry up and no flower will fade

In view of this, it need not surprise us that, as an immediate corollary to the definition in (44), we have the result below.

(46) **Corollary**

A noun phrase is a quasi-ideal iff the following schema is logically valid:

NP (VP$_1$ or VP$_2$) ↔ (NP VP$_1$ and NP VP$_2$).

With the aid of this test, it is easily shown that expressions of the forms *neither N* and *none of the N* are also to be regarded as quasi-ideals. To that end, it is sufficient to take the biconditionals in (47) and (48) into consideration.

(47) Neither musician laughs or coughs ↔

Neither musician laughs and neither musician coughs

(48) None of the boys scoffs or curses ↔

None of the boys scoffs and none of the boys curses

That both of these sentences have a valid character entails that the monotone decreasing quantifier which is associated with the subject, is in addition closed under (finite) unions. In other words, the two noun phrases in (47) and (48) act semantically as quasi-ideals.

Meanwhile, the suspicion arises that the notion of a quasi-ideal also has a counterpart. This is indeed the case. By way of illustration, we consider the following two conditionals.

(49) All monks rob and kill →

All monks rob and all monks kill

(50) All monks rob and all monks kill →

All monks rob and kill

There is no doubt that the validity of the conditional in (49) must be attributed to the monotone increasing nature of the expression *all monks*. This is not the case with the reverse proposition in (50). The fact that we have again a valid entailment, must instead be attributed to the circumstance that the monotone increasing quantifier which acts as the denotation of *all monks*, is also closed under (finite) intersections. Such quantifiers will henceforth be referred to as **quasi-filters** – a term which may not be customary within the theory of Boolean algebras, but which has gained some currency in modal logic.[16] For the sake of clarity we record this in the form of a definition.

(51) **Definition**

Let B be a Boolean algebra. A quantifier Q on B is said to be a **quasi-filter** iff for each two elements X and Y of the algebra B:

(a) if $X \cap Y \in Q$, then $X \in Q$ and $Y \in Q$;

(b) if $X \in Q$ and $Y \in Q$, then $X \cap Y \in Q$.

Noun phrases which are invariably interpreted by means of a quasi-filter on the VP-algebra, will accordingly be called quasi-filters.

The validity of the conditionals in (49) and (50) makes it clear that expressions of the form *all N* are to be regarded as quasi-filters. This is not to say that the property in question cannot manifest itself in a different way. The fact that (50) is the reverse of (49) entails that, as a proof of *all monks'* being a quasi-filter, we might as well have pointed to the validity of the biconditional in (52).

(52) All monks rob and kill ↔

   All monks rob and all monks kill

Once again, then, it need not surprise us that, as an immediate consequence of the definition in (51), we have the corollary below.

(53) **Corollary**

   A noun phrase is a quasi-filter iff the following schema is logically valid:

   NP (VP$_1$ and VP$_2$) ↔ (NP VP$_1$ and NP VP$_2$).

With the aid of this test, one can easily show that proper names and expressions of the form *the n N* also display the characteristic features of quasi-filters. To that end it is sufficient to take the biconditionals in (54) and (55) into consideration.

(54) Themistocles mourns and moans ↔

   Themistocles mourns and Themistocles moans

(55) The nine men grieve and whine ↔

   The nine men grieve and the nine men whine

The fact that each of these biconditionals is valid admits no other explanation than that the monotone increasing quantifier associated with the subject is in addition closed under (finite) intersections. In other words, the two noun phrases in (54) and (55) semantically act as quasi-filters.

We must not suppose that every monotone increasing quantifier is a quasi-filter. Surely not, for a short inspection reveals numerous cases in which the entailment NP (VP$_1$ and VP$_2$) → (NP VP$_1$ and NP VP$_2$) is valid, but its reverse is not. The next two conditionals serve as an illustration.

(56) Some fishermen waved and called →

   Some fishermen waved and some fishermen called

(57) Some fishermen waved and some fishermen called $\not\to$

Some fishermen waved and called

Evidently, it follows from the monotone increasing nature of the noun phrase *some fishermen* that the conditional in (56) must be accepted as valid. On the other hand, we are by no means justified in passing from the proposition *Some fishermen waved and some fishermen called* to *Some fishermen waved and called*. For if there are two fishermen who waved and two other fishermen who called, then the antecedent of the implication in (57) is true, but its consequent false. This shows that expressions of the form *some N* cannot be regarded as quasi-filters.

By means of a parallel argument it is easily established that not every monotone decreasing quantifier can be classified as a quasi-ideal. Indeed, there are situations in which the conditional NP (VP$_1$ or VP$_2$) → (NP VP$_1$ and NP VP$_2$) is valid, but its reverse is not. The next two sentences are good examples of what we have in mind.

(58) Not all knights rob or kill $\to$

Not all knights rob and not all knights kill

(59) Not all knights rob and not all knights kill $\to$

Not all knights rob or kill

It is clear that the conditional in (58) must be accepted as valid in virtue of the downward monotonic nature of the expression *not all knights*. On the other hand, one cannot legitimately pass from the proposition *Not all knights rob and not all knights kill* to *Not all knights rob or kill*. For if the class of knights is such that one half robs and the other half kills, then the antecedent of the conditional in (59) is true, but its consequent false. This suffices to establish that expressions of the form *not all N* are not quasi-ideals.

On the basis of the available tests, we can usually arrive at rather trustworthy judgments when we must decide whether a given monotonic noun phrase is either a quasi-filter or a quasi-ideal. For ease of survey, the outcomes of these tests have been collected in table 3. The twenty-two classes of noun phrases which are mentioned there must all be regarded as being either quasi-filters or quasi-ideals.

Table 3: Twenty-two classes of quasi-filters and quasi-ideals, with their Dutch counterparts

Quasi-filters

every N (**D**: ieder(e) N)
all N (**D**: alle N)
each N (**D**: elk(e) N)
both N
(**D**: beide N)
the n N (**D**: de n N)
the more than n N
(**D**: de meer dan n N)
the N [pl] (**D**: de N [pl])
the N [sg] (**D**: de N [sg])
everything (**D**: alles)
everyone (**D**: iedereen)
proper names

Quasi-ideals

no N (**D**: geen N)
neither N (**D**: geen van beide N)
none of the N (**D**: geen van de N)
none of the more than n N
(**D**: geen van de meer dan n N)
none of the N (**D**: geen van de N)
not a single N
(**D**: geen enkel(e) N)
not one N (**D**: niet één N)
nothing (**D**: niets)
no one (**D**: niemand)
only NP (**D**: alleen NP)
negated proper names

4. CONSISTENCY AND COMPLETENESS

It is well-known that there are considerable differences between sentential negation, on the one hand, and predicate negation, on the other. Less known is the fact that the logical relationship between both forms of negation depends entirely on the semantical nature of the subject. In order to convince ourselves, we do well to take the following two examples into consideration.

(60) At least two willows do not flower →

It is not the case that at least two willows flower

(61) Most weeping willows do not flower →

It is not the case that most weeping willows flower

One sees immediately that the conditional in (60) cannot be regarded as valid. For if the state of affairs is such that of the seven willows only four happen to flower, then the antecedent is true, but the consequent false. On the other hand, it is evident that the conditional in (61) must be accepted as valid. If we are willing to accept the truth of the statement *Most weeping willows do not flower*, then we shall also have to acknowledge that it is not the case that the majority of weeping willows flowers. What this means is that the quantifier associated with the noun phrase *most weeping willows* is invariably **consistent** in nature — consistent in the sense that it cannot contain a given set of individuals as well as the complement of that set. For the sake of clarity we give the following definition.[17]

(62) **Definition**

Let B be a Boolean algebra. A quantifier Q on B is said to be **consistent** iff for each element X of the algebra B:

if $-X \in Q$, then $X \notin Q$.

Noun phrases which invariably receive a consistent quantifier as their semantic value, will accordingly be referred to as consistent noun phrases.

The property of consistency can be formulated in more than one way. Indeed, it is readily established that the law of contraposition allows us to replace the definition in (62) by the alternative characterization in (63).

(63) **Definition**

Let B be a Boolean algebra. A quantifier Q on B is said to be **consistent** iff for each element X of the algebra B:

if $X \in Q$, then $-X \notin Q$.

In spite of this equivalence, we prefer the definition in (62), primarily because it affords us a handy way of establishing the corollary below.

(64) **Corollary**

A noun phrase is consistent iff the following schema is logically valid:

(1) NP (NEG VP) → NEG (NP VP)

This simple result is important, because it clearly shows that with a consistent noun phrase as subject the use of predicate negation invariably entails sentence negation.

From the fact that the implication in (61b) is valid, it follows immediately that noun phrases of the form *most N* are consistent. Do not suppose that this exhausts the matter, for one easily proves that proper names and expressions of the forms *both N*, *the n N*, *the N [sg]* and *the N [pl]* must also be regarded as belonging to the class of consistent noun phrases. In the following examples, the use of predicate negation invariably entails sentence negation.

(65) a Themistocles does not mourn →
It is not the case that Themistocles mourns

 b Both feet are not ulcerated →
It is not the case that both feet are ulcerated

 c The seventeen donkeys do not bray →
It is not the case that the seventeen donkeys bray

 d The scientists do not drink coffee →
It is not the case that the scientists drink coffee

 e The shopkeeper does not waste time →
It is not the case that the shopkeeper wastes time

Similarly, one easily shows that expressions of the forms *neither N*, *none of the n N* and *none of the N* are also consistent in nature. To this end, it is enough to take the conditionals in (66) into consideration.

(66) a None of the six donkeys does not bray →
It is not the case that none of the six donkeys brays

 b Neither foot is not ulcerated →
It is not the case that neither foot is ulcerated

 c None of the scientists does not waste time →
It is not the case that none of the scientists wastes time

That each of these entailments is valid, follows from the definitions of the quantifiers corresponding to the noun phrases in question. To give an example, if none of the scientists does not waste time, then it follows that they all waste time, which in turn means that it is not the case that none of them wastes time. Consequently, the conditional in (66c) must be accepted as valid.

The foregoing observations by no means imply that every noun phrase is consistent. The invalid implication in (60) clearly shows that expressions of the form *at least n N* do not belong to this class. In an analogous manner, one easily proves that noun phrases of the forms *all N* and *no N* also cannot be regarded as consistent. The next two examples, if interpreted as cases of regular negation, are both invalid.

(67) All students do not complain ↛
It is not the case that all students complain

(68) No child does not complain ↛
It is not the case that no child complains

By way of illustration, it should be noted that, when the universe does not contain any child, the statements *No child complains* and *No child does not complain* are both true, which means that the denial *It is not the case that no child complains* must be regarded as false. Similarly, if the universe happens to lack students, the two statements *All students complain* and *All students do not complain* must both be accepted as true, and hence the denial *It is not the case that all students complain* must be rejected as false.

In this connection, the behavior of partitive noun phrases is rather interesting. It requires no lengthy reflection to see that expressions of the form *at least n of the k N* are consistent iff $n > k/2$. As a special case of the general pattern we have the valid conditional in (69).

(69) At least three of the four children do not complain →
It is not the case that at least three of the four children complain

On the other hand, if we consider expressions of the form *(exactly) n of the k N*, then the property of consistency appears to manifest itself just in case $n \neq k/2$. That is to say:

(70) Six of the eight children do not complain →
It is not the case that six of the eight children complain

(71) One of the eight children does not complain →
It is not the case that one of the eight children complains

Finally, it should be easy to see that noun phrases of the form *at most n of the k N* are consistent only if $n < k/2$. In other words:

(72) At most one of the four children does not complain →
It is not the case that at most one of the four children complains

The logical behavior of partitive expressions thus appears to show some regularities. These find expression in three general laws concerning the phenomenon of consistency.

(73) **Laws of consistency for partitive expressions**

   (1) Expressions of the form *at least n of the k N* are consistent iff $n > k/2$.

   (2) Expressions of the form *(exactly) n of the k N* are consistent iff $n \neq k/2$.

   (3) Expressions of the form *at most n of the k N* are consistent iff $n < k/2$.

We must therefore conclude that, with a substantial number of partitive subject phrases, the use of predicate negation implies sentence negation.

With the aid of the foregoing test we can usually arrive at rather trustworthy judgments when it comes to deciding whether a given noun phrase does or does not enjoy the property of consistency. For the sake of clarity the outcomes of the test have been collected in table 4. The eighteen classes of noun phrases mentioned there must all be regarded as consistent. Such a catalogue, though at first sight merely of encyclopedic value, is important because we shall soon see that it leads to a coherent and complete account of the relationship between sentence negation and predicate negation.

Table 4: Eighteen classes of consistent noun phrases

most N	the N [sg]
the majority of the N	the N [pl]
at least n of the k N $(n > k/2)$	neither N
(exactly) n of the k N $(n \neq k/2)$	none of the n N $(n > 0)$
at most n of the k N $(n < k/2)$	none of the more than n N $(n > 0)$
both N	none of the no more than n N $(n > 0)$
the n N $(n > 0)$	none of the N
the more than n N $(n > 0)$	proper names
the no more than n N $(n > 0)$	negated proper names

It should be pointed out in this connection that the property of consistency shows a striking resemblance to the logical theorem known as **the law of contradiction**. Indeed, the principle in question is meant to exclude the possibility that two contradictory propositions are both accepted as true. For that reason it is usually stated as '$\sim (p \wedge \sim p)$'.

One sees immediately that the property of consistency is similar to the logical theorem in that it excludes that two sets X and $-X$ both belong to the quantifier. It will become apparent that this state of affairs has far-reaching consequences for our views on the different forms of negation.

It requires little reflection to realize that the property of consistency has a counterpart. In order to convince ourselves, we take the following two examples into account.

(74)   It is not the case that most tulips flower $\not\rightarrow$

Most tulips do not flower

(75)   It is not the case that Seneca plays chess $\rightarrow$

Seneca does not play chess

Clearly, the conditional in (74) cannot be regarded as valid. For if the state of affairs in the universe is such that half of all tulips flowers, then the antecedent is true, but the consequent false. On the other hand, the conditional sentence in (75) surely belongs to the class of valid statements. If we accept the truth of the statement *It is not the case that Seneca plays chess*, then we will also have to accept that Seneca does not play chess. This entails that the quantifiers which are associated with proper names invariably are complete in nature – complete in the sense that it cannot be that neither the complement of a given set nor that set itself is a member of the quantifier in question. For the sake of accuracy we record this in the form of a definition.[18]

(76)   **Definition**

Let B be a Boolean algebra. A quantifier Q on B is said to be **complete** iff for each element X of the algebra B:

if $X \notin Q$, then $-X \in Q$.

It is evident that the notion of completeness just introduced is the reversal of the notion of consistency mentioned before. This means that there are alternative characterizations of the property in question. Indeed, it is easily established that the law of contraposition allows us to replace the conditional in (76) by the equivalent statement 'if $-X \notin Q$, then $X \in Q$'. Yet, we shall stick to the original definition, primarily because of the following corollary.

(77) **Corollary**

A noun phrase is complete iff the following schema is logically valid:

(1) NEG (NP VP) → NP (NEG VP)

This elementary result is important because it expresses in a lucid way that with a complete noun phrase as subject the use of sentence negation invariably implies predicate negation.

From the fact that the implication in (75) is valid, it follows immediately that proper names are complete. In an analogous way, one easily shows that negated proper names are also complete in nature. This does not exhaust the stock, for a short search produces several other cases of completeness. The next two examples serve as an illustration.

(78) a It is not the case that at least half of all tulips flowers →
       At least half of all tulips does not flower
    b It is not the case that at most half of all cows has died →
       At most half of all cows has not died

There can be no doubt that both conditionals are valid. Indeed, if we accept the truth of the statement *It is not the case that at least half of all tulips flowers*, then we shall also have to accept that at least half of all tulips does not flower. Similarly, it is easily established that anyone who accepts the statement *It is not the case that at most half of all cows has died* as true will also be committed to the truth of *At most half of all cows has not died*. Consequently, we must conclude that noun phrases of the forms *at least half of all N* and *at most half of all N* both belong to the class of complete expressions.

For the sake of clarity, these results have been collected in table 5.

Table 5: Four classes of complete noun phrases

at least half of all N	at most half of all N
proper names	negated proper names

One sees immediately that two of the four classes of noun phrases mentioned are also consistent, namely proper names and their negations. This is important, because it follows from the relevant definitions that with a consistent and complete noun phrase as subject the use of sentence negation is equivalent to predicate negation. For that reason, the biconditional in (79) must be regarded as valid.

(79) It is not the case that Themistocles mourns ↔
Themistocles does not mourn

Indeed, it follows from the completeness of the expression *Themistocles* that the use of sentence negation entails predicate negation. Conversely, the consistent nature of the element in question guarantees that the use of predicate negation implies sentence negation. In this way, we can give a semantic explanation of the at first sight rather intricate relationship between both forms of negation.

It should be noted that the property of completeness bears a close relationship to the familiar logical theorem known as **the law of the excluded middle**. This principle is meant to exclude the possibility that two contradictory propositions are both rejected as false. For that reason it is usually stated as '$p \vee \sim p$'. One sees immediately that the property of completeness is similar to the logical theorem in that it excludes that two sets X and $-X$ both do not belong to the quantifier.

In terms of the properties of consistency and completeness, the relationship between sentence negation and predicate negation can be described adequately. To forestall any misunderstandings, we do well to express this in the form of two general laws concerning the use of both forms of negation.

(80) **Laws of negation**

a The use of sentence negation implies predicate negation just in case the subject of the sentence is complete in nature.

b The use of predicate negation implies sentence negation just in case the subject of the sentence is consistent in nature.

It goes without saying that, in the presence of a subject which is complete *and* consistent, the use of sentence negation is equivalent to predicate negation.

5. PRIME IDEALS AND ULTRAFILTERS

Among the noun phrases that are both consistent and complete, there are some which have the structure of a quasi-ideal. Such quantifiers are usually referred to as **prime ideals** or **maximal ideals**.[19] To be more precise:

(81) **Definition**

Let B be a Boolean algebra. A quantifier Q on B is said to be a **prime ideal** (**maximal ideal**) iff for each two elements X and Y of the algebra B:

(a) $X \cup Y \in Q$ iff $X \in Q$ and $Y \in Q$;

(b) $X \in Q$ iff $-X \notin Q$.

It turns out that the only noun phrases which invariably receive a prime ideal as their semantic value are negated proper names. Expressions of this type will accordingly be called prime ideals.

As an immediate corollary to the definition in (81), we have the following theorem.

(82) **Theorem**

Let B be a Boolean algebra and let Q be a quantifier on B. If Q is a prime ideal, then for each two elements X and Y of the algebra B:

$X \cap Y \in Q$ iff $X \in Q$ or $Y \in Q$.

With the aid of this result, one easily shows that the validity of the schema in (83) is necessary in order that a noun phrase be classified as belonging to the class of prime ideals.

(83) **Corollary**

If a noun phrase is a prime ideal, then the following schema is logically valid:

NP (VP$_1$ and VP$_2$) ↔ (NP VP$_1$ or NP VP$_2$).

It is clear that negated proper names act in accordance with the above test. To see this it is sufficient to take the following example into consideration.

(84) Not Themistocles mourns and moans ↔

Not Themistocles mourns or not Themistocles moans

That the biconditional in (84) must be regarded as valid is a consequence of the fact that the quantifier associated with the negated proper name *not Themistocles* has the structure of a prime ideal.

Among the noun phrases that are both consistent and complete, there are also some which have the structure of a quasi-filter. It is customary to refer to such quantifiers as **ultrafilters** or **maximal filters**.[20] That is to say:

(85) **Definition**

Let B be a Boolean algebra. A quantifier Q on B is said to be an **ultrafilter** (**maximal filter**) iff for each two elements X and Y of the algebra B:

(a) $X \cap Y \in Q$ iff $X \in Q$ and $Y \in Q$;

(b) $X \in Q$ iff $-X \notin Q$.

The only noun phrases which are invariably associated with a quantifier that has the structure of an ultrafilter are proper names. Expressions of this type will accordingly be called ultrafilters.

As an immediate corollary to the definition in (85), we have the following theorem.

(86) **Theorem**

Let B be a Boolean algebra and let Q be a quantifier on B. If Q is an ultrafilter, then for each two elements X and Y of the algebra B:

$X \cup Y \in Q$ iff $X \in Q$ or $Y \in Q$.

With the aid of this result, one easily shows that the validity of the schema in (87) is necessary in order that a noun phrase be classified as belonging to the class of ultrafilters.

(87) **Corollary**

If a noun phrase is an ultrafilter, then the following schema is logically valid:

NP (VP$_1$ or VP$_2$) $\leftrightarrow$ (NP VP$_1$ or NP VP$_2$).

It is clear that proper names act in accordance with the above test. To see this it is enough to take the following example into consideration.

(88) Themistocles mourns or moans $\qquad\qquad\qquad\leftrightarrow$

Themistocles mourns or Themistocles moans

That the biconditional in (88) must be regarded as valid is a consequence of the fact that the quantifier associated with the proper name *Themistocles* has the structure of an ultrafilter.

6. MONOTONIC FUNCTIONS

Thus far we have assumed that noun phrases must be regarded as quantifiers on the algebra of verb phrases. It is conceivable, however, that the semantic value assigned to expressions of this type is not a quantifier, but rather the characteristic function of a quantifier. Such a conceptual change immediately raises the question to what extent the usual notion of a function lends itself to the classifications discussed above. Surprisingly, this matter appears not to be as complex as one might at first expect. Let us begin by considering the special case of upward monotonicity. The fact that quantifiers of this type are closed under extension, entails that the associated characteristic function is such that assignment of the value 1 to an element X is invariably accompanied with assignment of the value 1 to each element Y which contains X. Put differently, if Q is a monotone increasing quantifier on the algebra of verb phrases, then its characteristic function $K_Q : P(U) \to 2$ has the property that the conditions $X \subseteq Y$ and $K_Q(X) = 1$ imply $K_Q(Y) = 1$. Do not suppose that this exhausts the matter, for in view of the composition of the Boolean algebra 2 it should be obvious that what the property in question amounts to is that whenever X is contained in Y, $K_Q(X)$ is contained in $K_Q(Y)$.[21] This state of affairs leads to the conclusion that, in general, a function f from a Boolean algebra B to a Boolean algebra B^* can be regarded as monotone increasing, just in case it preserves the inclusion relation. That is to say:

(89) **Definition**

Let B and B^* be two Boolean algebras. A function f from B to B^* is said to be **monotone increasing** iff for each two elements X and Y of the algebra B:

if $X \subseteq Y$, then $f(X) \subseteq f(Y)$.[22]

It is evident that such functions can also be given an alternative characterization. As a matter of fact, corresponding to theorem (36), we have the following result.

(90) **Theorem**

Let B and B^* be two Boolean algebras. The following statements about a function f from B to B^* are equivalent:

(a) f is monotone increasing;

(b) $f(X \cap Y) \subseteq f(X) \cap f(Y)$;

(c) $f(X) \cup f(Y) \subseteq f(X \cup Y)$.

We must not suppose that this exhausts the variety of available functions, for besides monotone increasing functions we can obviously also distinguish monotone decreasing functions. In that case it is the properties of monotone decreasing quantifiers that serve as our point of departure. Indeed, the fact that these collections are closed under inclusion entails that the associated characteristic function is such that assignment of the value 1 to an element Y is invariably accompanied with assignment of the value 1 to each element X which is contained in Y. In other words, if Q is a monotone decreasing quantifier on the algebra of verb phrases, then its characteristic function $K_Q : P(U) \to 2$ possesses the property that the conditions $X \subseteq Y$ and $K_Q(Y) = 1$ imply $K_Q(X) = 1$. In view of the nature of the Boolean algebra 2, it should be clear that what the property in question amounts to is that whenever X is contained in Y, $K_Q(Y)$ is contained in $K_Q(X)$. More precisely:

(91) **Definition**

Let B and B^* be two Boolean algebras. A function f from B to B^* is said to be **monotone decreasing** iff for each two elements X and Y of the algebra B:

if $X \subseteq Y$, then $f(Y) \subseteq f(X)$.

Needless to say, such functions can also be characterized in a different way. Indeed, analogous to theorem (30) we have the following:

(92) **Theorem**

Let B and B^* be two Boolean algebras. The following statements about a function f from B to B^* are equivalent:

(a) f is monotone decreasing;

(b) $f(X \cup Y) \subseteq f(X) \cap f(Y)$;

(c) $f(X) \cup f(Y) \subseteq f(X \cap Y)$.

At this point, the reader may protest that the distinction between monotone increasing and monotone decreasing functions must be regarded as an unnecessary complication. One should keep in mind, however, that the concept of a function is much more general than the rather limited notion of a quantifier. This is clear from the fact that natural languages as a rule have a variety of expressions which cannot be associated with a quantifier, but which nevertheless display the characteristic features of monotonicity. The next two conditionals may serve as an illustration.

(93) a No willow will die slowly →
        No blossoming willow will die slowly

  b All jonquils will blossom →
     All fertilized jonquils will blossom

Provided that the noun *blossoming willow* applies only to willows and the noun *fertilized jonquils* only to jonquils, the conditionals in (93) must both be accepted as valid. In other words, if the state of affairs in the universe is such that the class of blossoming willows is a subset of the class of willows and the class of unfertilized jonquils a subset of the class of jonquils, then we may legitimately pass from the propositions *No willow will die slowly* and *All jonquils will blossom* to the propositions *No blossoming willow will pass away* and *All unfertilized jonquils will flower*. These findings show that the logical behavior of the determiners *all* and *no* resembles that of monotone decreasing noun phrases, in spite of the fact that the semantic value of both expressions cannot be treated as a quantifier. In order to account for this resemblance, we must invoke the notion of a monotonic function. Indeed, it is not uncommon to find determiners being portrayed as functions which carry nouns into noun phrases. In accordance with this, such expressions are often identified semantically with a function from the algebra of nouns to the algebra of noun phrases – a state of affairs which admits no other interpretation than that a determiner associates with each element of the power set $P(U)$ a uniquely determined element of the power set $P(P(U))$. Once it is recognized that determiners are to be treated as functions, we have an explanation for the similarities between the logical behavior of monotone decreasing noun phrases and that of expressions like *all* and *no*. For if the semantic value of determiners is functional in nature, then the validity of the conditionals in (93) must be attributed to the circumstance that the functions associated with *all* and *no* are downward monotonic. As an illustration, we consider the case of the determiner *all*. It is easy to see that the monotone decreasing character of this element entails that the extension of the noun phrase *all jonquils* is contained in the extension of *all fertilized jonquils*. Stated differently, each set which is a member of the quantifier associated with *all jonquils* is also a member of the quantifier associated with *all fertilized jonquils*. From this it follows immediately that someone who considers the proposition *All jonquils will blossom* to be true must also accept the truth of *All fertilized jonquils will blossom*. For that reason, we may say that the validity of the conditional in (93b) is a consequence of the monotone decreasing nature of the determiner *all*. Needless to say, such reasoning is not limited to this single case, for in a completely analogous fashion the validity of the implication in (93a) can be attributed to the downward monotonic nature of the determiner *no*.

That the class of all such expressions has more members than *all* and *no*, is shown by the next two examples.

(94) a At most sixteen beggars have been convicted →
At most sixteen blind beggars have been convicted

b No more than ten beggars have been tortured →
No more than ten blind beggars have been tortured

Provided that the noun *blind beggars* applies only to what the noun *beggars* also applies to, the conditionals in (94) must both be accepted as true. Consequently, expressions of the forms *at most n N* and *no more than n N* must also be regarded as belonging to the class of monotone decreasing determiners.

It would surely be wrong to suppose that all determiners are downward monotonic, for it is easy to find expressions which do not have the property in question. The examples which follow speak for themselves.

(95) a Neither pedlar will be prosecuted ↛
Neither lame pedlar will be prosecuted

b None of the six artists was fined ↛
None of the six deaf artists was fined

Even if both pedlars are lucky enough not to be prosecuted, we are by no means justified in the conclusion that neither lame pedlar will be prosecuted, for the simple reason that the existence of just two pedlars does not necessarily entail the existence of just two lame pedlars. Similarly, when none of the six artists was fined, we cannot conclude that none of the six deaf artists was fined. This shows that expressions of the forms *neither N* and *none of the n N* do not belong to the class of monotone decreasing determiners.

The foregoing discussion is far from comprehensive, for besides downward monotonic determiners one also finds upward monotonic determiners, judging from the conditionals in (96).

(96) a At least one rich servant cries →
 At least one servant cries

 b Not all poor fishermen complain →
 Not all fishermen complain

On the condition that the noun *rich servant* is true only of servants and the noun *poor fishermen* only of fishermen, both conditionals must be considered valid. That is to say, if the universe is such that the class of rich servants is contained in the class of servants and the class of poor fishermen in the class of fishermen, then we may legitimately pass from the propositions *At least one rich servant cries* and *Not all poor fishermen complain* to the propositions *At least one servant cries* and *Not all fishermen complain*. What this shows is that the logical behavior of the determiners *at least one* and *not all* resembles that of monotone increasing noun phrases – something which admits no other explanation than that the functions associated with *at least one* and *not all* are likewise upward monotonic. Indeed, consultation of the relevant definition makes it clear that what this property amounts to is that the extension of the noun phrase *at least one servant* invariably contains the extension of the noun phrase *at least one rich servant*. In other words, each set which is a member of the quantifier associated with *at least one rich servant* must also be regarded as a member of the quantifier associated with *at least one servant*. Needless to say, this implies that someone who considers the proposition *At least one rich servant cries* to be true must also accept the truth of *At least one servant cries*. We may therefore say that the validity of the conditional in (96a) is a consequence of the monotone increasing nature of the determiner *at least one*. A parallel argument shows that the validity of the conditional in (96b) must be attributed to the upward monotonic character of the determiner *not all*.

That the class of all such elements contains more expressions than those of the forms *at least n* and *not all*, is demonstrated by the next two examples.

(97) a Several uninvited guests were treated unfriendly →
        Several guests were treated unfriendly
    b   More than twelve uninvited guests have collapsed →
        More than twelve guests have collapsed

Provided that the noun *uninvited guests* is true only of what the noun *guests* is also true of, acceptance of the antecedent must in each case lead to acceptance of the consequent. For that reason, expressions of the forms *several* and *more than n* must also be regarded as monotone increasing determiners.

This is of course not to say that all determiners are upward monotonic. Surely not, for natural language has a variety of expressions which cannot be analyzed in such a manner. In order to convince ourselves of this fact, we consider some examples.

(98) Neither lame pedlar will be prosecuted ↛
     Neither pedlar will be prosecuted

(99) None of the six deaf artists was fined ↛
     None of the six artists was fined

Even if both lame pedlars are lucky enough not to be prosecuted, we are by no means justified in the conclusion that neither pedlar will be prosecuted, since the existence of just two lame pedlars does not necessarily entail the existence of just two pedlars. Similarly, when none of the six deaf artists was fined, we cannot conclude that none of the six artists was fined. This shows that expressions of the forms *neither* and *none of the n* cannot be regarded as belonging to the class of monotone increasing determiners.

These and similar findings with regard to the laws which govern the logical behavior of determiners have been collected in table 6. The eighteen classes of expressions which are mentioned there must all be regarded as monotonic. It should be obvious that the logical properties of the determiner may be quite unlike those of the corresponding noun phrase. As a case in point, we consider the expressions *every* and *all*. When the semantical properties of these determiners are compared with those of noun phrases of the forms *every N* and *all N*, it is at once clear that one has downward monotonicity in the first case and upward monotonicity in the second. Things are different, however, when, instead of *every* and *all*, we consider their negations *not every* and *not all*, for now the determiners are monotone increasing and the corresponding noun phrases monotone decreasing.

Table 6: Eighteen classes of monotonic determiners in English, with their Dutch counterparts

Monotone increasing

not every (**D**: niet ieder(e))
not all (**D**: niet alle)
not each (**D**: niet elk(e))
sm (**D**: enkele)
at least n (**D**: minstens n)
some (**D**: sommige)
several (**D**: verscheidene)
more than n
(**D**: meer dan n)
some but not all
(**D**: sommige maar niet alle)

Monotone decreasing

every (**D**: ieder(e))
all (**D**: alle)
each (**D**: elk(e))
no (**D**: geen)
at most n (**D**: hoogstens n)
not a single (**D**: geen enkel(e))
only n (**D**: slechts n)
no more than n
(**D**: niet meer dan n)
not one
(**D**: niet één)

Even more surprising is the behavior of the composite determiner *some but not all*. By way of illustration, we take the conditional (100) into consideration.

(100) Some but not all contaminated pigs are being destroyed $\rightarrow$

Some but not all pigs are being destroyed

There is no doubt that the above implication must be accepted as valid. For if it is true that some but not all contaminated pigs are being destroyed, then it must also be true that some but not all pigs are being destroyed. This entails that the expression in question belongs to the class of monotone increasing determiners. On the other hand, noun phrases of the form *some but not all N* can neither be regarded as upward monotonic, nor as downward monotonic. Consequently, what we are here dealing with is a case in which the determiner possesses the property of upward monotonicity, but the corresponding noun phrase is devoid of any form of monotonicity at all.

We must not suppose that this is an exhaustive treatment of the different possibilities, for it requires little reflection to realize that the reverse situation may also arise. Indeed, natural language has a rather large group of determiners which are evidently not monotonic. Examples include not only expressions of the forms *both*, *neither*, *the n* and *none of the n*, but also elements like *many*, *most* and *(precisely) n*. In order to be convinced of this fact, examine the conditionals in (101) and (102).

(101) Many decayed houses will be pulled down $\not\to$

Many houses will be pulled down

(102) Many houses will be pulled down $\not\to$

Many decayed houses will be pulled down

It should be obvious that neither example can be accepted as valid. Indeed, it is easy to see that the intended demolition of many ruinous houses does not preclude the possibility that few houses will be pulled down and, reversely, that the intended demolition of many houses does not rule out the possibility that few decayed houses will be pulled down. For that reason, the expression *many* cannot be regarded as a monotonic determiner, nor can its negative counterpart *few*. In this light, we must also look at examples such as (103) and (104).

(103) Most obsolete engines will be replaced $\not\to$

Most engines will be replaced

(104) Most engines will be replaced $\not\to$

Most obsolete engines will be replaced

Using the same reasoning as we employed for the examples in (101) and (102), it is easily proved that the conditionals in (103) and (104) are also invalid. Consequently, the expression *most* cannot be regarded as a monotonic determiner.

Our last example relates to expressions of the form *(precisely) n*. To that end, one does well to take the next two conditionals into consideration.

(105) Precisely three poisoned storks will be killed $\not\to$

Precisely three storks will be killed

(106) Precisely three storks will be killed $\not\to$

Precisely three poisoned storks will be killed

It should be obvious that in neither case one can speak of a valid proposition. For if in addition to three poisoned storks two healthy ones will be killed, then the antecedent of (105) is true, but its consequent false. Likewise, the intended death of three storks, among which one poisoned one, is sufficient to reject the conditional in (106) as false. Therefore, no other conclusion can be drawn than that expressions of the form *(precisely) n* also do not belong to the class of monotonic determiners.

With the aid of the preceding test, we can usually arrive at rather trustworthy judgments when we must decide whether a given determiner is monotonic. Some of the outcomes have been collected in table 7. The eighteen classes of determiners mentioned there appear to be devoid of any form of monotonicity. This is not to say that the corresponding noun phrase must also be regarded as being non-monotonic. For it is easily established that determiners of the forms *almost all, both, many, the n, the more than n, the [sg], the [pl]* and *most* produce a monotone increasing noun phrase. Likewise, one easily proves that determiners of the forms *almost no, neither, few, none of the n, none of the more than n* and *none of the* result in a monotone decreasing noun phrase. Only in the case of *(precisely) n, all except n, an even number* and *an uneven number* is the corresponding noun phrase non-monotonic in nature.

Table 7: Eighteen classes of non-monotonic determiners in English, with their Dutch counterparts

almost all (**D**: vrijwel alle)

both (**D**: beide)

many (**D**: veel)

the n
(**D**: de n)

the more than n
(**D**: de meer dan n)

the [pl] (**D**: de [pl])

the [sg] (**D**: de [sg])

most
(**D**: de meeste)

almost no
(**D**: vrijwel geen)

neither (**D**: geen van beide)

few (**D**: weinig)

none of the n (**D**: geen van de n)

none of the more than n
(**D**: geen van de meer dan n)

none of the
(**D**: geen van de)

(precisely) n (**D**: (precies) n)

all except n (**D**: op n na alle)

an even number
(**D**: een even aantal)

an uneven number
(**D**: een oneven aantal)

7. ANTI-ADDITIVE, MULTIPLICATIVE AND ANTIMORPHIC FUNCTIONS

So far this short digression on the distinction between monotone increasing and monotone decreasing functions. Now it is necessary to consider the question of how the earlier notion of a quasi-ideal can be given a functional characterization. Surprisingly enough, the matter is not as complex as first expected. This becomes evident when we take the definition of a quasi-ideal into consideration. With the help of the relevant stipulations, one easily establishes that the associated characteristic function is such that the value assigned to the element $X \cup Y$ corresponds to the product of the values which are assigned to X and Y. Put differently, if Q is a quasi-ideal on the algebra of verb phrases, then the characteristic function $K_Q : P(U) \to 2$ has the property that $K_Q(X \cup Y)$ is invariably equal to $K_Q(X) \cap K_Q(Y)$. Such functions are sometimes referred to as anti-additive functions.[23]

(107) **Definition**

Let B and B^* be two Boolean algebras. A function f from B to B^* is said to be **anti-additive** iff for each two elements X and Y of the algebra B:

$$f(X \cup Y) = f(X) \cap f(Y).$$

Clearly, noun phrases which are associated with a quasi-ideal must be regarded as anti-additive from a functional point of view. It appears, however, that there are also some determiners which exhibit the behavior of an anti-additive function. By way of illustration, we consider the biconditionals in (108) and (109).

(108)   Every goat or donkey will be killed   ↔

   Every goat and every donkey will be killed

(109)   Not a priest or baker will be fired   ↔

   Not a priest and not a baker will be fired

There can be no doubt that both of the preceding propositions are valid. Indeed, anyone who regards one of the members of the biconditionals in (108) and (109) as true, must also accept the truth of the other member – a state of affairs which admits no other interpretation than that the determiners every and not a semantically behave as anti-additive functions. For if one regards the determiner as a functor and the noun as its argument, then the valid schema in (110) results.

(110) (DET (N$_1$ or N$_2$)) VP ↔ (DET (N$_1$) and DET (N$_2$)) VP

It is immediately clear that the above scheme can be interpreted in such a way that it satisfies the characteristic requirements of an anti-additive function.

This is not to say that every determiner is anti-additive in nature. Surely not, for natural language has a variety of expressions which do not obey the laws that govern the use of such elements. The next two conditionals serve as an illustration.

(111) Not all oxen or goats have been killed ↛

Not all oxen and not all goats have been killed

(112) Not all oxen and not all goats have been killed →

Not all oxen or goats have been killed

It is easy to see that the proposition in (111) is invalid. For if it is the case that all oxen, but not all goats have been killed, then the antecedent of the conditional in (111) is true, but its consequent false. For that reason, the expression *not all* cannot be regarded as belonging to the class of anti-additive determiners. On the other hand, it is a consequence of the monotone increasing nature of the determiner *not all* that the reverse proposition in (112) must be accepted as valid.

The preceding discussion is far from exhaustive, for the general notion of a quasi-filter can also easily be extended to the functional domain. Using the relevant definition, one proves without difficulty that the associated characteristic function is such that the value which is assigned to the element $X \cap Y$ is equal to the product of the values assigned to X and Y separately. In other words, if Q is a quasi-filter on the algebra of verb phrases, then its characteristic function $K_Q : P(U) \to 2$ has the property that $K_Q(X \cap Y)$ is invariably equal to $K_Q(X) \cap K_Q(Y)$. Functions of this nature are usually called **multiplicative** functions.[24] That is to say:

(113) **Definition**

Let B and B^* be two Boolean algebras. A function f from B to B^* is said to be **multiplicative** iff for each two elements X and Y of the algebra B:

$f(X \cap Y) = f(X) \cap f(Y)$.

It is evident that, from a functional point of view, noun phrases which act as quasi-filters must be regarded as being multiplicative. Curiously enough, it is exceptionally difficult to find a good example of a multiplicative determiner. This may rouse our suspicion as to whether there are any determiners which exhibit the properties of a multiplicative function. Indeed, it seems that natural language excludes such expressions on principle. Given the semantic constraints on the expressive nature of determiners, one can in fact prove that the observed gap is a logical one.[25]

The notion of a prime ideal, introduced in section 5, can likewise be given a functional characterization. With the help of the stipulations in (81), one easily establishes that the associated characteristic function is such that the value assigned to the element $X \cup Y$ corresponds to the product of the values assigned to X and Y, and the value assigned to the element $-X$, to the complement of the value assigned to X. Put differently, if Q is a prime ideal on the algebra of verb phrases, then the characteristic function $K_Q : P(U) \to 2$ has the property that $K_Q(X \cup Y)$ is invariably equal to $K_Q(X) \cap K_Q(Y)$ and that $K_Q(-X)$ is invariably equal to $-K_Q(X)$. Such functions will henceforth be referred to as antimorphic functions.

(114) **Definition**

> Let B and B^* be two Boolean algebras. A function f from B to B^* is said to be **antimorphic** iff for each two elements X and Y of the algebra B:
>
> (a) $f(X \cup Y) = f(X) \cap f(Y)$;
> (b) $f(-X) = -f(X)$.

We have seen that there are noun phrases whose associated quantifier acts, semantically, as a prime ideal. These expressions must therefore be classified as antimorphic. Within the category of determiners, however, it is difficult to find one whose logical behavior can be characterized as antimorphic. Again, it seems that natural language excludes such expressions on principle.

These findings with respect to the laws which govern the logical behavior of determiners have been collected in table 8. The five determiners mentioned there must all be understood as being anti-additive. It is immediately clear that there can be substantial differences between the behavior of the determiner, on the one hand, and that of the corresponding noun phrase, on the other. Characteristic examples are the expressions *every* and *all*. When we compare the semantical properties of these elements with those of noun phrases of the forms *every N* and

Table 8: Five anti-additive determiners in English, with their Dutch counterparts

every (**D**: ieder(e))   not a (**D**: geen enkel(e))
all (**D**: alle)   not one (**D**: niet één)
no (**D**: geen)

all N, it turns out that we are dealing with anti-additive expressions in the first case, but multiplicative expressions in the second. Things are different, however, when, in place of *every* and *all*, we consider the universal negations *no*, *not a* and *not one*, for now it is not only the determiner, but also the corresponding noun phrase which is anti-additive in nature. Even more surprising is the behavior of expressions as *both*, *each*, *the n*, *neither* and *none of the n*. In all of these cases, the determiner is clearly non-monotonic. On the other hand, noun phrases of the forms *both N*, *each N* and *the n N* exhibit a multiplicative character, as opposed to those of the forms *neither N* and *none of the n N*, which instead are anti-additive.

This description of the different possibilities is still not complete, for it is also possible that neither the determiner nor the corresponding noun phrase is multiplicative or anti-additive in nature. Expressions which belong to this class include *at least n*, *at most n*, *not all*, *some but not all*, *many*, *few*, *most* and *(precisely) n*. Following our earlier policy, a number of these results have been collected in table 9. On the basis of this survey, it is easy to see that the logical behavior of the determiner is wholly independent of that of the corresponding noun phrase. To forestall any misunderstandings, it should be pointed out that every multiplicative function is also monotone increasing. In an analogous way, one easily establishes that the class of anti-additive functions is a subset of the class of monotone decreasing functions and that the class of antimorphic functions is a subset of the class of anti-additive functions.

In the same way that a determiner can be associated with a function carrying sets of individuals into collections of such sets, a sentential connective can be assigned a function from the algebra of truth values, 2, to the power set algebra $P(2)$. It is not uncommon, for example, to find an expression like *and* being portrayed as a function which maps sentences into so-called adsentences. In accordance with this, the element in question will be associated semantically with a function that assigns the singleton set $\{1\}$ to the truth value 1, and the empty set to the truth

Table 9: Comparison of the logical behavior of determiners with that of the corresponding noun phrases

	Determiner	Noun phrase
at least n (**D**: minstens n)	mon. increas.	mon. increas.
some (**D**: sommige)	mon. increas.	mon. increas.
sm (**D**: enkele)	mon. increas.	mon. increas.
no (**D**: geen)	anti-additive	anti-additive
at most n (**D**: hoogstens n)	mon. decreas.	mon. decreas.
not a single (**D**: geen enkel(e))	anti-additive	anti-additive
not every (**D**: niet ieder(e))	mon. increas.	mon. decreas.
not all (**D**: niet alle)	mon. increas.	mon. decreas.
every (**D**: ieder(e))	anti-additive	multiplicative
all (**D**: alle)	anti-additive	multiplicative
some but not all (**D**: sommige maar niet alle)	mon. increas.	non-monotonic
nearly all (**D**: vrijwel alle)	non-monotonic	mon. increas.
both (**D**: beide)	non-monotonic	multiplicative
each (**D**: elk(e))	non-monotonic[26]	multiplicative
many (**D**: veel)	non-monotonic	mon. increas.
the n (**D**: de n)	non-monotonic	mon. increas.
most (**D**: de meeste)	non-monotonic	mon. increas.
almost no (**D**: vrijwel geen)	non-monotonic	mon. decreas.
not each (**D**: niet elk(e))	non-monotonic	mon. decreas.
neither (**D**: geen van beide)	non-monotonic	anti-additive
few (**D**: weinig)	non-monotonic	mon. decreas.
none of the n (**D**: geen van de n)	non-monotonic	anti-additive
(precisely) n (**D**: (precies) n)	non-monotonic	non-monotonic

value 0. What this means is that a sentence of the form *The dog barks and the cat meows* must be regarded as true just in case both of its component sentences are true. It requires little reflection to see that the

connectives *or*, *if* and *without* can be treated in an analogous manner. The following definition provides the necessary details.

(115) **Definition**

$And(0) = \emptyset \quad Or(0) = \{1\} \quad If(0) = \{0,1\} \quad Without(0) = \{1\}$
$And(1) = \{1\} \quad Or(1) = \{0,1\} \quad If(1) = \{1\} \quad Without(1) = \emptyset$

From this description it is immediately clear that the connectives *and* and *or* are multiplicative in nature; *if* and *without*, on the other hand, are anti-additive. These and similar findings have been collected in table 10.

Table 10: Comparison of the logical behavior of connectives with that of the corresponding adsentences

	Connective	**Adsentence**
and (**D**: en)	multiplicative	multiplicative
or (**D**: of)	multiplicative	multiplicative
if (**D**: als)	anti-additive	multiplicative
without (**D**: zonder (dat))	anti-additive	multiplicative

On the basis of this survey, it is easy to see that there can be substantial differences between the logical behavior of the connective and that of the corresponding adsentence. Characteristic examples are the expressions *if* and *without*. When we compare the semantical properties of these elements with those of adsentences of the forms *if S* and *without S*, it turns out that we are dealing with anti-additive expressions in the first case, but multiplicative expressions in the second. Things are different, however, when, instead of *if* and *without*, we consider the elements *and* and *or*, for now it is not only the adsentence, but also the corresponding connective which is multiplicative in nature.

8. LAWS OF NEGATIVE POLARITY

Some readers might be inclined to regard the functional perspective just introduced as an unnecessary complication. They should keep in mind that the notion of a function enables us to extend our investigations of polarity phenomena to arbitrary environments. In particular, it becomes clear in this way that the distinction between weak, strong and superstrong forms of negative polarity corresponds with that between monotone decreasing, anti-additive and antimorphic functions. In order to convince ourselves of this fact, we consider first the Dutch examples in (116).

(116)   a   *Hoogstens één kind zal een opstel hoeven te schrijven.*
             At most   one child will a   paper need   to write
             'At most one child need write a paper.'

       b   **Minstens één kind zal een verslag hoeven te schrijven.*
             At least   one child will a   report need   to write
             'At least one child need write a report.'

The contrast between (116a) and (116b) shows that the presence of the monotone increasing noun phrase *minstens één kind* is not sufficient to justify the occurrence of the weak polarity item *hoeven*. Apparently, it is only monotone decreasing expressions like *hoogstens één kind* that are able to license the element in question. This supposition is confirmed by the pattern which manifests itself in (117).

(117)   a   *Geen zuigeling zal de proeven hoeven te doorstaan.*
             No   infant   will the tests   need   to go through
             'No infant need go through the tests.'

       b   **Alle kinderen zullen een test hoeven te ondergaan.*
             All   children will   a   test need   to undergo
             'All children need undergo a test.'

Of the two phrases *geen zuigeling* and *alle kinderen*, it is only the first that can act as a licencing expression for *hoeven* - a state of affairs which must be attributed to the circumstance that *geen zuigeling* is downward monotonic and *alle kinderen* upward monotonic.

However, when we replace *hoeven* by the strong polarity item *ook maar iets*, a clear contrast manifests itself between licencing expressions of the form *hoogstens n N* and those of the form *geen N*. As an illustration we consider the examples in (118).

(118)   a   *Geen bemiddelaar zal ook maar iets bewerkstelligen.*
             No   mediator   will anything   accomplish
             'No mediator will accomplish anything.'

       b   **Hoogstens zes ouders zullen ook maar iets vernemen.*
             At most   six parents will   anything   hear
             'At most six parents will hear anything.'

The contrast between (118a) and (118b) shows clearly that only the anti-additive expression *geen bemiddelaar* is capable of licencing the occurrence of *ook maar iets*. This is by no means an accident, for as the sentences in (119) show, the strong polarity item *bijster* exhibits exactly the same characteristics as *ook maar iets*.

(119)   a   *Niet één leerkracht toonde zich bijster verontrust.*
Not one teacher showed himself very disturbed
'Not one teacher showed himself very disturbed.'

       b   **Slechts één leerling toonde zich bijster ingenomen.*
Only one student showed himself very pleased
'Only one student showed himself very pleased.'

The fact that the occurrence of *bijster* in (119b) produces an unacceptable result proves that the element in question requires the presence of an anti-additive expression elsewhere in the sentence.

In the light of such facts it is absolutely clear that there are certain regularities underlying both forms of negative polarity. These find expression in two general laws concerning the use of negative polarity items.

(120)   **Laws of negative polarity**

       a   Only sentences in which a monotone decreasing expression occurs, can contain a negative polarity item of the weak type.

       b   Only sentences in which an anti-additive expression occurs, can contain a negative polarity item of the strong type.

According to the first law, the presence of a monotone decreasing expression is a necessary condition for the appearance of negative polarity items of the weak type. On the other hand, the second law stipulates that negative polarity items of the strong type require the presence of an anti-additive expression.

In order to get a clear view of the domain of application of both laws, one does well to take the following examples into consideration.

(121)   a   *Geen kind dat ook maar iets bevroedt, zal iemand*
No child who anything suspects will someone
waarschuwen.
warn
'No child who suspects anything will tell someone.'

b *Ieder kind dat ook maar iets vermoedt, zal iemand*
   Every child who anything   suspects   will someone
   raadplegen.
   consult
   'Every child who suspects anything will consult someone.'

The occurrence of the strong polarity item *ook maar iets* is entirely acceptable in both sentences – a state of affairs which must be attributed to the anti-additive nature of the determiners *geen* and *ieder(e)*. However, if the expression in question is part of the main clause, then one of the two sentences becomes ungrammatical, as shown by the contrast in (122).

(122) a *Geen kind dat iets   bevroedt, zal ook maar iemand*
         No   child who something suspects will anyone
         waarschuwen.
         warn
         'No child who suspects something will tell anyone.'

     b **Ieder kind dat iets   vermoedt, zal*
         Every child who something suspects will
         ook maar iemand verwittigen.
         anyone   notify
         'Every child who suspects something will notify anyone.'

This is a consequence of the fact that the anti-additive determiner *ieder(e)* produces multiplicative noun phrases.

Things are different when we take the composite determiner *geen van de* into consideration, for now it is not the main clause, but the relative clause which excludes negative polarity items.

(123) a **Geen van de ukken   die ook maar iets zien, zal*
         None of the toddlers who anything   see will
         iemand waarschuwen.
         someone warn
         'None of the toddlers who see anything will tell someone.'

     b *Geen van de ukken   die iets zien,   zal*
         None of the toddlers who see something will
         ook maar iemand waarschuwen.
         anyone   warn
         'None of the toddlers who see something will tell anyone.'

It is easy to see that this follows from the non-monotonic nature of the expression *geen van de*. On the other hand, when we replace the occurrence of *geen van de* by *hoogstens zes* in examples such as (124), then the result is in both cases completely unacceptable.

(124) a **Hoogstens zes ukken   die ook maar iets zien, zullen*
         At most   six toddlers who anything   see   will
         iemand   roepen.
         someone call
         'At most six toddlers who see anything will call someone.'

  b **Hoogstens zes ukken   die iets   zien, zullen*
     At most   six toddlers who something see   will
     ook maarfliemand roepen.
     anyone   call
     'At most six toddlers who see something will call anyone.'

From this we must conclude that neither the monotone decreasing determiner *hoogstens zes* nor the monotone decreasing noun phrase *hoogstens zes ukken* is capable of triggering negative polarity items of the strong type.

The well-formed occurrence of the strong polarity item *ook maar iets* in (125) can likewise be explained in terms of the anti-additive nature of the connectives *als* en *zonder*.

(125) a *Als het kind ook maar iets bevroedt, zal het iemand*
         If the child anything   suspects will she someone
         waarschuwen.
         warn
         'If the child suspects anything, she will tell someone.'

  b *De man zal iemand waarschuwen zonder*
     The man will someone warn   without
     ook maar iets te bevroeden.
     anything   to suspect
     'The man will inform someone without suspecting anything.'

However, if the polarity item in question is part of the main clause, as in (126), then both sentences become ungrammatical.

(126) a *Als het kind iets   bevroedt, zal het
         If the child something suspects will she
         ook maar iemand waarschuwen.
         anyone   warn
         'If the child suspects something, she will tell anyone.'

     b *De man zal ook maar iemand waarschuwen zonder
        The man will anyone   warn   without
        iets   te bevroeden.
        something to suspect.
        'The man will inform anyone without suspecting
        something.'

This is a consequence of the fact that the anti-additive connectives *als* en *zonder* invariably produce multiplicative adsentences.

We must not suppose that this exhausts the matter, for the superstrong polarity item *one bit* requires the presence of an antimorphic expression, as shown by the examples in (127).

(127) a *Few clergymen liked the performance one bit.

     b *No politician liked the performance one bit.

     c The men didn't like the performance one bit.

The ungrammaticality of the sentences (127a) and (127b) must be attributed to the fact that neither *few clergymen* nor *no politician* belongs to the class of antimorphic expressions. The negative adverb *not (n't)*, on the other hand, is antimorphic; hence, the well-formed nature of the sentence in (127c).

As the ungrammatical examples in (128) show, the Dutch adjective *mals* 'tender' is also not content with a monotone decreasing or anti-additive expression. Instead, it requires the presence of the antimorphic adverb *niet* somewhere in the sentence.

(128) a *Weinig van zijn oordelen waren mals.
         Few   of his opinions were   tender
         'Few of his opinions were soft.'

     b *Niet één van zijn oordelen was mals.
        Not one of his opinions was tender
        'Not one of his opinions was soft.'

     c Zijn oordelen waren vaak niet mals.
        His opinions were often not tender
        'His opinions often weren't soft.'

In view of the additional constraints on the occurrence of polarity items such as *one bit* and *mals*, we must extend our account as follows.

(129) **Laws of negative polarity**

    a Only sentences in which a monotone decreasing expression occurs, can contain a negative polarity item of the weak type.

    b Only sentences in which an anti-additive expression occurs, can contain a negative polarity item of the strong type.

    c Only sentences in which an antimorphic expression occurs, can contain a negative polarity item of the superstrong type.

We are now in a position to answer the question that has guided us throughout. As the functional characterization in (92) shows, the logical behavior of monotone decreasing expressions is governed by one half of the first law of De Morgan and one half of the second law of De Morgan. This means that the class of monotone decreasing expressions is coextensive with the class of subminimal negations. By reference to (92) and the functional definition in (107) it can likewise be shown that the logical behavior of anti-additive expressions is determined by the first law of De Morgan as a whole and one half of the second law of De Morgan. Accordingly, the class of anti-additive expressions may be equated with the class of minimal negations. Finally, it should be noted that it follows from the set-theoretical theorem in (82) that antimorphic functions have the following property.

(130) **Theorem**

Let B and B^* be two Boolean algebras and let f be a function from B to B^*. If f is antimorphic, then
$f(X \cap Y) = f(X) \cup f(Y)$.

The above result, in combination with the functional characterization of antimorphic functions in (114), is sufficient to prove that the class of antimorphic expressions is identical to the class of classical negations. In other words, the hierarchy of subminimal, minimal, and classical negation, shown in table 11, is a linguistic reflection of the underlying hierarchy of monotone decreasing, anti-additive, and antimorphic functions. This completes our exposition.

Table 11: A hierarchy of negative expressions

Name	Logical properties
Expression of subminimal negation	(1) $f(X \cup Y) \subseteq f(X) \cap f(Y)$ (2) $f(X) \cup f(Y) \subseteq f(X \cap Y)$
Expression of minimal negation	(1) $f(X \cup Y) = f(X) \cap f(Y)$ (2) $f(X) \cup f(Y) \subseteq f(X \cap Y)$
Expression of classical negation	(1) $f(X \cup Y) = f(X) \cap f(Y)$ (2) $f(X) \cap f(Y) = f(X \cap Y)$ (3) $f(-X) = -f(X)$

NOTES

[1] The ideas explored in this paper have been presented at several occasions, among them the *Workshop on GPSG and Semantics* at the Technische Universität Berlin, February 1989, the *Workshop on Categorial Grammar* at the LSA Summer Institute, University of Arizona, Tucson, the *Dritte Sommerschule der deutschen Gesellschaft für Sprachwissenschaft*, Universität Hamburg, September 1989, the *Jahrestagung der deutschen Gesellschaft für Sprachwissenschaft*, Universität des Saarlandes, Saarbrücken, March 1990, the *Second European Summer School in Language, Logic and Information*, Katholieke Universiteit Leuven, August 1990, and the *Workshop on the Logic of Perceptual Reports*, Università degli studi di Milano, Gargnano, September 1990. I am indebted to Jay Atlas, Emmon Bach, Andrea Bonomi, Wojciech Buszkowski, Paolo Casalegno, Elisabet Engdahl, Fritz Hamm, Christa Hauenschild, Jack Hoeksema, Hans Kamp, Mark Kas, Ed Keenan, Manfred Krifka, Bill Ladusaw, Dick Oehrle, Víctor Sánchez Valencia, Pieter Seuren, Anna Szabolcsi, Birgit Wesche, Ton van der Wouden, Dietmar Zaefferer, Annie Zaenen and, above all, Johan van Benthem for valuable comments on earlier versions of the paper. The work reported here is part of a larger project, *Reflections of Logical Patterns in Language Structure and Language Use*, which is supported by the Netherlands Organization for Scientific Research (NWO) within the framework of the PIONIER-program.

[2] The distinction between the sentences in (1) and (2) was first discussed in Zwarts (1981: 39, 123–127), be it from a slightly different point of view. Additional discussion can be found in Hoeksema (1983: 427–432) and Zwarts (1986: 192–195, 313–319). It should be clear from the examples in (2) that the English negative polarity expression *anything (at all)* occurs in a larger set of environments than its Dutch counterpart *ook maar iets*. See Ladusaw (1979; 1980; and 1983) for discussion of the English data.

[3] The German examples involving the negative polarity item *sonderlich* (4c and

4d) are due to van Os (1989: 124). Kürschner (1983: 308–327) presents a comprehensive list of German negative polarity items, the only one which has appeared so far. Characteristic examples of the different types of polarity expressions in German can also be found in Krifka (1989). The interested reader may wish to consult Krifka (1990) as well, particularly in connection with the observed relationship between focus and certain classes of polarity items. In fact, this is what leads Krifka to adopt the framework of alternative semantics, developed by Rooth (1985) to account for the behavior of focus-sensitive expressions such as *only*.

[4] The laws in question are, of course, the familiar set-theoretical identities $-(X \cup Y) = -X \cap -Y$ and $-(X \cap Y) = -X \cup -Y$. Quine (1974: 69) speaks in this connection of the first, and the second, law of De Morgan, respectively.

[5] We ignore the fact that, in the intuitionistic propositional calculus, an entirely different interpretation is given to sentential negation. Readers who wish to acquaint themselves with this matter should consult Dummett (1977) and van Dalen (1986), among others.

[6] A description of the calculus of subminimal logic can be found in Hazen (1992) and Dunn (1993).

[7] The calculus of minimal logic was introduced by Johansson (1936). A short description of this system can be found in van Dalen (1986: 297–298), Gamut (1991: 139) and Dunn (1993: 25). Minimal negation is sometimes referred to as regular negation, a term which was introduced in Zwarts (1986: 351). The reader should note that our use of it has nothing to do with the way in which Seuren (1976) uses this notion. As a matter of fact, a significant part of the terminology employed in the present paper finds its origin in the study and classification of so-called *minimal models*, also known as *neighbourhood* or *Scott-Montague models*, in classical modal logic. See Chellas (1980) for a convenient introduction to this matter.

[8] A comparison of the conditionals in (9) and (10) shows that every logical law which governs the behavior of subminimal negation also governs the behavior of minimal negation.

[9] The examples in (15) are due to van Os (1989: 196). Additional discussion of the German polarity item *nennenswert* can be found in Biedermann (1969: 173).

[10] Jack Hoeksema points out that the Dutch adjective *onuitstaanbaar* 'unbearable' acts as a morphological counterpart of the composite verb *kunnen uitstaan*. In particular, the prefix *on-* 'un-' cannot be omitted (**uitstaanbaar*).

[11] The observations on the Dutch expression *mals* are due to Jack Hoeksema and have been discussed in van der Wouden (1994a, 1994b). Bill Ladusaw has supplied the English example *one bit*.

[12] Keenan and Faltz (1985) offer a detailed study of the role of Boolean algebras in the semantic analysis of natural languages.

[13] See Barwise (1979: 62) and Barwise and Cooper (1981: 184–185).

[14] Milsark (1977) uses *sm* to represent unstressed *some*. A very good discussion of the difference between *sommige* and *enkele*, the Dutch counterparts of stressed and unstressed *some*, is found in De Hoop and Kas (1989) and De Hoop (1990).

[15] The notion of an ideal is, of course, familiar from the theory of Boolean algebras. It involves a distinguished type of nonempty subset meeting the conditions in (44). See Sikorski (1969: 11) and Stoll (1974: 207). A detailed study and classification of ideals is provided by Stone (1937). The notion of a quasi-ideal is slightly more general in that it can also involve the empty set.

[16] See Chellas (1980: 215).

[17] See Zwarts (1991: 444).

[18] See Zwarts (1991: 447).

[19] See Stoll (1974: 211).

[20] See Chang and Keisler (1977: 143-144, 166).

[21] The relation of Boolean inclusion in the algebra 2 is defined in such a way that the zero element (0) contains only itself, whereas the unit element (1) contains both itself and the zero element.

[22] Such functions are sometimes said to be isotone. Their monotone decreasing counterparts, defined in (74), are accordingly referred to as antitone functions. See Birkhoff (1967: 3) and Stoll (1974: 55).

[23] See Chang and Keisler (1977: 307).

[24] See Bell and Slomson (1969).

[25] See Zwarts (1993) for a formal proof to this effect, using the assumptions and methods outlined in van Benthem (1986) and Zwarts (1983).

[26] Hoeksema (1986: 36-37) argues that the English determiner *each* differs from its Dutch counterpart *elk(e)* in that it is non-monotonic instead of anti-additive. Unlike *elk(e)*, *each* does not license negative polarity items in relative clauses, as shown by the ungrammaticality of *Each student who ever passed this test was killed by a mysterious disease*. Dutch *elk(e)*, on the other hand, is capable of licencing the strong polarity item *ook maar iets*: *Elk kind dat ook maar iets vermoedt, zal iemand waarschuwen* ('Each child that suspects anything will tell someone'). See Seuren (1985) for additional discussion.

REFERENCES

Barwise, J. (1979). 'On Branching Quantifiers in English.' *Journal of Philosophical Logic* **8**, 47-80.

Barwise, J. and R. Cooper (1981). 'Generalized Quantifiers and Natural Language.' *Linguistics and Philosophy* **4**, 159-219.

van Benthem, J. (1986). *Essays in Logical Semantics*. Dordrecht: Reidel.

Bell, J.L. and A.B. Slomson (1969). *Models and Ultraproducts*. Amsterdam: North-Holland.

Biedermann, R. (1969). *Die deutschen Gradadverbien in synchronischer und diachronischer Sicht*. Doctoral dissertation, University of Heidelberg.

Birkhoff, G. (1967). *Lattice Theory*. Third edition. Providence, Rhode Island: American Mathematical Society.

Chang, C.C. and H.J. Keisler (1977). *Model Theory*. Second edition. Amsterdam: North-Holland.

Chellas, B.F. (1980). *Modal Logic: An Introduction*. Cambridge: Cambridge University Press.

van Dalen, D. (1986). 'Intuitionistic Logic.' In: D. Gabbay and F. Guenthner (eds.), *Handbook of Philosophical Logic*. Volume III. Dordrecht: Reidel, 225-339.

De Hoop, H. (1990). 'On the Characterization of the Weak-Strong Distinction.' To appear in E. Bach, B. Jelinek, A. Kratzer, and B. Partee (eds.), *Cross-Linguistic Quantification*.

De Hoop, H. and M. Kas (1989). 'Sommige betekenisaspecten van enkele kwantoren, oftewel: enkele betekenisaspecten van sommige kwantoren.' *Tijdschrift voor Taal- en Tekstwetenschap* **9**, 31-49.

Dummett, M. (1977). *Elements of Intuitionism*. With the Assistance of R. Minio. Oxford: Oxford University Press.

Dunn, J.M. (1993), 'Star and Perp: Two Treatments of Negation.' Indiana University Logic Group, Preprint No. IULG-93-21, Indiana University, Bloomington. To appear in: James Tomberlin (ed.), *Philosophical Perspectives: Philosophical Logic*, Vols. 7-8.

Evers, A. (1975). *The Transformational Cycle in Dutch and German*. Doctoral dissertation, University of Utrecht.

Gamut, L.T.F. (1991). *Logic, Language, and Meaning. Volume I: Introduction to Logic*. Chicago: The University of Chicago Press.

Hazen, A.(1992) 'Subminimal Negation.' Philosophy Department Preprints 1/92, University of Melbourne, Melbourne.

Hoeksema, J. (1983). 'Negative Polarity and the Comparative.' *Natural Language and Linguistic Theory* **1**, 403-434.

Hoeksema, J. (1986). 'Monotonicity Phenomena in Natural Language.' *Linguistic Analysis* **16**, 25-40.

Hoppenbrouwers, G. (1983). *Negatief en Positief Polaire Elementen in de Taal: Een Onderzoek naar het Syntactisch en Semantisch gedrag van Negatief- en Positief Polaire Elementen*. M.A. thesis, University of Nijmegen.

Keenan, E.L. and L.M. Faltz (1985). *Boolean Semantics for Natural Language*. Dordrecht, Reidel.

Krifka, M. (1989). 'Some Remarks on Polarity Items.' D. Zaefferer (ed.), *Semantic Universals and Universal Semantics*. Dordrecht, Foris.

Krifka, M. (1990). 'Polarity Phenomena and Alternative Semantics.' In: M. Stokhof and L. Torenvliet, eds., *Proceedings of the Seventh Amsterdam Colloquium*. Amsterdam: Institute for Language, Logic and Information, 277-301.

Kürschner, W. (1983). *Studien zur Negation im Deutschen*. Tübingen: Narr.

Ladusaw, W.A. (1979). *Polarity Sensitivity as Inherent Scope Relations*. Doctoral dissertation, University of Texas, Austin. Reproduced by the Indiana University Linguistics Club. Also published, New York: Garland Press, 1980.

Ladusaw, W.A. (1980). 'On the Notion *Affective* in the Analysis of Negative-Polarity Items.' *Journal of Linguistic Research* **1**, 1-16.

Ladusaw, W.A. (1983). 'Logical Form and Conditions on Grammaticality.' *Linguistics and Philosophy* **6**, 373-392.

Milsark, G.L (1977). 'Toward an Explanation of Certain Peculiarities of the Existential Construction in English.' *Linguistic Analysis* **3**, 1-29.

van Os, C. (1989). *Aspekte der Intensivierung im Deutschen*. Tübingen: Narr.

Pullum, G.K. and G. Gazdar (1982) 'Natural Languages and Context-Free Languages.' *Linguistics and Philosophy* **4**, 471-504.

Quine, W.V. (1974). *Methods of Logic*. Third edition. London: Routledge and Kegan Paul.

Rooth, M. (1985). *Association with Focus*. Doctoral dissertation, University of Massachusetts, Amherst.

Seuren, P.A.M. (1976). 'Echo: een studie in negatie.' In: G. Koefoed and A. Evers (eds.), *Lijnen van Taaltheoretisch Onderzoek: Een Bundel Oorspronkelijke Opstellen Aangeboden aan Prof. Dr. H. Schultink*. Groningen: Tjeenk Willink, 160-184.

Seuren, P.A.M. (1985). *Discourse Semantics*. Oxford: Blackwell.

Sikorski, R. (1969). *Boolean Algebras*. Third edition. Berlin: Springer.

Stoll, R.R. (1974). *Sets, Logic, and Axiomatic Theories*. Second edition. San Francisco: Freeman.

Stone, M.H. (1937). 'Algebraic Characterization of Special Boolean Rings.' *Fundamenta Mathematicae* **29**, 223-303.

van der Wouden, T. (1994a). 'Polarity and 'Illogical Negation'. In: M. Kanazawa and C.J. Piñón, eds., *Dynamics, Polarity, and Quantification*. CSLI Lecture Notes 48. Stanford: Center for the Study of Language and Information, 17-45.

van der Wouden, T. (1994b). *Negative Contexts*. Doctoral dissertation, University of Groningen.

Zwarts, F. (1981). 'Negatief polaire uitdrukkingen I.' *GLOT: Tijdschrift voor Taalwetenschap* **4**, 35-132.

Zwarts, F. (1983). 'Determiners: A Relational Perspective.' In: A.G.B. ter Meulen (ed.), *Studies in Modeltheoretic Semantics*. Dordrecht, Foris, 37-62.

Zwarts, F. (1986). *Categoriale Grammatica en Algebraïsche Semantiek: Een Onderzoeknaar Negatie en Polariteit in het Nederlands*. Doctoral dissertation, University of Groningen.

Zwarts, F. (1991). 'Negation and Generalized Quantifiers.' In: J. van der Does and J. van Eijck (eds.), *Generalized Quantifier Theory and Applications*. Amsterdam: Dutch Network for Language, Logic and Information, 443-462.

Zwarts, F. (1993). 'The Syntax and Semantics of Negative Polarity.' Manuscript, University of Groningen.

JAAP VAN DER DOES

SUMS AND QUANTIFIERS

1. AIMS

The present article is on the semantics of plural noun phrases. Perhaps the semantics of no category is studied as thoroughly as that of noun phrases. Yet, the resulting theory of generalised quantifiers is mainly developed by disregarding the fact that most noun phrases are plural. Since it restricts itself to properties of 'plain' individuals rather than of sums or groups, it does not elucidate the typical phenomena of statements about such collections. Conversely, the familiar proposals concerning the semantics of plurals normally concentrate on a small number of noun phrases and leave unclear which options there are in collectivising the theory of generalised quantification.

Here I study systematic ways to combine the standard theory of quantification with the sum theory of collections. The research is carried out within an extensional type theory. In such a framework the theories can be connected by giving ways to transform determiners in type $((et)((et)t))$, i.e., relations between sets, to ones in type $((et)(((et)t)t))$, i.e., relations between sets and sets of sets. I assume for simplicity that common nouns only hold of individuals (denote sets) and that only verb phrases are collective (denote sets of sets). Given that collections viewed as sums may be identified with sets, such 'lifted' determiner denotations are suitable to be used in a collective setting.

There are two reasons why I do not treat the alternative theory of collections as groups. Firstly, the sum approach is easier to handle, and there is no obstacle to transfer the results obtained here to the more involved group setting (cf. Van der Does (1992, 12–14)). Secondly, Schwarzschild's (1992) arguments, which leave little room for groups, are rather convincing.

1.1. Two sources of readings

Whatever the preferred theory of collections may be, the literature has basically two strategies to obtain collective and other readings. On the first and oldest strategy, called the NP strategy here, the noun phrase is the main locus to generate the readings (Bartsch (1973), Bennett (1974), Scha (1981), Verkuyl (1981)). In contrast, a more recent strategy works on the assumption that the readings should be generated within the

VP by means of (c)overt modification. This so-called VP strategy is introduced by Link (1983; 1991) and refined by Lønning (1987; 1989) and Roberts (1987), among others. The third option, where the readings of complex sentences depend functionally on the readings of both categories (and perhaps on that of others), is, I think, the correct one (cf. Van der Does (1992, ch. 4)). Roberts comes close to this view where she writes that 'distributivity is a property of predications, combinations of a subject and an object' (Roberts (1987, 100)). However, for the simple transitive sentences studied here it is enough to discern the above two strategies.

It may seem that the VP strategy, with its emphasis on modification, is less interesting when the connection between quantification and collectives is at stake. This is not so, for the problem still remains of how to deal with arbitrary noun phrases. On this view each noun phrase or class of noun phrases should be treated in a single way. But which ways are used in the literature and do they allow a satisfactory generalisation? Moreover, both the NP and VP strategy should be studied since we want to know how they compare, logically as well as empirically.

To enable such a comparison the differences between the two approaches, though real, should be kept at a minimum. I will use the fact that noun phrases often denote sets of verb phrase extensions. So, the VP strategy can to a large extent be mimicked within the NP strategy by combining the different verb phrase modifications with the one treatment of noun phrases. In this way different readings of noun phrases result which may be contrasted with the ones proposed by the NP strategy. (It so happens that conversely the readings given by the NP strategy can be obtained systematically by use of exactly the same modifiers used within the VP strategy.)

1.2. Three readings, six lifts

Closely related to the question of where the readings come from is the more empirical question of which kind of readings occur and how they should be modeled. Most semanticists would grant that at least a collective and a distributive or 'atomic' reading exist. Less attention has been paid to what I call a neutral reading, but I study this reading separately.

One of the reasons why neutral readings need special care is that it is not entirely clear how to model them. Scha (1981) and Gillon (1987; 1990) take some statements about collections to be neither distributive nor collective but kind of intermediate. E.g., (1) cannot be distributive, for single individuals do not gather.

(1)   Five thousand people gathered near Amsterdam

But (1) does have a neutral reading, which is used to describe one or more gatherings with a view to the precise number people involved in them. As we shall see, this precision is not available on its collective reading.

However, the most straightforward way to formalise the neutral reading quickly leads to unwelcome truth conditions. For instance, on its neutral reading a noun phrases cannot combine with a complex verb phrase in the usual way. I try to remedy this by considering some alternatives involving partitions, minimal covers, and so-called pseudo-partitions. I shall argue that none of these alternatives are appropriate, and hence that on its neutral reading a noun phrase does not take scope over complex verb phrases. On the other hand, this reading is the likely candidate to be used in non-iterative polyadic quantification, such as the cumulative or branching variants. By way of example I show how to deal with cumulative readings in a collective setting.

Three readings for each of the two strategies gives a sum total of six lifts to generate them from the familiar denotations. These lifts capture most of the semantical observations found in the literature. To be sure, I do not claim that each determiner allows all the readings. However, I do hold that the readings can be acquired uniformly for all the determiners that do allow them. It is this uniformity which enables us to compare the readings by looking at logical behaviour, scopal behaviour, and quantificational force.

1.3. Main results

Using the results obtained along these lines, I argue that in case of simple sentences the NP strategy is empirically more adequate than the VP strategy. In its purest form the VP strategy takes the collective reading as basic and generates the other readings by means of verb phrase modification. The collective readings which have been proposed in the literature treat the noun phrase so that it leaves the verb phrase outside of its scope. Here the determiner in a noun phrase, if present, rather functions in an adjectival way. For example, numerals select the collections from a noun of a particular size, and similarly for the other determiners. In contrast, the NP strategy allows for more variation in handling the noun phrase. Most of the times it has the verb phrase within its scope (on the distributive and neutral readings), but sometimes it does not (on the collective reading). It is precisely this difference which makes the distributive and neutral reading given by the NP strategy superior to those of the VP strategy. On these readings one is interested respectively in the individuals that have a property *simpliciter* or which partake in a collection having a property. But the relevant individuals are only determined as required if the verb phrase is within the scope of the noun phrase. The conclusion seems to be that without further ado the VP strategy in its purest form is not feasible.

On the other hand, it is held against the NP strategy that not all readings result from noun phrase ambiguities. The problem arises with some conjoined verb phrases, which may only be partly marked for distributivity. Since I do not concern myself with conjunction in the following, I make some remarks on this matter here.

Dowty (1986) observes that if modification is included in a NP denotation, the distributivity of a verb phrase becomes an all–or–nothing issue. Sentence (2), which resembles the examples given by Dowty, is adapted from Lasersohn (1989):

(2)   *a.*   Four men met in a bar and had a beer
      b.   Four men$_1$ are such that they$_1$ met in a bar and each of them$_1$ had a beer

In (2a) the first conjunct of *to meet in a bar and have a beer* is collective and the second distributive. Does this force us to hold that the readings come from the modified VP conjuncts? Not necessarily, for in the common analysis (2b) of (2a) the collectivity or distributivity of the conjuncts may be due to the noun phrases 'they' and 'each of them' (cf. Van der Does (1992, 83-85)). The anaphoric link between these noun phrases and the main subject could be established by means of quantifying in or a similar such device. At any rate, the differences between this and the modification approach are negligible, as the modifiers result from the different readings of the quantifier 'all' by swapping its noun and verb argument.

Note that on both approaches there is a threat of over generation. In case of the NP strategy the reading of the main subject may not combine well with the conjoined VP denotations. Whereas the VP strategy should preclude further modification of the complex VP. A convenient way to handle this problem is the use of a feature system as is given in Van der Does (1992, ch. 4). In such a system, whether a complex expression is distributive, collective or neutral depends functionally on its constituting categories. Mainly to preclude over generation, I hold that the reading of a complex sentences should not be attributed to a single category but be determined compositionally.

1.4. Overview

In section 2, I give a quick overview of the models used in the sum theory of collections and show how they are represented within the extensional type theory opted for here. Even at this point I stress that the application of simple type shifts which embed objects of lower level into a collective environment is beneficial. Section 3 studies the treatments of numerals by Scha and Link, the two main proponents of the NP and the VP strategy. With a view to handling arbitrary noun phrases, I analyse their proposals in terms of the familiar numeral denotations from generalised quantifier theory. The next section is on determiners. I introduce the six lifts to make determiners suitable for a collective VP, show that they can be generated from two basic lifts by means of modification, and give some examples of lifted determiners. The examples are used to show which lift gives the appropriate collective reading. Section 5 maps the logical relations between the different readings for different kinds of determiner. It also makes a choice among the two treatments of distributive and neutral readings by comparing their quantificational force. Yet, the neutral reading receives further attention in section 6 with a view to its rather special scopal behaviour. As we go along, we also obtain information to what extent neutral readings could be used to reduce the number of readings of a sentence (cf. Verkuyl and Van der Does (1991)).

In this article, the focus is mainly on the empirical side of simple plural noun phrases. Definite as well as more complex plural noun phrases are studied in Van der Does (1992). One could also take a logical stance, where arbitrary lifts from type $((et)((et)t))$ to type $((et)(((et)t)t))$ are studied in order to find constraints to single out the reasonable ones. Here one would also like to know which alternatives there are for such familiar notions as conservativity and the like. Moreover, one would like to characterise the results of the lifts as the unique determiners having certain properties. The readers interested in these issues may consult Van der Does (1992, ch. 5). There one also finds the proofs of propositions, which are just stated here.

1.5. Tools and notational conventions

In this article I often interchange set theory and type theory without much notice. That one may do so, follows from the well–known equivalence of sets and their characteristic functions. I keep the explicit typing of variables at a minimum by use of some notation:

variables	type
$x, y, z, \ldots$	e
$X, Y, Z, \ldots$	(et)
$R^n, \ldots$	e^n
$\mathbf{X}, \mathbf{Y}, \mathbf{Z}, \ldots$	$((et)t)$
$\mathbf{R}^n, \ldots$	$(et)^n$
$D, \ldots$	$((et)((et)t))$
$\Delta, \ldots$	$((et)(((et)t)t))$

Here α: $\alpha^0 = t$ and $\alpha^{n+1} = (\alpha \alpha^n)$. The variables may have primes or subscripts as usual.

2. THE LOGICAL FRAMEWORK

The core insight which made people work on the semantics of plurals is captured in the following principle:

> Some properties of collections cannot be reduced to properties between their individual members.

An example of such a property is *to play the 'Große Fuge'*, as in:

(3)   The musicians played the *'Große Fuge'*

Plainly, the musicians were able to perform the composition in virtue of their individual achievements and quality. Still, (3) records a fact over and above the complex relationships between the musicians during the performance. It is the fact that to play this fugue is a joint venture.

2.1. CAJS–models

Several authors have addressed the question of how to model collective readings. It is felt that the collections should comply with three principles that 'incorporate all the intuitions about the behaviour of plural objects in natural language' (Link (1991)):[1]

Atomicity Each collection must be the unique combination of all individuals constituting it.

Completeness It should be possible to combine collections into a single new one.

Atoms Individuals have to reappear as a limiting case; as those collections which consist of just one item (the *atoms* of a domain).

Among the structures which satisfy these requirements are the complete atomic join semilattices – CAJS's for short. Link (1983) introduces the idea to replace the familiar domains of discourse, which consist of just individuals, by CAJSs. I do not give definitions, but the main advantage of using algebraic domains is that they enable to capitalise on 'a striking similarity between collective predication and predication involving mass nouns' (Link (1983, 302)).

In the present setting, where mass terms are disregarded, one may as well use a particular kind of set–theoretic CAJS, namely those with a domain of the form $\wp^+(X)$, X a set.[2] The elements of $\wp^+(X)$, the non–empty subsets of X, are to model collections; individuals d appear as singletons $\{d\}$, the atoms of $\wp^+(X)$; the operation assembling sets of collections into a new one is union; and as to atomicity, indeed, for each set Y one has:

(4) $$Y = \bigcup\{\{d\} : d \in Y\}$$

In (4) it is assumed that union is of arbitrary sets of sets and not just of pairs of sets, otherwise atomicity would only be guaranteed for finite sets. Given this much, one defines:

Definition 2.1. (CAJS–models) *Let X be a non–empty set. A CAJS–model $\mathcal{M}$ is an ordered tuple:*

$$\langle \wp^+(X), \mathrm{AT}(X), \bigcup, \subseteq, [\![-]\!] \rangle$$

The set $\mathrm{AT}(X) (= \{\{d\} : d \in X\})$ contains the atoms of $\wp^+(X)$. The interpretation function $[\![-]\!]$ assigns a collection: $[\![c]\!] \in \wp^+(X)$, to each constant c, and an n–place relation among collections: $[\![R^n]\!] \subseteq \wp^+(X)^n$, to each n–ary relation sign R^n.

Models come with formal languages, but I shall not give one in full detail. Rather, I introduce relations, constants and the like as we go along, and deal with them directly in terms of their interpretations. Given that the noun 'musicians' denotes a set of atoms, (3) is formalised by:

$$[\![play\ the\ 'Große\ Fuge']\!](\bigcup [\![musicians]\!])$$

As is done more often, *the* is taken to return the collection obtain from the noun. Note that the property *to play the 'Große Fuge'* is attributed to the set of musicians instead of to its members. It is often assumed that this is enough to model the collective reading of (3).

2.2. Type theory

As said, the explicit use of algebraic domains for the purpose of modeling collective readings, originated with Link (1983), and presently this technique is very popular. But there also has been an alternative tradition that works within the extensional type theory with basic types e (entities) and t (truth values), and compound types $(\alpha\beta)$ (functions mapping type α objects onto type β objects). The tradition can be traced back to Bartsch (1973) and Bennett (1974), among others. For reasons given shortly, type theory will in this article be my main instrument too. Therefore, I shall now discuss some strategies showing that all that can be done with CAJS–models can be done as well within type theory.

In a CAJS–model, relation signs are interpreted according to the most complex case: without exception relations are between arbitrary collections. Using a strategy of collectivisation in analogy with Van Benthem (1991, ch. 12), this can also be simulated within type theory. For example, let R be a two place relation sign of type $(e(et))$. In a CAJS–model its interpretation will be a relation between elements of $\wp^+(X)$, which are sets. Due to the fact that this domain is, so to speak, of type (et), one could therefore say that the type of R's interpretation $[\![R]\!]$ is $((et)((et)t))$ rather than $(e(et))$. But then a uniform change in the types assigned to expressions achieves the same effect, as follows:

- convert all e's in the types of expressions into (et);
- interpret the resulting expressions as is usual for type theory.

This strategy capitalises on the main characteristic of CAJS–models, or of Scha's (1981) system for that matter: that the distinction between individuals and collections is blurred. The reason for wanting this identification is that some expressions, e.g. the verb *to make music*, pertain to individuals and collections alike so that a type distinction between individuals and collections combined with a rigid category–to–type assignment enforces one to give such verbs two lexical entries: one interpreted in type (et) another in type $((et)t)$. Similarly, proper names, which intuitively take their denotation in the set of entities $\mathbf{D}_e$, can be conjoined in a non–Boolean way with NPs such as *the boys*, which may denote the set of boys in $\mathbf{D}_{(et)}$. Again, multiple lexical entries seem to be called for. Some feel that the ambiguities imposed on these expressions are only motived by the logical apparatus.

Changing the semantics to a richer environment, the question comes to the fore of how the new semantics relates to the old, and particularly whether there are systematic ways to connect them. In case of the CAJS–models this is indeed so, as can be show within type theory by means of type changes. The definition of these models can be seen to involve the following shift in types:

$$(et) \Rightarrow ((et)t)$$

It tacitly uses the type shift operators:

$$\wp^+ := \lambda X \lambda Y.\ Y \subseteq X \wedge Y \neq \emptyset$$
$$\text{AT} := \lambda X \lambda Y.\ Y \subseteq X \wedge |Y| = 1$$

which transform sets – objects of type (et) – into sets of sets – objects of type $((et)t)$. In fact, these operators play a prominent role in the literature on plurals: they are Link's pluralisation operator and Scha's atomiser, respectively.[3] Similarly, the new denotation of proper names results from a use of 'Quine's function,' which embodies the type change: $e \Rightarrow (et)$:

$$I := \lambda x \lambda y.\ x = y$$

This function transforms an individual into the corresponding singleton, so that we get for proper names c the denotation $\lambda \mathbf{X}.\mathbf{X}(I([\![c]\!]))$ (proper names have no other readings).

Even these simple examples suggest that type theory is well–suited to study collectivity. For our present purposes it is particularly useful, since it gives a framework to transform the standard semantics to the richer collective setting in a uniform way.

3. NUMERALS

Numerals are a prime source of collective readings, and indeed their semantics figures prominently in the literature. Here I shall focus on the semantics given by Scha (1981) and Link (1983; 1991) together with one inspired by Gillon (1987). These semantics leave opaque how the numeral denotations in type $((et)(((et)t)t))$ relate to the ones of type $((et)((et)t))$ given in generalised quantifier theory. I shall remedy this by formulating the systems within type theory in terms of the usual denotations:

(5) $\quad \mathbf{n}_{((et)((et)t))} := \lambda X \lambda Y. |X \cap Y| = n$

This, in turn, suggests six lifts from type $((et)((et)t))$ to type $((et)(((et)t)t))$ by means of which an arbitrary determiner may receive different readings on the basis of its standard denotation. This way of proceeding has the important advantage that the collective semantics of determiners gets connected with generalised quantifier theory.

To analyse the treatment of numerals in Scha (1981) and Link (1983; 1991), much ground can be covered by studying the simple sentence:

(6) $\qquad$ Four men lifted two tables

I discuss which readings of (6) can be detected. As we go along, we learn where Scha and Link locate the quintessence of collectivity, and whether they live up to their own opinions.

3.1. Scha

The title 'Distributive, Collective and Cumulative Quantification' of Scha (1981) makes plain that he thinks distributivity and collectivity to reside in the NP. An inspection of his semantics shows that complex NPs have these properties in a derivative sense: it is the determiners which receive different readings in this respect. A numeral (**exactly**) n, in particular, has three denotations: a distributive, a collective and a neutral one. Using my own notation and names they are:[4]

$$D_1 \quad \lambda X \lambda \mathbf{Y}. |\{d \in X : \mathbf{Y}(\{d\})\}| = n$$
$$C_2^a \quad \lambda X \lambda \mathbf{Y}. \exists Y \subseteq X \, [|Y| = n \wedge \mathbf{Y}(Y)]$$
$$N_2 \quad \lambda X \lambda \mathbf{Y}. |\bigcup \{Y \subseteq X : \mathbf{Y}(Y)\}| = n$$

These readings can be rewritten in terms of the numeral denotation in (5):

$$D_1 \quad \lambda X \lambda \mathbf{Y}. \mathbf{n}(X)(\bigcup(\mathbf{Y} \cap \mathrm{AT}(X)))$$
$$C_2^a \quad \lambda X \lambda \mathbf{Y}. \exists Z \subseteq X \, [\mathbf{n}(X)(Z) \wedge Z \in \mathbf{Y}]$$
$$N_2 \quad \lambda X \lambda \mathbf{Y}. \mathbf{n}(X)(\bigcup(\mathbf{Y} \cap \wp(X)))$$

Depending on how the NUM in an NP is marked, a sentence:

$[_S [_{NP_1} \text{ NUM N}] [_{VP} \text{ V } [_{NP_2} \text{ NUM N}]]]$

could have the nine readings in table 1 (entry form: $NP_1 NP_2$).

$D_1 D_1$	$D_1 N_2$	$D_1 C_2^{em\ a}$
$N_2 D_1$	$N_2 N_2$	$N_2 C_2^{em\ a}$
$C_2^a D_1$	$C_2^a N_2$	$C_2^a C_2^a$

Table 1: *nine readings*

In section 6 we shall see that some of these readings are unwanted. To give a first indication of what they amount to, we have a closer look at three of them: $D_1 D_1$, $N_2 N_2$, and $C_2^a C_2^a$.

(7) a. $|\{d \in [\![man]\!] : |\{d' \in [\![table]\!] : [\![lift]\!](\{d\})(\{d'\}))| = 2\}| = 4$
    b. $|\bigcup\{X \subseteq [\![man]\!] : |\bigcup\{Y \subseteq [\![table]\!] : [\![lift]\!](X)(Y)\}| = 2\}| = 4$
    c. $\exists X \in [\![four\ man]\!] \exists Y \in [\![two\ table]\!] : [\![lift]\!](X)(Y)$

On the $D_1 D_1$ reading of (6) one has (7a): four men each lifted each of two tables; which speaks for itself. The $N_2 N_2$ reading of (6) gives (7b), which says that there are four men forming collections M and that for each such M there are two tables from which the collections of tables are formed which M lifted. Link (1991) calls these readings 'partitional'. But in a partition the collections do not overlap, whereas N_2 does not require this. The $C_2^a C_2^a$ reading of (6), finally, is of a different nature altogether. Shortening, e.g., $\exists X[X \subseteq [\![man]\!] \wedge |X| = 4 \wedge \phi]$ to: $\exists X \in [\![four\ man]\!][\phi]$, one gets (7c). Now (6) states that a collection of four men lifted a collection of two tables.

Table 1 has nine readings, but in this count I disregarded scope ambiguities of NPs. As in Scha's 'strict version' – i.e., his formal system without the rule F4, – the order of the quantifiers is that of the corresponding NPs in (6). The 'loose version' of Scha does allow scope ambiguities and in that system (6) has eighteen readings. Apart from these, there is the so-called cumulative reading in which the NPs are independent of each other. It states that the number of table lifting men is four and the number of man lifted tables is two. In case of numerals some of these readings are equivalent, but for arbitrary determiners this need not be so.

3.2. Link

In his 'Plural' (1991) Link is concerned, among many other things, with showing that sentences like (6) are less ambiguous than Scha would have it.[5] He counts eight readings, some of which are equivalent due to the particular determiners used.

How does Link go about this? He stresses that distributivity is a lexical feature which appears primarily in the head noun of an NP and the head verb of a VP, an observation which can also be found in Link (1983, 310). This is significant, because it disallows distributivity to occur, say, just at the level of a VP. If distributivity is a lexical feature, a complex VP can only be distributive in a derivative sense, namely in as far as this property is passed on to the VP by its immediate constituents and the way they are combined.

In contrast with Scha, Link does not see distributivity and collectivity as lexical features of determiners. Yet his calculation of the ambiguity of (6) is based on this assumption:

> ...an indefinite PNP gives rise to three different readings, one distributive and two collective. [···] Now I have already expressed doubts as to whether I should really distinguish the simple collective [C_2^a] and the partitional reading [N_2]. Be this as it may, I am going to ignore the latter one here. This brings us back to eight different cases... Link (1991)

The calculation is in conflict with the supposition that distributivity is a lexical feature of verbs, but one can make sense of it by calling an NP *distributive* if it binds a distributive argument and *collective* otherwise. Then Scha and Link differ in the number of readings they attribute to an NP. Link's razor leisurely cuts down Scha's distinction between a neutral and a collective reading to leave us C_2^a only.[6] As a result (6) gets eight readings, but one may wonder whether the choice made can be argued for empirically.

To model that the distributivity of an NP depends on the distributivity of the argument it binds, Link introduces the verb modifier δ besides the other operators in (8) for two–place relations (Link (1991)):[7]

(8) $\quad \delta \quad := \quad \lambda \mathbf{X} \lambda Y.\ \text{AT}(Y) \subseteq \mathbf{X}$
$\quad\quad\ \bullet\bullet \quad := \quad \lambda \mathbf{R}^2.\ \mathbf{R}$
$\quad\quad\ \delta\bullet \quad := \quad \lambda \mathbf{R}^2 \lambda X \lambda Y.\ \forall x \in X\ \mathbf{R}(\{x\})(Y)$
$\quad\quad\ \bullet\delta \quad := \quad \lambda \mathbf{R}^2 \lambda X \lambda Y.\ \forall y \in Y\ \mathbf{R}(X)(\{y\})$
$\quad\quad\ \delta\delta \quad := \quad \lambda \mathbf{R}^2 \lambda X \lambda Y.\ \forall x \in X\ \forall y \in Y\ \mathbf{R}(\{x\})(\{y\})$

As to the relational operators, $\delta\bullet$ makes a two–place relation distributive in its first argument and leaves the other one unaffected, and similarly for the other operators. Now, the general scheme of a simple transitive sentence is:

(9) $NP_1[\lambda X.NP_2[\lambda Y.DO(V)(X)(Y)]]$

In (9), DO varies over the relational operators $\bullet\bullet, \delta\bullet, \bullet\delta, \delta\delta$. So, the scheme justifies (6) to have eight readings: there are four instantiations of DO for both orders of the NPs.

The story does not end here. A closer look at Link (1991) shows that his formal system allows (6) to have more readings than the eight listed. Lønning (1987; 1989) and Roberts (1987) have observed that the conviction that distributivity is a matter of the verb is countered by some of the logical forms given. Using a type theoretical analogue, the subject wide–scope doubly distributive reading of (6) is formalised in (10):

(10) $\exists X \in [\![four\ man]\!][\delta(\lambda Y.\exists Z \in [\![two\ table]\!][\bullet\delta([\![lift]\!])(Y)(Z)])(X)]$

On this reading, (6) states that there is a collection of four men and that for each member m in this collection there is a collection of two tables each of which are lifted by m. In terms of verb categories, the distributivity in (10) is non–lexical: it is a property of the VP *to lift two tables*.[8] This makes plain that Link selects his readings from the scheme (11) rather than from (9):

(11) $NP_1[\lambda X.DO_1(\lambda Y.NP_2[\lambda Z.DO_2(\mathbf{V})(Y)(Z)])(X)]$

Here DO_2 is as before, while DO_1 can be either δ or $\lambda \mathbf{X}.\mathbf{X}$. What has gone unnoticed is that scheme (11) gives a sum total of sixteen possible readings; the previous eight for each of δ and $\lambda \mathbf{X}.\mathbf{X}$. Some of these readings are undesirable, like those in which DO_2 is set to $\delta\delta$ and DO_1 to δ with the effect that an argument place is marked for distributivity twice. It is not clear, though, how they can be precluded when working with verb modifiers.

One way to circumvent the over generation in Link's system is Scha's proposal: distributivity and collectivity are lexical features of determiners.[9] To this end, a denotation for **n** could be defined with a built–in use of δ, as in (12a) and its equivalent (12b):

(12)   *a.* $\lambda X \lambda \mathbf{Y}.\ \exists Z \subseteq X\,[|Z| = n \wedge \delta(\mathbf{Y})(Z)]$
         b. $\lambda X \lambda \mathbf{Y}.\ \exists Z \subseteq X\,[|Z| = n \wedge \mathrm{AT}(Z) \subseteq \mathbf{Y}]$

Recall that this is how the VP strategy is mimicked within the NP strategy. Formulated in terms of the type $((et)((et)t))$ denotation of **n** this becomes:

$$D_1^a \quad \lambda X \lambda \mathbf{Y}.\ \exists Z \subseteq X\,[\mathbf{n}(X)(Z) \wedge \text{AT}(Z) \subseteq \mathbf{Y}]$$

With D_1^a numerals at hand, the $D_1^a D_1^a$ reading of (6) still reduces to (10) while the infelicitous readings are blocked. In D_1^a the marking of an argument place for distributivity is connected with binding it. Since double bindings are impossible, double distributivity markings are too.

On this view, Link's treatment of numerals is seen as:

- opting for Scha's collective C_2^a only;
- interchanging Scha's D_1 for the newly distributive D_1^a.

However, there is a reading generated by the scheme 11 which cannot be obtained by use of the distributive NP denotation.[10] It is the reading where DO_1 is the identity and DO_2 $\delta\delta$. It makes (6) equivalent to (13):

(13) $\quad \exists X \in [\![\textit{four man}]\!] \exists Z \in [\![\textit{two table}]\!] : \text{AT}(X) \times \text{AT}(Z) \subseteq [\![\textit{lift}]\!]$

How serious a defect is it that (13) cannot be generated in this way? I'm inclined to think that it is no defect at all. In fact (13) is the branching reading of (6) as proposed by Barwise (1979) for the case of MON↑ quantifiers (cf. also Hoeksema (1983, appendix)). But recent research has shown that the branching reading is much more complex. In particular, it is argued by Sher (1990) and Spaan (1993) that some notion of maximality is involved; a notion which is absent in case of collective readings. For this reason I think that we better treat the non–iterative forms of quantification separately. Also, within a collective framework I surmise that these forms of quantification use the neutral rather than the distributive readings of the quantifiers. In the next section I give a first indication of what these neutral readings look like.

3.3. Getting mixed–up

Sentences with large numerals often have an intermediate or neutral reading, which is neither distributive nor collective. Sentence (14) is an example adapted from Link (1991):[11]

(14)   Half a million children gathered all over the country

This sentence will be true even if the collection of children did not gather as a whole; there could be many subgatherings that may or may not overlap. The N_2 numerals of Scha come close to modelling this reading. However, it requires that only groups of children gathered, and this seems too strict. I do not think (14) is false, if some adults join the children.

Gillon (1987) has similar intuitions. His observations imply that (15) should be valid:

(15) Hammerstein and Rodgers wrote a musical together
Rodgers and Hart wrote a musical together
$\Rightarrow$ At least three composers wrote some musicals

Here, too, the most natural explanation is in terms of neutral readings.

I propose to model the neutral reading by means of the 'partaking in' operator π (cf. Link (1987)):

$$\pi := \lambda \mathbf{X} \lambda Y.\ Y \subseteq \bigcup \mathbf{X}$$

Using either a C_2^a or a N_2 numeral with a π-marked VP, the conclusion of (15) is formalised by (16a-b), which are synonymous to their primed neighbours:

(16) a. $\exists X \in [\![\text{at least three composers}]\!][\pi([\![\text{write some musicals}]\!])(X)]$
 a'. $\exists X \in [\![\text{at least three composers}]\!][X \subseteq \bigcup [\![\text{write some musicals}]\!]]$
 b. $|\bigcup \{X \subseteq [\![\text{composer}]\!] : \pi([\![\text{write some musicals}]\!])(X)\}| \geq 3$
 b'. $|\bigcup \{X \subseteq [\![\text{composer}]\!] : X \subseteq \bigcup [\![\text{write some musicals}]\!]\}| \geq 3$

Note that neither of the denotations restricts the VP to collections of composers. On both readings composers may have collaborated with others to write a musical.

Applied to transitive verbs, the π-operator leads to the problem of double marking noted earlier for the δ-operator. Again it can be solved by incorporating the use of the operator into the meaning of a numeral. As a result, two other denotations are introduced:[12]

$$\begin{aligned}
N_3 &:= \lambda X \lambda \mathbf{Y}.\ |\bigcup \{Z \subseteq X : \pi(\mathbf{Y})(Z)\}| = n \\
&= \lambda X \lambda \mathbf{Y}.\ |\bigcup \{Z \subseteq X : Z \subseteq \bigcup \mathbf{Y}\}| = n \\
N_3^a &:= \lambda X \lambda \mathbf{Y}.\ \exists Z \subseteq X [|Z| = n \wedge \pi(\mathbf{Y})(Z)] \\
&= \lambda X \lambda \mathbf{Y}.\ \exists Z \subseteq X [|Z| = n \wedge Z \subseteq \bigcup \mathbf{Y}]
\end{aligned}$$

This ends my discussion of numerals. In the next section I show how the insights obtained here can be generalised to give a semantics for arbitrary plural noun phrases.

4. DETERMINERS

This following question is central to this section:

> Do systematic and empirically satisfying ways exists in which the determiners of type $((et)((et)t))$ can be related to their readings in type $((et)(((et)t)t))$?

As a first answer, I propose six lifts suggested by the treatment of numerals, three for the NP and three for the VP approach. Although there are other options – we shall encounter some in section 6, – these seem the most reasonable ones. Note that if both strategies were feasible, excessive ambiguity would result. An intransitive sentence such as

(17)   Most of the men made music

would have an upperbound of six readings (one for each lift). And for transitive sentences the situation is even worse. The sentence

(18)   All men lifted some tables

would get at most seventy–three readings !:

> (six × six NP readings × two scope orderings)
> + one cumulative reading

It is as of old, when people were taught differences.

Here this embarrassment of riches is to some extent eliminated; on each strategy a determiner has at most three readings. Yet one may find the number of readings still too high (at most nine for a transitive sentence if the neutral reading is confined to the cumulative reading). In trying to attain a further reduction of readings, one could address an underlying methodological issue, namely:

> Where exactly does the line of demarcation run between proper readings and mere models realizing a reading?
> Link (1991)

An answer to this question cannot result from a mere inspection of one's idiolect. Instead, one should use both logical results and empirical arguments to reduce the readings to the few, if any, which somehow encompass the others. The other 'readings' could then be seen as types of verifying situations to be promoted to explicit readings only if lexical items demand.

My agenda looks as follows. The lifts are introduced in section 4.1, and section 4.2 indicates their usefulness by means of some examples. In section 5, the strengths and weaknesses of the lifts are compared. I investigate the logical relationships between the readings for arbitrary and for monotonic determiners, besides their quantificational force. The important issue of neutral readings and scope is discussed in section 6. This section also addresses the question of how the neutral readings can be used to effect a reduction in ambiguity.

4.1. Type lifting operators

A first step towards a general semantics for plural noun phrases consists in rewriting the numeral denotations in terms of their standard denotation in type $((et)((et)t))$. In section 3, the following denotations were given:[13]

$$D_1 \quad \lambda X \lambda Y. \, \mathbf{n}(X)(\bigcup(\mathbf{Y} \cap \mathrm{AT}(X)))$$
$$N_2 \quad \lambda X \lambda Y. \, \mathbf{n}(X)(\bigcup(\mathbf{Y} \cap \wp(X)))$$
$$N_3 \quad \lambda X \lambda Y. \, \mathbf{n}(X)(X \cap \bigcup \mathbf{Y})$$
$$D_1^a \quad \lambda X \lambda Y. \, \exists Z \subseteq X \, [\mathbf{n}(X)(Z) \wedge \mathrm{AT}(Z) \subseteq \mathbf{Y}]$$
$$C_2^a \quad \lambda X \lambda Y. \, \exists Z \subseteq X \, [\mathbf{n}(X)(Z) \wedge Z \in \mathbf{Y}]$$
$$N_3^a \quad \lambda X \lambda Y. \, \exists Z \subseteq X \, [\mathbf{n}(X)(Z) \wedge Z \subseteq \bigcup \mathbf{Y}]$$

This manner of presenting the numerals suggests uniform procedures for turning a determiner of type $((et)((et)t))$ into one of type $((et)(((et)t)t))$, as are captured by the lambda–abstracts in (19):

(19) $\quad D_1 \quad \lambda D \lambda X \lambda Y. \, D(X)(\bigcup(\mathbf{Y} \cap \mathrm{AT}(X)))$
$\quad\quad\;\; N_2 \quad \lambda D \lambda X \lambda Y. \, D(X)(\bigcup(\mathbf{Y} \cap \wp(X)))$
$\quad\quad\;\; N_3 \quad \lambda D \lambda X \lambda Y. \, D(X)(X \cap \bigcup \mathbf{Y})$
$\quad\quad\;\; D_1^a \quad \lambda D \lambda X \lambda Y. \, \exists Z \subseteq X \, [D(X)(Z) \wedge \mathrm{AT}(Z) \subseteq \mathbf{Y}]$
$\quad\quad\;\; C_2^a \quad \lambda D \lambda X \lambda Y. \, \exists Z \subseteq X \, [D(X)(Z) \wedge Z \in \mathbf{Y}]$
$\quad\quad\;\; N_3^a \quad \lambda D \lambda X \lambda Y. \, \exists Z \subseteq X \, [D(X)(Z) \wedge Z \subseteq \bigcup \mathbf{Y}]$

The lifts N_2 and N_3 are also in Van Benthem (1991, 67–68), which made me aware of the virtues of using lifts for this purpose.

The names of the lifts carry information on how they function. The letter 'D' stands for distributive, 'C' for collective, and 'N' for neutral. The superscript 'a' indicates that the 'old' determiner leaves the VP argument outside of its scope. These lifts are called the a lifts, and the other ones the non-a lifts. The subscripts, finally, point to the way in which the noun and the verb phrase extension are related to each other. 1: only the atoms formed out of the noun extension matter; 2: only the collections formed out of the noun extension matter; 3: all members in the noun extension matter that occur in a collection in the verb phrase extension. The determiner lifts are distributed over the two approaches as follows. On the NP strategy we have D_1, C_2^a, and as yet two options for the neutral reading: N_2 and N_3. On the VP strategy we have D_1^a, C_2^a, and N_3^a. So the strategies coincide in their treatment of collective readings.

The system behind the determiner names can be brought to the fore by considering some equivalent forms. The lifts D_1^a and N_3^a can also be obtained by combining C_2^a with the application of a modifier δ or π to its VP argument. This is particularly plain when using the format:

$$D_1^a \quad \lambda D \lambda X \lambda \mathbf{Y}.\ D(X) \cap \wp(X) \cap \delta(\mathbf{Y}) \neq \emptyset$$
$$C_2^a \quad \lambda D \lambda X \lambda \mathbf{Y}.\ D(X) \cap \wp(X) \cap \mathbf{Y} \neq \emptyset$$
$$N_3^a \quad \lambda D \lambda X \lambda \mathbf{Y}.\ D(X) \cap \wp(X) \cap \pi(\mathbf{Y}) \neq \emptyset$$

Analogously, the non-a lifts can be presented in a uniform manner, now obtaining D_1 and N_3 from N_2 by means of δ or π:[14]

$$D_1 \quad \lambda D \lambda X \lambda \mathbf{Y}.\ D(X)(\bigcup(\delta(\mathbf{Y}) \cap \wp(X)))$$
$$N_2 \quad \lambda D \lambda X \lambda \mathbf{Y}.\ D(X)(\bigcup(\mathbf{Y} \cap \wp(X)))$$
$$N_3 \quad \lambda D \lambda X \lambda \mathbf{Y}.\ D(X)(\bigcup(\pi(\mathbf{Y}) \cap \wp(X)))$$

Another way to present the non-a lifts stresses that they mainly differ in the ways the type $((et)t)$ VP is restricted to the type (et) noun:

$$D_1 \quad \lambda D \lambda X \lambda \mathbf{Y}.\ D(X)(\bigcup(\mathbf{Y}|_X^1))$$
$$N_2 \quad \lambda D \lambda X \lambda \mathbf{Y}.\ D(X)(\bigcup(\mathbf{Y}|_X^2))$$
$$N_3 \quad \lambda D \lambda X \lambda \mathbf{Y}.\ D(X)(\bigcup(\mathbf{Y}|_X^3))$$

Here the functions $|^i$ ($1 \leq i \leq 3$) of type $((et)(((et)t)((et)t)))$ are defined by:

$$|^1 := \lambda X \lambda \mathbf{Y}.\ \mathbf{Y} \cap \mathrm{AT}(X)$$
$$|^2 := \lambda X \lambda \mathbf{Y}.\ \mathbf{Y} \cap \wp(X)$$
$$|^3 := \lambda X \lambda \mathbf{Y}.\ \lambda Y \exists Z[\mathbf{Y}(Z) \wedge Y = Z \cap X]$$

In set notation $|^3$ can be written as $\lambda X \lambda \mathbf{Y}.\{X \cap Z : Z \in \mathbf{Y}\}$. The notation: $\mathbf{Y}|_X^i$ instead of $|^i(X)(\mathbf{Y})$ derives from the fact that the functions are used to restrict a set $\mathbf{Y}$ to a set X.

Proposing determiner lifts is one thing, but it remains to be argued whether they make sense, or if not generally, whether their application should be restricted to particular occasions. This question is addressed in section 5 and 6. For now, I give an impression of how the lifts work by inspecting the lifted forms of a few determiners.

4.2. Some examples

In this section I have a closer look at the lifted variants of **all**, **some**$_{pl}$, **not all**, **at most four** and of the higher–order determiner **most**. I use **some**$_{pl}$ to pay special attention to the logical behaviour of the collective and neutral readings. The lifted singular determiners, like **every** and **some**$_{sg}$, are discussed separately.

All, the$_{pl}$ The plural determiners **all** and **the**$_{pl}$ of type $((et)((et)t))$ denote the relation: $\lambda X \lambda Y. X \subseteq Y$.[15] As a consequence, their a lifts are of the form (20a), or equivalently (20b):

(20)   a. $\lambda Y \lambda Z.\ \exists X\,[Y = X \land \text{OP}(\mathbf{Z})(X)]$
           b. $\lambda Y \lambda Z.\ \text{OP}(\mathbf{Z})(Y)$

Here 'OP' varies over δ, π and $\lambda \mathbf{X}.\mathbf{X}$. Spelling out the details, the lifts of **all** can be summed up in a table:

(21) $D_1(\mathbf{all}) = \lambda X \lambda \mathbf{Y}.\ \text{AT}(X) \subseteq \mathbf{Y}\ \ \ = D_1^a(\mathbf{all})$
        $N_2(\mathbf{all}) = \lambda X \lambda \mathbf{Y}.\ X \subseteq \bigcup(\mathbf{Y} \cap \wp(X))$
        $C_2^a(\mathbf{all}) = \lambda X \lambda \mathbf{Y}.\ \mathbf{Y}(X)$
        $N_3(\mathbf{all}) = \lambda X \lambda \mathbf{Y}.\ X \subseteq \bigcup \mathbf{Y}\ \ \ = N_3^a(\mathbf{all})$

Note that swapping the arguments of the D_1 and the N_3 reading respectively gives δ and π. This simple observation shows that conjoined VPs which are only partly marked for distributivity or neutrality can be handled in essentially the same way on the VP as on the NP strategy (cf. section 1.3).

Some of the denotations in (21) are also familiar from Scha (1981, 491). He grants **all** a distributive and a collective reading, which are respectively captured by $D_1(\mathbf{all})$ and $C_2^a(\mathbf{all})$. The C_2^a reading of **all** also gives Scha's interpretation of **the**; i.e. the $\in$–relation which leaves noun extensions unaffected. For example, (22a) is formalised by (22b-c):

(22)   a.   The sheep flocked
           b. $C_2^a(\mathbf{all})(\llbracket sheep \rrbracket)(\llbracket flock \rrbracket)$
           c. $\llbracket flock \rrbracket(\llbracket sheep \rrbracket)$

It is nice to see that this use of **the**, which at first appeared so different, can be seen as a lifted form of 'low–level' **all**, thus accounting for the feeling that these determiners are closely related. This is not to say that the determiners function alike in all circumstances. E.g., only (23a) has a collective reading (Dowty (1986)):

(23)   *a.*   The trees get thinner in the middle
        b.   All trees get thinner in the middle

Some$_{pl}$ As is usual, I take **some**$_{pl}$ in type $((et)((et)t))$ to be equivalent with **at least two**. Its lifts are:

(24) $D_1(\mathbf{some}_{pl}) = \lambda X \lambda \mathbf{Y}. |\mathrm{AT}(X) \cap \mathbf{Y}| \geq 2 \qquad\qquad = D_1^a(\mathbf{some}_{pl})$
      $N_2(\mathbf{some}_{pl}) = \lambda X \lambda \mathbf{Y}. |\bigcup(\mathbf{Y} \cap \wp(X))| \geq 2$
      $C_2^a(\mathbf{some}_{pl}) = \lambda X \lambda \mathbf{Y}. \exists Z \subseteq X\, [|Z| \geq 2 \wedge Z \in \mathbf{Y}]$
      $N_3(\mathbf{some}_{pl}) = \lambda X \lambda \mathbf{Y}. |X \cap \bigcup \mathbf{Y}| \geq 2 \qquad\qquad = N_3^a(\mathbf{some}_{pl})$

As a result, the C_2^a reading of sentence (25) may be compared with two neutral readings: N_2 and N_3.

(25)   Some trumpet players jammed
            $\exists Z \subseteq [\![\textit{trumpet player}]\!]\, [|Z| \geq 2 \wedge Z \in [\![\textit{jam}]\!]] \quad C_2^a$
            $|\bigcup([\![\textit{jam}]\!]) \cap \wp([\![\textit{trumpet player}]\!]))| \geq 2 \quad N_2$
            $|\bigcup([\![\textit{jam}]\!]) \cap [\![\textit{trumpet player}]\!]| \geq 2 \quad N_3$

In this comparison I shall mainly concentrate on the logical behaviour of the readings. This will show that the neutral readings cannot do duty as collective readings.

On the collective reading of a sentence, one would expect some inferences to be invalid. For instance, assuming that Miles and Chet are trumpet players, while Wayne and Stan are saxophonists, the inference (26) should fail:

(26)   Miles and Wayne jammed together
            Chet and Stan jammed together
    $\not\Rightarrow$ Some trumpet players jammed together

Consequently, N_3, which makes the inference valid, does not give a collective reading. That N_2 does invalidate (26), is due to its sensitivity for 'CN–pure' collections. Relative to the first argument of a determiner, only the collections formed from its extension are counted relevant. However, in as far as the pure CN–collections of a VP are concerned, $N_2([\![\mathrm{DET}]\!])([\![\mathrm{CN}]\!])$ and $N_3([\![\mathrm{DET}]\!])([\![\mathrm{CN}]\!])$ behave alike. This explains why both make (27) valid:

(27)   Miles made music and Chet made music
        ⇏   Some trumpet players made music together

So, N_2 cannot be used for collective readings either. This leaves C_2^a the one determiner lift that models these readings.

Of course, I do not conclude that N_2 and N_3 are useless. Although plural NPs are a necessary ingredient for sentences to have collective readings, their use is in no way sufficient. As we have seen in section 3.3, plural NPs have a neutral use which exhibits a certain insensitivity towards the structure of collections. And it is here where N_2 and N_3 should be put to work.

Not all, at most four   It is sometimes felt that MON↓ determiners are intrinsically distributive but this is not so. Sentence (28a) has a collective reading in that it might mean (28b):

(28)   a.   Not all heroines came together
         b.   Some heroines came together but not all

An inspection of the lifts shows that (28b) can be had via (29a), i.e., $C_2^a(\mathbf{not\ all})$, which makes it mean (29b):

(29)   a. $\lambda X \lambda \mathbf{Y}.\ \exists Z \subseteq X[X \cap \overline{Z} \neq \emptyset \wedge Z \in \mathbf{Y}]$
      b. $\exists Z \subseteq [\![heroine]\!][[\![heroine]\!] \cap \overline{Z} \neq \emptyset \wedge Z \in [\![come\ together]\!]]$

As is shown by (30), the MON↓ **at most four** has a collective reading, too, which is paraphrased by (30b).

(30)   a.   At most four heroines came together
         b.   All collections of heroines which came together, contained at most four heroines

The paraphrase (30b) of (30a) is obtained by means of the dual of C_2^a defined by:

$$\widetilde{C_2^a} := \lambda D \lambda X \lambda \mathbf{Y}.\ \sim C_2^a(\sim D)$$
$$= \lambda D \lambda X \lambda \mathbf{Y}.\ \forall Z \in \wp(X) \cap \mathbf{Y}[D(X)(Z)]$$

Applied to **at most four** this lift gives (30a) the meaning (31):

(31) $\forall Z \in \wp([\![heroine]\!]) \cap [\![come\ together]\!] : |[\![heroine]\!] \cap Z| \leq 4$

Sentence (30a) is one of the simplest which asks for universal quantification over collections (see Link (1987) for a discussion).

Most It has been observed that **most** only has distributive uses in which it quantifies over atoms or individuals (Roberts (1987)). Do (32a,b) have collective readings?

(32)   a.   Most boys came together
               b.   Most of the boys came together

I agree with Roberts that (32a) is a bit queer. If it should be granted a meaning at all, one should use the neutral N_3:

$$N_3(\mathbf{most}) = \lambda X \lambda \mathbf{Y}.\ |X \cap \bigcup \mathbf{Y}| > |X \cap \overline{\bigcup \mathbf{Y}}|$$

But a collective reading of (32b), with its partitive construction, is perfectly in order and can be obtained via a C_2^a lift to get the truth conditions:

$$\exists Z \subseteq \llbracket boy \rrbracket\ [|Z| > |\llbracket boy \rrbracket \cap \overline{Z}| \wedge Z \in \llbracket come\ together \rrbracket]$$

Atomic and intrinsic distributive determiners Let us call a DET *atomic* iff it satisfies the following form of conservativity in type $((et)(((et)t)t))$:

CONS$_1$ In type $((et)(((et)t)t))$ a determiner Δ is CONS$_1$, iff for all X, **Y**:

$$\Delta(X)(\mathbf{Y}) \Leftrightarrow \Delta(X)(\mathbf{Y} \cap \mathrm{AT}(X))$$

NPs are atomic, iff they are generated from an atom, or iff they are formed from an atomic determiner. Examples are proper names like 'Woody' or NPs with the determiners **every** and **some**$_{sg}$. Atomic determiners do not permit collective readings because they do not combine with collective predicates.[16] The sentences in (33) are all senseless:

(33)   a.   *Woody flocked
                 b.   *Every bird flocked
                 c.   *Some bird flocked

In order to account for this, one could make uninterpretability correspond to a categorial misfit. Then one uses the following fact: if atomic NPs take their denotation in $\mathbf{D}_{((et)t)}$ type theory prohibits them to combine with collective predicates, since these take their denotation in $\mathbf{D}_{((et)t)}$ too. The same would hold for proper names. This move has been made in the literature, e.g. Bennett (1974)), but there are good reasons why people tend to reject it nowadays:

1. Some verbs, like *to play chess*, combine with atomic and non–atomic NPs alike.
2. Atomicity is not preserved under non–Boolean coordination; e.g.:

$$\left.\begin{array}{l}\text{Tony and Chick} \\ \text{A drummer and a pianist}\end{array}\right\} \text{jammed together}$$

It is hard to see how 1 or 2 can be obtained, using the common typings of NPs without further ado. Here I shall discuss only 1, since 2 involves non–Boolean coordination which is not treated in this article.

To solve 1, Scha (1981), Link (1983), and others have used the fact that collections as sets always enforce a worst case: type $((et)t)$. They interpret all VPs at this level. The task is now to choose a determiner lift which enable atomic NPs to combine with mixed predicates. But this lift should preclude the NPs to associate with collective predicates to form contingent statements.[17] All this is achieved by allowing proper names to be lifted by the function $\lambda x \lambda y. x = y$, and to obtain other atomic NPs via D_1. Given that *to flock* is collective, the non–contingent (34a-c) result:

(34)   a. $\{[\![veronica]\!]\} \in [\![flock]\!]$
                b. $\text{AT}([\![sheep]\!]) \subseteq [\![flock]\!]$
                c. $\text{AT}([\![sheep]\!]) \cap [\![flock]\!] \neq \emptyset$

Since the predication in D_1^a is always of the form (34b), this lift will result in non–contingency too.

As it happens, on using D_1 the techniques of Russell/Bennett and of Scha yield the same truth conditions for sentences with conservative determiners, for then:

$$\mathbf{D}(X)(Y) \Leftrightarrow D_1(\mathbf{D})(X)(\text{AT}(Y))$$

This is a point in favour of D_1, since D_1^a has the equivalence for conservative MON↑ determiners only.

In my opinion, the strategy to make unwell–formed sentences logical validities or contradictories is conceptually not very appealing. Another way to deal with this problem is to use variety features that can mark expressions for distributivity, collectivity and so forth. Sentences require agreement, since an NP and a VP of different variety cannot combine with each other. Then, (33a-c) cannot even be formed, since atomic NP are distributive while the VP *flocked* is collective. Van der Does (1992, ch. 4) introduces such a feature system, also to solve the problems of over generation noted in section 1.3.

To summarise this section, the examples have shown that only C_2^a yields collective readings. As yet we have no sufficient ground to choose among the two distributive and the three neutral readings given by the strategies. This issue will occupy the next sections. Besides, the first part of section 5 studies the logical relationships between determiner readings in $((et)(((et)t)t))$.

5. ON THE BATTLEFIELD

5.1. Maps of readings

The question of Link (1991) – 'Where exactly does the line of demarcation run between proper readings and mere models realizing a reading?' – suggests a logician's route to reduce ambiguity: go and search for readings which encompass the others and use these unless lexical items force you to do otherwise. This will involve an investigation on how the lifted forms of a determiner relate logically (a topic which is of interest regardless). Here, I adopt the global view on determiners, which makes them functors associating with each domain E the determiner $\mathbf{D}_E$ of type $((et)((et)t))$. The notion of the relative strength of lifted determiners is made precise in the standard manner:

Definition 5.1. (relative strength) *Let L and L' be operators of type*

$$(((et)((et)t))\ ((et)(((et)t)t)))$$

By definition a determiner $\mathbf{D}$ satisfies: $L \longrightarrow L'$, if for all domains E:

$$L(\mathbf{D}_E) \subseteq L'(\mathbf{D}_E)$$

The L' reading of $\mathbf{D}$ is at most as strong as its L reading, if $\mathbf{D}$ satisfies $L \longrightarrow L'$. I write $L \equiv L'$, just in case $L \longrightarrow L'$ and $L' \longrightarrow L$.

Using the arrow–notation, we can draw the maps of readings for arbitrary and for monotone determiners. Proposition 5.2. shows that for arbitrary determiners a weakest reading can always be found.[18]

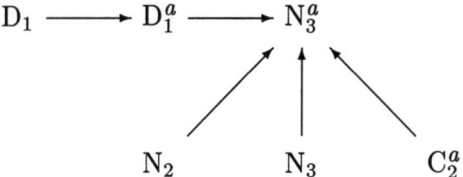

Figure 1: *arbitrary determiners*

Proposition 5.2. *Every determiner satisfies the arrows in figure 1.* □

Of course, the situation may be different for determiners of a particular kind. The map of readings for MON↑ determiners, for example, has a nice symmetry about it.

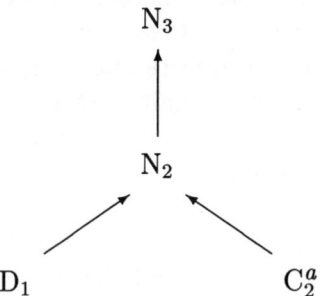

Figure 2: MON↑ *determiners*

Proposition 5.3. *Each* MON↑ *determiner* **D** *satisfies the map in figure 2. Besides this, one has: $D_1^a \equiv D_1$ and $N_3^a \equiv N_3$.* □

The map for MON↓ determiners is asymmetric again.

Proposition 5.4. *Each* MON↓ *determiner* **D** *satisfies the map in figure 3, and also: $D_1^a \equiv N_3^a$.* □

From a logical point of view it is natural to ask whether there are converses to proposition 5.3. and 5.4.. The answer is given in Van der Does

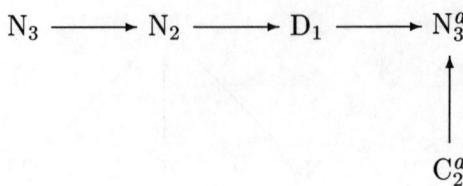

Figure 3: MON↓ *determiners*

(1992, ch. 5), where it is shown that the maps in figure 2 and 3 are typical of conservative MON↑ and MON↓ determiners, in that order.

For now a more important question is: what do the maps tell us with respect to the strategy suggested by Link? A weakest reading is available; namely, N_3^a which is equivalent to N_3 on the MON↑ determiners and to D_1^a on the MON↓ ones. It remains to be seen, though, whether this reading is empirically defensible. If so, it will be *the* candidate to model neutral readings. Otherwise, we are left in general with five readings: D_1, D_1^a, N_2, C_2^a and N_3. This, again, would require us to show which lift gives the best way to capture the distributive reading, D_1 or D_1^a. We should also ask whether it is necessary to discern two neutral readings, N_2 and N_3.

In sum, we have to make observations which give more insight into the behaviour of the distributive and the neutral readings as they are proposed by the NP and the VP strategy. A choice is made in the ensuing section on the quantificational force of determiners.

5.2. *Quantificational force*

It is quite clear that the lifts induce a semantic change in the determiner denotations. So, how does a determiner function when it is lifted to $((et)(((et)t)t))$? More precisely, does it still determine quantities in an accurate way? And if not, is this modification of the standard meaning desirable?

That the numerals need not behave alike on different readings, is shown by example (35) adapted from Lønning (1987, 205):

(35) *a.* Yesterday, exactly five boys bought a boat together in the shop
    b. Yesterday, exactly five boys each bought a boat in the shop
    c. Yesterday, 836 people bought a boat at the trade fair

In case of (35a,b) the total number of boys that bought a boat in the shop during the day may well be more than five. But for (35c), where the number of boat buying clients is an issue, this is impossible.

The explanation is simple. The collective reading in (35a) is about an unspecified collection of exactly five boys, while the distributive (35b) restricts the count to boys who bought a boat all by themselves. Both statements leave the possibility of other groups of boys that bought a boat. In contrast, (35c) is sort of neutral. Here one is not so much interested in whether the people bought a boat by themselves or with others, the sum total of people that bought a boat is at stake. On this reading one discards the structure of collections and just counts the relevant people.

To see which lifts function as required in this respect, I have listed the six readings of (36) as they are obtained from the lifts of **exactly three**:

(36)   Exactly three brothers are gossiping
$|\bigcup(\llbracket gossip \rrbracket \cap \text{AT}(\llbracket brothers \rrbracket))| = 3$ D_1
$|\bigcup(\llbracket gossip \rrbracket \cap \wp(\llbracket brother \rrbracket))| = 3$ N_2
$|\bigcup(\llbracket gossip \rrbracket) \cap \llbracket brother \rrbracket| = 3$ N_3
$\exists X \subseteq \llbracket brother \rrbracket [|X| = 3 \wedge \text{AT}(X) \subseteq \llbracket gossip \rrbracket]$ D_1^a
$\exists X \subseteq \llbracket brother \rrbracket [|X| = 3 \wedge X \in \llbracket gossip \rrbracket]$ C_2^a
$\exists X \subseteq \llbracket brother \rrbracket [|X| = 3 \wedge X \subseteq \bigcup(\llbracket gossip \rrbracket)]$ N_3^a

Examining the formulae, one would expect none of the a readings to give a correct total count: on these readings the numerals leave the verb phrase extension outside their scope. And indeed, focussing on quantities the a readings in (36) rather mean:

(37)   At least three brothers are gossiping

The reason is that they allow the existence of other collections of gossiping brothers, whose members are left uncounted (cf. Van Benthem (1986, 52), Lønning (1987, 205)). However, this change in meaning should not just be attributed to the a–lifted determiners, for a similar change takes place in case of D_1 and N_2: $D_1(\mathbf{n})$ counts the members of $\text{AT}(X)$ in **Y** discarding Xs in larger **Y**-collections, while $N_2(\mathbf{n})$ fails to count the Xs in mixed **Y**-collections. Only $N_3(\mathbf{n})$, which 'X-rays' the collections, does not miss any of the relevant Xs.

Note, by way of digression, that there is a more surprising reason why an explanation in terms of the a–use of a determiner fails: all lifts are equivalent to lifts in which the determiners are treated in this way. This is shown using the uniform formats of D_1, N_2 and N_3 in terms of the restricting functions given in section 4.1 (for convenience the lifts are temporally renamed L_i with $i \in \{1, 2, 3\}$):

$$L_i \quad \lambda D \lambda X \lambda \mathbf{Y}.\ D(X)(\bigcup(\mathbf{Y}|_X^i))$$

Three alternative lifts using the restriction functions are:

$$M_i \quad \lambda D \lambda X \lambda \mathbf{Y}.\ \exists Z \subseteq X[D(X)(Z) \wedge \exists \mathbf{Z}\ \text{cv}\ Z[\mathbf{Z} = \mathbf{Y}|_X^i]]$$

Here, $\mathbf{Z}$ cv Z means that $\mathbf{Z}$ *covers* Z; that is: $\bigcup \mathbf{Z} = Z$. As it happens, for each i the lifts are equivalent to each other:

Proposition 5.5. *All determiners satisfy:* $L_i \equiv M_i$. □

Proposition 5.5. reminds us of the fact that although in a lift a determiner may leave the VP outside its scope, it could still be equivalent to a lift where this is not so. As always, the relevant factor for a determiner is the relation that obtains between its N and VP argument.

Let us return to the main argument. We have seen that for the collective (35a) the change in meaning is just as it should be. The determiner is set to work to specify the size of an unspecified collection of boys which has the property expressed by the VP. All this is realised by C_2^a. On the distributive reading (35b), the predication should be restricted to the relevant individuals (atoms), and the count of these individuals should be correct: exactly five, no more no less. This accuracy is given by D_1 but is beyond reach of D_1^a. In fact, all a lifts turn an arbitrary determiner $\mathbf{D}$ into a determiner $L(\mathbf{D})$ which is MON↑ in type $((et)(((et)t)t))$, so that for all X, $\mathbf{X}$ and $\mathbf{Y}$:

$$L(\mathbf{D})(X)(\mathbf{X})\ and\ \mathbf{X} \subseteq \mathbf{Y} \Rightarrow L(\mathbf{D})(X)(\mathbf{Y})$$

Often such a transformation is undesirable.[19] The conclusion to draw is that Scha's distributive reading of numerals does generalise to arbitrary determiners, whereas Link's treatment does not. In other words, the NP strategy treats the distributive reading empirically more adequate than the VP strategy.

One may hope to save D_1^a by claiming that distributive readings of sentences result from the combination of a distributive NP with a distributive VP; i.e. one of the form $\delta(\llbracket\text{VP}\rrbracket)$. Then one should compare the lifts on such VPs and see if they fare better in this limited area. But they do not:

Proposition 5.6. *Restricting attention to distributive VPs, one has for arbitrary and for* MON↓ *determiners:*

$$D_1 \equiv N_2 \equiv N_3 \text{ and } D_1^a \equiv C_2^a \equiv N_3^a$$

But for MON↑ *determiners total equivalence results:*

$$D_1 \equiv N_2 \equiv N_3 \equiv D_1^a \equiv C_2^a \equiv N_3^a$$

□

Even though distributive VPs give a massive collapse of readings, proposition 5.6. shows that they still leave D_1^a non–equivalent to the properly counting non–a lifts in the crucial non–MON↑ cases. Hence the earlier observation is left unaffected. In my opinion this is a serious defect of the approach to distributivity as it is found, e.g., in Link's treatment of non–monotonic numerals and in Lønning (1987). Non–MON↑ determiners are used distributively when the focus is on the precise number of individuals involved in a predication. But as it stands this precision cannot be had within this framework.

Exactly the same argument shows that the neutral readings N_2 and N_3 given on the NP approach are to be preferred to N_3^a which mimics the neutral reading of the VP approach. But can we make a further choice among N_2 and N_3? This section leaves the impression that N_3 gives all that is required, since it is the only one properly counting all the relevant members. However, this very fact makes the resulting reading too weak. Sentence (14), here repeated as (38), should be false if there are half a million families gathering with their one and only child, and not with any of the other families:

(38)   Half a million children gathered all over the country

But N_3 would make it true. For this reason I opt for N_2 which only counts the members of gatherings consisting of just children. This does not mean that (38) would be false in a situation where there are also mixed gatherings of children with others. Though, for the children to be relevant for the truth of (38) they should form a subgathering of just children.

For all we know now, distributive readings should be obtained from D_1, collective readings from C_2^a, and neutral readings from N_2. These are precisely the readings proposed by the NP strategy. However, the article is not yet finished: there are some subtleties having to do with neutral readings and scope.

6. NEUTRAL READINGS AND SCOPE

In the literature based on Link, there is consensus on which readings of (39) exist:

(39)   Four men lifted two tables

Either the four men lifted the tables all alone or they did it all together; intermediate or neutral readings are often disregarded. In case they are considered, one tends to be in favour of reducing them to the collective reading (cf. Lasersohn (1989), Lønning (1991)). But in the foregoing section I have argued that the reductions as they are proposed in the literature are infelicitous. The reason is that neutral readings of (39) occur in the rare but possible situations where the precise number of table lifting men is at stake, regardless of whether they have acted alone or with others. And for (39) as for other sentences with neutral readings this precision is beyond the given reductions to collective readings.

The observation that neutral readings occur is not new. As we have seen, Scha's N_2 reading of numerals derives from a similar intuition, and such readings formed the core of the debate of Gillon against Lasersohn. What is absent, however, is a logical semantics which models them satisfactorily.

If on neutral readings quantification is the issue, why can't we use N_2, which counts all the relevant members? Whatever the truth conditions of (39) are, it is commonly understood that on its subject wide scope reading ('sws' for short) at most eight tables could be involved. Hence the subject can never have a N_2 reading. In the previous section I have shown that on this reading – using N_2 in its M_2 guise – (39) is equivalent to:

(40) $\exists X \subseteq [\![four\ man]\!]\ \exists \mathbf{Y}\ \text{cv}\ X : \mathbf{Y} = [\![lifts\ two\ tables]\!] \cap \wp([\![man]\!])$

But then the number of tables may vary from two (= two × the cardinality of the poorest cover $\{\{X\}\}$ of a four element set X) to thirty-two (= two × the cardinality of its richest cover: $\wp(X)$)! Plainly, N_2 is an inappropriate reading of the subject in a transitive sentence.

A simple way to deal with this embarrassment is to take it as a knock–down argument against the intermediate reading N_2 intends to model. In my opinion this would be too crude, if only because neutral readings of intransitive sentences abound. Moreover, the argument against a N_2 reading of the subject having wide scope does not extend to the object having narrow scope. On the contrary, (41a, sws) even seems to favour it:

(41)   a.   Four men lifted at most two tables together
       b.   Thesa lifted exactly two tables

Sentence (41) can be used to describe a situation in which a collection of four men lifted one table, then another, then both of them, but no more. And such truth conditions of (41a) are best captured by means of its $C_2^a N_2$ reading. Also in case the subject is a proper name, as in (41b), this suggestion works well. Then, the neutral object reading should be equivalent to its distributive reading. As it stands this is not so since the meaning of *to lift* is unconstrained. But adding the meaning postulate (42a) or even the weaker (42b):

(42)   a. $\forall x, Y [[\![lift]\!](\{x\})(Y) \Rightarrow \forall Z \subseteq Y : [\![lift]\!](\{x\})(Z)]$
       b. $\forall x, Y [[\![lift]\!](\{x\})(Y) \Rightarrow \forall y \in Y : [\![lift]\!](\{x\})(\{y\})]$

the set $\lambda Y. [\![lift]\!](\{[\![Thesa]\!]\})(Y)$ will be distributive. Proposition 5.6. states that for such predicates the N_2 and D_1 reading are identical.[20] Given (42), (41b) has the meaning required. In all such cases, the rule seems to be: NPs which allow neutral readings are neutral when they have narrow scope.

The observations lead us to consider alternatives of N_2 which circumvent the scope problem noted. Using the fact that the N_2 reading can be written as in (43):[21]

(43) $\lambda D \lambda X \lambda \mathbf{Y}. \exists Z \subseteq X[D(X)(Z) \wedge \exists \mathbf{Z} \text{ cover } Z[\mathbf{Z} = \mathbf{Y} \cap \wp(X)]]$

I discuss three variants by strengthening the notion of cover to that of partition, minimal cover, and pseudo–partition, respectively. Although the pseudo–partitional reading of an NP comes close to what we want, it has unattractive properties too. For this reason I hold that there is no satisfactory neutral reading which may take scope over complex VPs. Instead, the neutral readings of NPs should be used in case of non–iterative quantification. In particular the cumulative reading is well–suited to be treated in this way, and gives a defensible stance in the debate between Gillon and Lasersohn.

6.1. Alternative neutral readings

Looking closer at the above counter-example to the use of N_2, we see that the problem is this: the cardinality of an arbitrary cover may exceed that of its underlying set and the restriction function used may allow this distortion of quantificational information. The problem can be solved in one go if we can restrict the quantification in (40) to a kind of cover, call it cover*, with the property:

(44) *If* **Y** *covers* X, then* $|\mathbf{Y}| \leq |X|$

Here I shall consider three such covers, which relate as follows:

$$partitions \subseteq minimal\ covers \subseteq pseudo\text{-}partitions$$

Partitions Partitions are covers whose members, all non-empty, do not overlap. The two extreme partitions of a set X are $\text{AT}(X)$ and $\{\{X\}\}$, respectively corresponding to the distributive 'all Xs by themselves' and the collective 'all Xs together'. Since partitions may be thought of as identifying members of X with each other in a particular way, they satisfy (44). And indeed, restricting the quantification over covers in N_2 to quantification over partitions, (39, sws) will again be about two up to eight tables.

However, the restriction to partitions seems too strong. For suppose, following Gillon (1987), that the composers are Hammerstein, Rodgers and Hart. Suppose also that Rodgers collaborated with Hammerstein and with Hart to write musicals, but that the composers did not write a musical together nor all by themselves. Then the partitional reading of NPs makes the sentence (45) false:

(45) Three composers wrote some musicals

The reason is that the set

(46) $\{\{Hammerstein, Rodgers\}, \{Rodgers, Hart\}\}$

does not partition the set $\{Hammerstein, Rodgers, Hart\}$. This indicates that the neutral reading of an NP should not preclude overlapping collections, and that a weaker alternative to the use of partitions should be sought.

Minimal covers Adapting Gillon's suggestion to deal with set denoting NPs, one could restrict the quantification over covers to the so-called minimal covers. By definition, a minimal cover is a cover which does not have covers as real parts.[22]

Definition 6.1. (minimal covers) *A set* **Y** *minimally covers a set* X *– notation:* **Y** *mc* X, *– iff:*

- **Y** cv X
- $\forall \mathbf{Z}\ cv\ X[\mathbf{Z} \subseteq \mathbf{Y} \Rightarrow \mathbf{Z} = \mathbf{Y}]$

Note that minimal covers, which have partitions as a special case, may contain overlapping collections. In particular, on the minimal cover reading of NPs (45) will be true, since the set (46) does minimally cover the set

$$\{Hammerstein, Rodgers, Hart\}$$

Van der Does (1992, ch. 5) shows that minimal covers satisfy (44). Altering N_2 as indicated, (39a, sws) will be about two to eight tables – as common intuition has it, – while at the same time collections are allowed to overlap.

What we have seen above, is that the partitional reading of NPs solves the scope problem of neutral readings of transitive sentences. But it does not give a satisfactory semantics to intransitive sentences, where the use of N_2 was unproblematic. The minimal cover reading of an NP shows a similar pattern. For instance, the minimal cover reading of *the managers*, as it derives from $N_2(\mathbf{all})$, will give (47a) the truth conditions (47b):

(47) a. The managers came together
  b. $\exists \mathbf{Y}$ mc $[\![manager]\!] : \mathbf{Y} = [\![come\ together]\!] \cap \wp([\![manager]\!])$

It is conceivable, though, that the gathering of managers was used by some efficient ones, say Ploeger and Timmer, to have a 'subgathering'. Hence it should be possibly that:

$$[\![come\ together]\!] \cap \wp([\![manager]\!]) = \{[\![manager]\!], \{ploeger, timmer\}\}$$

But this is not minimal, since $\{[\![manager]\!]\}$ will do to cover it. So, (47b) wrongly predicts (47a) to be false then (a referee of Lasersohn (1989) gave a similar counterexample to Gillon (1987)).

Pseudo–partitions Since minimal covers are not satisfactory either, let us finally have a look at the weakest kind of cover which satisfy (44). They are the pseudo–partitions of Verkuyl and Van der Does (1991):

Definition 6.2. (pseudo–partitions) *A set* **Y** *pseudo–partitions a set* X *if and only if* **Y** *covers* X *and* $|\mathbf{Y}| \leq |X|$.

Pseudo–partitions point to the main reason why stronger notions of covers are considered. Linguistically, their use makes the interesting claim that in allowing the determiner to leave the VP outside its scope, as is common to do in this area, we have to ensure that its quantificational information is preserved when passing to the part where the VP is treated.[23]

Again, it is unclear whether pseudo–partitional NPs are entirely felicitous in case of intransitive sentences. Consider the variation (48a) of (47a) whose truth conditions on the pseudo–partitional reading is given by (48b):

(48) a. Four managers came together
 b. **four**($[\![manager]\!]$)($[\![come\ together]\!] \cap \wp([\![manager]\!])$)
    $\wedge\ |[\![come\ together]\!] \cap \wp([\![manager]\!])| \leq 4$

Allowing for subgatherings of the gathering reported on by (48a), one should argue why there may be at most four of those, as is stipulated by the second conjunct of (48b). In this connection Verkuyl (1994) defends a 'once counted, always counted' principle. The idea is that in disregarding multiple occurrences of one and the same manager, we discern at most four gatherings to establish the truth of (48). This means that the number of gatherings is strongly dependent on the perspective under which we regard them. However, as soon as the existence of gatherings is not entirely dependent on us, the principle cannot be used to explain the bound. Then the number of gatherings and the number of people involved in these gatherings may vastly differ, just because we count persons not their occurrences.

The behaviour of the pseudo–partitional reading of an NP as the subject of a transitive sentence also leaves room for debate. On such a use the claim would be that (49c) could describe the minimal situation sketched by (49a-b):

(49)   a. Richard and Harry each lifted two tables
  b. Richard and Ellen lifted two tables together
  c. Three people lifted two tables

Semanticists tend to have varying judgments on whether (49c) can be so used. According to Verkuyl (Verkuyl and Van der Does (1991, 27)) this use is acceptable, and Gillon (1990) has similar judgments. The reason would be that (49c) could report on situations where it is checked which people have fulfilled the minimal duty of lifting two tables (e.g., the paymaster of a removal company may have such qualms).[24] In contrast, Lasersohn (1989) and Lønning (1991, 43) hold that a sentence like (49c) could not be so used, and I agree (cf. Verkuyl and Van der Does, ibidem). On the other hand, Hoeksema (p.c.) observes that this kind of verifying situation is less troublesome when sentences are explicitly modified as in (50a), and the same is true for (50b):

(50) a. Three people lifted two tables alone or with others
 b. Three people lifted two tables; namely, Richard and Harry alone, and Richard together with Ellen.

These observations focus on the main advantage of using pseudo-partitional NPs. In section 4.1, I have shown that wherever the readings come from, they can always be taken to result from a (tacit) use of modifiers like δ. But (50) reminds us of the fact that natural language has many more ways to modify a VP. Should each of these modifiers give rise to a different reading? But if not, why restrict attention to the familiar 'each' and 'together'?[25] Because of the different kinds of modification, it is desirable to have an NP denotation which is compatible with each of them. Without overt modification this denotation must determine the relevant quantities, but it should leave us underinformed as to what situation is described.

Could we go one step further and hold that such a denotation could be used to give a reduction of ambiguity? Then the NPs which are not intrinsically distributive would just have this one reading, since it encompasses the situations described by means of the distributive and the collective reading. This position is defended in Verkuyl and Van der Does (1991). But apart from the objectionable truth conditions exemplified by means of (48) and (49), this proposal makes sentences too adaptive to the situations they describe. The following dialogue, for instance, is coherent:

(51) A : Four men lifted at most two tables. To be precise, John, Gustav, Larry, and Tom did so all by themselves.
 B : No that's not true. They lifted at most two tables together.

Suppose that B is right. It is reasonable to hold then that A's first sentence is false, even before he used the second sentences to be more informative. But if the sentence is unambiguous this cannot be accounted for, since the collective lifting of the pianos would make it true. For me this road to a vague but less ambiguous paradise is now closed.[26]

Let us recapitulate what we have achieved up till now. I have argued for a neutral reading of an NP which is used when the precise determination of quantities is at stake. This neutral reading should be obtained by means of a general principle from the common denotation of a determiner in type $((et)((et)t))$. In case of intransitive sentences the neutral reading can be had without pain by use of N_2. But the N_2 reading of the subject of a transitive sentence, when widely scoped, will embarrass even the most tolerant semanticist. It has been shown in the previous section that N_2 can be seen to involve an existential quantification over covers, and I have discussed restrictions to stronger kinds of cover in the hope that they will yield a defensible neutral reading of plural NPs. The weakest such restriction is given by the pseudo–partitions of Verkuyl and Van der Does (1991). Their use comes close to what is required but remains debatable. For (i) they put a restriction on the number of subevents of the event described, and (ii) the resulting truth conditions seem too liberal.

Nevertheless, we should not conclude that the neutral readings of NPs, with their generous attitude towards non–distributive and non–collective predication, should be excluded. In the above, I have tried to stay close to the N_2 reading of an NP under the assumption that it should be able to take scope over other NPs. But it is precisely this assumption which is to be challenged. On the neutral reading of sentences with more than one NP, the NPs cannot have scope over each other. Yet, this allows the cumulative reading to occur on the basis of relations between sets. (Scha only considers distributive variants of this reading.) Indeed, in the next section I argue that N_2 should be used in this scope independent way to model neutral readings.[27]

6.2. *Cumulative readings*

On the cumulative reading, (52a) gets the truth conditions given by (52b):

(52) a. Three people lifted two tables
 b. **three**($[\![people]\!]$)($\bigcup \text{DOM}([\![lift]\!] \cap \wp([\![thing]\!]) \times \wp([\![table]\!]))) \wedge$
    two($[\![table]\!]$)($\bigcup \text{RG}([\![lift]\!] \cap \wp([\![people]\!]) \times \wp([\![thing]\!])))$

Here the following notions are used:

$$[\![thing]\!] := \mathbf{D}_e$$
$$\text{DOM} := \lambda \mathbf{R} \lambda X \exists Y.\ \mathbf{R}(X)(Y)$$
$$\text{RG} := \lambda \mathbf{R} \lambda Y \exists X.\ \mathbf{R}(X)(Y)$$

The content of (52) may be paraphrased by:

> The collections of people which lift a collection of tables are made up of three people, and the collections of tables which are lifted by a collection of people are made up of two tables.

That is, one restricts attention to the collections of people which lifted tables. Given this part of *to lift*, the first conjunct of (52) merges the collections of people in its domain and sees if the sum total of their members is three, and similarly for the second conjunct.

It remains to be shown how the cumulative reading for arbitrary determiners can be obtained via the mechanisms of lifting. Moreover, there are some well-known problems with this kind of reading, if one wants to comply with a principle of compositionality and at the same time give sentences a reasonable syntactic structure (Scha (1981) does the former but not the latter). A proposal to deal with these matters is in Van der Does (1992, ch. 4). For now, I shall use my claim to take a stance in the Gillon/Lasersohn debate.

In Gillon (1987) neutral readings are argued for by means of the sentence (53):

(53)   Hammerstein, Rodgers and Hart wrote musicals

Gillon observes that (53) could be true if, as in fact, Rodgers collaborated with one of the others, even in the circumstance that none of the composers wrote a musical all by himself.

According to Lønning (1991), (53) does not sustain the claim that neutral readings are called for. In contrast to the predicate *to write a musical*, he takes *to write musicals* to be distributive; that is, from (53), e.g., (54) follows:

(54)   Rodgers wrote musicals

This is correct, but it only shows that Gillon's example is not well-chosen. Some semanticists hold that the bare plural in the predicate of (53) does not carry quantificational information. If this is so, the predicate *to write musicals* is distributive and hence unsuitable to sustain Gillon's claim. But what about (55)?:

(55)   Hammerstein, Rodgers and Hart wrote some musicals

This would be true, or so I think, even if Hammerstein and Rodgers wrote exactly one musical together, as did Rodgers and Hart, while none of them wrote any other musical. Then we neither have a distributive nor a collective predication.

I have already rejected Gillon's solution in terms of minimal covers, so it must be shown how the neutral reading of (55) comes about. I claim that this reading is the cumulative one based on relations between sets. Sentence (55) states that the people involved in writing musicals were Hammerstein, Rodgers and Hart and that the total number of the musicals they wrote, collectively or otherwise, is at least two. Note that on this reading (56) is no consequence of (55), as it should not.

(56)   Rodgers wrote some musicals

Since proper names denote atoms, this non–inference is a general phenomenon of cumulative readings.

7. CONCLUSIONS

In this article I studied different ways in which the semantics of simple plural noun phrases could be developed. Some of the main questions are: which readings does a statement about collections have, where do these readings come from, how are they modeled? For the sentences studied here two strategies are distinguished. One locates the source of the readings in the NP, the other in the VP. For each of these strategies I discerned three readings: a distributive, a collective, and a neutral reading. The strategies and their readings are studied in a systematic way by means of six lifts instantiating the type change:

$$((et)((et)t)) \Rightarrow ((et)(((et)t)t))$$

In this way the different semantics for plural noun phrases are obtained from the standard denotations of their determiners in type $((et)((et)t))$. The lifts are distiled from the treatments of numerals by Scha and Link, the main proponents of the NP and the VP strategy. The present set up connects the sum theory of collections with generalised quantifiers theory in a uniform way. This has the important virtue of allowing a simple comparison between the different proposals. I have obtained the following insights.

Most semanticists grant the existence of a collective and a distributive reading. *Pace* the treatment of groups, the collective reading is adequately captured by C_2^a. This reading derives from Scha's collective denotation of numerals rewritten in terms of their $((et)((et)t))$ denotation. As to the distributive and neutral reading, I argued that their main function is respectively to determine with precision the individuals which have a certain property, or which occur in a collection with that property. In case of the distributive reading this accuracy is given by D_1, which derives from Scha's distributive reading of numerals, but not by D_1^a, which generalises Link. The lift D_1^a fails to do this duty when applied to non–MON↑ determiners, which are often the crucial cases. Similarly, the precision required on the neutral reading is captured by N_2 but not by N_3^a. The D_1, C_2^a, and N_2 reading are generalisations of the numeral readings proposed on the NP strategy. I conclude that for the sentences considered in this article the NP strategy is superior to the VP strategy. However, for more complex sentences I think we have to compute the reading of a complex expression compositionally from the readings of its constituting expressions (cf. section 1, or Van der Does (1992, ch. 4)).

The neutral reading of an NP is used to determine the individuals partaking in a relation, independent of whether they do so on their own or as a member of a collection. Although the use of an N_2 reading is unproblematic for simple intransitive sentences, it is problematic in case of transitive sentences. In particular, it does not comply with the common intuition that 'four men lifted two tables' is about eight tables at most. It is not straightforward to find a logical semantics where neutral readings of NPs allow complex VPs within their scope. I have considered some alternatives involving an existential quantification over partitions, minimal covers and pseudo–partitions. The conclusion was that the partitional and the minimal cover reading of an NP are too strict. The pseudo–partitional reading comes close to what is required but it has some troublesome aspects. Firstly, it puts a bound on the number of subevents of the events described, which is only defensible if this number is dependent on the perspective under which the event is regarded. Secondly, it would make sentences like the following acceptable: 'Four men lifted two tables; namely John together with Luke, and Peter together with Thomas.' But quite a few semanticists find this a bit strange, and I agree. I conclude that the NP of an intransitive sentence and the NP of a transitive sentence with narrow scope may have a neutral reading, but not so the NP of a transitive sentence which has wide scope. Both NPs in a transitive sentence can only be neutral in case of non–iterative polyadic quantification. For example, in a collective setting the cumulative reading generalises N_2 to transitive sentences in a way which leaves the scope of the NPs independent of each other.

All in all we have the following situation. Disregarding scope ambiguities, the noun phrases in a transitive sentence $[_S \text{NP}_1 \ [_{VP} \ \text{TV NP}_2]]$ induce the seven readings (entry form: NP_1NP_2):

$$D_1D_1, \ D_1C_2^a, \ D_1N_2, \ C_2^aD_1, \ C_2^aC_2^a, \ C_2^aN_2, \text{ the cumulative one}$$

If scope is allowed, the number is twelve (twice the first six plus the cumulative reading). It appeared however that the NP with narrow scope favours a neutral reading. If so, there are three readings without scope,

$$D_1N_2, \ C_2^aN_2, \text{ the cumulative one}$$

But with scope the number of readings is five.

ACKNOWLEDGEMENTS

This work has been supported by ESPRIT Basic Research Action 3175. A previous and rather different version of this article, called 'Among Collections', appeared in Van der Does [1991] together with comments by Jan Tore Lønning and Remko Scha. Van der Does [1992, ch. 2] is a revision of this earlier version, which makes use of and reacts to the helpful remarks of Lønning and Scha. The present article is a revision of Van der Does [1992, ch. 2], which also contains material from Van der Does [1992, ch. 4]. I would like to thank Johan van Benthem, Jeroen Groenendijk, Jan Tore Lønning, Remko Scha, Martin Stokhof, Frank Veltman, Henk Verkuyl, two anonymous referees, and the members of the workshop on plurals in Tübingen, December 1991, for comments and discussions.

NOTES

[1] The date of this publication is misleading. It has been available as a typescript since 1984.

[2] See Landman (1989, 568–571) for convincing arguments why one should use this kind of CAJS.

[3] As it happens, these authors both use '*' to denote their operator.

[4] The idea behind the labeling is explained in section 4.1. For now, it suffices to say that the 'D' stands for distributive, 'C' for collective, and 'N' for neutral. Scha

speaks of two collective readings. In section 4.2 it will appear that this terminology is misleading: the C_2 numerals (here called N_2) do not give rise to collective readings.

[5] The main aim of Link (1983) is to formalise the similarities between mass terms and plurals.

[6] Link (1991) does not discern among C_2^a and N_2 'for methodological reasons'. The important differences in their logical behaviour does not justify this decision.

[7] For technical convenience I have omitted the requirement that Y be non–empty. In introducing the relational modifiers separately I have followed Link, but they can also be defined from δ (cf. Van der Does (1992, 70)).

[8] Roberts (1987) argues that the distributivity of the VP is lexical: it results from a (c)overt use of *each*. But how to justify the use of $\bullet\delta$ along these lines?

[9] The formalisation of so-called variety agreement in Van der Does (1992, ch. 4) is another system to preclude double markings.

[10] I am indebted to one of the referees here.

[11] Since Link (1991) does not discern among C_2^a and N_2, he presumably takes (14) to be collective.

[12] According to Lønning (1991) both these readings are wrong. They incorrectly validate the inference:

John and Harry ate three pizzas
$\not\Rightarrow$ John ate three pizzas

This observation is correct, I think, for the VP strategy. Then there is no good reason why the modification of the VP in premise and conclusion should differ. The case is different for the NP strategy, where the observation presumes that both NPs should have the same reading. But since the NPs are different this need not be so. The NP in the conclusion may even lack the reading assumed for the premise. Proper names, in particular, do not have the neutral reading: $\lambda \mathbf{X}.[\![john]\!] \in \bigcup \mathbf{X}$. And their standard denotation $\lambda \mathbf{X}.\mathbf{X}(\{[\![john]\!]\})$ does invalidate the inference.

[13] In case of N_3, I gave an equivalent form.

[14] There is an interesting context dependent variant of N_2 in which the power set operator is changed for a function F with for all X: $F(X) \subseteq \wp(X)$. $F(X)$ is a set of contextually given collections formed out of the members of the noun extension. Whenever $F(X) \subseteq \text{AT}(X)$ we have a distributive reading. And if $F(X)$ is a singleton we have the 'witness' version of the collective reading describing a contextually given collection. As we shall see in section 6, the remaining possibility for $F(X)$ is problematic in case of transitive sentences.

[15] One may wonder whether an explicit marking for plurality in the semantics of NPs should be used; e.g., as in $\lambda X \lambda Y. X \subseteq Y \wedge |X| > 1$. I choose not to, for often such markings do not give correct truth conditions under negation. In using a plural NP it is rather presupposed that there is a plurality of the required kind; a presupposition which may disappear when forming complexes.

[16] Atomicity and collectivity have strong ties with syntactic number. Since the fit is not perfect, I prefer to use the semantical terminology.

[17] In three- or four-valued semantics, unwell-formed sentences could be taken as un- or overdefined. But in a two-valued semantics, as is used here, the usual option is to make them uninformative; i.e., to let their interpretation be either universally valid or unsatisfiable.

[18] Recall that the proofs are in Van der Does (1992, ch. 5).

[19] This observation is related to the fact that defining a determiner $\mathbf{D}'$ in terms of a determiner $\mathbf{D}$ by means of $\mathbf{D}'(X)(Y) \Leftrightarrow_{def} \exists Z \subseteq Y : \mathbf{D}(X)(Z)$ makes $\mathbf{D}'$ MON↑. The a lifts are higher typed variants of this scheme.

[20] Lønning (1991) discusses the possibility of always giving the NP with narrow scope a neutral reading, but rejects it. His main objection is that the neutral reading of (41b), as induced by the object NP, must be equivalent to the distributive one. I have shown how this can be had by means of meaning postulates.

In his discussion, Lønning (1991) proposes to obtain the neutral object reading via verb modification combined with a C_2^a reading of an NP. His solution is as problematic as N_3^a is in that its fails to determine quantities correctly in the crucial non–MON↑ cases. Lønning is well aware of this and suggests to try to settle the matter by means of topic/focus articulation. Instead, I prefer using N_2, which gives a simple and fully rigorous solution.

[21] Recall that **Z** covers Z iff $\bigcup \mathbf{Z} = Z$.

[22] With regard to definite NPs, Gillon argues that neutral readings abound: each minimal cover of such an NP gives a new reading. In the present set up, where we existentially quantify over cover*, they are used to give but one reading of the NPs which allow neutrality.

[23] Note that the observations made below with respect to pseudo–partitions also hold for partitions and minimal covers. Also, there is a context dependent variant of the pseudo–partitional reading:

$$\lambda D \lambda X \lambda \mathbf{Y}.\ D(X)(\bigcup(\mathbf{Y} \cap F(X))) \wedge |\mathbf{Y} \cap F(X)| \leq |\bigcup(\mathbf{Y} \cap F(X))|$$

This is the context dependent version of N_2 with the extra requirement that the contextually given set of collections $F(X)$ with property **Y** has at most the size of the set of the members of such collections.

[24] Verkuyl (1992) has some other examples where these intermediate situations are easier to get.

[25] I am indebted here to Henk Verkuyl.

[26] The context dependent version of the pseudo–partitional reading defined in footnote 23 is better of. It allows us to say that A took $F(X)$ to be different from what it really was.

[27] There are other forms of polyadic quantification which leave the NPs independent of each other. For instance, resumptive quantification – which I take to be a special case of cumulative quantification, – or branching quantification. Since cumulative quantification is primarily used to focus on quantities, I restrict myself to this form here.

It has been suggested in the literature that the use of the cumulative reading is superfluous, since it should be reducible to a doubly collective reading (Partee, Link, Roberts (cf. Roberts (1987, 148-149)), Lønning (1991)). This is not so, for such a proposal does not work in case of non–MON↑ determiners.

REFERENCES

Bäuerle, R., Schwarze, C. & von Stechow, A. (eds.) (1983): *Meaning, Use, and Interpretation of Language.* Berlin.

Bartsch, R. (1973): 'The Semantics and Syntax of Number and Numbers' In Kimball (ed.) (1973, 51-93).

Barwise, J. (1979): 'On Branching Quantifiers in English' *Journal of Philosophical Logic* **8**, 47 – 80.

Bennet, M.R. (1974): *Some Extensions of a Montague Fragment of English*. Dissertation, University of California, Los Angeles.

Benthem, J. van (1986): *Essays in Logical Semantics*. Dordrecht.

Benthem, J. van (1991): *Language in Action*. Amsterdam.

Benthem, J. van, and A. ter Meulen (eds.) (1984): *Generalized Quantifiers in Natural Language*. Dordrecht.

Does, J.M. van der (ed.) (1991): *Quantification and Anaphora II*. DYANA deliverable 2.2.b, Edinburgh.

Does, J.M. van der (1992): *Applied Quantifier Logics: Collectives, Naked Infinitives*. Dissertation, University of Amsterdam, Amsterdam.

Does, J.M. van der (1993): 'On Complex Plural Noun Phrases' In Kanazawa and Pinon (1994).

Does, J.M. van der and Eijck, J. van (eds.) (1996): *Quantifiers, Logic, and Language*. Lecture Notes, Vol. 54. Stanford, California: CSLI Publications. Distributed by Cambridge University Press.

Dowty, D. (1986): 'A Note on Collective Predicates, Distributive Predicates, and *All*' In Marshall (ed.) (1986).

Gärdenfors, P. (ed.) (1987): *Generalized Quantifiers: Linguistic and Logical approaches*. Dordrecht.

Gillon. B. (1987): 'The Readings of Plural Noun Phrases in English' *Linguistics and Philosophy* **10**, 199 – 219.

Gillon. B. (1990): 'Plural Noun Phrases and their Readings: A Reply to Lasersohn' *Linguistics and Philosophy* **13**, 477 – 485.

Groenendijk, J., T. Janssen and M. Stokhof (eds.) (1981): *Formal Methods in the Study of Language (Part I & II)*. Amsterdam.

Hoeksema, J. (1983): 'Plurality and Conjunction' In ter Meulen (ed.) (1983, 63–83).

Kanazawa, M. and C. Piñón (eds) (1994): *Dynamics, Polarity and Quantification* CSLI Lecture Notes, No. 48, Stanford.

Kimball, J.P. (ed.) (1973): *Syntax and Semantics (Volume 2)*. New York.

Landman, F. (1989): 'Groups I & II' *Linguistics and Philosophy* **12**, 559 – 605 and 723 – 744.

Lasersohn, P. (1989): 'On the Readings of Plural Noun Phrases' *Linguistic Inquiry* **20**, 130 – 134.

Link, G. (1983): 'The Logical Analysis of Plural and Mass Terms: a Lattice-theoretical Approach' In Bäuerle *et al.* (eds.) (1983, 302–323).

Link, G. (1987): 'Generalized Quantifiers and Plurals' In Gärdenfors (ed.) (1987, 151–180).

Link, G. (1991): 'Plural' In Wunderlich and Von Stechow (eds.) (1991).

Lønning, J.T. (1987): 'Collective Readings of Definite and Indefinite Noun Phrases' In Gärdenfors (ed.) (1987, 203–235).

Lønning, J.T. (1989): *Some Aspects of the Logic of Plural Noun Phrases*. Dissertation, University of Oslo, Oslo.

Lønning, J.T. (1991): 'Among Readings. Some Comments on 'Among Collections'' Does, J.M. van der (ed.) (1991, 37–51).

Marshall, F. (ed.) (1986): *ESCOL 86*. Ohio State University, Columbus.

Meulen, A.G.B ter (ed.) (1983): *Studies in Modeltheoretic Semantics*. Dordrecht.

Roberts, C. (1987): *Modal Subordination, Anaphora and Distributivity* Dissertation, University of Amherst, Amherst.

Scha, R. (1981): 'Distributive, Collective and Cumulative Quantification' In Groenendijk *et al.* (eds.) (1981, 483–512).

Scha, R. (1991): 'Afterthoughts on Collections' In Does, J.M. van der (ed.) (1991, 53–58).

Schwarzschild, R. (1992): 'Types of Plural Individuals' *Linguistics and Philosophy* **15**, 641 – 675.

Sher, G. (1990): 'Ways of Branching Quantification' *Linguistics and Philosophy* **13**, 393 – 422.

Spaan, M. (1993): 'Parallel Quantification' ILLC Prepublication series, LP–93–01. Also in Does, J.M. van der and Eijck, J. van (eds.) (1996).

Verkuyl, H.J. (1981): 'Numerals and Quantifiers in X'-syntax and their Semantic Interpretation' In Groenendijk *et al.* (eds.) (1981, 567–599).

Verkuyl, H.J. (1992): 'Some Issues in the Analysis of Multiple Quantification with Plural NP's' OTS Working Papers OTS–WP–TL–92–005.

Verkuyl, H.J. (1994) 'Distributivity and Collectivity: A Couple at Odds' In Kanazawa and Piñón (eds.) (1994).

Verkuyl, H.J. and Does, J.M. van der (1991): *The Semantics of Plural Noun Phrases* ITLI prepublication LP–91–07, Amsterdam 1991. Also in Does, J.M. van der and Eijck, J. van (eds.) (1996).

Wunderlich, D. and von Stechow, A. (eds.) (1991): *Semantics. An International Handbook of Contemporary Research*. Berlin and New York.

HENK J. VERKUYL

SOME ISSUES IN THE ANALYSIS OF MULTIPLE QUANTIFICATION WITH PLURAL NPs

1. INTRODUCTION

On the assumption that (1) is syntactically of the form (2), three important issues involved in theory formation about multiple quantification and plurality announce themselves:

(1) Four boys lifted three tables

(2) NP_1 [V NP_2]

(a) how many readings are to be assigned to (1); (b) may NP_1 be scopally dependent on NP_2; and (c) is NP_2 always scopally dependent on NP_1?

Leading theories about (1) seem to be reading–happy: some of them assign at least nine readings to it. There is also a tradition in which (1) is seen as a sentence underinforming language users. Adherents to this position argue that one should try to capture its property of allowing a wide range of verifying situations. Surely, for each verifying situation the proper entailments should come out, but this does not mean that one has to let a separate reading correspond to a (particular sort of) verifying situation. The most extreme position in the latter tradition has been adopted in Verkuyl & Van der Does (1991), which says that (1) has just one reading expressing an interpretive scale from purely collective to purely distributive. In the present paper, I shall discuss some problems with respect to this position.

Scope reversal tends to blur the discussion about readings. To say that NP_2 in (2) may have scope over NP_1, results in doubling the number of readings: (i) $NP_1(\ldots NP_2 \ldots)$, as in (2) itself, where NP_1 has wide scope over NP_2; and (ii) $NP_2(\ldots NP_1 \ldots)$, by some rule giving NP_2 a structural position from which it can have wide scope over NP_1. In the standard analysis of the quantificational structure of (2) scopal ambiguity is an accepted phenomenon. It was also accepted in Montague's PTQ, where second order techniques allow the NP_2 in (3) to "quantify in" from its prominent place to the place of the variable, semantically obtaining wide scope over NP_1 in the resulting representations, where NP_i are quantifiers binding a variable x_i.

(3) NP_2 [NP_1 [x_1 [V x_2]]]

(4) NP_1 [NP_2 [x_1 [V x_2]]]

283

F. Hamm and E. Hinrichs, (eds.), Plurality and Quantification, 283–319.
© 1998 *Kluwer Academic Publishers. Printed in the Netherlands.*

Modern versions of Montague grammar, such as Keenan & Faltz (1985), distinguish two logical forms for sentences like (5) where (6) is seen as "underlying", whereas (7) is derived by some operation:

(5) All participants get a medal

(6) $\lambda Y \forall x[\text{Participant}(x) \to Y(x)](\lambda x_1.\exists y[\text{Medal}(y) \land \text{Get}(x_1,y)])$

(7) $\lambda Y \exists y[\text{Medal}(y) \land Y(y)](\lambda x_2.\forall x[\text{Participant}(x) \to \text{Get}(x,x_2)])$

In the Logical Form–component of Chomsky grammar, a rule of Quantifier Raising applies to (2) and moves the quantifier NP_2 from its position inside the sentential structure into the one in (3) leaving behind a variable x_2. In the other reading, (4), NP_1 has wide scope over NP_2.

There has been an extensive debate about whether or not scopal exchange is necessary and justified for the analysis of natural language. After all, (8) represents just one of the situations captured by (9) itself, so if one wants to interpret "on the sleeves" of surface structure (5), then representations like (8) or (7) seem rather artificial, from the linguistic point of view.

(8) $\exists y[\text{Medal}(y) \land \forall x[\text{Participant}(x) \to \text{Get}(x,y)]]$

(9) $\forall x[\text{Participant}(x) \to \exists y[\text{Medal}(y) \land \text{Get}(x,y)]]$

Yet, the assumption of scope ambiguity is still part and parcel of the standard treatment of multiple quantification, even though there have been attacks on its usefulness for the analysis of natural language expressions (e.g. Reinhart 1985). The remaining obstacle against the idea of dropping scopal exchange entirely, appears to be sentences like (10), discussed in e.g. Landman & Moerdijk (1983), where the wide scope reading (11) for *every participant* seems to be required to make sure that there may be as many medals as participants:

(10) A medal is available (at the finish) for every participant

(11) $\forall x[\text{Participant}(x) \to \exists y[\text{Medal}(y) \land \text{Available\_for}(y,x)]]$

More closely to format (2), sentences like (12) also seem to motivate the existence of (13) as a separate reading next to (14).

(12) A bunny assisted all guests

(13) $\forall x[\text{Guest}(x) \to \exists y[\text{Bunny}(y) \land \text{Assist}(x,y)]]$

(14) $\exists y[\text{Bunny}(y) \land \forall x[\text{Guest}(x) \to \text{Assist}(x,y)]]$

One of the aims of this paper is to show that the interpretations expressed by (11) and (13) can be obtained without scope reversal. If this goal is achieved, it will have effects on the issue of how many readings are to be assigned to (1).

The third issue is whether or not the quantificational structure of a sentence of the form (2) is to be analyzed on the basis of some asymmetrical ("scope works from left to right") relation R. There are two variants: (15) and (16). In (16), R creates asymmetry between the two arguments by holding between NP_1 and the VP–structure created by the assemblage of V and NP_2:

(15) $R(NP_1, NP_2)$

(16) $R(NP_1,(V\ NP_2))$

Given (15) or (16) as the default case where NP_1 has scope over NP_2, the only problematic case left (after having accepted the argument with respect to (10), that is) is the one in which there is a separate reading of sentences with multiple quantification requiring that R be neutralized so that the quantifying expressions NP_1 and NP_2 are interpreted completely independent of one another. This is a claim made by Hintikka (1974), Barwise (1979), Scha (1981), Van der Does (1992), among others.

The third issue is strongly tied up with the first one, and it can be treated along with it, provided the issue of scopal ambiguity is settled first. This will be done in the next section.

2. BARENESS AND SCOPAL AMBIGUITY

In Verkuyl (1981), it was proposed to derive NPs like *a medal* and *two medals* in sentences such as:

(17)   A medal went to Leo

(18)   Leo got two medals

on the basis of the type–logical structure:

(19) N^0 $\langle e, t \rangle$
       NUM $\langle \langle e, t \rangle, \langle \langle e, t \rangle, t \rangle \rangle$
       N^1 $\langle \langle e, t \rangle, t \rangle$
       DET $\langle \langle \langle e, t \rangle, t \rangle, \langle \langle \langle e, t \rangle, t \rangle, t \rangle \rangle$
       N^2 $\langle \langle \langle e, t \rangle, t \rangle, t \rangle$

It was assumed that the abstract morphemes SG (singular) and PL (plural) belong to the category of Numerals. They take a Noun to form a N^1. As *two* is inherently "plural", we do not need PL. Thus, *a medal* was analyzed as: a[SG[medal]], and *two medals* as: ∅[two[medal]].

Sentence (17) can be derived as shown in (20) if we (temporarily) treat *went to Leo* as a one-place predicate to keep things as simple as possible. The derivation gives a direct interpretation by the standard function $[\![\ ]\!]$.[1]

(20)
N^0	medal	$[\![medal]\!]$
NUM	SG	$\lambda Y \lambda X[X \subseteq Y \wedge \|X\| = 1]$
N^1	SG(medal)	$\lambda Y \lambda X[X \subseteq Y \wedge \|X\| = 1]([\![medal]\!])$
		$\lambda X[X \subseteq [\![medal]\!] \wedge \|X\| = 1]$
DET	a	$\lambda Q \lambda P \exists W[Q(W) \wedge P(W)]$
N^2	aSG(medal)	$\lambda Q \lambda P \exists W[Q(W) \wedge$
		$P(W)](\lambda X[X \subseteq [\![medal]\!] \wedge \|X\| = 1])$
		$\lambda P \exists W[[W \subseteq [\![medal]\!] \wedge \|W\| = 1] \wedge$
		$P(W)]$
VP	go to Leo	$\lambda X.X \subseteq [\![go\_to\_Leo]\!]$
S	a medal go to L.	$\lambda P \exists W[W \subseteq [\![medal]\!] \wedge \|W\| = 1 \wedge$
		$P(W)](\lambda X.X \subseteq [\![go\_to\_Leo]\!])$
		$\exists W[W \subseteq [\![medal]\!] \wedge \|W\| = 1 \wedge$
		$W \subseteq [\![go\_to\_Leo]\!]]$

The derivation ends with the information (21) that there is a set W which is a singleton subset of the set of medals and which is a subset of the set of those things that went to Leo.[2]

(21) $\exists W[W \subseteq [\![medal]\!] \wedge \|W\| = 1 \wedge W \subseteq [\![go\_to\_Leo]\!]]$

When *go_to* is written out as a two-place predicate, (22) results:[3]

(22) $\exists W[W \subseteq [\![medal]\!] \wedge \|W\| = 1 \wedge [\![go\_to]\!](Leo)(W)]$

This analysis of (17) serves its purpose well because it makes it possible to define an important aspectual notion on the basis of the factual presence of cardinality information on W, in this case by the cardinality statement $\|W\| = 1$. NPs expressing cardinality either explicitly (numerals) or implicitly (*many, some, more than 3, several, at most twenty,* etc.) can be characterized as expressing a Specified Quantity of A, where A is the N-denotation $[\![N]\!]$, in this case $[\![medal]\!]$. One may abbreviate this semantic property by the (meta–)feature [+SQA]. Any NP of the form

(23) $\lambda P \exists W [W \subseteq [\![N]\!] \wedge r(|W|, m) \wedge P(W)]$

introduces a set W whose membership is specified (a) by a cardinality statement of the form $r(|W|, m)$, where $r \in \{<, \leq, \geq, >, =\}$ and m is a positive integer, and (b) by the fact that W is involved in the predication P. An NP meeting the conditions (a) and (b) is [+SQA].[4]

If an NP is [+SQA], it is predicted to contribute to terminative aspect, as it does in (24) — (27), where the combination of the terminative a–sentences with the durational adverbial *for hours* leads to the well-known aspectual blocking of the single event reading, so that one is to interpret the sentence as expressing forced repetition (or sometimes forced stretching), as indicated by #:

(24)   a.   A medal went to Leo
       b.   # For hours a medal went to Leo

(25)   a.   The medal went to Leo[5]
       b.   # For hours the medal went to Leo

(26)   a.   Some medals went to Leo
       b.   # For hours some medals went to Leo

(27)   a.   At least three medals went to Leo
       b.   # For hours at least three medals went to Leo

Some NPs do have a [–SQA]–specification, as in:

(28)   a.   No medal went to Leo
       b.   For hours no medal went to Leo

(29)   a.   Medals went to Leo
       b.   For hours medals went to Leo

Both a–sentences are durative, though for different reasons. Sentence (28) is to be interpreted as a statement about W being the empty set: it expresses that the empty subset of the set of medals went to Leo. Zero cardinality of W leads to durative aspectuality.

As far as (29) is concerned, it is striking that the [–SQA]–behaviour of *medals* is not restricted to bare plurals only. In fact, it can be argued that all regular [+SQA]–NPs systematically show this bare–like behaviour:

(30)   When the soldiers came into town I stayed inside

(31) The general first dropped the infantry soldiers and then the marines

(32) I moved the cube to the left

Sentence (30) may pertain to a group of soldiers, say Harry, Tom and Bruce. When these three soldiers came into town, I stayed inside. But suppose that we are inhabitants of this town which is near a NATO–basis, which contains soldiers as well as sailors. Now, (30) may mean that when members of the first category came in, I stayed inside, possibly opposed to what happened when members of the category of sailors visited the town. Likewise, (31) may pertain to a dropping of Harry, Tom and Bruce, after which a contextually given group of (say, ten) marines was dropped, or it may say something about the general as a "meat grinder": he dropped an unspecified amount of soldiers and then an unspecified amount of marines. It is clear that the definiteness pertains to the category, not to the elements contained by it. The same applies to (32): in the Tarski game invented by Barwise and Etchemendy at desktop the Macintosh computer has a folder containing documents each of which (on opening it) shows a square on which cubes, dodecahedra, and tetrahedra may be located. One may change the position of these objects on the square with the help of the cursor. Sentence (32) may pertain to just one document in which I moved the cube (the only one or the identified one) to the left. However, (32) may also be used to report about a task which I did on all the documents, the task being to move the cube to the left in all documents when there was one (of the desired kind). Thus, "bareness" may occur both in the definite singular and definite plural, expressing itself in unboundedness ot the category or categories. The same applies to NPs like *some saucers*, *several etchings*, *at least three medals*, etc. as I shall demonstrate shortly.

There is a clear aspectual difference between the two readings: the "Harry, Tom and Bruce"–reading is terminative, whereas the other one is durative:

(33) For hours the soldiers came into town

(34) For hours the general dropped the soldiers, and then for the rest of the afternoon the marines

Terminative #–repetition in (33) is only obtained if the soldiers is taken as [+SQA], i.e. if *the soldiers* is interpreted in terms of a cardinality statement $|W| = m$ (m determined by the context set, in this case 3). However, on the durative interpretation an unbounded number of members of a contextually identified category came in. Likewise, the [+SQA]–reading of *the soldiers* in (34) is blocked or it must bring about forced aspectual repetition, but the "bare" [-SQA]–reading for *the soldiers* and *the marines* allows the general to drop members of the category soldiers continuously, after which he went on dropping an unbounded number of the other category, the marines.

This phenomenon is aspectually interesting because the translations of (33) and (34) into Slavic languages such as Polish show that the relevant difference of interpretation is brought out in the verbal system, as aspectual differences do in these languages.[6]

That is, for the [-SQA]–reading of the two sentences one needs to use the imperfective aspect, whereas for the [+SQA]–interpretation of (30) and (31) the perfective aspect is required. Hence, the perfective translation of (33) and (34) is blocked in e.g. Polish.

As said, the "bare" behaviour of NPs shows up systematically, as a sort of "shadow" [-SQA]–system counterparting the [+SQA]–use of NPs:

(35) a. Luce sold three etchings
     b. For years Luce sold three etchings

(36) a. Luce sold that etching
     b. For years Luce sold that etching

(37) a. Leo won the bronze medal
     b. For years Leo won the bronze medal

Sentence (35-b) would get a #–interpretation if its (35-a)–part would mean that Luce sold three unique token etchings. However, a natural [-SQA]–reading of (35-b) is that she sold an unbounded number of tokens from three different etchings. The same applies to (36) and (37); it is even very hard to interpret (37-b) with a forced repetition, because our knowledge of the world tells us that every token–medal won is new.

It is impossible to derive a sentence like (29) on the basis of the presence of a PL–marker belonging to num in (19), because pl is semantically defined as: $\lambda Y \lambda X [X \subseteq Y \wedge |X| > 1]$.[7]

This would yield (38) for the NP *medals*:

(38) $\lambda P \exists W [W \subseteq [\![medal]\!] \wedge |W| > 1 \wedge \mathcal{P}(W)]$

The problem now is that (38) characterizes medals as [+SQA], due to the presence of the $|W| > 1$–information. Therefore it was proposed in Verkuyl (1993) to interpret e.g. the plural NP *three etchings* in (35) as:

(39) $\lambda P \exists W \exists \mathcal{W}[W = \bigcup \mathcal{W} \subseteq [\![etching]\!] \land |\mathcal{W}| = 3 \land \mathcal{P}(W)]$

which says that there is a W which is the union of a collection $\mathcal{W}$ consisting of three subsets of W.[8]

In this way, no information about the cardinality of W itself is available. As it is the presence of cardinality information about W which makes an NP [+SQA], this analysis correctly predicts that on the "bare" interpretation sentences like (35-a) are durative. In this way, it is also explained why — given our knowledge of competitions — the most natural meaning of (37) is a durative one, which is that for years Leo acquired an (unbounded) number of token medals, as many times as he won the third prize.

My claim now is that "bare–like" NPs have the following format:

(40) $\lambda P \exists W \exists \mathcal{W}[W = \bigcup \mathcal{W} \subseteq [\![N]\!] \land r(|\mathcal{W}|, n) \land \mathcal{P}(W)]$

This expresses that no cardinality information is given about W itself. Thus, $r(|Q|, n)$ gives information about the number of elements of the collection $\mathcal{W}$.

This being said as a first step towards the solution of the scope reversal problem, it is necessary to first embark on the issue of the reduction of readings, and then to fine–grain (40) by giving more information about the relation R between NP_1 and NP_2 in (15) or (16), which is another way of saying that we need to be more specific about how W is involved in the predication $\mathcal{P}$.

3. THE ONE READING HYPOTHESIS

Scha (1981) claims that sentences like (1) *Four boys lifted three tables* have nine readings, whereas Link (1983) claims to count up to eight possible readings, which reduce to six because they are logically equivalent. Van der Does (1992: 31–33) points out that because Scha (1981) does not exclude the possibility of some rule of focus forcing us into a salient wide scope reading for *five sandwiches* or *three tables*, eighteen readings are produced. He also shows that in general Link is committed to sixteen possible readings (again with some reduction). In Verkuyl & Van der Does (1991), it is argued that contrary to what Scha and Link claim, sentences like (1) must be analyzed as underinforming language users as to the precise way in which the situation described took place in a particular model. Thus the number of readings is reduced considerably, in fact to just one. This will be called the *One Reading Hypothesis*. It says that the interpretation of the subject NP four boys of (1) would capture a scale of interpretive possibilities leading from completely collective to completely distributive, as illustrated in Figure 1, where collective and distributive are only used as pre-theoretic descriptive terms.

Figure 1:

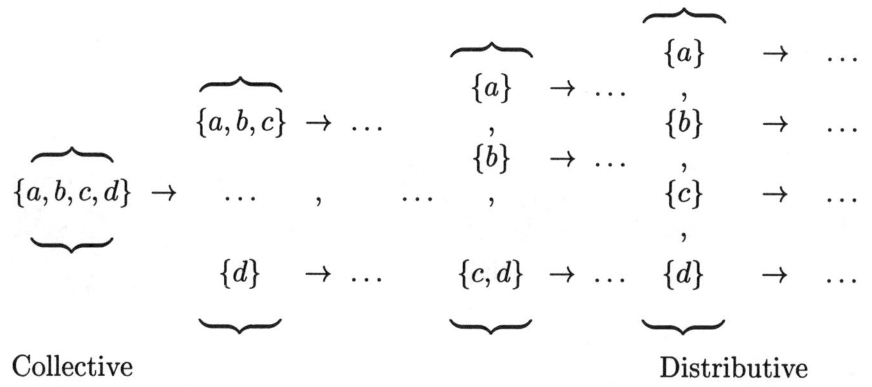

$$
\{a,b,c,d\} \to \ldots \;,\; \begin{Bmatrix} \{a,b,c\} \to \ldots \\ \{d\} \to \ldots \end{Bmatrix} \;,\; \begin{Bmatrix} \{a\} \to \ldots \\ \{b\} \to \ldots \\ \{c,d\} \to \ldots \end{Bmatrix} \;,\; \begin{Bmatrix} \{a\} \to \ldots \\ \{b\} \to \ldots \\ \{c\} \to \ldots \\ \{d\} \to \ldots \end{Bmatrix}
$$

Collective $\hspace{6cm}$ Distributive

According to Verkuyl & Van der Does (1991) sentences like (1) have the one reading given in (41) in which the existential quantifier of the external argument has scope over the quantifier of the internal argument.

(41) $\exists Z[Z \subseteq \llbracket boy \rrbracket \land |Z| \quad = \quad 4 \land \exists \mathcal{P} ps Z[\mathcal{P} \quad =$
$\{V \cap \llbracket boy \rrbracket | \exists W[W \subseteq \llbracket table \rrbracket \land |W| = 3$
$\land \exists \mathcal{Q} ps W [\mathcal{Q} = \{U \cap \llbracket table \rrbracket | \llbracket lift \rrbracket (U)(V)\}]]\}]]$

The formula in (41) is more complicated than the formulas in the preceding section by the presence of information of the form $\exists \alpha ps \beta$, where α is identified as a collection of subsets of β, in particular a partition.[9]

For the time being, 'ps' is to be read for 'partitions'. Below the underlying equivalence relation required for a partition will be identified and then it will become clear that Verkuyl & Van der Does in fact used a weaker form of partitioning, called pseudo-partitioning. As it now stands, (41) says that there is a set Z of four boys and that Z is partitioned into a collection $\mathcal{P}$ such that for each of the elements ("cells") of $\mathcal{P}$, i.e. the partitioned subsets V of Z, there is a set W of 3 tables where W is partitioned by the subsets of W lifted by V such that each of the cells U of the collection $\mathcal{Q}$ is involved in the lift-predication.

On the basis of the lexical definitions in (42) and the syntactic structure in Figure 2, the denotation of the NP three tables in (41) can be derived:

(42) ⟦∅⟧   :λDλXλR.∃W[W⊆X ∧ D(X)(W) ∧
              ∃QpsW[Q = R|$_X$]]
      ⟦three⟧ :λXλY.|X∩Y| = 3
      ⟦table⟧ :{$t_1, t_2, \ldots, t_n$}

Figure 2:

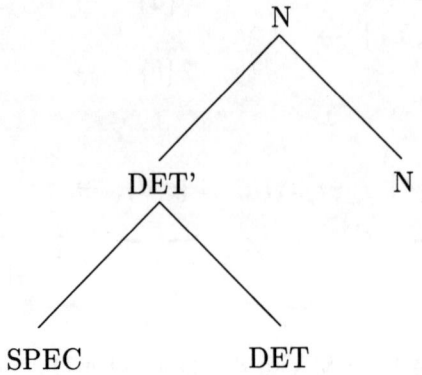

NP–derivation:

Spec(Det) ⤳ ⟦∅⟧⟦three⟧
= λDλXλR.∃W[W⊆X ∧ D(X)(W) ∧ ∃QpsW[Q = R|$_X$]](λXλY.|X∩Y| = 3)
= λXλR.∃W[W⊆X ∧ λXλY.|X∩Y| = 3(X)(W) ∧ ∃QpsW[Q = R|$_X$]]
= λXλR.∃W[W⊆X ∧ |W| = 3 ∧ ∃QpsW[Q = R|$_X$]]

⟦∅⟧(⟦three⟧)(⟦table⟧)
= λXλR.∃W[W⊆X ∧ |W| = 3 ∧ ∃QpsW[Q = R|$_X$]](⟦table⟧)
= λR.∃W[W⊆⟦table⟧ ∧ |W| = 3 ∧ ∃QpsW[Q = R|$_{⟦table⟧}$]]

The NP is of type ⟨⟨⟨e, t⟩, t⟩, t⟩, the N of type ⟨e, t⟩. Hence DET' is of type ⟨⟨e, t⟩, ⟨⟨⟨e, t⟩, t⟩, t⟩⟩. DET itself is of type ⟨⟨e, t⟩, ⟨⟨e, t⟩, t⟩⟩. The indefinite SPEC ensures that the NP *three tables* existentially introduces a set W which is a subset of ⟦N⟧. The Van Benthem-problem is solved because SPEC contains the restriction on the predicate R written as R|$_X$ and defined as R|$_X$:= {X∩Z|Z∈R}, where X = ⟦N⟧. The VP ⟦*lift three tables*⟧ is derived as follows:

VP–derivation:

$\lambda V(\lambda \mathcal{R}.\exists W[W\subseteq[\![table]\!] \wedge |W| = 3 \wedge \exists \mathcal{Q}psW[\mathcal{Q} = \mathcal{R}|_{[\![table]\!]}]](\lambda U.[\![lift]\!](U)(V)))$
$= \lambda V \exists W[W\subseteq[\![table]\!] \wedge |W| = 3 \wedge \exists \mathcal{Q}psW[\mathcal{Q} = \lambda U.[\![lift]\!](U)(V)|_{[\![table]\!]}]]$
$= \lambda V \exists W[W\subseteq[\![table]\!] \wedge |W| = 3 \wedge \exists \mathcal{Q}psW[\mathcal{Q} = \{U \cap [\![table]\!] | [\![lift]\!](U)(V)\}]]$

(41) is obtained by applying (43) to the last line of the VP–derivation.

(43) $\lambda \mathcal{S}.\exists Z[Z\subseteq[\![boy]\!] \wedge |Z| = 4 \wedge \exists \mathcal{P}psZ[\mathcal{P} = \mathcal{S}|_{[\![boy]\!]}]]$

What (41) says is that there are two sets Z and W and that each of them is possibly partitioned so that there is some (yet unidentified) relationship R between the partitioned subsets of Z and W. Recall that cardinality information about Z and W is a determinant for terminative aspect. This can be expressed in terms of Figure 3.

Figure 3:

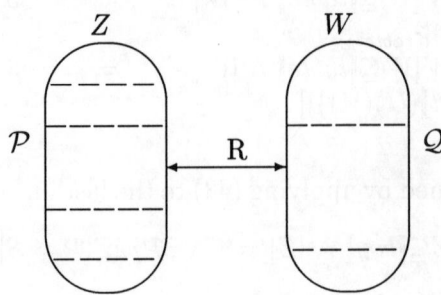

The number of cells of $\mathcal{P}$ and $\mathcal{Q}$ are directly dependent on the cardinalities of Z and W, so if $|\mathcal{P}| = k$ and $|Z| = m$, then $1 \leq k \leq m$.

Sentence (1) fundamentally underinforms about what happened with the four boys in a particular model: if no further information is available one will never know exactly what happened, e.g. how many tables were involved. The four boys may have operated as a set or as four singletons or in any other combination allowed by $1 \leq k \leq 4$. Again, one does not know what happened, but there must have been a partition of some sort.

Let us first see what the analysis of (1) as (41) contributes to an understanding of sentences like (44) allowing for an interpretation in which four winners received a medal.

(44) A medal went to four winners

This can be obtained without the fronting of four winners:

(45) $\exists W [W \subseteq \llbracket medal \rrbracket \wedge |W| \quad = \quad 1 \wedge \exists \mathcal{P} ps W [\mathcal{P} \quad =$
  $\{V \cap \llbracket medal \rrbracket | \exists Z [Z \subseteq \llbracket winner \rrbracket$
  $\wedge |Z| = 4 \wedge \exists \mathcal{Q} ps Z [\mathcal{Q} = \{U \cap \llbracket winner \rrbracket | \llbracket go\_to \rrbracket (U)(V) \}]]\}]]$

(46) $\exists W \exists \mathcal{W} [W = \bigcup \mathcal{W} \subseteq \llbracket medal \rrbracket \wedge |\mathcal{W}| \quad = \quad 1 \wedge \exists \mathcal{P} ps W [\mathcal{P} \quad =$
  $\{V \cap \llbracket medal \rrbracket | \exists Z [Z \subseteq \llbracket winner \rrbracket \wedge |Z| \quad = \quad 4 \wedge \exists \mathcal{Q} ps Z [\mathcal{Q} \quad =$
  $\{U \cap \llbracket winner \rrbracket | \llbracket go\_to \rrbracket (U)(V) \}]]\}]]$

In (45), there is one singleton set W which is (trivially) partitioned into a collection $\mathcal{P}$ containing one singleton V (= W) such that for V there is a set of four winners. Note that (45) allows that V first went to winner1, then to winner2, but also to four winners as a group, or partitions of this group. In (46) there is a set W construed from the union of a singleton–collection of subsets of [[medal]], such that the go_to relation holds between a partition of this collection and members of a collection $\mathcal{Q}$ of subsets of the set [[winner]]. It is clear that (46) is a situation in which W would contain four medals so that there is a 1 medal : 1 winner interpretation. Is it also possible for (46) to express that say three medals went to four winners? I think it is, because e.g. one gold medal may go to a team whereas each of the individual members is a winner. In fact, the whole range between 1 and 4 token–medals contained by W is allowed (without it being expressed explicitly). Note also that on this reading, (44) does not exclude that each of the four winners received more than one medal, as is more clearly demonstrated in sentences like (47):

(47)   A computer supported four of our colleagues

It may mean that in every place where our colleagues went (individually) on their trip a computer was available to support them there. My colleague Eric, for example, visited eight places, and in each of them there was a computer supporting him, so there were eight computers supporting him.[10]

Two points are important. The first one, is that two readings are distinguished: they are distinguished with respect to the presence or absence of cardinality information about W. One might also speak about a [+SQA]–reading and a [−SQA]–reading. The second point is that W can be partitioned in both cases, even to the point of a 1:1 relation between the members of $Dom(R)$ and $Ran(R)$ in Figure 3. Essential is that on the [−SQA]–reading one cannot tell what the partition looks like, because there is no information about the membership of W.

On the [−SQA]–reading, sentences like (48) are treated as in (49):[11]

(48)   A medal went to all participants

(49) $\exists W \exists \mathcal{W}[W = \bigcup \mathcal{W} \subseteq [\![medal]\!] \wedge |\mathcal{W}| = 1 \wedge \exists \mathcal{P}ps W[\mathcal{P} = \{V \cap [\![medal]\!]\} | \exists Z[Z = [\![participant]\!] \wedge \exists \mathcal{Q}ps Z[\mathcal{Q} = \{U \cap [\![participant]\!]\} | [\![go\_to]\!](U)(V)\}]]\}]]$

(50)   For hours a medal went to all participants

On this reading, (48) expresses that members of W went to subsets of

Z, possibly in a 1:1–way, but also in a 1:many–way (subgroups of participants involved) and a many:1–way (some participants have received more than one medal). Note that (50) on its durative interpretation expresses that for hours whoever was participant received a medal, the (forced) terminative interpretation being that for hours one token medal repeatedly went to all participants.[12]

4. PROBLEMS WITH THE ONE READING HYPOTHESIS

The *ps*–information in (41) can be made more explicit by considering the expression $\exists \mathcal{P} ps X$ as equivalent with $X = \bigcup \mathcal{P}$ plus some additional constraint. Verkuyl & Van der Does (1991) discussed three possible constraints on the condition of the form $X = \bigcup \mathcal{P}$:[13]

(51)   a.   no constraint (cover)
       b. $|\mathcal{P}| \leq |X|$ (pseudo–partition)
       c.   for all Z, if $X = Z$ and $Z \subseteq Y$, then $Z = Y$ (minimal cover)
       d.   for all $U, V \in \mathcal{P}, U \cap V = \emptyset$ (partition)

They proposed (51-b) rather than (51-d) in view of sentences like (52):

(52)   Five children came upstairs

which may verify a situation in which one child came upstairs, then the second one, after which the first one went down to open the door for the remaining three and came upstairs with them. Thus, (51-b) makes it possible for individuals to belong to more than one member of $\mathcal{P}$.[14]

So, *ps* in (41) became: 'pseudo–partitions'. Position (51-a) is even weaker than Gillon (1983) who proposed (51-b) in order to deal with sentences like *Hammerstein, Hart and Rogers wrote some musicals*. Hammerstein and Hart wrote jointly, and Hart and Rogers worked together, but never the three of them. As I do not see empirically interesting differences between pseudo–partitions and minimal covers, I will ignore the latter and not the former because aspectually the constraint $|\mathcal{P}| \leq |X|$ is important.

A choice between (51-b) and (51-d) is very difficult to make because decisions must be made with respect to the question of whether or not lexical properties count as idiosyncrasies. For example, the semantics of a sentence like (53), which is represented by (54), allows for all intermediate situations.[15]

(53)   Two girls ate five sandwiches

(54) $\exists Z[Z \in [\![2girls]\!] \wedge \exists \mathcal{P}psZ[\mathcal{P} = \{V \cap [\![girl]\!] | \exists W[W \in [\![5sandwiches]\!]$
$\wedge \exists \mathcal{Q}psW[\mathcal{Q} = \{U \cap [\![sandwich]\!] | [\![eat]\!](U)(V)\}]\}]]$

It even allows that the girls each had two sandwiches and shared the fifth one. The normal lexical characterization of the verb *eat* demands that one should exclude interpretations in which sandwich s_1 is completely eaten by girl$_1$ and also by girl$_2$. In contrast with this, one may have a fully distributive reading of (1) *Four boys lifted three tables* even though there happens to be just one set of three tables: (1) may apply to a situation in which boy$_1$ lifted three tables on Monday, boy$_2$ the same three tables on Tuesday, etc.

The fact that such an interpretation is to be excluded in the case of (53) should not be taken as structurally important (e.g. one may wish to talk about gods who eat sandwiches which have been eaten by other gods). In other words, even though it is attractive to translate the lexical difference between *eat* and *lift* in terms of a difference between a partition and a pseudo–partition, it seems more rewarding to treat (53) and (1) analogously as long as possible to see whether structural factors are involved. In the remainder I shall often use the *ps*–notation without distinguishing between a pseudo–partition and a partition, because other aspects of the semantic structure are being discussed. So, it is only when the distinction between (51-b) and (51-d) is at issue, that I shall make it. The formula in (41) appears adequate for the full scale of possibilities on a scale like Figure 1 if the *ps*–relation is taken as a genuine partition: its meaning ranges from one set of four boys relating to one set of 3 tables on the one hand, and four singletons relating each to three different singletons. The strict partition interpretation captures all intermediate verifying situations of Figure 1, e.g. situations in which one or more boys lifted together or one of more tables were lifted together. The same applies to (54). It is only outside the range of Figure 1 that the need for an unconstrained cover, and according to Van der Does (1992), the need for different readings is to be argued for. This is because, given our scheme (55)

(55) $\exists Z[\ldots \wedge \exists \mathcal{P}psZ[\mathcal{P} = \{U \cap [\![N]\!] | \exists W(\ldots \exists \mathcal{Q}psW)\}]]$

it is predicted that each member of the collection $\mathcal{P}$ picks out a member of the collection $\mathcal{Q}$ which may be the unit set Z itself. That is $Z_1 \rightarrow W_1$ and $Z_2 \rightarrow W_2$, where Z_1 and W_2 may or not overlap ('$\rightarrow$' = 'buy–relates to'). This leads to problems for sentences like:[16]

(56)   Three boys bought a boat

(57) Three policemen transported two prisoners

(58) Four boys shared three pizzas

These problems arise only if one interprets (56) as expressing that two boys (John and Bill) bought a boat and that a third boy (Harry) also bought a boat. Likewise there is a problem if one interprets (57) as pertaining to three or four prisoners. On the other hand, Lønning (1991) says that (58) may pertain to a situation in which John, Bill and Harry shared two pizzas and Harry shared a pizza with a girl, and (55) fails to account for this. Let us start out with the last case.

I do not think that Lønning's (58) is a genuine counterexample. It cannot be interpreted in the way he does, unless one introduces means to distinguish two token–occurrences of Harry, say $Harry_1$ and $Harry_2$. Suppose (58) is used e.g. by some person behind the counter of some restaurant who deduces from her notes that during the day four boys have shared three pizzas. The woman behind the counter may speak about four boys, but her notion of four boys is different from those who know that only three boys were really involved. This situation is factually the only way to let Lønning make his point, but it is clear then that (58) pertains now to four representatives (e.g. the counter notes) for four or less boys, or more neutrally to boy–occurrences. This has consequences for the construal of the set X in (55), because in this way (58) may even pertain to just one boy who happens to be counted as four boys. But here it is important to observe that on this token–occurrence analysis (55) turns out to be the proper mechanism again. On the assumption that Z contains four different boy–occurrences (possibly construed from 1 to 4 boys in some way), the proper prediction is made. Note that (55) in the non–token–occurrence construal of X properly allows an interpretation in which John, Bill and Harry shared two pizzas among each other and Tom shared a pizza with a girl.[17]

I shall come back to some problems with the phenomenon of quantifying over token–occurrences below in section 6.

So, (56) and (57) remain as a stumblestone, because (55) predicts that two boys may form a cell of X involved in the predicate 'buy a boat', whereas the third boy form a second cell of X. Can we solve this problem without giving up asymmetry of R? There is also Van der Does (1992) arguing that (52) *Five children came upstairs* should be able to express that the number of 'coming upstairs'–events may exceed the number of children. Why not fifty times? So he weakens the constraints on $X = \bigcup \mathcal{P}$ to zero obtaining a cover (cv).

These two problems made Van der Does (1992) decide to step back into the position in which three readings are distinguished, (59), (60) and a cumulative one (which will be spelled out later on):

(59) distributive reading:
$[\ \exists Z[Z \in [\![4boys]\!] \land \exists \mathcal{P}cvZ[\mathcal{P} = ATOM([\![boy]\!]) \cap \{V | \exists W[W \in [\![3tables]\!] \land \exists \mathcal{Q}cvW[\mathcal{Q} = \{U \cap [\![table]\!] | [\![lift]\!](U)(V)\}]]\}]]]$

(60) collective reading:
$[\ \exists Z[Z \in [\![4boys]\!] \land \exists \mathcal{P}cvZ[\mathcal{P} = \{V | \exists W[W \in [\![3tables]\!] \land \exists \mathcal{Q}cvW [\mathcal{Q} = \{U \cap [\![table]\!] | [\![lift]\!](U)(V)\}]]\}]]]$

In the cumulative reading, the dependency of Y from members of X is completely neutralized. It says that the total number of boys in the universe of discourse involved in lifting is 4 and that the total number of tables lifted is 3. This tripartition of readings still constitutes a considerable reduction when compared with Link and Scha.

The weakening of the constraints in (51) is orthogonal to the need of strengthening them in case the temporal structure of the sentences is drawn into account explicitly, as I shall show below. Multiple quantification from the point of view of aspectual behaviour was studied in Verkuyl (1988). In fact, Verkuyl & Van der Does (1991) was an attempt to deal first with atemporal denotations completely atemporally so that a solid ground was obtained on which one might build insight into temporal factors involved in multiple and plural quantification. However, from Verkuyl (1988) it was clear that indices may play a crucial role for a better understanding of what is involved in the interpretation of sentences in which temporal and atemporal structure interact. In the next section, a brief survey will be given of the role given to indices in construing semantic objects expressing the asymmetry of (16).

5. ASPECTUAL ASYMMETRY AND INDICES

The need for an asymmetric approach to multiple quantification in Verkuyl (1987;1988) is motivated by the underlying aspectual theory which requires among other things that a VP may express terminative aspectuality without an external argument NP. The VP *to eat three sandwiches* itself is terminative and this can be explained by assuming that this results from combining information expressed by the verb with information expressed by its internal argument. As pointed out in Verkuyl

(1988; 1993) there are several arguments favouring the idea of asymmetry among which the fact that resultative clauses which contribute to terminativity are always oriented to the internal argument and never to the external argument NP, and the fact that a typical VP–phenomenon such as idiomatization shows that literal (i.e. compositionally formed) meanings often differ aspectually from their idiomaticized counterparts.

My aspectual theory is located in the localistic tradition which attributes to the verb a crucial role in the construal of a semantic structure in which time structure interacts with atemporal structure. In Verkuyl (1978), it was argued that for an NP denoting an individual undergoing a change, one may semantically define a Path. In Verkuyl (1988) it was proposed to analyze an external argument denotation in terms of a function π which assigns to each of its individual member a pair consisting of an index and a subset of the denotation of the internal argument. This function can be defined as follows:[18]

DEFINITION 1: The function $\pi : \mathbf{D}_e \to \mathbf{D}_L^N$ is defined by:

(61) $\quad x \mapsto \ell, where\ \ell = \{\langle i, p \rangle | [\![AT(p)(x)]\!]_{M,i} = 1\}$

N is taken as a set of indices representing intervals, $\mathbf{D}_L$ is the domain of spatial coordinates p, and $\ell \in \mathbf{D}_L^N$. AT is a two–place relation between x and a spatial coordinate p. It determines x's position p at a certain index i. A spatial coordinate is a point in one of the so–called "semantic fields", i.e. in a set of semantic values ranging over spatial positions, possession, identity, circumstance, etc., in the sense of Gruber (1975) and Jackendoff (1990). Definition 1 attempts to bring the localistic tradition in which change expressed by sentences is taken in terms of "movement" along a path, under the model–theoretical umbrella. The idea is the following. Given (61), one might picture out the events described in (62) and (63) both in terms of the resulting path–structure as illustrated in Figure 4.

(62)   John flew to three cities

(63)   Judith ate five sandwiches

Figure 4:

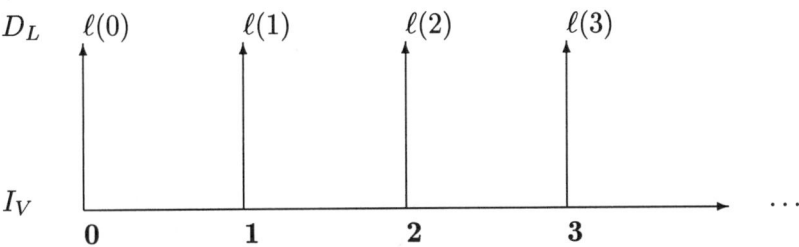

Suppose that John had three flights.[19] Then at each counting point after point zero, he was in one city. Each $\ell(i)$ is a spatial position, or in a mental projection thereof, as e.g. in Clark 1973. [20]

Generalization over the different semantic fields makes it possible to use Figure 4 for the analysis of sentences like (63). It represents just one of the situations in which (63) is true, i.e. the one in which she went through the set of five sandwiches in three successive phases. The only thing required by the generalization is to define the equivalence relation which partitions the set Z of five sandwiches as: 'counting as being involved at the same index'.[21]

On the basis of Definition 1 the following definition is relevant:

DEFINITION 2: $I_V := \{(0,k) \in \mathbf{R} | k \in N\}$

The relation between $\mathbf{N}$ and I_V is accounted for by the Entier function $Ent : \mathbf{R} \rightarrow \mathbf{N}$ defined as: for all $x \in \mathbf{R}$, $Ent(x) = y$ where $y \in \mathbf{N}$ and $y \leq x \leq y+1$. A natural analogue is to see the set of indices $I(I \subseteq \mathbf{N})$ associated with a verb as a value on an odometer in a car put at zero at the start of the drive and showing say the natural number 378. This (ordinal) number is a *representative*. It not only represents all elements in $\mathbf{R}$ belonging to (0,378), but also those which may (theoretically) belong to the interval (378,378.999...).

This position with respect to the aspectual structure makes it possible to explain terminative aspect: the interval structure I_V contributed by the verb is built up from point zero with the help of indices from $\mathbf{N}$, is dependent on the cardinality of the partitioning. The cardinality of the partitioned collection of subsets of Z, the set of five sandwiches in (63), can never exceed the cardinality of Z itself. Thus, John's flying to three cities in (62) is terminative in the same way as Judith's eating five sandwiches in (63). An instantiation of one of the possibilities expressed by (63) is given in Figure 5.

Figure 5:

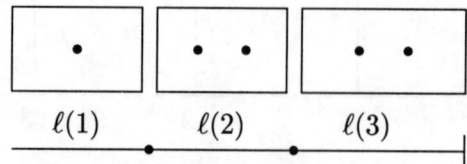

It is clearly a metaphoric way of saying that in verifying this particular situation Judith "goes through" a finite, discrete, in this case three membered partitioning of the set of five sandwiches. Another way of saying this is that — given a sense of progress in time expressed by the verb — there is some underlying temporalization: each $\ell(i)$ is connected to a (ultimately temporal) index i. It is clear that (63) expresses just one of the many possible different ways of going through the eating of five sandwiches. This is exactly the reason why Verkuyl & Van der Does (1991) introduced the existential quantifier $\exists QpsW$ in its (simplified) representation:

(64) $\exists W[W \subseteq [\![sandwich]\!] \wedge |W| = 5 \wedge \exists QpsW[Q = \{U \cap [\![sandwich]\!] | [\![lift]\!](U)(\{j\})\}]]$

That is, the representation warrants that there is a Q, but it does not say how it looks like. Sometimes this is decided by modifiers such as *one-by-one*.[22]

The formal representation of the indices in versions of (64) which are relevant for the analysis of aspectuality, involves intensionalizing the otherwise extensional NP–denotation ($\exists W$) by making the sets U of the collection Q in (64) dependent on indices induced by the verb. A formalization would carry too far away from the main line of argument (see Verkuyl 1993), and for the present discussion it would have no sense because the points at issue can be explained more informally. It suffices to observe that Q introduced by $\exists QpsW$ in (63) is seen as the result of applying the function ℓ in (61) to a domain of indices yielding (indexed) subsets of W.

6. TWO PARTICIPANCY FUNCTIONS

The function π in Definition 1, rewritten as (65) commits to scheme (16) because x corresponds to NP_1 and ℓ to the pair $[V\ NP_2]$.

(65) $x \mapsto \ell$ where $\ell : \mathbf{N} \to \mathbf{D}_L$ defined as $\ell(i) = p$ such that $[\![AT(p)(x)]\!]_{M,i} = 1$

Verkuyl (1988) called π a participancy function because π determines the way in which the members of the external argument denotation participate in the predication. It was proposed to allow only two functions π: an injective function denoted by π_i and a constant function denoted by π_c. In this way, the extensional nature of the subject NP position was underscored by requiring that each individual belonging to the NP_{ext}-denotation be assigned its own unique image (its own Path, so to say), as in (66), where the function π is spelled out for each x.

(66) $x_1 \mapsto \ell_1 : \mathbf{N} \to \mathbf{D}_L$
         $x_2 \mapsto \ell_2 : \mathbf{N} \to \mathbf{D}_L$
         $x_3 \mapsto \ell_3 : \mathbf{N} \to \mathbf{D}_L$
         ...

When π is an injection, then for all $i, j, x_i \neq x_j \Rightarrow \ell_i \neq \ell_j$. When π is a constant function, then for all $i, j, x_i \neq x_j \Rightarrow \ell_i = \ell_j$. The two variants of π not only cover all the forms of multiple quantification between the two poles of Figure 1, but they also shed some light on cases like (56) and (57).

In Verkuyl (1988), the type–logical status of NPs was left unspecified because it did not play an important role. Hence, in $boy_1 \mapsto \langle 1, table_1 \rangle, \langle 2, table_{2,3} \rangle$, boy_1 would stand for an individual and $table_1$ for $\{table_1\}$. In the present context π might be defined as taking singletons rather than individuals as its input, so in that case boy_1 and $table_1$ both would represent singletons.

It is important to underscore that the meaning of $\mapsto$ in the application of the functions π_i and π_c is not 'be completely involved in' but rather 'be involved in'. An adequate paraphrase would be something like 'execute lifting activities'. The sense of completeness is not inherent to *lift* itself, it is contributed by the cardinality information expressed by the arguments of the verb in question.

(67)   One boy lifted a table

(68)   Four boys lifted a table

It is indeed hard to escape from the "complete involvement"–interpretation which says that boy_1 is the only actor involved in the lifting of $table_1$ whereas $table_1$ is not lifted by other individuals (at the time with respect to which (67) is true). However, to assign such a "1:1–sense" to *lift* as part of its meaning would be misleading. The verb *lift* in (68) must be able to express that each of the four boys did just a part of the total activity needed to lift the table (It may even be used to describe a situation in which three boys actually happened to lift the table whereas the fourth one opened the door, prevented scratching, and directed the lifting). This also means for the table that it did not relate to just one lifting individual. Due to the fact that it should be used in sentences like (68), the verb *lift* must be characterized as being vague with respect to complete involvement of the individuals making up the denotations of its arguments. More in general, the degree to which individuals that are part of the argument denotation, are involved in the predication is left unspecified by the verb itself; it is filled in by the arguments (cf. Carlson 1978; Roberts 1987). Hence $\mapsto$ means 'sufficiently involved in the predication to speak of participancy'.

An analysis based on (66) makes it possible to vary over members of $\mathbf{N}$ and $\mathbf{D}_L$. Thus, the function value $\langle 1, table_1 \rangle$ is different from both the pair $\langle 1, table_2 \rangle$ and the pair $\langle 2, table_1 \rangle$. This enlarged degree of freedom solves the problem of there being just three tables in (1), as exemplified by (69), where I will write natural numbers as subscripts of indices i, j and k in order to distinguish them properly:

(69) $boy_1 \mapsto \{\langle i_1, table_1 \rangle, \langle i_2, table_{2,3} \rangle\}$
$boy_2 \mapsto \{\langle j_1, table_1 \rangle, \langle j_2, table_{2,3} \rangle\}$
$boy_3 \mapsto \{\langle i_1, table_2 \rangle, \langle i_2, table_1 \rangle, \langle i_3, table_3 \rangle\}$
$boy_4 \mapsto \{\langle k_1, table_{1,2,3} \rangle\}$

This configuration meets the conditions of π_i because for each individual boy x in the NP domain, there is a different unique function value $\ell(x)$. The configuration (70), abbreviated as (71) is yielded by π_c as one of a variety of interpretations in which all boys relate to a constant function value:

(70) $boy_1 \mapsto \{\langle i_1, table_1 \rangle, \langle i_2, table_{2,3} \rangle\}$
$boy_2 \mapsto \{\langle i_1, table_1 \rangle, \langle i_2, table_{2,3} \rangle\}$
$boy_3 \mapsto \{\langle i_1, table_1 \rangle, \langle i_2, table_{2,3} \rangle\}$
$boy_4 \mapsto \{\langle i_1, table_1 \rangle, \langle i_2, table_{2,3} \rangle\}$

(71) $boy_{1,2,3,4} \mapsto \{\langle i_1, table_1 \rangle, \langle i_2, table_{2,3} \rangle\}$

π_c also allows cases like (72):

(72) Three men bought two houses

It is very hard to get reliable judgments on its meaning: people differ in their opinions (even within themselves). In particular, the problem seems to be that the cardinality of the external argument is higher than that of the internal argument. Note that (72) cannot be interpreted as (73) because (73) cannot be obtained by an injective function.

(73) $man_{1,2} \mapsto \{\langle i_1, house_1 \rangle\}$
      $man_3 \mapsto \{\langle i_1, house_2 \rangle\}$

(74) $man_{1,2,3} \mapsto \{\langle i_1, house_{1,2} \rangle\}$

But π_c may yield (74). In this way, joint ownership is not excluded because one may allow internal structure in which two of the three men were acting jointly. Essential for (74) is that there be something which brings the three men together in one collection: three men satisfy the predicate 'buy two houses', but whether they were involved as a set of three does not matter. The only way for me to interpret (72) in the way described here, is the situation in which e.g. someone is reporting about the total sum total of men with respect to a predicate 'buy two houses'. In this way, there is some cumulativity involved in a function π_c. This point is important enough to consider it again with an eye on the π_c-situation (75) verifying (57):

(57) Three policemen have transported (today's) two prisoners

(75) $policeman_{1,2,3} \mapsto \{\langle i_1, prisoner_{1,2}\rangle\}$

In (75), three policemen were involved in the transportation of two prisoners, but the collective task may have spread out over, say the whole evening as i_1 represents an interval. There are two interesting scenarios in this respect: (a) $policemen_{1,2}$ transported $prisoner_1$ at about 6.30 p.m and $policemen_3$ transported $prisoner_2$ at about 11.45 p.m.); (b) $policemen_{1,2}$ transported $prisoner_1$ at about 6.30 p.m, and $policemen_{1,3}$ transported $prisoner_2$ at about 11.45 p.m.). In the latter case, $policeman_1$ carried out two transports. Note that in this case, (75) also solves Gillon's problem if it would turn up in *Three men wrote two musicals* (Hammerstein = man_2, Rodgers = man_1, Hart = man_2, and i is an index covering a period of time.

In both cases considered, there is some shared property organizing the individual men and policemen into some set. This "setting" property could be 'house buying', or 'transportation duty', or the like. It seems provided by contextual information about the index, not by the sentence itself. Recall that index i_1 *represents* an R–interval in which the prisoners are involved in the predication. Of course, one could require that the situation described in the preceding paragraph be covered by (76) rather than by (75), but this would ignore the nature of indices representing intervals.

(76) $policeman_{1,2,3} \mapsto \{\langle i_1, prisoner_1\rangle, \langle i_2, prisoner_2\rangle\}$

The representation of an interval by a natural number, which is what we do when we represent e.g. natural days by numbering them, should give sufficient room for the situation in which given a group of three policemen two of them relate to one prisoner and a third policemen to a second prisoner. In this perspective, it would be simply misleading to require for (57) a common transport activity on the part of all the men for the whole interval. The sentence underinforms us by using a representative (index) and thus provides for a lot of possible ways in which the transport relations actualized.

Other examples show first that the π–functions do their job properly, but also that Verkuyl & Van der Does need not surrender immediately:

(77)   Three cars crossed a bridge (and they are now in this area)

(78)   Three women have killed a burglar

Firstly, (77) may mean (say for a police–team following a number of gangster cars on the map of Amsterdam) that two cars (simultaneously or not) have crossed the Berlage–bridge and a third car the Amstel–bridge. Likewise, (78) may mean that Jet and Koosje have killed a burglar who entered their home, whereas one day later Klazien killed a burglar. Sentence (78) is said by a police officer focussing on the information that on his list there were three women involved in the same sort of situation, namely killing a burglar. So lexical properties of the verb may be decisive for a judgment about (58) and (72). I will come back to this point in the next section.[23]

7. QUANTIFYING OVER

Returning to (52) *Five children came upstairs*, if this sentence is used to report about the number of children (each of them having a different name) the temporal relevance of the predicate appears to be of no importance: five children belong to the set of individuals who came upstairs. If, however, (52) reports on the event structure, the cardinality information associated with *five children* restricts the temporal structure of [[*five children came upstairs*]], because a genuine partition is required. The first question is: do we quantify differently in both cases. The second question is: is a distinction between cover, pseudo–partition, minimal cover and partition related to a difference between "temporal interpretation" and "atemporal interpretation"?

The first problem is also raised by (79) and by (80).

(79)   Ole lifted three tables

(80)   Fourteen Peugeots 309 crossed the bridge this morning[24]

In (79), the situation could have been something like:

(81) $Ole \mapsto \{\langle i_1, table_1\rangle, \langle i_2, table_1\rangle, \langle i_3, table_1\rangle\}$

That is, Ole might have lifted one and the same table three times. Admittedly, this is not the most normal interpretation of (79), but it is easy to get in the context of say physical trainings: in the course of the evening, Ole has fulfilled his duty of lifting three tables, and (79) reports about that. A different case seems to be (80) which in the context of traffic counting may turn out to pertain to say six Peugeots 309 if we would go by the number plate: some of them crossed the bridge more than once.

Sentence (80) gives a partial answer to Van der Does' objection. If there happened to be only six cars (i.e. six different number plates), the total number of crossing indices may not exceed 14. That is, if we talk about indexed occurrences of cars, the cardinality information 14 indeed determines the maximum of indices present in the temporal structure contributed by the verb. It is only if (80) happens to speak about 14 different cars (i.e. with 14 different number plates), that Van der Does' point can be made: if we interpret (80) knowing that there are 14 different cars having crossed the bridge this morning, there might be room for each of them to have crossed the bridge more than twice. But note that in this case the temporal structure is completely suppressed: it is only the number of individuals which is at stake.

The distinction between indexed and non–indexed counting is important, though it is often made invisible by the specific lexical properties of the verb. In *Sixty Peugeots 309 were sold this morning* it is pragmatically excluded, but in *Sixty Peugeots 309 were sold this year*, Van der Does' interpretation allowing more than sixty sellings is very hard to get.

In view of the discussion about (56) *Three boys bought a boat*, it was observed that lexical properties of the predicate *buy* are involved. But it is not only properties of the verb that matter:

(82)   Three theaters have a Sol LeWitt–painting in the main hall

Sentence (82) seemingly excludes the interpretation that two theatres have the same Sol LeWitt–painting and a third theater a different one. This would come out even more clearly if we talk about three original Rembrandt paintings. But as Sol LeWitt is a conceptual artist, it is perfectly okay to interpret (82) as being about two paintings. In other words, a difference between the NPs *Sol LeWitt–painting* and *Rembrandt–painting* may be involved in the judgment about partitioning in (55). Thus, it may be concluded that the difference between pseudo–partitioning and partitioning is not a structural matter but a matter of all sorts of restrictions involving lexical knowledge. In general, it seems affirmed by the fact that sentences like:

(83)   This salesman sold fourteen Peugeots 309

may be true even if this salesman sold five Peugeots twice because these were sold back on part exchange. A genuine partition is only possible if one quantifies over index–dependent Peugeots. In fact, this is the only way to get fourteen events, which is necessary in view of the continuation *... and fourteen times he made his customers happy*.

A formal characterization of the problem of what sort of entities we quantify over, might proceed along the lines of extending representations like (41) to (84), as in Verkuyl (1993):

(84) $\exists Z [Z \subseteq [\![boy]\!] \wedge |Z| = 4 \wedge \exists \mathcal{P} ps Z [\mathcal{P} = \{V \cap [\![boy]\!] | \exists \mathbf{W}[\mathbf{W} \subseteq (\mathbf{N} \times [\![table]\!]) \wedge |\mathbf{W}| = 3 \wedge \exists \mathbf{Q} ps \mathbf{W}[\mathbf{Q} = \ldots]]\}]]$

where the bold–faced $\mathbf{W}$ is a set and $\mathbf{Q}$ a collection of sets of pairs of indices and sets of individuals, respectively. As said before, it would add nothing to the present discussion to present this machinery here in detail. It suffices to observe that stative verbs such like *hate* are not analyzed as having a additive function of the sort defined in Definitions 1 and 2 above: their indices are kept at zero (or to a fixed point). It is certainly relevant to observe therefore that Van der Does contention that (52) *Five children came upstairs* is true if each of the five children came upstairs say more than five times, holds only good if we interpret (52) atemporally, i.e. reduce the verb *come upstairs* to a stative verb by abstracting away from its temporal structure because the attention is directed to mere arithmetical quantification over concrete entities. In that interpretation (52) does no longer express terminative aspectuality. Thus the "mere cover"–interpretation is only possible if the repetitive #–marker of *Five children came upstairs for an hour* is absent. This sentence means that the total number of children satisfying the predicate 'come upstairs' is five measured over an interval of an hour. (This interpretation is quite natural if I give a one–hour report about a couple of movies in which I had things to count). It does not matter how many times they came upstairs. This would suggest that on this interpretation (84) the values of the indices are kept at zero (as we might talk about different models with different time structures).

In general, I would like to observe that the discussion about (minimal) covers and (pseudo–)partitions will make sense only if we allow a sentence to vary over this range, dependent on whether we speak temporally or atemporally. In other words, one should not reject the notion of a minimal cover because there are clear cases where a partition is more appropriate, but one should face the situation in which even one sentence may have a weaker or a stronger constraint on the partitioning dependent on factors like (a–)temporality, the presence or absence of focus, etc. This question will be picked up again in the course of the next section.

There is another aspect of the present issue which deserves some attention: the question of whether entailments can be effected by different ways of quantifying. For example, although there are close semantic correspondences between active and passive sentences, it might be useful to explore the fact noted in Chomsky (1965) that their quantificational structure differs considerably.

(85)   Everyone in this room knows two languages

(86)   Two languages are known by everyone in this room

Sentence (85) allows a variety of languages, whereas the most salient interpretation of (86) restricts the number of languages to 2. Likewise, the present analysis of sentences like (1) and (87) in terms of π_i and π_c implies that there are important differences of meaning:

(1)   Four boys lifted three tables

(87)   Three tables were lifted by four boys

Whereas in (1) there may be twelve tables, there are just three tables in (87). Likewise, there are just four boys in (1) but there may be twelve boys in (87). This empirical fact is explained by the asymmetry involved and by the fact that the subject position is taken extensionally. According to Schein (p.c.), native speakers clearly see an entailment relation between sentences like (1) and (87). It is suggested then that they have a most salient interpretation available, which helps them to make the entailment. I do not think one is forced into such a conclusion. If people want to make an entailment between two sentences they are looking for a constant element in the premises. So, guided by the fact that the passive requires three tables they narrow down on the number of tables in (87). The same applies to the boys. Note that different empirical judgments do not harm this analysis. Chomsky (1965:224) does not seem to exclude the possibility that (85) and (86) have the same deep structure. Thus, he would allow twelve tables in (87). However, also in this case the only way to make an entailment is to fix the meaning of *three tables* in the first sentence under consideration and then to transfer this particular interpretation to the second one.

8. CUTTING THE READING PIE DIFFERENTLY

At the beginning of this paper, it was suggested that three issues are involved in the analysis of sentences like (1). Many more issues have arisen. In this last section, I would like to try to reconsider the first issue 'how many readings should be assigned to (1)' again in order to see whether some reshuffling may be necessary.

In a way, the "One" in what was called the *One Reading Hypothesis* of Verkuyl & Van der Does (1991) is somewhat misleading in that it might only apply to the reduction of readings captured by Figure 1. If Scha's cumulative reading is indeed logically independent of the other ones, then the One Reading Hypothesis either fails to capture it or fails to have shown that it can be reduced to format (55).

(55) $\exists X[\ldots \wedge \exists \mathcal{P} ps X[X = \{U \cap [\![N]\!] | \exists Y (\ldots \exists \mathcal{Q} ps Y)\}]]$

Van der Does (1992) is convinced that the cumulative reading cannot be got by (55) because it presents the $\exists X$ (if partitioned by the unit set) as a collective in Scha's sense. In other words, it would allow that in a model in which Scha's (88) is true,

(88)   600 Dutch firms have 5000 American computers

there are other Dutch firms having American computers. Scha's cumulative reading is properly paraphrased by saying that the total number of Dutch firms having American computers is 600, and the total number of American computers had by Dutch firms is 5000. Van der Does (1992: 54) analyzes (88) as follows:

(89) $[\![600]\!]([\![Dfirm]\!])(\bigcup DOM([\![have]\!]\cap \wp[\![Dfirm]\!])\times \wp([\![Amco]\!])))$
$\wedge$ $[\![5000]\!]([\![Amco]\!])(\bigcup RG([\![have]\!]\cap \wp[\![Dfirm]\!])\times \wp([\![Amco]\!])))$

and (89) gives indeed this paraphrase: the determiner $[\![600]\!]$ relates the set $[\![Dfirm]\!]$ to the set of those who stand in the have–relation to members of $[\![Amco]\!]$, and $[\![5000]\!]$ relates the set $[\![Amco]\!]$ to those individuals who are had by members of $[\![Dfirm]\!]$. As long as there is no satisfactory answer for the problem of how to account for the problem of (55) allowing that more than 600 firms in the interpretation domain have American computers, Verkuyl & Van der Does have wrongly ignored the cumulative reading. This is what Van der Does (1992:56) concludes forcefully.

Yet, it is appropriate to make some further remarks about cumulativity, possibly preparing the road for the recalcitrant who wants to see cumulativity as a special case of a more general phenomenon. First of all, note that cumulativity does not occur in the following sentences:

(90) These 600 Dutch firms have those 5000 American computers

(91) 600 Dutch firms have those 5000 American computers

(92) These 600 Dutch firms have 5000 American computers

Scha (pers. comm.) agrees with this observation. He also agrees with my conclusion that cumulativity in Scha's sense can be said to arise only if the two NPs involved are indefinite. I mention this in order to make sure that I do not misrepresent Scha's view on cumulativity: it really only shows up in sentences like (88), not in sentences like (90) — (92). So, why is it that it is tied up with double indefiniteness or with indefiniteness? And why is it, that it does not seem to work in typical "counting contexts" like the following: we are interested to know how many companies are owned by how many families in this country, and in particular how these companies are distributed over the families. So we say that

(93) 4 families own 5000 companies, 600 families own 6000, and 1000 families own 6500

Here we know that there are thousand families and what (93) says is that 4 of them own 5000 companies, and that the next 596 families own 1000. So, now several question arise, e.g. is there ordinality involved in (93) and may be in (88). Or, is the sentence *4 families own 5000 companies* cumulative indeed? And if not, why not? The last question is not so innocent as it looks like, because it reveals a problem connected with the fact that a separate reading is given for a situation in which *4 families* pertains to some group of families owning companies and a situation in which it pertains to the only families owning companies. So, the question becomes: why does this sort of cumulativity not occur in sentences like (52) *Five children came upstairs* or is there a cumulative reading in case the five children in question happen to be the only children in the domain? And if we would affirm this, wouldn't it mean the notion of cumulativity is tied up with the situation in which it happens to be the case that an indefinite NP incidentally covers all members of its $[\![N]\!]$. Is it necessary to have a separate reading for incidental situations?

I do not intend to answer these questions here. I raise them only to suggest that the notion of cumulativity is based on an artificial distinction. Scha proposed it on top of the notions of distributivity and collectivity, because these two notions were accepted standardly. Suppose that there were no such distinction. Would the property of cumulativity then have led to a separate reading? Or could it have been seen as the manifestation of a more general phenomenon, namely that indefinite NPs may or may not cover all the members of their $[\![N]\!]$-denotation (restricted to the predicate in two place predications), so that they get some "definiteness feature", because an "all (the)–meaning" is expressed?

Let us now add to these questions the question raised in the preceding section: does a choice between different sorts of partitioning involve temporal considerations? It certainly does, because for e.g. (52) Van der Does' cover interpretation (they may have come up fifty times) makes only sense in a complete atemporal setting, in which one is interested in the number of children rather than in what was going on. If the sentence is interpreted in a temporal setting, then the notion of termination inherent to *came upstairs* requires a pseudo–partitioning or a partitioning. As said, a choice between the two sorts is in fact trivial: one may partition completely if one obeys the rule 'Once Counted in a cell, Always Counted'. Verkuyl & Van der Does (1991) offered an atemporal analysis of multiple quantification, to keep in touch with atemporal treatments like Scha (1981), Link (1983), Gillon (1987) and others. However, if atemporal interpretations are seen as special cases — by suppressing the indices —, say, a different light is thrown on the issue of quantification leading to the asymmetric scheme (16), in which the members of the external argument denotation relate to pairs containing indices rather than to individuals or sets thereof. The functions π_i and π_c may be seen as the general format which capture both temporality and atemporality expressed by sentences. On the external argument side of the asymmetric scheme (55)

(55) $\exists X[\ldots \wedge \exists PpsX[X = \{U \cap [\![N]\!] | \exists Y(\ldots \exists QpsY)\}]]$

it would mean that X in $\exists PpsX$ is the domain of π_i or π_c so that always a partitioning in singletons is obtained, whereas the internal argument part behind the | should be adapted so as to contain pairs of indices and parts of the NP–denotation, as illustrated in (84).

The questions raised suggest a different cutting of the reading pie. Let us therefore try to get rid of the (basically atemporal) distinction between distributive and collective readings. I am aware of the fact that people do not like to give up traditional terms which seem to serve their purpose well, but I think that we do not have to give them up, but rather ought to give them back their original meaning, which is basically lexical. *Every*, *each* are distributive operators in English, whereas *together* may be seen as a collective one. In particular, a determiner like *every* may be seen as a modifier on the ps–relation in structures of the form (55) by requiring that the atoms (singletons) are involved in the range of π. Note that this requirement is "empty" in the case of *A medal went to every winner* in the sense that in (94) the $\exists PpsZ$ of the [−SQA]–reading would contain an unbounded number of singletons: [25]

(94) $\exists Z \exists \mathcal{Z}[Z = \bigcup \mathcal{Z} \subseteq [\![medal]\!] \wedge |\mathcal{Z}| = 1 \wedge \exists PpsZ[\mathcal{P} = \{V \cap [\![medal]\!]| $
$ATOM([\![winner]\!]) \subseteq \{U|go\_to(U)(V)\}\}]]$

Somewhere in the discussion about multiple and plural quantification the two terms were applied to NPs as a whole. In my view, the determiner *every* is distributive in that it explicitly requires that the predicate be applied to atoms in the NP–denotation, but this does not mean that the NP of which it is part is distributive *sui generis*. And certainly, to give every NP a distributive reading because some of the determiners are distributive, is simply misleading. Why should *three children* have a distributive reading just because *every* and *each* are distributive operators? Why should *three children* not simply mean that no information is given about the way the individual children are involved in the predication?

If one allows oneself these heretical thoughts, one might do away with the distinction between distributive and collective as a structural distinction based on atomicity on the one hand and the unit set on the other hand. Instead, the π-functions above may be seen as introducing a fundamentally different division based on the natural distinction between an injection and a constant function. Natural, because the two π-functions are intimately connected: they share the same domain and co-domain, and they are extremes in an interesting way. For π_i each individual argument has a different image, for π_c it has the same image. Difference and sameness are linguistically relevant notions.

Even though it follows from the examples given, the function π_i cannot be called distributive in the sense e.g. defined in Link (1983), though it applies to the atoms of the external argument denotation; but π_c also operates on atoms. Moreover, π_i turns out to be able to cover the whole range of Figure 1, as shown in (95):

(95) $boy_1 \mapsto \{\langle i_1, table_1\rangle, \langle i_2, table_2\rangle, \langle i_3, table_3\rangle\}$
$boy_2 \mapsto \{\langle i_1, table_2\rangle, \langle i_2, table_3\rangle, \langle i_3, table_1\rangle\}$
$boy_3 \mapsto \{\langle i_1, table_3\rangle, \langle i_2, table_1\rangle, \langle i_3, table_2\rangle\}$
$boy_4 \mapsto \{\langle i_3, table_{1,2,3}\rangle, \langle i_2, table_1\rangle, \langle i_3, table_2\rangle\}$

So, it seems as if π_i can be understood as distributivity in the sense of covering the scale of Figure 1. This interpretation of the notion of distributivity is developed in Verkuyl (1994).

One may argue that (95) is a collective enterprise, say a circus act involving four boys and three tables. Especially, if one interprets i_k as a second counting point of an interval including i_{k-1} (as one should, cf. Figure 4 and Definitions 1 and 2 above), the situation is a collective one. This example shows that the term 'collective' is logically independent of the quantification structure, because (95) can also stand for a situation in which the boys acted totally independently from one another. That is, at i_1 and i_2 the tables were at different places and the boys did not know each other and i_3 was sufficiently long to allow boy_4 to go to the place where the tables were. In my view, this shows that the terms distributive and collective are not very useful for the overall–analysis of quantificational structure. One should restrict their use to specific lexical information which plays its fine–graining role in the semantic structure.

Should one get rid of π_c? I do not think so, because it deals properly with cases lying outside the range of Figure 1, as shown with the help of (57) and (75). Moreover, by this it partially covers the sort of cumulativity we observe in Scha's notion, because sentences like (72) and (57) "totalize": the total sum of men buying two houses is three, or the total sum of policemen having transported two prisoners is three. Sentences like (72) are used cumulativily to establish categories on the basis of predicate 'buy n houses'; (72) may be extended by ... *and eight couples bought three houses*. It seems to me that an analysis of the notion of cumulativity along this lines might be interesting, because there appears to be a sort of lower level (atemporal) cumulativity. At any rate it could contribute to a better understanding of the phenomenon observed by Scha.

ACKNOWLEDGEMENTS

I would like to thank Jaap van der Does, Marcus Kracht, and Joost Zwarts for their comments on a previous version, Remko Scha for a long discussion about cumulativity, and Barry Schein for a discussion about distributivity and collectivity.

NOTES

[1] In the present paper, the variables U, V, W, X, Y and Z will be used for sets, i.e. semantic objects of type $\langle e, t \rangle$, whereas the variables $\mathcal{P}, \mathcal{Q}, \mathcal{R}, \mathcal{S}$ and $\mathcal{W}$ will be used for collections of sets, i.e. for semantic objects of type $\langle \langle e, t \rangle, t \rangle$.

[2] There is a problem with this analysis pointed out by Van Benthem which is that an "adjectival analysis" of the NP as in Verkuyl (1981) can never deal correctly with the meaning of (exactly) *n medals* because any formula of the form $\exists W[\ldots|W| = n \ldots]$ is bound to give an at least–meaning due to the presence of the existential quantifier in front of it. This problem was solved in Verkuyl & Van der Does (1991): DET and NUM are to be taken together in one node, as will be discussed later on. As the issue of the wide scope of NP_2 is independent of the Van Benthem-problem, I will continue to use the derivation in the present section to make the point at issue.

[3] In Verkuyl (to appear), (21) is written as $\exists Z[Z = [\![Leo]\!] \cap \{Leo_j\} \wedge \exists W[W \subseteq [\![medal]\!] \wedge |W| = 1 \wedge [\![go\_to]\!](Z)(W)]]$, because proper names are analyzed as resulting from an intersection of a contextually definite singleton and the set of those who bear the name Leo.

[4] For the determiners under analysis, $|W| = k$ where $r(k, m)$, and $k, r \in N$, though of course its membership in one of the number systems is dependent on how fine-grained the determiner is, e.g. as in *2.576 sandwiches*. At any rate, one has to generalize over measuring values of mass terms (cf. Bunt (1981;1985), Link (1984), Krifka (1987)). If a quantifying NP expresses a certain measuring unit $|W|_\alpha$, it will stand for a certain finite and non–empty value k along a certain dimension α. In the present paper α will be restricted to values in N.

[5] Here the set W is already identified in the domain of interpretation. I will write this as $\exists! W$.

[6] Verkuyl (1993) gives examples from these and other languages in which the ambiguity comes out in the verbal system rather than in the NPs as in English and Dutch.

[7] Or $|X|\geq 1$, if one would follow Ojeda (1990).

[8] $W = \bigcup W \subseteq [\![etching]\!]$ is short for $W = \bigcup W \wedge W \subseteq [\![etching]\!]$.

[9] The use of the equation — though somewhat redundant — is motivated by the fact that e.g. the expression $Q = \{U \cap [\![table]\!] | \ldots\}$ may express that all cells of the partition are covered (totally affected) by the lift- predication. So, there is a possibility for a sentence to express partial affectedness by means of $Q \supset \{U \cap [\![sandwiches]\!] | \ldots\}$, or indeterminacy by $Q \supseteq \{U \cap [\![carts]\!] | \ldots\}$, as in (i) *Judith ate from the sandwiches*, and (ii) *John pushed three carts*.

[10] The durative reading shares some properties with donkey-sentences, as shown in (i) *For hours the bronze medal went to a Dutch skater.* Suppose that I am watching videotapes each of which contains skating matches. My task is to report which medal went to which nationality. After a while someone wants to know about my findings and I can report (i) about the series of tapes. Note that there can be a tape without there being Dutch skaters or even without bronze medals (say the second and third both got the silver one). Yet, (i) reports duratively about all the tapes and should be paraphrased as: for hours the situation was such that if I came into a tape (a model) and if there was a bronze medal, it went to a Dutch skater if there was one). The importance of (i) is that sentences with singular NPs express plurality.

[11] The difference between *go_to* and *be available* is that *go_to* is a verb which brings out the difference between the two readings more clearly than *be available*, because one can make an appeal to a terminative test. In Verkuyl & Van der Does (1991) *all* is treated as $\emptyset + INC$, where $\emptyset$ is defined as in (41) and INC as $\lambda X \lambda Y [|X \cap Y'| = 0]$.

[12] Taking a union of a collection containing one singleton is somewhat inappropriate to demonstrate the full impact of this analysis, but one can easily see its effect for the interpretation of sentences like *Mary sold those three etchings for years*. On the lowest level-interpretations (there are three tokens which were sold repeatedly), one may stick to $\exists Z[Z \subseteq [\![etching]\!] \wedge |Z| \geq 3 \ldots]$, but the more natural interpretation in which Mary sold an unbounded number of tokens from three different (type-)etchings appears to be covered by the higher level representation $\exists Z \exists \mathcal{Z}[Z \subseteq \bigcup \mathcal{Z} \subseteq [\![etching]\!] \wedge |\mathcal{Z}| \geq 3 \ldots]$. The loss of structure by the application of $\bigcup$ may require some proportion over the sets involved, but this seems to me a pragmatic matter. Cf. Verkuyl (1993) for many more details.

[13] Cf. Van der Does (1992: 51–57) for a more detailed discussion.

[14] From 1984 onwards, I myself had been defending partitioning, but I had no satisfactory answer to Van der Does' observation with respect to *Five children came upstairs*.

[15] $\exists Z[Z \in [\![2girls]\!] \wedge \ldots$ is short for $\exists Z[Z \subseteq [\![girl]\!] \wedge |Z| = 2 \wedge \ldots$.

[16] These counterexamples against $\exists \alpha ps \beta$ were adduced by Verkuyl (1988), Lasersohn (1989), Lønning (1991) and Van der Does (1992). Lønning (1991) wrongly attributes this to what he sees as the formal representation brought about by the One Reading Hypothesis for the sentences under discussion, namely the asymmetrical $\exists Z[\ldots \wedge \exists \mathcal{P}(\ldots \forall V \in \mathcal{P} \exists W(\ldots))]$. Van der Does (1992:84f.) shows that Lønning is wrong because in $\exists Q ps W[Q = \{U \cap [\![sandwich]\!] | \ldots\}]$ the equation is bidirectional. In other words, for every cell V of a (pseudo-)partition $\mathcal{P}$ there is a set W. This works satisfactorily because if V_1 relates to W_1 and V_2 relates to W_2, W_1 and W_2 may overlap partially or completely, dependent on whether a verb allows this, as we have seen with *eat* and *lift*.

[17] Apart from that, the use of the verb share is much more complicated than Lønning admits: the boys may share the pizzas among themselves) or others may be involved as well, in which case the sentence expresses two different share- predications.

[18] In the following I use definitions used in Verkuyl (1993). They are simplified

in order to avoid the explication of things that do not play a role in the discussion here. Rather than **N** one might take $\mathbf{D}_i$ as a set of indices isomorphic to **N**. Also, **R** will be taken rather than **Q** even though Van Benthem (1983) pointed out that **Q** is sufficient.

[19] Note that he might have had two flights (say, one to Atlanta, and the other to Dallas and Fort Knox).

[20] In Gruber's, Jackendoff's and my own work $\mathbf{D}_L$ is taken as a set of positions in the mental domain, a domain which is projected from positions in "the real world". Different philosophical interpretations of the localistic framework are possible.

[21] Judith may have cut her five sandwiches into say twenty parts and have eaten from them indiscriminately. Yet, it would be odd to use positive integers in NPs if there fails to be a corresponding structure. Using natural numbers signals that the speaker is counting in units of a certain size. It is not necessary to play naive physics by treating *5 sandwiches* in terms of rationals because sandwiches happen to consist of mass. There seems to be a law saying that in natural language our use of the number system is as "rough–grained" as conversation allows.

[22] As observed earlier $\{j\}$ is a short–hand version for $\exists!V[V = [\![Judith]\!] \cap \{j\}\ldots]$. Van der Does (p.c) suggests that a better way to represent proper names would be $\lambda \mathcal{P}[|[\![Judith]\!] \cap C_i| = 1 \wedge \mathcal{P}([\![Judith]\!] \cap C_i)]$, where C is a context set in the sense of Westerståhl (1985). It says that given a valuation at an index i a definite context set intersects with the set of Judiths and picks out an identified singleton.

[23] Evidently, it is much harder in (i) *Three boys bought two boats* to get four boats involved in two transactions. Is it possible to think in (ii) *Three cars have crossed two bridges* of three or four bridges? At the police office where the actions of a number of cars are followed carefully on the radar screen and the position map, (ii) can be interpreted as a summing up a report about three cars: each of them have crossed two bridges, but the first and second car both crossed (simultaneously) first the Berlage bridge and then the Amstelbridge, whereas the third car crossed the Utrechtse bridge and the Waterloo–bridge. Admittedly, (i) and (ii) are not the most appropriate vehicles to express the mixed–joint participancy of the three boys and the three cars, but in my view it is possible to construe contexts in which they serve their purpose well.

[24] Sentences like these have been discussed recently in Krifka (1990) in a different framework in which notions of event semantics are used to deal with token–occurrences. In Verkuyl (1984; 1988) a completely different route was taken. The relevant observations are made in Carlson (1978) and Gupta (1980), and in Verkuyl (1976) in which sentences like *For hours Den Uyl handed the Labour badge to congress–goers* was discussed. This sentence is durative if it expresses that Den Uyl handed an unspecified number of tokens of the Labour badge to anyone who was a congress-goer. Verkuyl (1984) discussed cases like *Hey, look there is my pen* pointing at a pen lying in the shop–window and similar to my own Waterman pen in my pocket. In all these seemingly disparate cases, "blueprints" are used, but essentially two different ways of counting are involved: Boolean and arithmetical. For example, the Den Uyl sentence is about one badge *and* about many badges.

[25] Here again I ignore the presence of indices in the VP–structure because their presence do not add to the point made here and their absence does not hide shortcomings (see Verkuyl 1993 for details).

REFERENCES

Barwise, J. (1979): 'On Branching Quantifiers in English'. In: *Journal of Philosophical Logic* **8**, 47–80.

Benthem, J.F.A.K. van (1983): *The Logic of Time. A Modeltheoretic Investigation into the Varieties of Temporal Ontology and Temporal Discourse.* Reidel: Dordrecht.

Benthem, J.F.A.K. van (1986): *Essays in Logical Semantics.* SLAP 26. Reidel: Dordrecht.

Bunt, H.C. (1981): *The Formal Semantics of Mass Terms.* Doct. Dissertation University of Amsterdam.

Bunt, H.C. (1985): 'The Formal Representation of (Quasi-) Continuous Concepts'. In: R. Moore & G. Hobbes (eds.), *Formal Theories of the Common Sense World*, 37–70.

Carlson, G.N. (1978): *Reference to kinds in English.* Dissertation UMASS, Amherst.

Chomsky, N. (1965): *Aspects of the Theory of Syntax.* The MIT Press: Cambridge, Mass.

Clark, H.H. (1973): 'Space, Semantics and the Child'. In: T.E. Moore (ed.), *Cognitive Development and the Acquisition of Language.* Academic Press: New York, 27–64.

Does, J. van der (1992): *Applied Quantifier Logics.* Dissertation University of Amsterdam.

Gillon, B.S. (1987): 'The Readings of Plural Noun Phrases in English'. In: *Linguistics and Philosophy* 10, 199–219.

Gillon, B.S. (1990): 'Plural Noun Phrases and Their Readings: A Reply to Lasersohn'. In: *Linguistics and Philosophy* 13, 477–485.

Gupta, A. (1980): *The Logic of Common Nouns. An Investigation in Quantified Model Logic.* Yale University Press: New Haven.

Gruber, J.S. (1976): *Lexical structures in Syntax and Semantics.* North-Holland: Amsterdam.

Hintikka, J. (1974): 'Quantifiers vs. Quantification Theory'. In: *Linguistic Inquiry* **5**, 153–177.

Jackendoff, R.S. (1990): *Semantic Structures.* The MIT Press: Cambridge, Mass.

Keenan, E.L. & L.M. Faltz (1985): *Boolean Semantics for Natural Language.* SLL 23. Reidel: Dordrecht.

Krifka, M. (1987): 'Nominal Reference and Temporal Constitution: Towards a Semantics of Quantity'. In: J. Groenendijk, M. Stokhof & F. Veltman (eds.), *Proceedings of the Sixth Amsterdam Colloquium* April 13–16 1987, 153–173.

Krifka, M. (1990): 'Four thousand Ships Passed Through the Lock: Object-Induced Measure Functions on Events. In: *Linguistics and Philosophy* **13**, 487–520.

Landman, F. & I. Moerdijk (1983): 'Compositionality and the Analysis of Anaphors'. In: *Linguistics and Philosophy* **6** , 89–114.

Lasersohn (1989): 'On the Readings of Plural Noun Phrases'. In: *Linguistic Inquiry* **20**, 130–134.

Link, G. (1984): 'Plural'. In: D. Wunderlich & A. von Stechow (eds.), *Handbook of*

Semantics. W. de Gruyter: Berlin.

Lønning, J.T. (1989): 'Some Aspects of the Logic of Plural Noun Phrases'. Department of Mathematics, University of Oslo. Cosmos Report 11.

Lønning, J.T. (1991): 'Among Readings. Some Comments on 'Among Collections'. In: J.M. van der Does (ed.), Quantification and Anaphora II. DYANA deliverable 2.2.b. Edinburgh, 37–51.

Ojeda, A.E. (1990): *Linguistic Individuals.* Linguistics Program. UCDavis.

Reinhart, T. (1985): *Anaphora and Semantic Interpretation.* The University of Chicago Press: Chicago.

Roberts, C. (1987): *Modal Subordination, Anaphora, and Distributivity.* Unpublished Ph.D. University of Amherst.

Scha, R. (1981): 'Distributive, Collective and Cumulative Quantification'. In: J.A.G. Groenendijk, T.M.V. Janssen & M.B.J. Stokhof (eds.), *Formal Methods in the study of Language.* MCT 136: Amsterdam, 483–512.

Verkuyl, H.J. (1976): 'Interpretive Rules and the Description of the Aspects'. In: *Foundations of Language* **14**, 471–503.

Verkuyl, H.J. (1978): 'Thematic Relations and the Semantic Representation of Verbs Expressing Change'. In: *Studies in Language* **2**, 199–233.

Verkuyl, H.J. (1981): 'Numerals and Quantifiers in Xbar-Syntax and their Semantic Interpretation'. In: J.A.G. Groenendijk, T.M.V. Janssen & M.J. B. Stokhof (eds.), *Formal Methods in the study of Language.* MCT 136: Amsterdam, 567–599.

Verkuyl, H.J. (1984): *Verdiepingen in taal.* Veen: Utrecht.

Verkuyl, H.J. (1987): 'Nondurative Closure of Events'. In: J.A.G. Groenendijk, D. de Jongh and M.J.B. Stokhof (eds.), *Studies in Discourse Representation Theory and the Theory of Generalized Quantifiers. Proceedings of the 5th Amsterdam Colloquium on Formal Semantics 1984.* Foris: Dordrecht, 87–113.

Verkuyl, H.J. (1988): 'Aspectual Asymmetry and Quantification'. In: V. Ehrich & H. Vater (eds.), *Temporalsemantik. Beiträge zur Linguistik der Zeitreferenz.* Niemeyer: Tübingen 1988, 220–259.

Verkuyl, H.J. (1989): 'Aspectual Classes and Aspectual Composition'. In: *Linguistics and Philosophy* **12**, 39–94.

Verkuyl, H.J. (1993): *A Theory of Aspectuality. The Interaction between Temporal and Atemporal Structure.* Cambridge University Press.

Verkuyl, H.J. (1994): 'Distributivity and Collectivity: A Couple at Odds.' In: M. Kanazawa and C.J. Piñón (eds.), *Dynamics, Polarity and Quantification.* CSLI Publications: Stanford, 49–80.

Verkuyl, H.J. & J. van der Does (1991): 'The Semantics of Plural Noun Phrases'. IILC-paper.

Westerståhl, D. (1985): 'Logical Constants in Quantifier Languages'. In: *Linguistics and Philosophy* **8**, 387–413.

CHRISTINE MICHAUX

REDUCING THE COORDINATION OF DETERMINERS: SOME PRINCIPLES

1. INTRODUCTION

In order to classify the collectives in French, we had in [Michaux 91] elaborated a series of syntactic tests. Among those was the "reduction test", a test which consisted in reducing the coordination of two identical collectives combined with two different defining complements to a single collective combined with the two defining complements coordinated. The reduction scheme can thus be illustrated as follows:

coll. a + (def. compl. x *et/ou* def. compl. y)
is reduced to
(coll. a + def. compl. x) *et/ou* (coll. a + def. compl. y)

The idea was to examine the semantic consequences of such a syntactic test on the various collective types previously encountered[1]. We then realized that the test is indeed semantically crucial since, depending on which type of collectives it is applied to and on the type of coordinator (*et/ou*), the reduced expression is equivalent or not to the original expression. We notice for example that with the same coordinator those collectives that can be assimilated to quantifiers react differently, as far as their semantic content is concerned, than those that cannot. Compare the following sets of sentences:

1. *Dans les rues traînaient une flopée de gosses affamés et une flopée de femmes au regard vide*
   → is semantically equivalent to
   Dans les rues traînaient une flopée de gosses affamés et de femmes au regard vide

2. *Un tas de Belges et un tas de Français vous diront qu'ils ne parlent pas la même langue*
   → is semantically equivalent to
   Un tas de Belges et de Français vous diront qu'ils ne parlent pas la même langue

3. *une assemblée de fonctionnaires et une assemblée de légionnaires*
   → is not semantically equivalent to
   une assemblée de fonctionnaires et de légionnaires

4. *un tas de feuilles et un tas de sable*
   → is not semantically equivalent to
   un tas de feuilles et de sable

We also note that changing the coordinator can imply, within the same group of collectives, a semantic difference. Contrast the following sentences:

1. *une gorgée d'eau et une gorgée de vin*
   → is not semantically equivalent to
   une gorgée d'eau et de vin

2. *une gorgée d'eau ou une gorgée de vin*
   → is semantically equivalent to
   une gorgée d'eau ou de vin

Furthermore, when applying the same test to other types of determiners, we can immediately note that not all of them distribute nor reduce the same way.

1. *Il lui a acheté un jouet et un manteau*
   → the reduction leads to the syntactically incorrect sentence:
   * *Il lui a acheté un jouet et manteau*

2. *Il lui a acheté beaucoup de livres et beaucoup de cahiers*
   → is semantically equivalent to
   Il lui a acheté beaucoup de livres et de cahiers

In this paper, we intend to systematically examine the syntactic reaction of each determiner to the reduction test. For each determiner and coordinator, we compare the semantic content of the unreduced and the reduced expressions and try to determine what are the (syntactic?) criteria that intervene in this semantic equivalence or change. We finally analyse the semantic differences implied by the use of a particular coordinator rather than by the use of another.

The various steps that lead to a classification of the determiners according to their syntactic reaction to the reduction test are the answers to the following questions:

1. Is it syntactically possible to reduce the original expression?

2. If the reduced expression is syntactically acceptable, is there a stylistic difference between the two? A semantic difference?

2. REDUCING THE COORDINATION OF DETERMINERS

2.1. Reducing coordinations in et

2.1.1. "Syntactically unreducable determiners"

As mentioned in the preceding section, one of the first criteria that plays a role in our classification consists in checking whether the reduction of the original coordination leads to a syntactically correct expression. When applying the reduction test to the list of determiners, it appears indeed that for some determiners the reduction of the coordination is not syntactically correct. For example, the sentence *Il a pris un bout de papier et un crayon et s'est mis à griffonner quelques mots illisibles* does not allow the original coordination to be reduced. (∗ *Il a pris un bout de papier et crayon et s'est mis à griffonner quelques mots illisibles*)

If the last sentence is indeed syntactically unacceptable, the reduction of this type of determiner does not however systematically lead to such an unacceptable sentence. It is indeed very common to find sentences including the coordination of the indefinite article in the singular that are syntactically correct when reduced. For example, the sentence:

Il a rencontré un écrivain et un philosophe au Trocadéro samedi soir
can be syntactically reduced to
Il a rencontré un écrivain et philosophe au Trocadéro samedi soir

However, if the second sentence is syntactically correct, it is also semantically different from the original sentence. In the first sentence, two distinct individuals were met (a philosopher and a writer); in the second sentence, only one individual was met, this person sharing both the properties of being a philosopher and a writer at the same time.

This semantic difference comes from the fact that the two coordinated defining complements of the original sentence are "homogeneous" terms. By "homogeneous", we mean that they symbolize properties that can be simultaneously true of a same entity (object or individual). The sentence then must concern "des individus détenant à la fois les propriétés désignées par les noms coordonnés." Cf. [Milner 78:90]

This in turn means that the original coordinated terms have become coreferential in the reduced sentence. The fact that the two coordinated terms refer to a single entity in the reduced sentence can be further illustrated by the following example:

Il a rencontré un philosophe et un écrivain au Trocadéro samedi soir. Ceux-ci étaient tous les deux attablés devant un verre de vodka
→ the reduction leads to the syntactically incorrect sentence:
* *Il a rencontré un philosophe et écrivain au Trocadéro samedi soir. Ceux-ci étaient tous les deux attablés devant un verre de vodka*

We can then draw up a list of the characteristics of a first type of determiners: the reduced expression is either syntactically incorrect or, if it is syntactically acceptable, it is modified as far as the semantic content is concerned. This semantic change arises from the possibility the coordinated terms have of being homogeneous.

These peculiarities are shared by other determiners such as:

the indefinite article in the plural

1. *Il a toujours adoré manger une tartine de confiture avec des bananes et des cacahuètes*
   → the reduction leads to the syntactically incorrect sentence:
   * *Il a toujours adoré manger une tartine de confiture avec des bananes et cacahuètes*

2. *Lors de la foire du livre à Bruxelles, il a eu l'occasion de rencontrer des écrivains et des philosophes de grande renommée*
   → is not semantically equivalent to
   Lors de la foire du livre à Bruxelles, il a eu l'occasion de rencontrer des écrivains et philosophes de grande renommée

the definite article in the singular

1. *Dès qu'ils ont aperçu la voiture et la caravane, les fans se sont mis à hurler*
   → the reduction leads to the syntactically incorrect sentence:
   **Dès qu'ils ont aperçu la voiture et caravane, les fans se sont mis à hurler*

2. *Il a fini par obtenir une interview du directeur d'entreprise et du baron que je t'avais présentés*
   → is not semantically equivalent to
   Il a fini par obtenir une interview du directeur d'entreprise et baron que je t'avais présenté
   → the reduction leads to the syntactically incorrect sentence:

* *Il a fini par obtenir une interview du directeur d'entreprise et baron que je t'avais présentés*

Other determiners belong to this category in the sense that they share the same syntactic and semantic peculiarities as those previously emphasized. They form in fact a subset of that group because they can form syntactically correct reduced sentences even when their coordinated terms are not homogeneous. Compare the following sentences:

1. *Il connaît très bien les frères et les soeurs du Premier Ministre*
   → is semantically equivalent to
   Il connaît très bien les frères et soeurs du Premier Ministre

2. *Il connaît très bien les soeurs et les frères du Premier Ministre*
   → the reduction leads to the syntactically incorrect sentence:
   * *Il connaît très bien les soeurs et frères du Premier Ministre*

3. *Il a eu l'honneur d'être invité par les philosophes et les écrivains les plus prestigieux de notre époque*
   → is not semantically equivalent to
   Il a eu l'honneur d'être invité par les philosophes et écrivains les plus prestigieux de notre époque

4. *Les ouvriers et les cadres qui ont été licenciés par l'entreprise ont décidé de mener une série d'actions de protestation*
   → is not semantically equivalent to
   Les ouvriers et cadres qui ont été licenciés par l'entreprise ont décidé de mener une série d'actions de protestation

The first two sets of sentences illustrate that, as might not appear at first sight, *les* cannot be syntactically reduced if the coordinated terms are not homogeneous (third group of sentences) or defined by a relative clause that insists on the togetherness of the action (fourth group of sentences). In fact the reduced sentence in the first example is correct seemingly because the coordinated terms form an idiomatic expression. This is well illustrated by the sentence of the second example, which in its reduced form happens to be syntactically unacceptable just because the coordinated terms have been reversed.

Milner [Milner 78:91] had already mentioned the possibility of reducing the coordination of some determiners by using a relative clause that focusses on the idea of group constituency.

If adding a relative clause allows the reduced coordination to be syntactically correct, it still implies a semantic change. In the fourth group of sentences, the first sentence is characterized by two distinct groups of individuals that have been fired and have decided to protest. In the reduced sentence, the overall idea is that a single group of "mixed" individuals have decided to react.

It should be noticed in this context that the definite and plural criteria play an essential role at this stage. Consider the following sentences:

Les quelques chercheurs et les quelques assistants qui avaient résisté à la première crise financière ont finalement été congédiés faute de subsides
→ is not semantically equivalent to
Les quelques chercheurs et assistants qui avaient résisté à la première crise financière ont finalement été congédiés faute de subsides

By introducing the definite article in the plural before the determiner *quelques*, it becomes possible to add a relative clause that insists on the fact that the individuals share the properties evoked in the relative clause. Without the definite article, the reduced sentence even if it contains the same type of relative clause is somehow sloppy.

Plurality also plays a crucial role as far as the "relative clause solution" is concerned. Compare the sentences:

1. *Les ouvriers et les cadres qui ont été licenciés par l'entreprise ont décidé de mener une série d'actions de protestation*

2. * *L'ouvrier et cadre qui ont été licenciés par l'entreprise ont décidé de mener une série d'actions de protestation*

In the second sentence, the coordinated entities are single entities which seems to make it difficult to play with mixed groups. Intuitively we feel that it is easier to obtain heterogeneous sets when the coordinated terms are themselves in the plural than when they are isolated entities. This particular phenomenon is similar to what happens when we reduce the coordination of numerals. Contrast the following sets of examples:

1. *Il a assisté à la mise à mort des trois vachettes et des trois taureaux qu'il avait élevés lui-même avec tant de patience*
→ is not semantically equivalent to

*Il a assisté à la mise à mort des trois vachette(?s) et taureau(?x)²
qu'il avait élevés lui-même avec tant de patience*

2. *Jean a assisté à la mise à mort de plusieurs vachettes et plusieurs taureaux qu'il avait élevés lui-même avec beaucoup de patience*
→ is not semantically equivalent to
Jean a assisté à la mise à mort de plusieurs vachettes et taureaux qu'il avait élevés lui-même avec beaucoup de patience

When the numerals are reduced and defined by a relative clause of the "group constituency" type, the implied semantic change is more precise than is the case with determiners like *les* or *plusieurs*. In the first set of examples, whereas the original sentence refers to two groups of three objects each, the reduced sentence refers to a single group composed of three entities, the only constraint being that this group should contain at least one bull. With determiners like *plusieurs* on the other hand (second set of examples), whereas the original sentence refers to two distinct sets, the reduced sentence refers to a single mixed group, the constituents of which we do not know much about as far as the quantity is concerned.

For all of these determiners then, the reduction of the coordination implies at least (with homogeneous terms or a relative clause focussing on the idea of togetherness) a semantic change. This change is more or less precise depending on the determiners involved. Notice that with greater numerals (such as ten), the group constitution becomes less precise as far as the proportion each entity represents within the mixed group is concerned.

2.1.2. "Syntactically reducable determiners"

There exists a second group of determiners for which the reduction of the coordination does not cause any syntactic problem. Within this category, a further distinction can be made between those for which the reduction implies a semantic change and those for which the reduced expression has exactly the same meaning as the original.

No semantic change This category mainly contains the determiners that combine with the particle *de*. Consider the following examples:

1. *Beaucoup de parents et beaucoup d'enseignants ne sont pas conscients de l'importance du sport pour l'équilibre psychique des enfants*
→ is semantically equivalent to

Beaucoup de parents et d'enseignants ne sont pas conscients de l'importance du sport pour l'équilibre psychique des enfants

2. *Il a acheté beaucoup de sable et beaucoup de ciment*
   → is semantically equivalent to
   Il a acheté beaucoup de sable et de ciment
   → the reduction leads to the syntactically incorrect sentence:
   * *Il a acheté beaucoup de sable et ciment*

3. *Quand il va au Trocadéro, il rencontre souvent beaucoup de philosophes et beaucoup d'écrivains*
   → is semantically equivalent to
   Quand il va au Trocadéro, il rencontre souvent beaucoup de philosophes et d'écrivains
   → is not semantically equivalent to
   Quand il va au Trocadéro, il rencontre souvent beaucoup d'écrivains et philosophes

These sentences show first of all that the reduction does not cause any syntactic problem. It also demonstrates that the meaning of the original sentence is completely preserved as long as the particle *de* is not dropped. It seems indeed that this particle plays an important role in the sense that it either preserves the syntactic acceptability of the reduced sentence or its semantic equivalence when the coordinated terms are homogeneous.

A whole series of determiners belong to this group. Consider the following sentences:

? *La plupart des écrivains et la plupart des philosophes qu'ils ont invités sont d'origine russe*
   → is semantically equivalent to
La plupart des philosophes et des écrivains qu'ils ont invités sont d'origine russe
   → is not semantically equivalent to
? *La plupart des philosophes et écrivains qu'ils ont invités sont d'origine russe*

Notice that the first example of this set tends to show that stylistically speaking the reduced sentence is better than the original one.

1. *Il a survécu avec un peu d'eau et un peu de pain*
   → is semantically equivalent to

Il a survécu avec un peu d'eau et de pain
→ the reduction leads to the syntactically incorrect sentence:
* *Il a survécu avec un peu d'eau et pain*

2. ? *Il a préféré n'inviter que peu d'amis et peu de collègues*
   → is semantically equivalent to
   Il a préféré n'inviter que peu d'amis et de collègues
   → is not semantically equivalent to
   Il a préféré n'inviter que peu d'amis et collègues

The same phenomenon is true of coordinated noun phrases in *bon nombre de, la majorité de, une grande quantité de*:

La souris s'est enfuie avec un morceau de fromage et un morceau de pomme
→ is semantically equivalent to
La souris s'est enfuie avec un morceau de fromage et de pomme
→ the reduction leads to the syntactically incorrect sentence:
* *La souris s'est enfuie avec un morceau de fromage et pomme*

We must add to this category a couple of determiners that share the same features except that they do not combine with the particle *de*. For example:

1. *Chaque professeur de math et chaque professeur de langue ont reçu un dictionnaire. Les autres professeurs ont reçu une montre*
   → is semantically equivalent to
   Chaque professeur de math et professeur de langue ont reçu un dictionnaire

2. *chaque écrivain et chaque philosophe*
   → is not semantically equivalent to
   chaque écrivain et philosophe

Notice that the lack of particle is important in the case the coordinated terms are homogeneous since then there is automatically a semantic change.

Consider a few more examples:

1. *Tout réalisateur et tout cinéaste se doit d'aller voir le dernier film de Madonna*

→ is not semantically equivalent to
Tout réalisateur et cinéaste se doit d'aller voir le dernier film de Madonna

2. *Tous les artistes peintres et tous les cinéastes que nous avons rencontrés partaient en vacances à Bagdad*
→ is semantically equivalent to
Tous les artistes peintres et les cinéastes que nous avons rencontrés partaient en vacances à Bagdad
→ is not semantically equivalent to
Tous les artistes peintres et cinéastes que nous avons rencontrés partaient en vacances à Bagdad

Again, when there is no particle, the semantic change is systematic when the coordinated terms are homogeneous. The last sentence show that *les* can play the same role as *de* in the preceding examples since it preserves the semantic equivalence when it is not dropped.

To this class, we must finally add the collectives. The collectives that do not imply any semantic change after reduction are those that can be assimilated to quantifiers: *tapée* or *tas* when the latter plays the role of a quantifier.

1. *Sur toutes les plages de France des tapées de jeunes filles et des tapées de jeunes garçons font bronzette à longueur de journées*
→ is semantically equivalent to
Sur toutes les plages de France des tapées de jeunes filles et de jeunes garçons font bronzette à longueur de journées
→ the reduction leads to the syntactically incorrect sentence:
* *Sur toutes les plages de France des tapées de jeunes filles et jeunes garçons font bronzette à longueur de journées*

2. *Des tas de Belges et des tas de Français vous diront qu'ils ne parlent pas la même langue*
→ is semantically equivalent to
Des tas de Belges et de Français vous diront qu'ils ne parlent pas la même langue
→ the reduction leads to the syntactically incorrect sentence:
* *Des tas de Belges et Français vous diront qu'ils ne parlent pas la même langue*

Semantic change This class is again characterized by a syntactically correct reduction but, this time, the reduction implies a semantic change.

REDUCING THE COORDINATION OF DETERMINERS

In this class we find the collectives of measure:

Ajoutez une cuillerée de pili-pili et une cuillerée de poivre de Cayenne
→ is not semantically equivalent to
Ajoutez une cuillerée de pili-pili et de poivre de Cayenne
→ the reduction leads to the syntactically incorrect sentence:
* *Ajoutez une cuillerée de pili-pili et poivre de Cayenne*

This class also contains the collectives–quantifiers when they can be assimilated to the "true" collectives:

Pendant la récréation, les enfants ont accumulé un grand tas de vieux chapeaux et un grand tas de vieux souliers
→ is not semantically equivalent to
Pendant la récréation, les enfants ont accumulé un grand tas de vieux chapeaux et de vieux souliers
→
? *Pendant la récréation, les enfants ont accumulé un grand tas de vieux chapeaux et vieux souliers*
→ the reduction leads to the syntactically incorrect sentence:
* *Pendant la récréation, les enfants ont accumulé un grand tas de chapeaux et souliers*

The third sentence tends to show that when the coordinated terms are defined by a similar adjective it is syntactically possible to drop the particle. However, when the particle is lacking, the original meaning is altered since the distinct groups of the original sentence now form a single mixed group.

Finally this class contains the "true" collectives:

Il a été convoqué par l'assemblée des philosophes et l'assemblée des écrivains
→ is not semantically equivalent to
Il a été convoqué par l'assemblée des philosophes et des écrivains
→ is not semantically equivalent to
Il a été convoqué par l'assemblée des philosophes et écrivains

2.2. Reducing coordinations in *ou*

In order not to make this part too heavy, we only emphasize the characteristic differences between the use of the two coordinators. When applying the reduction test to coordinations in *ou*, one notices indeed a whole lot of similar phenomena that would not be worth reconsidering in this section. However, the semantics itself of the coordinator *ou* implies a number of restrictions when compared to the syntactic and semantic behaviour of reduced expressions in *et*.

First of all, the interpretation of coordinations in *ou* is semantically speaking more limited than the interpretation of those in *et*. It is indeed more difficult to grasp the reality underlying an expression whose coordination is in *ou*. Compare the following sentences:

1. *J'ai colmaté les trous de la clôture avec du carton et de la ficelle*

2. *J'ai colmaté les trous de la clôture avec du carton ou de la ficelle*

In the first sentence, the interpretation is direct: the fence has been repaired using cardboard and string. In the second sentence however the interpretation remains vague since it is not sure what the repair looks like. Does the sentence mean that the repairer used alternatively cardboard and string depending on the type of holes in the fence? Or did he use cardboard and string in each hole anyway?

Secondly, since the semantics of *ou* implies a choice between alternatives, it is not possible to resort to the coreferential properties of homogeneous terms. This in turn means that whereas with coordinations in *et*, the reduced sentence was syntactically correct but semantically different, with coordinations in *ou*, the reduced expressions are hardly semantically interpretable and syntactically clumsy. Compare the following sets of sentences:

1. *Il a rencontré un philosophe et un écrivain au Trocadéro*
   → is semantically different from
   Il a rencontré un philosophe et écrivain au Trocadéro

2. *Il a rencontré un philosophe ou un écrivain au Trocadéro.*
   →
   * *Il a rencontré un philosophe ou écrivain au Trocadéro*

In the first set of sentences, the original sentence expresses the meeting of two individuals each of whom has a particular property. In the reduced sentence, the meeting occurs with a single individual sharing both the properties of being simultaneously a philosopher and a writer. On the other hand, in the second set of sentences, the first sentence means that the subject met either a philosopher or a writer, that is that he met only one individual, this person only having one property. In the reduced sentence, the only interpretation that seems possible is that the subject met one single individual who has the property of either being a philosopher or a writer, the speaker wanting this last bit of information to remain unclear. In any case, even if this interpretation is plausible, it is rather awkwardly expressed syntactically speaking.

One should finally note that since the coordination of two homogeneous terms does not allow a different semantic interpretation in the case of a coordination in *ou*, the use of a relative clause insisting on the idea of group constituency does not provide a different semantic interpretation either.

The semantics of *ou* has finally another impact on the semantic interpretation of noun phrases coordinated with *ou*. Since coordinations in *ou* imply an alternative, the "mixed group" interpretation becomes indeed impossible. Contrast the following sets of sentences:

1. *un tas de feuilles et un tas de sable*
   → is semantically different from
   un tas de feuilles et de sable

2. *un tas de feuilles ou un tas de sable*
   → is semantically equivalent to
   un tas de feuilles ou de sable

In the first set of sentences, the first sentence refers to two different piles, one of leaves and one of sand, whereas the reduced sentence refers to a single pile made up of sand and leaves mixed together. On the other hand, in the second set of sentences, the second sentence refers to the same reality as the first one. In each case, we have indeed the choice between two piles, each pile either containing only sand or only leaves. The same is true of all collectives referred to as "true" collectives in [Michaux 91] and is explained by the fact that *ou* requires a separation between entities rather than a mixture.

3. INTERVENING CRITERIA: SUMMARY

3.1. *"Syntactically unreducable determiners"*

The indefinite article in the singular and the plural and the definite article in the singular

- *un(e), la, le, des*

- their reduction always leads to a syntactically incorrect sentence.

- exceptions: if the coordinated defining complements are homogeneous terms, the reduction is syntactically possible but implies a semantic change (only true of coordinations in *et*).

The numerals and the definite determiners in the plural

- *les, plusieurs, quelques*

- *les* appears in reduced form in some idiomatic expressions (only with coordinations in *et*).

- if the coordinated defining complements are homogeneous, the reduction is syntactically possible but implies a semantic change (only with coordinations in *et*).

- when combined with a relative clause that emphasizes the idea of togetherness, the reduction is syntactically possible but implies a semantic change (only with coordinations in *et*).

3.2. *"Syntactically reducable determiners"*

3.2.1. No semantic change

determiners that are followed by the particle *de*:

- examples: *beaucoup, peu, un peu, la plupart, la moitié, un morceau, une grande quantité, bon nombre, la majorité*, the collectives–quantifiers when they are quantifiers (*un tas*), the collectives that can always be assimilated to quantifiers (*flopée*).

- the particle *de* plays a crucial role: either to preserve the semantic content when the coordinated terms are homogeneous (only with coordinations in *et*), or to preserve the syntactic acceptability when the coordinated terms are not homogeneous.

determiners not followed by the particle *de*:

- *chaque, tout*: semantic change when the coordinated terms are homogeneous (only with coordinations in *et*)

- *tous les*: when *les* is preserved, there is no semantic change; when it is not preserved, a semantic change appears (only with coordinations in *et*; with coordinations in *ou*, it leads to a syntactically incorrect sentence).

3.2.2. Semantic change

The "true" collectives (*assemblée*) and the collectives–quantifiers when it plays the role of a "true" collective (*tas*):

- with coordinations in *et*: without the particle *de*, the reduced expression becomes syntactically unacceptable except if the two coordinated terms are homogeneous. In this particular case, the two sentences are semantically equivalent.

- with coordinations in *ou*: there is no semantic change between the unreduced sentence and the reduced one.

The collectives of measure (*gorgée*):

- with coordinations in *et*: without the particle *de*, the reduced expression is syntactically unacceptable. When the particle is preserved, the reduced sentence is not semantically equivalent to the original one.

- with coordinations in *ou*: there is no semantic change and the reduced expression is syntactically acceptable.

4. CONCLUSION

The syntactic and semantic consequences of the reduction test allow us to draw a list of important observations:

First of all, a distinction must be made between coordinations in *et* and coordinations in *ou*. Even without considering the application of the reduction test, coordinations in *ou* become much more quickly vague as far as their semantic content is concerned. It is indeed more difficult to grasp the reality underlying a noun phrase whose coordination is in *ou*. This limitation becomes even more obvious after the application of the reduction test. Because the semantics of *ou* implies a choice between alternatives, the "homogeneous terms" interpretation becomes impossible. The same is true with the "mixed group" interpretation. When applying the reduction test to coordinations in *ou*, the obtained sentences are thus more often syntactically incorrect than it is the case with coordinations in *et*. It appears consequently to be of prime necessity to render formally this difference.

For coordinations in *et*, the reduction of the coordination of determiners has led to a distinction between three groups:

1. the syntactically unreducable determiners: to form a syntactically correct reduced expression, they need either homogeneous coordinated terms or a relative clause that insists on the idea of group constituency. In any case, the reduction implies a semantic change.

2. the syntactically reducable determiners that preserve the original meaning when reduced: for those the particle they combine with is essential since it either preserves the syntactic acceptability of the reduced sentence or the semantic equivalence between the original sentence and the reduced one.

3. the syntactically reducable determiners for which the reduction causes a semantic change: this group contains "true" collectives or those that can be assimilated to "true" collectives.

We can finally distinguish between two types of semantic changes:

1. the original sentence refers to two distinct groups; the reduced sentence refers to a single group composed of the individuals of the original sentence but mixed (*les ouvriers et les cadres* → *les ouvriers et cadres*) (*un tas de feuilles et un tas de sable* → *un tas de feuilles et de sable*). In this case the proportion of the entities mixed together are more or less precise depending on the determiners involved.

2. the original sentence refers to two distinct entities; the reduced sentence refers to a single entity sharing the properties of the two coordinated terms of the original sentence (*des écrivains et des philosophes* → *des écrivains et philosophes*). This semantic change is caused by the possibility the two coordinated terms of the original sentence have of being homogeneous.

ACKNOWLEDGEMENTS

This text presents research results of the Belgian National incentive program for fundamental research in artificial intelligence initiated by the Belgian state – Prime Minister's Office – Science Policy Programming.

The scientific responsibility is supported by its authors. I would like to thank Professor Marc Dominicy for the criticisms and suggestions offered on this paper.

NOTES

[1] See [Michaux 91]

[2] Notice that the noun forms remain ambiguous. In this case, the ambiguity disappears orally. But with words that have a peculiar plural form such as *cheval-chevaux*, it is not clear how the plural noun phrase should be expressed.

REFERENCES

Gross, M. (1986): *Grammaire transformationnelle du français. Syntaxe du nom.* Cantilène.

Michaux, Ch. (1990): *Le pluriel dans la langue française: présentation des données.* Rapport Interne, Université de Liège.

Michaux, Ch. (1991): The Collectives in French: a Linguistic Investigation, *Linguisticae Investigationes* **16**, 99-12.

Milner, J . (1978): *De la syntaxe à l'interprétation. Quantités, insultes, exclamations.* Le Seuil, Paris.

JOÃO ANDRADE PERES

ISSUES ON DISTRIBUTIVE AND COLLECTIVE READINGS

1. QUESTIONS AND ASSUMPTIONS

The formal semantics of plurals – which goes back to at least Bennett (1974) – has the work of Link (namely, 1983 and 1984) as a crucial landmark. His ideas about a lattice–theoretical definition of the domain of discourse undoubtedly shed a new light on the thought about plurality in natural languages and was the origin of a rich literature. However, several questions that derive precisely from the wealth of the denotations made available by Link's new framework have not yet, to my knowledge, been addressed in a systematic way and thus remain unanswered. Three of such questions will be addressed here:

(i) given the variety of individuals that can be in the denotations of nominals – simple atoms, complex atoms and i–sums –, what individuals can count for a distributive reading (henceforth, DR), or, reducing to the really puzzling point, can i–sums be the relevant individuals in $A \cap B$, where A and B are the sets denoted by the relevant nominal and the relevant predicative expression?

(ii) under what (linguistic) circumstances can – atomic or non–atomic – individuals in the denotation of a nominal structure become parts of a plural individual being considered in a collective reading (henceforth, CR)?

(iii) what are the factors that determine whether or not an NP can be assigned a DR, a CR or both?

Before concentrating on the above questions – (i) and (ii) in section 2, and (iii) in section 3 –, I will roughly characterise in the following paragraphs the framework that I am presupposing for dealing with natural language nominal plurals. In its basic features, this is the framework devised in Link's work.

a. It is assumed that plurality – in particular in what regards nouns – can be viewed from at least three points of view: morphological, syntactic and semantic. The purely morphological plural is taken to be a value in a lexical feature Number, which is considered not to have any semantic import (examples of purely morphological plural involve nouns like *glasses*, *scissors* and *trousers*). As for the syntactic plural – due to agreement –, it is as well taken to be semantically irrelevant. Finally, the semantic plural – the only that will be on focus here – is taken to always involve a change in denotation induced by a rule of pluralization. This complies with Link's advice that "morphological change in pluralization" (which clearly regards the just mentioned "semantic plural", not the one that was identified as "purely morphological") be taken seriously (cf. 1983: 306).

b. Following **a.** above, basic common nouns are taken to denote sets of atoms, regardless of being morphologically singular or plural in the lexicon, while those nouns that undergo pluralization are taken to denote the join semilattice generated by the set of atoms denoted by the corresponding basic expression (regardless of the initial morphological number of this expression). Link's star operator – "*" – will be used to signal the logical translation of a pluralized noun. The same would apply for intersective adjectives.

c. In accordance with what is stated in **a.** above, the plural of verbs or other predicative expressions that give rise to verb phrases is taken not to have any semantic import, only agreement being involved.

d. In accordance with the assignment of denotations described in **b.**, the universe of discourse is defined as a complete and atomic join semilattice. The (in Link's terminology) "individual sums" that have ordinary individuals – **simple atoms** – as their atomic parts are in a one-to-one correspondence with **complex atoms**. Complex atoms and individual sums will be called **collective individuals** (or **pluralities**, as Link called them).

e. Nouns are divided into two semantic subclasses: the subclass of those nouns that denote sets of simple atoms (like *book, boy, student* and *woman*), and the subclass of those nouns that denote sets of complex atoms (like *committee, flock, group,* and *team*).

f. Semantic subclasses of verbs are defined in terms of the sorts of individuals – simple or complex atoms, collective individuals or any combination of these – that their denotations admit in connection with their arguments. These subclasses are exemplified as follows:

predicative expressions like *be a student, cry, smile,* and *snore* are **atomic** with respect to their only argument;

predicative expressions like unary *disperse, gather* and *meet* are *collective* with respect to their only argument;

predicative expressions like binary *include* are **collective** with respect to their first argument and **neutral** – a word borrowed, with basically the same sense, from Kamp and Reyle (1993) – with respect to their second argument;

predicative expressions like binary *disperse* and *gather* are **neutral** with respect to their first argument and **collective** with respect to their second argument;

predicative expressions like binary *build, buy, carry, lift* and *fit (in)* are **neutral** with respect to both their arguments;

predicative expressions like unary *be students* (to be translated by * student') are **neutral** with respect to their only argument; furthermore, they exhibit the special property of always denoting a join semilattice, for which reason they will be called **join semilattice**d predicative expressions (or, for short, given that only one kind of latticed structure will be relevant, **latticed** predicative expressions).

g. Quantifiers are conceived in terms of the Theory of Generalized Quantifiers. In particular, those quantifiers that are not to be considered as (genuine) polyadic quantifiers are taken to denote relations between sets. Therefore, all the relevant properties of relations that quantifiers exhibit – which can be deduced from their formal definitions – are available in the system.

h. It is assumed that a number of **readings of noun phrases** is available, which are assigned according to combinations of **properties** of the expressions involved. A reading of a noun phrase is to be taken in this context as a set of conditions on the (possibly but not exclusively lattice–theoretical) sorts of individuals that are to be taken as relevant in the process of combining the meaning of the noun phrase with that of a predicative expression. Only two of these sets of conditions will be considered here: the distributive reading and the collective (or group) reading. Given the denotation Q of a quantifier and, as above, sets A and B denoted, respectively, by the relevant nominal and the relevant predicative expression, the following assertions apparently capture the core of the notions of DR and CR, despite the fact that further restrictions can be imposed:

(i) the relevant formula is assigned a DR if there is a truth condition stating that $A \cap B$ is in accordance with the condition established in the definition of the quantifier, which ranges from $A \cap B = \emptyset$ to $A \cap B = A$ and may involve the cardinality of $A \cap B$ or the ratio between $A \cap B$ and A;

(ii) the relevant formula is assigned a CR if there is a truth condition stating that $A \cap B$ has to have as a member a collective individual which has a number of atomic or non–atomic parts that are members of A (but not necessarily of $A \cap B$), this number being in accordance with the formal definition of the quantifier.

2. QUANTIFICATION OVER INDIVIDUAL SUMS?

Let us, for the sake of simplicity, assume that adjectives and prepositional modifiers do not play any particular role in the determination of the Boolean characteristics of the relevant entities involved in DR's and CR's. On the contrary, let us raise the hypothesis that relative clauses play some role of that kind. Accordingly, subsection 2.1 will focus on nominals without any modifiers, while nominals with relative clauses will be the object of subsection 2.2. In both cases, we will start by semantically analysing structures where i–sums apparently aren't computable elements, and then move to the discussion of cases that have been – or will now be – claimed to require the computation of i–sums, either as members of the sets being quantified over or as non–atomic parts of collective individuals.

2.1. *Distributive and Collective Readings with Non–Relativized Nominals*

2.1.1. Readings Involving Atoms and Suprema

Sentences (1) – (3) below will be the point of departure for the definition of (what I will assume to be) typical truth conditions for the kind of syntactic structures to be discussed in this section. It should be noticed that at this point ambiguity issues – to which we will return in section 3 – are not of central concern. Accordingly, attention will not be paid to the variation of predicators.

(1) The students are falling asleep.

(2) The students carried the stone upstairs.

(3) The students gathered for a party.

In all three cases the plural noun *students* is taken to denote the join semilattice generated by the denotation of the singular noun *student*. Let us represent this latter set of simple atoms by S and the join semilattice at stake by $/S/_\cup$. If we take $\underline{A}$ to be the set of atoms in the universe, $\bigvee(X)$ to be the supremum of any set X, and F, C and G to be the sets denoted by the VP's (in sentences (1), (2) and (3), respectively), then the truth conditions for sentences (1), (2) and (3) can be stated, respectively, as follows, where the symbol "$[\![\ ]\!]$" is to be taken as the function assigning values to the non–logical constants:

(1) a. $([\![{}^*\text{student}']\!] \cap \underline{A}) \subseteq F$ i.e. $(/S/_\cup \cap \underline{A}) \subseteq F$.

(2) a. $([\![{}^*\text{student}']\!] \cap \underline{A}) \subseteq C$ i.e. $(/S/_\cup \cap \underline{A}) \subseteq C$.
   b. $\{\bigvee([\![{}^*\text{student}']\!])\} \subseteq C$ i.e. $\{\bigvee(/S/_\cup \cap \underline{A})\} \subseteq C$

(3) a. $\{\bigvee([\![{}^*\text{student}']\!])\} \subseteq G$ i.e. $\{\bigvee(/S/_\cup \cap \underline{A})\} \subseteq G$.

(1)a. and (2)a. instantiate a DR [1] – the second requiring different events and intervals of time –, while (2)b. and (3)a. instantiate a CR. If the truth conditions for the three sentences are well represented, this means that strong restrictions are being imposed on the selection of individuals. In other words, the DR can involve only the atoms in the relevant semilattice, while the CR can involve only its supremum. All the individuals that stand between this supremum and those atoms have no role whatsoever in the meaning computation of sentences involving the given quantifier (*the*). In fact, apparently no formula involving this quantifier in the relevant position can have the following as truth conditions, regardless of whatever the set B is denoted by:

(4) $/S/_\cup \subseteq B$

(5) $(\{X_0 \subseteq /S/_\cup : \bigvee(X_0) = \bigvee(/S/_\cup)\} \cap \{X_1 \subseteq /S/_\cup : X_1 \subseteq B\}) \neq \emptyset$

The latter condition states that there is at least one subset of the join semilattice generated by the set of student–atoms which has the same supremum as the semilattice itself and which is in the denotation of the relevant predicative expression. If neither of the above conditions is appropriate as a truth condition for a formula involving (plural) *the*, none of the following definitions, where E is the universe, would be appropriate for that quantifier:

(6) $[\![\text{the}']\!](A) = \{X_0 \subseteq E : A \subseteq X_0\}$
(7) $[\![\text{the}']\!](A) = \{X_0 \subseteq E : \bigvee(A \cap X_0) = \bigvee(A)\}$

Instead, what is needed is something like (8):

(8) $[\![\text{the}']\!](A) = \{X_0 \subseteq E : (A \cap \underline{A}) \subseteq X_0\} \cup \{X_1 \subseteq E : \{\bigvee(A)\} \subseteq X_1$

The family of sets denoted by the class of NP's under analysis is defined in (8) as the union of two families of sets – the family of those sets that contain all the atoms in the denotation of the nominal expression (involving or not modifiers) and the family of those sets that contain the supremum of the denotation of the nominal expression.

If we substitute some other quantifier for *the*, the parsimony in the use of i–sums remains unchanged, the only difference being that, in most cases, it is not the supremum of the semilattice that is involved in the truth conditions. Take plural *some* as an example:

(9)   Some students are falling asleep.

(10) Some students carried the stone upstairs.

(11) Some students gathered for a party.

The truth conditions would now be the following, where $e_m \cup e_n$ (with m, n any natural numbers) represents the join of the individuals e_m and e_n, or, in other words, the supremum of the set $\{e_m, e_n\}$:

(9) a. $\#((\llbracket *\text{student'}\rrbracket \cap \underline{A}) \cap F) > 1$ i.e. $\#((/S/_\cup \cap \underline{A}) \cap F) > 1$

(10) a. $\#((\llbracket *\text{student'}\rrbracket \cap \underline{A}) \cap C) > 1$ i.e. $\#((/S/_\cup \cap \underline{A}) \cap C) > 1$
    b. $\{e_1 \in (\llbracket *\text{student'}\rrbracket \cap C) : \#(\{e_{10} \in A : e_{10} \cup e_1 = e_1\}) > 1\} \neq \emptyset$

(11) a. $\{e_1 \in (\llbracket *\text{student'}\rrbracket \cap G) : \#(\{e_{10} \in A : e_{10} \cup e_1 = e_1\}) > 1\} \neq \emptyset$

Conditions (9)a. and (10)a. state that the number of atoms in the relevant intersection has to be greater than 1. Conditions (10)b. and (11)a. state that there has to be in the relevant intersection at least one collective individual such that the number of its atomic parts is greater than 1. Accordingly, the appropriate definition for the quantifier (plural) *some* would be as follows:

(12) $\llbracket \text{some'}\rrbracket(A) = \{X_0 \subseteq E : \#((A \cap \underline{A}) \cap X_0) > 1\} \cup \{X_1 \subseteq E : \{e_1 \in (A \cap X_1) : \#(\{e_2 \in \underline{A} : e_2 \cup e_1 = e_1\}) > 1\} \neq \emptyset\}$

According to this definition, a formula involving the quantifier *some* in the relevant position is true if and only if at least one of two conditions is verified: (i) the intersection of the two argument sets contains more than one atom or (ii) the intersection of the two argument sets contains at least one member whose number of atomic parts is greater than 1^2.

ISSUES ON DISTRIBUTIVE AND COLLECTIVE READINGS 345

2.1.2. Readings Possibly Involving Individual Sums

The data discussed in the previous section could be tackled without involving i–sums in distributive readings. I will now briefly mention two cases of non–relativized nominals that have been claimed to require that i–sums be the relevant entities for such readings. The first one is from (Link 1987: 160):

(13)   All competing companies have common interests.

According to Link, this is an example of "genuine plural quantification", that is, "quantification over i–sums" (cf. *ib.*). Once one assumes that i–sums can be the individuals at stake in the relevant interpretation, the crucial question to be answered regards which i–sums play a real role in the meaning computation. Link's answer is apparently given in the definition of the noun phrase *all men* in what he considers to be its "genuine plural quantification" reading, given in (14) below – cf. Link (*op. cit.*: 163) –, where subscripted g stands for Link's marker of genuine plural quantification, E is the universe of discourse and $[\![^*\text{man}]\!]$ is the join semilattice generated by the set of atoms in $[\![\text{man}]\!]$:

(14) $[\![\text{all}_g \text{ men}]\!] = \{X \subseteq E : [\![^*\text{man}]\!] \subseteq X\}^3$

The corresponding definition for *all competing companies* would require that in (13) "what one is talking about (...) is any group of competing companies" (cf. *ib.*). In other words, the sentence is taken to universally quantify over the members of some semilattice. Now, the important point, is the composition of such semilattice. Although Link does not explore the issue, he gives a hint as to the relevant structure, in a note where he casts doubt on the results obtained with his definition: "Especially with the vague quantifiers most and many the truth of a $Q_\oplus$ reading might be difficult to assess, and one cannot even be sure whether it gives the right result at all. So imagine there are only seven firms that are in competition; then we would have to look already at $2^7 - 8 = 120$ proper i–sums to decide if the majority of them share interests internally" (*ib.*, p. 178, n. 5)[4]. However, in my view, a still more relevant problem remains unsolved in Link's conception, which has to do with situations where more than one the group of competing companies is in the model. What would in this case be the denotation of *all competing companies*? Since one certainly doesn't want to have to deal with spurious i–sums made up from companies that are not in competition with each other, the denotation of *competing companies* can simply not be a semilattice.

The denotation of an expression like *all competing companies* has to face the fact that a symmetric relation is involved, as it would be the case if the nominals were *children of same age* – an example due to Link[5] – *brothers, co-authors, friends, neighbours, partners, roommates, twins* or *parallel streets*. It seems to me that a possible way for reaching an appropriate definition of the relevant noun phrases is one that takes the corresponding binary relations as a point of departure. In what concerns the nominal *competing companies*, its denotation can easily be derived from the binary relation denoted by the predicative expressions *be a competitor of* or *compete with*. Taking this relation to be R, the first step to produce the new denotation would consist in obtaining all the maximal sets of companies in which some symmetric relation R', such that $R' \subseteq R$, is defined. Obviously, each of these sets contains all the companies that can be considered to be competitors of each other in some economic and geographic domain. However, it is not required that such sets form a partition of the set of companies involved. Now, it is possibly just the suprema of these sets that are needed in the denotation of *competing companies*, not other smaller i–sums. In fact, it seems to me that the preferred interpretation of sentence (13) is one where the objects of predication are the largest (in lattice–theoretical terms) plural individuals formed by companies that are competitors in some domain. Of course, in the particular case of the given predicative expression – *have common interests* –, one wants to ensure that the property applies to all the "smaller" i–sums, which is trivially guaranteed by its partial distributivity (that is, its application to any i–sums that are a subpart of an i–sum to which it also applies). Furthermore, in case the predicate is not partially distributive, as in (15)–(17) below, again only the mentioned maximal i–sums are required to be in its denotation.

(15)   All competing companies eventually generate a new company.

(16)   All former housemates gather for an annual party.

(17)   All twins organise activities together.

If the interpretations that I suggested are the relevant ones, Link's claim that in these cases the plural quantification at stake is a quantification over i–sums – contrary to the cases that were discussed in section 2.1.1., where only atoms and suprema were involved – remains undisputed. However, since the i–sums required by such quantification are autonomous, in the sense that they don't have to be associated in a lattice–theoretical structure, one can apparently conclude that the need for the strong quantification over i–sums that is exhibited in a definition like (14) remains to be proven.

The second of the two cases mentioned at the beginning of this section is extracted from Gillon (1987: 211), who found inspiration in data from Higginbotham (1981):

(18)   The men wrote operas.

One can easily see how Gillon's description of the semantics of sentence (18) in terms of the set–theoretical notion of **cover** can translate into a lattice–theoretical approach. Accordingly, one can assert that, according to Gillon's interpretation, that sentence can be true either in the distributive case – where the atoms in ⟦men⟧ are in the denotation of *wrote operas* –, or in the collective case – where the supremum of ⟦men⟧ is in the denotation of ⟦wrote operas⟧ –, or, finally, in the case where the supremum of the intersection of ⟦men⟧ and ⟦wrote operas⟧ equals the supremum of ⟦men⟧. This third possibility accounts, for instance, for the case where the relevant entities are the atom Handel, the atom Mozart and the i–sum formed out of Gilbert and Sullivan.

I think that Gillon is right in his claims about the subject noun phrase. However, it seems to me that the object phrase may raise some interesting problems if one wants to stick to a treatment of plurals à la Link. Notice, in fact, that sentence (18) can be true given any positive number of operas written by the above mentioned operatic authors. Accordingly, if Handel and Mozart had written just one opera each and Gilbert and Sullivan had not written any opera separately and only one together, the plural *operas* would have to be considered as a dependent plural, that is, as a semantically irrelevant plural. Suppose now that at least one of the – singular or collective – authors wrote more than one opera and that at least one of the other authors wrote just one opera. This is the kind of situation that is somehow hard to treat in a straightforward manner.

Given this sort of problem, I think that an alternative way should be tried to account for Gillon's "intermediate readings". One possibility is the consideration of a sentence like (18) as giving rise to Scha's cumulative reading. In this case, the bare plural *operas* would have to be taken to mean "some (indeterminate) number of operas", in any case "more than one opera". Besides the distributive case – where each man mentioned in the subject noun phrase wrote more than one opera –, the sentence could then convey the information that all the men were involved in writing at least one opera (to the end) and that the final product of the group taken together – in the cumulative, not in the collective sense – is more than one opera (formally, the image of the set of atomic and collective composers at stake under the relation 〚write〛 has an intersection with the set of (atomic) operas with cardinality greater than 1).

If the cumulative treatment turns out to be a satisfactory one, then, contrary to Link's data, Gillon's don't even seem to require any instance of quantification over i–sums, which of course reinforces the idea that no evidence has so far been given to support the claim that the full range of a semilattice construct – as expressed in definition (14) above – is required for a meaning computation. In order to further evaluate the legitimacy of this conclusion, we will now move to the consideration of noun phrases with relativized nominals.

2.2. Distributive and Collective Readings with Relativized Nominals

2.2.1. Atom–Based Readings

The most obvious cases of indisputable **atom–based readings** with relativized nominals are those in which the relevant predicate in the relative clause is atomic in the argument that matters. Let us call these readings **direct atom–based readings**. Contrasting with these are the readings I will call **indirect atom–based readings**, in which the relevant predicate in the relative clause is or can be interpreted collectively in the argument that matters, although the quantification affecting the truth value of the main clause is over the atomic parts of the collective individual.

The sentences in (20)–(22) illustrate direct cases. The logical translations accompanying them are given in an extension of the Logic with Generalised Quantifiers of Barwise and Cooper (1981). The following values for logical operators have to be kept in mind: "$*$" is Link's operator for building the translation of plurals ($〚{}^*\beta〛 = /〚\beta〛/_\cup$); "$\alpha$" is an operator that selects only the atoms in any set $〚{}^\alpha\beta〛 = 〚\beta〛 \cap \underline{A}$, where $\underline{A}$ is the set of atoms in the universe); "σ" is an operator that selects the i–sums in some set $〚{}^\sigma\beta〛 = 〚\beta〛 \cap (E \setminus \underline{A})$, where $\underline{A}$ is as before, E is the universe, and the zero individual is always excluded from any denotation). The VP translation appears in a simplified form.

(19)   a.   the students who swim

         b. the'(*λx[*student'(x) ∧ swim'(x)])
(20) a. The students who swim are healthy.
     b. the'(*λx[*student'(x) ∧ swim'(x)])(*healthy')
(21) a. The students who swim bought a life jacket.
     b. the'(*λx[*student'(x) ∧ swim'(x)])($^{\alpha}$buy_a_life_jacket'(x))
     c. the'(*λx[*student'(x) ∧ swim'(x)])($^{\sigma}$buy_a_life_jacket'(x))
(22) a. The students who swim met (yesterday).
     b. the'(*λx[*student'(x) ∧ swim'(x)]) ($^{\alpha}$meet')
     c. the'(*λx[*student'(x) ∧ swim'(x)])($^{\sigma}$meet')

Given appropriate meaning postulates for *student'* and *meet'*, one stating that the first expression can only denote sets of simple atoms – that is, non-collective individuals – and another stating that there can only be collective individuals in the denotation of the second expression, the formula in (22)b. is a contradiction, as it should be, although the grammar does not block it up to the stage of meaning computation.

The indirect atom–based readings are exemplified by sentences (23) and (24), where the unique argument of the predicate in the relative clause has to be interpreted collectively.

(23) Some of the students who met are swimmers.

(24) Some of the students who met joined to rent a car.

In (23), we have a distributive reading over a subset of atomic parts of one i–sum denoted by the nominal *students who met*. We can assign this reading the label **distributive cross–collective reading**. In (24), we have a collective reading involving one i–sum built up from a subset of atomic parts of the i–sum denoted by the same nominal. This reading can be labelled **collective cross–collective reading** or, for short, **subcollective reading**.

2.2.2. Readings Possibly Involving Individual Sums

The structures that will be discussed in this subsection include relative clauses whose relevant predicate is not atomic with respect to the argument bound by the relative pronoun. Instead, it is either collective or neutral. In terms of interpretation judgements, the issue is whether or not the sentences under analysis are instances of quantification over i–sums.

(25) a. The students that rented a car paid by cheque.
b. All (of) the students that rented a car paid by cheque.
c. Some (of the) students that rented a car paid by cheque.
d. Most (of the) students that rented a car paid by cheque.
e. Two thirds of the students that rented a car paid by cheque.

According to my intuitions, all the sentences in (25) – possibly with some reluctance in what concerns (25)e. – accept a distributive reading that does not require the individuals in the denotations of the relativized nominals to be atoms. In other words, the entities being quantified over can be atoms as well as i–sums. I believe these sentences are perfectly appropriate to describe situations where it is known that several individuals rented a car and that some of these individuals were collective entities, in case this distinction is totally irrelevant. This could be the case, from the point of view of the person who spent the day renting cars to students and who, on doing his accounting at the end of the day, uses one of the above sentences. Some other contexts may help to support this claim:

(26) All the students that rented a computer also rented a printer.

(27) Most of the students that prepared the Math exam together are planning to do the same for the Chemistry exam.

(28) Some of the students that were able to lift a piano were also able to lift a car.

The particular behaviour of cardinal numerals, which definitely rule out a distributive reading over i–sums – as shown in (29) below – should not constitute any surprise, given the well–known idiosyncrasies that characterise this class in different respects.

(29) Five of the students who rented a computer also rented a printer.

In what concerns collective readings, it should be noticed that they are also available when the right predicates are present. In fact, none of the sentences represented in (30) below appears to require that only atoms be involved in the denotation of the nominals.

(30) The / all (of) the / most of the / some of the / students that rented a computer will be meeting tomorrow in order to define a user schedule.

Again, what the data in this section have shown is that quantification over i–sums is required for their meaning computation. However, once more such quantification does not necessarily involve a semilattice of i–sums – much less with atoms – as is required by definition (14). Accordingly, the data that, to my knowledge, have been discussed so far in the literature only prove two facts regarding i–sums: (i) that they are required for collective readings; (ii) that sets of i–sums (possibly independent of each other in terms of their composition) can be quantified over. It remains to be proven that any interpretation of a natural language sentence requires that all the i–sums in a join semilattice denoted by some nominal construct have to be – not trivially, that is, not due to inferential properties of the predicator – in the denotation of the VP.

3. HYDRAS: UNEXPLORED (IM)POSSIBILITIES

We now turn to the second question announced in section 1, which concerns the circumstances under which atomic and non–atomic individuals in the denotation of a nominal structure become parts of a plural individual being considered in a collective reading. Such possibility arises namely with the conjoined NP's with relative clauses that were named **hydras** in Link (1984) – exemplified in (31) below (cf. *op. cit.*: 246). These are one of the kinds of nominal structures that, given their syntactical complexity and the wealth of the (lattice–theoretically defined) available domain, can give rise to ambiguities involving atom–based readings and non–atom–based readings. Yet, as it seems to be the case with simpler nominals, apparently no systematic account of the possible readings elicited with these structures has thus far been attempted.

(31) All the *students* and some of the *professors* who had met in secret joined in underground activities after the coup d'état.

Together with a rather problematic syntax for this sentence[6], Link (1984) assigned it one single reading, which I will informally express in the following terms:

(32) at some point in the past, presumably before a given coup d'état, a group formed by students and professors met in secret; at a later point, after that coup d'état, a new group, formed by all the students and some of the professors of the previous group joined in underground activities

It seems quite evident that this is not the only reading that one can think of, given the various possible ways of composing the value of the relative clause with the values of the conjoined NP's. My point is that, if this is the case, then either all the readings have to be made explicit in the process of computing the meaning of the sentence, or else some general restrictions have to apply which separate the real readings from implausible or ultimately unavailable readings. The first step to be taken is the enumeration of conceivable readings, that is, readings that are initially available, before any (possibly universal) restrictions apply.

In order to fully explore the semantic potential of hydras, we should not ignore the case where the relative clause distributes over the conjoined NP's, although its semantics is rather straightforward. Such distribution is clearly the case in a sentence like the following:

(33)   The boy and the girl that are swimming are Chinese.

The reading at stake can be accounted for either assuming that the subject NP is the result of an ellipsis of the relative clause in the left conjoined NP or that the relative clause is adjoined to the higher NP, although semantically it independently applies to both conjoined NP's. This second possibility – which is favoured by the required agreement – can be dealt with by means of a free predicative variable to be inserted in the translation of each of the conjoined NP's, a strategy that was first suggested by Bach and Cooper (1978) in order to account for languages where restrictive relative clauses are never (or are generally not) adjacent to the NP on which they semantically operate[7]. Such variable would be replaced by the predicative expression built up from the relative clause. The adoption of such a technical strategy requires that (presumably) every NP is assigned (at least) two alternative translations, only one of them being computed. (34) below, where P is a variable of type $<e,t>$ and "$\Rightarrow$" is to be read as "translates into", illustrates the two possible translations for an NP like *the boy*:

(34)   a.   [$_{NP}$ the boy] $\Rightarrow$ the'(boy')
        b.   [$_{NP}$ the boy] $\Rightarrow$ the'(λx[boy'(x) $\wedge$ P(x)])

Following the Bach–Cooper strategy, the translation of sentence (33) would include the following steps, where the translation of the VP is simplified:

(35)   a.   [$_{NP}$[$_{NP}$ the boy] and [$_{NP}$ the girl]] $\Rightarrow$ [the'(λx_1 [boy'(x_1)$\wedge$ P(x_1)])$\wedge$ the'(λx_2 [girl'(x_2)$\wedge$ P(x_2)])]

ISSUES ON DISTRIBUTIVE AND COLLECTIVE READINGS 353

b. $[_{NP}[_{NP}[_{NP}$ the boy] and$[_{NP}$ the girl]] $[_{F'}$ that are swimming]]
$\Rightarrow \lambda P[\text{the'}(\lambda x_1 \ [\text{boy'}(x_1) \wedge \ P(x_1)]) \wedge \ \text{the'}(\lambda x_2 \ [\text{girl'}(x_2) \wedge P(x_2)])](\lambda x_3[\text{swimming'}(x_3)]) \ = \ [\text{the'}(\lambda x_1 \ [\text{boy'}(x_1) \wedge \text{swimming'}(x_1)]) \wedge \text{the'}(\lambda x_2 \ [\text{girl'}(x_2) \wedge \ \text{swimming'}(x_2)])]$

Returning to Link's sentence in (31), let us replace *all* with *some*, just in order to make the intuitive meaning computation simpler. Besides, let us substitute two collective nouns (*team* and *commission*) for the atomic nouns *professor* and *student*. This second modification of Link's sentence takes into account the fact that the relevant predicates – *meet* and *join* – are collective in their unique argument, and is aimed at eliciting all the possible readings, namely those that involve distribution (of the predication induced by the relative clause) over the conjoined NP's. Accordingly, sentence (36) – which apparently exhibits as high a degree of complexity as it can be reached regarding the issues and the kind of structures under discussion – will now be the object of scrutiny instead of (31):

(36) Some of the teams and some of the commissions that had met in secret joined in underground activities after the coup d'état.

Before any restrictions apply, there are five possibilities concerning the Boolean characterisation of the entities to which the relative clause applies. In this particular case, given the nouns being used, they can be:

A – complex atoms (*team*–atoms and *commission*–atoms), a possibility that would be ruled out if the verbs were still *meet* and *join* and the nouns were *professor* and *student*;

B – two individual sums, one having teams and the other commissions as atomic parts;

C – one set of atoms given by the first noun and one individual sum given by the second noun;

D – one set of atoms given by the second noun and one individual sum given by the first noun;

E – one single individual sum whose atomic parts are more than one team–atom and more than one commission–atom.

These five cases are schematically represented in Table 1, where the letters a, b, c, d, e and f stand for the relevant teams, and g, h, i, j, k and l stand for the relevant commissions. According to my intuitions, cases C and D, which correspond to an asymmetric behaviour of the two NP's regarding the choice of entities – atoms in one case, and one individual sum in the other – are to be ruled out. In fact, it seems that the selections of semantic values at stake do not constitute a real possibility for the meaning computation of the conjoined NP's. In view of an explanation, one can hypothesise that such a semantic configuration violates a general principle of symmetry in the processing of meaning in natural languages, similar to what has been suggested for anaphora interpretation – for instance, in Lightfoot (1982).

In case B, a collective reading with respect to the relative clause is being assigned to both conjoined NP's. This is a case that I believe will not get unanimous judgements. At the moment I am writing, my choice favours the rejection of the reading (and I will not change the text tomorrow morning). Let us check a few more data involving both collective and non–collective individuals:

(37) Some of the boys and some of the girls who joined to organise a party are neighbours.

(38) Some of the boys and some of the girls who joined to sing madrigals will be meeting later to sing Bach cantatas.

(39) Some of the trios and some of the quartets that joined to sing madrigals will be meeting later to sing Bach cantatas.

TABLE I

	relevant entities in the denotation of N_1 and the relative clause	relevant entities in the denotation of N_2 and the relative clause
A	a, b, c, d, e, f	g, h, i, j, k, l
B	$\bigvee(\{a,b,c,d,e,f\})$	$\bigvee(\{g,h,i,j,k,l\})$
C	a, b, c, d, e, f	$\bigvee(\{g,h,i,j,k,l\})$
D	$\bigvee(\{a,b,c,d,e,f\})$	g, h, i, j, k, l
	relevant entity defined out of the denotations of N_1, N_2 and the relative clause	
E	$\bigvee(\{a,b,c,d,e,f,g,h,i,j,k,l\})$	

I don't think that sentence (37) can refer to two parties, and the same would apply if the bare plural *parties* were substituted for *a party*. Similarly, it seems rather implausible that in sentence (39) independent groups of male and female singers are being mentioned.

If these judgements are right, this would mean that a strong constraint is imposed on hydras, namely that the conjoined NP's cannot be

ISSUES ON DISTRIBUTIVE AND COLLECTIVE READINGS

assigned independent group readings with respect to the relevant predication of the relative clause. In what concerns the property expressed by the VP, at least three possibilities seem to be available:

(i)   – the property is applied to atoms;

(ii) – the property is applied to at least two individual sums whose atomic parts originate in different entities – in one case those involved in the denotation of one noun, in the other case those involved in the denotation of the other noun;

(iii) – the property is applied to a single individual sum whose atomic parts originate in the different entities involved in the denotation of both nouns.

The combination of all the unrestricted possibilities concerning the relative clause and those concerning the VP gives rise to fifteen readings. However, if we rule out cases B, C and D in Table I, the number reduces to six. All the fifteen combinations are given in Table II, where "R" stands for "reading". The "before (the coup d'état)" areas of the table – marked with the capitals A, B, C, D and E – contain the relevant entities to which both the common noun and the relative clause apply, and are therefore in the denotation of the relativized nominal (N', whose denotation, depending on the strategy chosen for composing its meaning and that of the VP, may have to be assigned a richer structure in lattice–theoretical terms,). As for the "after (the coup d'état)" parts, they contain arbitrarily chosen entities to which the VP applies, according to the cardinality condition expressed by the quantifier. Notice that Link's only reading corresponds to the rightmost column in the E part of the table.

TABLE II

before(A)	N'$_1$: a, b, c, d, e, f		N'$_2$: g, h, i, j, k, l
	R$_1$	***R$_2$**	**R$_3$**
after	a b c g h i	$\bigvee(\{a,b,c\})$ $\bigvee(\{g,h,i\})$	$\bigvee(\{a,b,c,g,h,i\})$
before(B)	N'$_1$: $\bigvee(\{a,b,c,d,e,f\})$		N'$_2$: $\bigvee(\{g,h,i,j,k,l\})$
	***R$_4$**	***R$_5$**	***R$_6$**
after	a b c g h i	$\bigvee(\{a,b,c\})$ $\bigvee(\{g,h,i\})$	$\bigvee(\{a,b,c,g,h,i\})$
before(C)	N'$_1$: a, b, c, d, e, f		N'$_2$: $\bigvee(\{g,h,i,j,k,l\})$
	***R$_7$**	***R$_8$**	***R$_9$**
after	a b c g h i	$\bigvee(\{a,b,c\})$ $\bigvee(\{g,h,i\})$	$\bigvee(\{a,b,c,g,h,i\})$
before(D)	N'$_1$: $\bigvee(\{a,b,c,d,e,f\})$		N'$_2$: g, h, i, j, k, l
	***R$_{10}$**	***R$_{11}$**	***R$_{12}$**
after	a b c g h i	$\bigvee(\{a,b,c\})$ $\bigvee(\{g,h,i\})$	$\bigvee(\{a,b,c,g,h,i\})$
before(E)	[N'$_1$...N$_2$]' : $\bigvee(\{a,b,c,d,e,f,g,h,i,j,k,l\})$		
	R$_{13}$	***R$_{14}$**	**R$_{15}$**
after	a b c g h i	$\bigvee(\{a,b,c\})$ $\bigvee(\{g,h,i\})$	$\bigvee(\{a,b,c,g,h,i\})$

The crucial question to be asked is whether or not a principled way exists that allows speakers – as always, most of them – to rule out a subgroup of readings (or, alternatively, to accept a subgroup of readings). I suggested above that cases C and D might be a violation of some general principle of symmetry. As for case B, its rejection could be an application of a general principle of "semantic processing simplicity" that, in this case, would prevent the consideration of two different individual sums, each given by one of the nouns (restricted by the relative clause). Assuming that some explanation can be found for cases B, C and D along these or similar lines, let us now concentrate on cases A and E, which are put together in Table III.

TABLE III

before(A)	N'$_1$: a, b, c, d, e, f		N'$_2$: g, h, i, j, k, l
	R_1	*R_2	R_3
after	$a\ b\ c$	$\bigvee(\{a,b,c\})$	$\bigvee(\{a,b,c,g,h,i\})$
	$g\ h\ i$	$\bigvee(\{g,h,i\})$	
before(E)	$[N'_1...N_2]'$: $\bigvee(\{a,b,c,d,e,f,g,h,i,j,k,l\})$		
	R_{13}	*R_{14}	R_{15}
after	$a\ b\ c$	$\bigvee(\{a,b,c\})$	$\bigvee(\{a,b,c,g,h,i\})$
	$g\ h\ i$	$\bigvee(\{g,h,i\})$	

If the judgements expressed in this table are sound, the interesting point is the fact that, again, a principle of semantic processing simplicity appears to be operating, leading in both cases – R_2 and R_{14} – to the rejection of the readings that require the definition of more than one individual sum, built up either from two sets of atoms (case A) or from one single individual sum (case E). The legal choice for case A, in which the relative clause distributes over the two NP's, appears to read as follows with respect to the VP: "choose between: (i) a distributive reading applying to both NP's (first column), and (ii) a collective reading involving a single individual sum defined out of the denotations of the two (relativized) nouns (third column)". As for what appears to be the rule for case E, in which the relative clause applies to a single individual sum, it can possibly be expressed in these terms: "given the initial individual sum, choose between: (i) a distributive reading applying to individuals that are in the denotation of the two nouns and that are also atomic parts of the initial individual sum (first column), and (ii) a collective reading involving a single individual sum defined out of the denotations of the two nouns and which is a part of the initial individual sum (third column)".

4. SELECTION OF READINGS

In this section, I will address the third question in section 1, which concerns the factors that determine whether or not an NP can be assigned a DR, a CR or both. The history of the attempt to systematically account for the variation between these two readings, which again goes back at least to Bennett (1974), is well documented in Roberts (1987). An obvious conclusion to which different authors have come is that predicates play a crucial role in the assignment of DR's and CR's. Besides, some authors have also tried to define subclasses of determiners in relation to their preference for DR's or CR's. For example, Scha (1981) makes a distinction between distributive and collective determiners and in Kamp's work a distinction appears between quantificational and non–quantificational determiners, which is based on the same grounds. It is therefore quite natural to think that what crucially determines the assignment of a reading is the combination of properties of determiners (or, equivalently, quantifiers) and properties of predicates. This is the general idea I will try to enunciate here. It can be rephrased in more detail as follows: with respect to an argument position, the assignment of a DR or a CR depends on properties of the predicate relative to that argument position and on properties of the relevant determiner.

In what concerns the properties of determiners, I believe they can be those that have been extensively described in the theory of natural quantifiers, namely in Barwise and Cooper (1981) and van Benthem (1986). Regarding the role of predicates in the assignment of readings, I came to the conclusion that the relevant properties have to do with the Boolean structure of the denotations of the predicate. In what follows, I will define five of these properties: the property of being **atomic** (abbreviated AT), the property of being **join semilatticed** (abbreviated SL), the property of being **divisible** (a designation inspired by the "fallacy of division", abbreviated DIV), the property of being **quasi–divisible** (abbreviated Q–DIV) and the property of being **indivisible** (abbreviated INDIV):

AT: A predicate is **atomic** with respect to its ith argument if the sets of ith coordinates of its non–empty extensions are sets of atoms (cf. *distributive* predicates in Link).
Examples: *student', cry', smile', snore'*.

SL: A predicate is **join semilatticed** with respect to its ith argument if the sets of ith coordinates of its non–empty extensions are atomic join semilattices.
Examples: **student', *group'*.

DIV: A predicate is **divisible** with respect to its ith argument if, when some individual is in the ith set of coordinates of a non–empty extension of the predicate, so are all the members of the principal ideal generated by the set containing it, except for the zero element (cf. "distributive predicates" in Hoeksema (1983)).
Examples: *fit in* and *house*, with respect to their first argument.

Q–DIV: A predicate is **quasi–divisible** with respect to its ith argument if, when some individual is in the ith set of coordinates of a

ISSUES ON DISTRIBUTIVE AND COLLECTIVE READINGS 359

non–empty extension of the predicate, so are all the members of the principal ideal generated by the set containing it, except for the atoms and the zero element (cf. *predicates closed under subgroups* in Hoeksema 1983).
Examples: *disperse, gather, meet* – intransitive, with respect to their only argument; transitive, with respect to their second argument.

INDIV: A predicate is **indivisible** with respect to its ith argument if, when some individual is in the ith set of coordinates of a non–empty extension of the predicate, no other member of the principal ideal generated by the set containing that individual, except itself, is in that set of coordinates.
Examples: *build, buy, carry, give, lift, own, rent*, with respect to their first argument.

It should be clear that there are predicates which don't exhibit any of the above properties. Examples of these are *include* (with respect to its first argument) and *weigh more two hundred kilos*.

Table IV contains a sketch of a standard assignment of collective and distributive readings, which is certainly subject to cross–linguistic variation. Considering the paramount importance of dealing with as much accurate judgements as possible – and the considerable difficulty in getting them –, I will now, as a measure of prudence, take Portuguese as the object language. The following conventions are being used in the Table: Q–AT (an Table IV contains a sketch of a standard assignment of collective and distributive readings, which is certainly subject to cross–linguistic variation. Considering the paramount importance of dealing with as much accurate judgements as possible – and the considerable difficulty in getting them –, I will now, as a measure of prudence, take Portuguese as the object language. The following conventions are being used in the Table: Q–AT (an abbreviation for **atomic quantifier**) designates the property of being a quantifier that denotes a relation between sets whose domain – the one involving the denotations of the common noun – only contains sets of atoms (of course, these quantifiers never give rise to collective readings); Q–DEF (an abbreviation for **definite quantifier**) designates the property of being a quantifier that denotes a relation between sets whose domain, as stated in the definition of the quantifier, never contains the empty set; S-N stands for "strong negative" or irreflexive; "EXACT" and "INEXACT" account for the absence or presence of expressions like *less than* or *more than* in the form of the cardinal or rational numeral; plural existential quantifiers (corresponding to plural *some*) are taken to imply *not all*, which has as a consequence that they are not increasing monotone; a plus signal marking a given combination of argument place and quantifier means that, besides a DR, a CR is possible in that case, while the minus signal means that only the DR is allowed. Each Portuguese expression is given the closest English translation.

TABLE IV

HYPOTHESIS OF A STANDARD ASSIGNMENT OF COLLECTIVE AND DISTRIBUTIVE READINGS IN PORTUGUESE

	[AT ∨ SL] smile (intrans.)	[—] include (1st arg.)	[INDIV] buy (1st arg.)	[Q-DIV] meet (intrans.)	[DIV] fit in (1st arg.)
[Q-AT] todo_o (every) o (the$_{sg}$) um (a) nenhum (no)	−	−	−	−	−
[Q-DEF ∧ ¬Q-AT] ambos (both)	−	−	−	−	+
¬[Q-DEF ∧ ¬Q-AT] ∧ [S-N ∨ MON↑ ∨ MON↓] todos (all) quase todos (nearly all) muitos (many) poucos (few) INEXACT NUMERALS (CARDINAL AND RATIONAL)	−	−	−	+	+
[WEAK ∧ ¬[MON↑ ∨ MON↓]] alguns (some$_{pl}$) uns (some$_{pl}$) uns tantos (a few) EXACT NUMERALS (CARDINAL AND RATIONAL)	−	−	+	+	+
[Q-DEF ∧ ¬Q-AT] os (the$_{pl}$) os <u>n</u> (the <u>n</u>)	−	+	+	+	+

The observation of Table IV reveals some interesting regularities (possibly too many). On the side of predicates, it suggests that the more a predicate involves the parts of a collective individual – in the sense of also applying to some or all of its parts –, the more it gives rise to collective readings. Possibly, this empirical fact can be the object of some sharp interpretation on a mathematically inspired theoretical approach, which I am not able to devise. On what concerns quantifiers, the distinctions are less clear–cut in terms of known properties. In fact, *ambos* (*both*) has exactly the same semantic properties as *os n* (*the n*), although it behaves in a completely idiosyncratic manner[8]. Of course, the definite quantifiers *os* (*the*) – with or without a specification of cardinality – and *ambos* (*both*) can be distinguished in terms of the semantic and syntactic central role that the first play in many languages, including English and Portuguese, that is, the role of building the referential basis on which other quantifiers – like rational numerals, and, in Portuguese, *ambos* (*both*) obligatorily – can operate. This role extends to all sorts of so–called partitive constructions, in fact assigning the quantifiers with *os* (*the*) a status of **nuclear quantifiers** in at least the above mentioned languages.

It should be noted that the combinations of factors considered so far are necessary but not sufficient conditions for an assignment of readings. Indeed, other factors can elicit or block a given reading, as can be seen with the following pairs of sentences:

(40)   Five boys bought a bike.

(41)   Five boys bought this bike.

(42)   Five boys ate a chocolate bar.

(43)   Five boys ate the chocolate bar.

According to Table IV, all these sentences are ambiguous between a DR and a CR regarding the first argument, given that both *buy* and *eat* are indivisible predicates in that argument. Obviously, this assignment of readings is not appropriate for sentences (42) and (44), due to the fact that the relations denoted by *buy* and *eat* are functional from the second to the first argument when a single interval of time is being considered for the truth evaluation, which blocks the distributive reading. Presumably, it is the same property that blocks the wide scope reading of the object NP in Scha's sentence given in (45). However, if *have* is replaced by *use*, as in (46), the reading becomes available. Notice that, in contrast to *have*, the predicate *use* is not functional from its second to its first argument.

(44) Six hundred Dutch firms have five thousand American computers.

(45) Six hundred Dutch firms use five thousand American computers.

Very likely, the sketch of reading assignments given in Table IV will have to undergo deep revisions and become somewhat less "perfect"[9]. However, it seems to me that the line of research I have tried to suggest here is worth being pursued, namely in view of integrating other factors that may play some role in the licensing or blocking of noun phrase readings.

NOTES

[1] Remko Scha (in the 1991 Tübingen meeting and in personal communication) recalled his exclusively collective treatment of *the* in his 1981 paper, and disagreed with my assigning of DR's to NP's with *the*. He illustrated his argument with the sentence *The boys danced with the girls*, where one should avoid the (according to him) undesired reading saying that each of the boys danced with all the girls, and only get the CR. I stick to my position, considering two reasons. In the first place, I don't think that such DR should be ruled out, since it accounts for perfectly plausible situations (suppose, for instance, that in our situation there are six boys and two girls...). In the second place, it seems to me that the notion of CR is inadequate to cover the cases where each boy danced with one or more girls, as I think is Scha's idea. In fact, what we have in such cases is, I think, precisely Scha's 1981 "cumulative reading", which is available with many quantifiers other than the numerals that he concentrated on, therefore not being restricted to "sentences with indefinite noun phrases", as Scha seemed to believe at the time (cf. *ib.*, p. 484). As for the notion of CR – using the same sentence as an illustration –, I would like to keep it for the case where the group of boys dances with the girls as a group, not individually, while the girls are also probably – but not necessarily – being taken as a group (think, for instance, of any kind of collective folk dance).

[2] An obvious consequence of the kind of definitions of quantifiers allowing CR's that I have been discussing is that the mathematical properties of quantifiers – namely, properties of relations – that have been discussed in recent years – for example, in van Benthem (1986) and earlier work – will have to be inferred only from the part of the definition that concerns atoms.

[3] Considering that *man* is not akin to any symmetric relation, it is hard to see what relevant data would be covered by this ("genuine plural quantification") definition of the denotation of all men. In fact, the truth condition included in (14) would give the right results with formulas like *all men are men* or *all men are human beings*, where the predicative nominals can easily be taken to denote join semilattices, but even these cases can have simpler solutions that don't require quantification over a full semilattice.

[4] $Q_\oplus$ stands for "a semantic theory of plurals" that incorporates the treatment of what Link considers to be "genuine plural quantification" (cf. *ib.*, p. 160).

[5] The expressions *competing companies* and *children of same age* are given by Link together with *demonstrations*, which I would rather consider a collective noun of the same sort as *team*.

[6] In Peres (1987), a fully compositional treatment of this kind of hydras is proposed.

[7] This strategy was explored in Peres (1987 and 1989) for treating the semantics of hydras.

[8] I find some disagreement among English speakers about the behaviour of *both*, namely with respect to the alleged ambiguity between a DR and a CR with a sentence like *Both houses cost £50.000*, mentioned in a Longman dictionary (*Dictionary of the English Language*, 1984). In Ladusaw (1982), both is unambiguously treated, much in the same way that is fit for Portuguese *ambos*.

[9] During the presentation of this paper at the Tübingen meeting, Hans Kamp offered the sentence *Every paper that you gave me fit in my briefcase* (or one very close to it), suggesting that, even with *every* – a maximally distributive quantifier –, a predicate like *fit (in)* might give rise to a CR. I tend to think that Kamp's kind of sentence does not exactly involve a CR, requiring instead that different events be taken into account. In this case, the sentence would not mean that all the papers were put together in the briefcase, but rather that they were put there one after the other and that all the attempts to do so were successful up to the last paper.

REFERENCES

Bach, E. & R. Cooper (1978): 'The NP-S Analysis of Relative Clauses and Compositional Semantics', *Linguistics and Philosophy* **1**, 145–150.

Barwise, J. & R. Cooper (1981): 'Generalised Quantifiers and Natural Languages', *Linguistics and Philosophy* **4**, 159–220.

Bennett, M. (1974/1975): *Some Extensions of a Montague Fragment of English*. PhD diss., UCLA. Dist. Indiana University Linguistics Club, 1975.

van Benthem, J. (1986): *Essays in Logical Semantics*. D. Reidel, Dordrecht.

Gillon, B. (1987): 'The Readings of Plural Noun Phrases in English', *Linguistics and Philosophy* **10**, 199–219.

Higginbotham, J. (1981): 'Reciprocal Interpretation', *Journal of Linguistic Research* **1**, 97–117.

Hoeksema, J. (1983): 'Plurality and Conjunction' In A. Ter Meulen (ed.) *Studies in Modeltheoretic Semantics*. Foris, Dordrecht.

Kamp, H. & U. Reyle (1993): *From Discourse to Logic, An Introduction to Modeltheoretic Semantics of Natural Language, Formal Logic and Discourse Representation Theory*. Kluwer, Dordrecht.

Ladusaw, W. A. (1982): 'Semantic Constraints on the English Partitive Construction' In D. P. Flickinger, M. Macken & N. Wiegand (eds.) *Proceedings of the First West Coast Conference on Formal Linguistics*. Department of Linguistics, Stanford University.

Lightfoot, D. (1982): *The Language Lottery, Toward a Biology of Grammars*. The MIT Press, Cambridge, MA.

Link, G. (1983): 'The Logical Analysis of Plurals and Mass terms: A Lattice-theoretical Approach' In R. Bäuerle, C. Schwarze & A. von Stechow (eds.) *Meaning, Use and Interpretation of Language*. de Gruyter, Berlin.

Link, G. (1984): 'Hydras, On the Logic of Relative Constructions with Multiple Heads' In F. Landman & F. Veltman (eds.) *Varieties of Formal Semantics.* Foris, Dordrecht.

Link, G. (1987): 'Generalized Quantifiers and Plurals' In P. Gärdenfors (ed.) *Generalized Quantifiers, Linguistic and Logic Approaches.* D. Reidel, Dordrecht.

Peres, J. (1987a): *Para uma Semântica Formal da Quantificação Nominal Não-Massiva.* Dissertation, University of Lisbon.

Peres, J. (1987b/1989): 'A semantic argument for an NP–S' analysis of relative structures' In W. Bahner, J. Schildt e D. Viehweger (eds.) *Proceedings of the Fourteenth International Congress of Linguists, Berlin/GDR, August 10 – August 15, 1987.* Akademie–Verlag, Berlin.

Roberts, C. (1987): *Modal Subordination, Anaphora and Distributivity.* Dissertation, University of Massachusetts, Amherst.

Scha, R. (1984): 'Distributive, Collective and Cumulative Quantification' In J. Groenendijk, T. M. V. Janssen & M. Stokhof (eds.) *Truth, Interpretation and Information.* Foris, Dordrecht.

INDEX OF SUBJECTS

abstract morpheme, 286
accomplishment, 4, 55–57, 106, 107
achievement, 55, 56, 106, 107
active sentence, 309
activity, 4, 55–58, 65–68, 80, 81, 107
additive role, *see* thematic role
additivity, 80, 81, 83
adjective
    affirmative, 171
    collective, 152
    distributive, 152
    homogeneous, 152
    predicative, 156
    restrictive, 171
    subsective, 150, 151, 171
    transparent, 156
adsentences, 226, 228
    multiplicative, 233
agent role, *see* thematic role
Aktionsart, 4, 5, 16, 55–58, 64, 66, 72, 80, 82–87, 90, 92–94, 102, 103, 105–107, 109
    calculus, 58, 82, 84, 93, 94, 106
algebra
    Boolean, 6, 120, 126, 127, 137, 143, 193, 201, 214, 215, 236
    atomic, 27
    complete atomic, 24, 165, 167–169
    of noun phrases, 193, 216
    of nouns, 216
    of truth values, 226
    of verb phrases, 193, 194, 200, 201, 214, 215, 223–225

algebraic semantics, 24, 44
ambiguity, 3, 9, 32, 35, 36, 117, 128, 242, 247, 255, 262, 273
anaphora, 36, 39, 43, 118, 354
    anaphoric link, 242
    anaphoric reference, 118
    plural, 20, 21, 25–26
    resolution, 2, 25
antecedent, 141
anti-additive determiner, *see* determiner
anti-additive function, *see* function
anti-additive noun phrase, *see* noun phrase
anti-quantifier, 24, 37
antimorphic adverb, 233
antimorphic function, *see* function
aspect, 11, 12, 106, 286
    durative, 287
    imperfective, 289
    perfective, 289
    terminative, 287, 299, 301, 309
associativity, 138
asymmetry, 300, 310, 313, 316
atemporal, 299
atomicity, 124
atomless, 124
axiomatic semantics, 124, 163
    axioms of propositions, 134
    axioms of truth, 134, 135

bare plural noun phrase, *see* noun phrase
bottom element, 142

CAJS-model, 244–247

cardinality, 286–288, 290,
    293–295, 301, 305, 307
  information, 286
categorial grammar, 173
Categorial Unification
    Grammar, 85
category mistake, 127, 135, 144
characteristic function, *see*
    function
characteristic role, *see* thematic
    role
classical negation, *see* negation
collection, 22
collective determiner, *see*
    determiner
collective noun, 12, 14, 364
collective predicate, *see*
    predicate
collective reading, *see* reading
collective/distributive
    ambiguity, 36, *see also*
    distributivity
collective/distributive
    distinction, 4, 23, 32,
    see also distributivity
collectivity, 1, 8, 12, 16, 247,
    248, 250, 251, 261,
    279, 312, 315
complement, 142
complete noun phrase, *see*
    noun phrase
complete quantifier, *see*
    quantifier
completeness, 125, 204,
    209–211, 245
compositionality, 119, 125
conjunction reduction, 13,
    321–337
connective
    anti-additive, 228, 232, 233

multiplicative, 228
  sentential, 226
consistency, 7, 204, 205,
    207–209, 211
consistent noun phrase, *see*
    noun phrase
consistent quantifier, *see*
    quantifier
constant role, *see* thematic role
coordination, 12, 261, 321–337
coreference, 113
count term, 124, 143
cover, 10–12, 33–36, 269, 270,
    274, 296, 307, 309, 347
  minimal, 10, 33, 128, 241,
    269–271, 276, 277,
    280, 296, 307, 309
  partition, 10, 11, 35, 128,
    241, 269–271, 277,
    280, 291, 294–297,
    301, 302, 307–309,
    312, 313, 316
  pseudo-partition, 10, 33,
    35, 241, 269, 270,
    272–274, 277, 280,
    291, 296, 297,
    307–309, 312, 316
cumulative predicate, *see*
    predicate
cumulative reading, *see* reading
cumulative role, *see* thematic
    role
cumulativity, 12, 65, 66, 70, 71,
    73, 75, 79, 84, 311,
    312, 315

definable completeness, 137
definable ordering, 138
definite, 126
  non-denoting, 113, 126,
    139, 163, 169

denotable, 120, 139–141, 146, 147, 151, 153, 154, 170
determiner
    anti-additive, 224–226, 231, 237
    collective, 12, 358, *see also* collectivity
    conservative, 243, 261, 264
    distributive, 260, 313, 358
    lifted, 243
    monotone, 219, 220, 222, 255, 262
    monotone decreasing, 42, 216–218, 232, 259, 263, 264, 267
    monotone increasing, 4, 9, 43, 218–220, 224, 261, 263, 264, 266, 267, 279
    multiplicative, 225, 226
    non-monotone, 221, 222, 226, 237
    non-monotone increasing, 37–39, 41, 43, 267, 277, 280
    plural, 21, 36, 42, 43, 257
    relative strength, 9, 262
    scope of, 39
Discourse Representation Theory (DRT), 2, 4, 20, 25, 26, 32, 37–39, 58, 60, 63, 64, 74, 78, 87, 95
    accessibility of discourse referent (DRF), 95
    discourse referent (DRF), 58, 59, 61–64, 78, 86, 87, 95, 98, 102, 107
    DRS, 58–61, 63, 78, 85–87, 89, 91–93, 95, 98, 101–103, 107, 109
    DRS-construction algorithm, 5, 58, 85, 94, 98, 106
    partial embedding function, 60
distributive predicate, *see* predicate
distributive reading, *see* reading
distributivity, 1–3, 8, 12, 16, 22–24, 28, 32, 37, 83, 240, 242, 248, 250–252, 257, 261, 267, 279, 312, 315
    temporal distributivity, 72, 79, 94, 103, 105
    temporal simultaneity, 103, 105
ditransitive verb, 144
divisive predicate, *see* predicate
divisivity, 65–71, 75, 79, 83, 84
domain
    algebraic, 245, 246
    atomic, 124
    plural, 116
    sub-domain, 167
downward heredity, 58, 73

ellipsis, 118
external argument, 291, 305

feature logic, 107
fine-grainedness, 126
floated quantifier, *see* quantifier
focus, 309
free logic, 126, 127, 140
Frege Structure, 115, 126, 166
Frege structure, 6
function
    additive, 308

anti-additive, 8, 192, 223, 224, 226, 229, 234
antimorphic, 192, 223, 225, 226, 229, 234
antitone, 237
characteristic, 214, 215, 223–225
constant, 303, 314
continuous, 165
distributive, 314
Entier, 301
injective, 303, 314
isotone, 237
monotone, 192
monotone decreasing, 7, 215, 216, 223, 226, 229, 234
monotone increasing, 7, 214–216, 223, 226
multiplicative, 224–226
participancy, 303
functional application, 86
functional composition, 86
fusion, *see* least upper bound

general model, 137
generalized conjunction, 129, 145
generalized quantification, *see* quantification
generalized quantifier, *see* quantifier
Generalized Quantifier Theory (GQT), 20, 24, 37, 40, 42, 243, 248, 276, 341
generics, 57, 106
genuine plural quantification, *see* quantification
goal role, *see* thematic role
gradual role, *see* thematic role
group, 1–3, 22, 28–31, 295

structured, 128

heterogeneity, 75, 92–94, 102, 103, 105
heterogeneous event description, 55, 64, 73, 80, 82, 106
heterogeneous event type, 64, 86, 106
heterogeneous reading, *see* reading
hierarchy of negative expressions, 8, 182, 192, 235
homogeneity, 65, 66, 70, 71, 74, 75, 83, 84, 91–94, 102, 103, 105, 106
homogeneous event description, 55, 64, 66, 72, 73, 77, 79, 82, 92, 106
homogeneous event type, 58, 64, 79, 86, 106
homogeneous predicate, *see* predicate
homogeneous reading, *see* reading
hydra, 15, 351, 352, 354, 364

ideal, 236
idempotence, 138
imparfait, 106
indefinite noun phrase, *see* noun phrase
index, 300
individual
    atomic, 22, 44, 339, 351
    collective, 340, 342, 348, 349, 354, 362
    individual sum (i–sum), 2, 14, 15, 22, 24, 27–31, 34, 35, 37, 39–44, 57,

339, 340, 342, 344–351, 355–357
intensional, 5
non-atomic, 351
non-collective, 354
plural, 14, 339, 346, 351
infinitival form, 191
intensional subject, 114
intensionality, 1
intermediate-level reading, *see* reading
internal argument, 291, 300, 305
internal ordering, 138
interval, 306, 314
interval semantics, 55, 69
intonation, 31
intransitive verb, 144, 147, 150
intuitionistic propositional calculus, 236
iterative reading, *see* reading

join, 172

kind, 57
KL–ONE, 64
knowledge representation formalism, 64

Lønning's Plural Logic (PL), 2, 24, 25
Ladusaw–Fauconnier Generalization, 7
lambda calculus, 131, 165
  $\lambda\beta$-calculus, 133
  untyped, 131
lattice, 24, 44, 58, 60, 65, 115, 137, 143
  complete, 165
  join semilattice, 15, 59, 245, 340–343, 351, 358, 363

semilattice, 58, 65, 343–346, 348, 351
law of contradiction, 208
law of excluded middle, 211
laws of consistency, 208
laws of contraposition, 205, 209
laws of DeMorgan, 7, 8, 181–183, 234, 236
laws of negation, *see* negation
least upper bound, 60, 120, 127, 343, 344, 346, 347
lexical feature, 250, 251
licencing expression, 186–189, 229
lift, 240, 241, 243, 254–257, 259–262, 264–266, 276, 279, 316
limit, 165
Link's Logic of Plurality (LP), 1, 14, 22, 24, 26–29, 31, 32, 34, 37, 39
logical form, 284
logical paradox, 126

mass term, 1, 6, 16, 24, 26, 56, 82, 84, 119–126, 129, 137, 150, 157, 158, 164, 279
material part-relation, 66, 67, 69
maximal filter, *see* ultrafilter
maximal ideal, *see* prime ideal
meaning postulate, 269
mereology, 2, 6, 27, 30, 31, 65, 66, 136–138
  mereological property, 113
minimal logic, 236
minimal model, 236
minimal negation, *see* negation
mixed predicate, *see* predicate
mixed reading, *see* reading

modal logic, 201, 236
model-theoretic semantics,
    124–126, 163
modifier, 302
    cumulative, 152
    distributive, 152
    homogeneous, 153
    plural property, 155
    singular property, 155
    transparent, 156
monadic second order logic, 24,
    27
monotone decreasing quantifier,
    see quantifier
monotone determiner, see
    determiner
monotone function, see
    function
monotone increasing quantifier,
    see quantifier
monotone noun phrase, see
    noun phrase
Montague Grammar, 20
multiplicative determiner, see
    determiner
multiplicative function, see
    function
multiplicative noun phrase, see
    noun phrase

natural kind, 22
negation, 121, 179
    classical, 8, 183, 192, 234,
        235
    laws of, 211
    minimal, 8, 181–184, 186,
        187, 189, 191, 192,
        234–236
    predicate, 204–206, 208,
        210, 211
    regular, 206, 236
    sentential, 204–206, 208,
        210, 211, 236
    subminimal, 8, 181–186,
        188, 189, 191, 192,
        234–236
negative adverb, 183, 191, 233
negative polarity item, 7, 16,
    177–179, 183, 185,
    186, 190
    laws of negative polarity, 8,
        184, 192, 228, 230, 234
    strong, 8, 177, 183, 184,
        187, 189, 190, 192,
        228–232, 234, 237
    superstrong, 8, 191, 192,
        228, 234
    weak, 8, 177, 183–185, 187,
        189, 190, 192,
        228–230, 234
neighbourhood, 236
neutral reading, see reading
non-denoting noun phrase, see
    noun phrase
non-monotone determiner, see
    determiner
non-monotone increasing
    predicate, see
    predicate
non-monotone noun phrase, see
    noun phrase
noun phrase
    anti-additive, 223, 226
    bare plural, 4, 5, 11, 56,
        57, 92, 98, 102, 103,
        106, 109, 275, 287,
        290, 347
    collective, 250
    complete, 210–212, see also
        completeness
    conjunction, 12, 16, 130,

351–354
consistent, 205–208, 210–212, *see also* consistency
definite, 114, 126, 280
definite plural, 11, 288
definite singular, 288
distributive, 250, 252, 261, 266, 273, 313
indefinite, 37, 311, 312, 363
indefinite plural, 44
indefinite singular, 37
monotone, 196, 222
monotone decreasing, 194–199, 216, 219, 220, 222, 232
monotone increasing, 195, 196, 198, 199, 203, 218, 219, 229
multiplicative, 224, 226, 231
non-denoting definite, 6
non-monotone, 222
partitive, 207, 208
plural, 14, 16, 87, 92, 106, 239, 243, 253, 255, 259, 274, 276, 279
quantized, 106
singular, 316
noun phrase strategy, 239–243, 252, 254, 257, 266, 268, 276, 277, 279
numeral, 241, 247, 286

object role, *see* thematic role
one reading hypothesis, 11, 12, 16, 283, 290, 291, 296, 310, 316
ontology, 1, 2, 26, 27, 57, 67, 69, 74, 107, 108, 113, 115, 117, 119, 122–125, 163, 171
homogeneous, 119, 121, 124, 125, 129
inhomogeneous, 119
operator
abstraction, 59, 62, 63, 79, 80, 91, 98
iteration - ITER, 57, 72–75, 78, 79, 94, 105, 108
join, 169
partaking in - π, 253
plural operator - *, 59, 60, 107, 278, 340, 348
sum operator - σ, 348
summation, 138
supremum, 137, 138, 140, 158
type shifting, 3
verb modifier - δ, 250, 253

partition, *see* cover
partitive construction, 27, 260
partitive noun phrase, *see* noun phrase
passé simple, 106
passive sentence, 172, 309, 310
past progressive, 106
path, 300
plural character, 22, 36
plural determiner, *see* determiner
plural noun phrase, *see* noun phrase
plural object, 22, 26, 28
plural quantification, *see* quantification
plural term, 22
plurality, 1
possible world, 130

predicate
    collective, 25, 36, 41, 43, 260, 261, *see also* collectivity
    cumulative, 41, 65, 70, 71, 73, 75, *see also* cumulativity
    distributive, 23, 35, 36, 40, 42–44, 75, *see also* distributivity
    divisive, 65, 68, 73, *see also* divisivity
    homogeneous, 73, *see also* homogeneity
    mixed, 26, 261
    non-monotone increasing, 43
    quantized, 65
    temporally distributive, 103
    temporally simultaneous, 103
predicate negation, *see* negation
predication, 1, 287, 290, 291, 303, 304, 306, 312, 313, 316
    opaque, 130
    self, 126, 127, 135
presupposition, 126
prime ideal, 192, 211, 212, 225
principle of compositionality, 275
proper name, 117, 118, 198, 202, 206, 210, 212, 213, 247, 260, 269, 279, 317
    negated, 210
property
    cumulative, 142, 153
    disjunctive, 121
    distributive, 117
    modifier, 115, 116, 118, 124, 130, 146, 149, 151, 152, 154, 155, 158, 163, 165
    universal, 131
property modification, 6
propositional attitude, 114

quantification
    arithmetical, 309
    generalized, 1
    genuine plural, 14, 15, 345, 363
    multiple, 283–285, 299, 303, 312, 313
    non-iterative, 269
    over i–sums, 345, 346, 348–350
    plural, 14, 16, 25, 27, 43, 299, 313, 346
    polyadic, 241, 278, 280
    singular, 19
quantificational force, 243, 255, 264
quantifier
    complete, 209
    consistent, 205
    distributive, 364
    floated, 23, 96
    generalized, 2, 20, 21, 28, 37–39, 42, 239
    monotone, 192
    monotone decreasing, 193–195, 197, 200, 201, 203, 215
    monotone increasing, 37, 38, 194, 195, 198, 201, 202, 214, 252
    plural existential, 360

raising, 284
quantifier scope ambiguity, 11
quantifying in, 242
quantized noun phrase, *see*
    noun phrase
quantized predicate, *see*
    predicate
quasi-filter, 192, 199, 201–204, 224
quasi-ideal, 192, 199, 200, 203, 204, 211, 223, 236

reading
    branching, 241, 252
    collective, 3, 5, 10, 11, 14, 15, 28, 29, 33, 35, 36, 83–85, 87, 92, 96, 98, 128, 240, 241, 243, 244, 246, 247, 250, 252, 256–260, 262, 265–268, 273, 276, 279, 280, 283, 313, 339, 341, 342, 348–351, 354, 357–364, *see also* collectivity
    cumulative, 5, 10–12, 36, 58, 95, 96, 98, 103, 108, 241, 249, 254, 269, 274–276, 278, 280, 299, 310, 311, 347, 348, 363, *see also* cumulativity
    distributive, 3–5, 9–12, 14, 15, 23, 24, 28, 33–36, 83, 85, 96, 97, 104, 106, 128, 150, 164, 240, 241, 243, 250–252, 257, 262, 264–267, 269, 275–277, 279, 280, 283, 297, 313, 339, 341, 342, 345, 347–350, 357–364, *see also* distributivity
    durative, 316
    group, 354
    heterogeneous, 83, 94, *see also* heterogeneity
    homogeneous, 82, 83, 94, *see also* homogeneity
    intermediate-level, 2, 16, 28, 29, 252, 268, 347
    iterative, 66, 74
    mixed, 3, 33–35
    neutral, 9, 10, 240, 241, 243, 252, 253, 256–258, 262, 264, 265, 267–271, 274–277, 279, 280, 349
    [+SQA], 289, 295
    [-SQA], 289, 295, 313
    temporally distributive, 84, 87, 90, 92, 98, 101–103, 106
    temporally simultaneous, 84, 87, 92
    wide scope, 268
reduction test, 12–14, 321–323, 332, 335, *see also* conjunction reduction
reference, 132
regular negation, *see* negation
relative clause, 15, 231, 325–327, 333, 334, 336, 342, 351–357
repetitive, 309
resultative clause, 300

scope
    narrow, 159
    reversal, 283

INDEX OF SUBJECTS

scopal ambiguity, 283–285
    wide, 283, 284
scope of determiner, *see*
    determiner
Scott model, 165
Scott-Montague model, 236
second-order logic, 137
self application, 125
semantic field, 300
sense, 132
sentential negation, *see*
    negation
simple past, 106
singular quantification, *see*
    quantification
Situation Theory, 20
soundness, 125
standard proposal, 3, 33
state, 55, 58, 64, 107
stative verb, 308, 309
subinterval property, 55, 65, 69, 72
subminimal logic, 236
subminimal negation, *see*
    negation
sum, 120
    mereological, 123
sum theory, 243
summative role, *see* thematic role
summativity, 81
supremum, *see* least upper bound
symmetry, 138

temporal, 299
temporal discourse-heterogeneity, 4, 76, 80
temporal discourse-homogeneity, 4, 75, 77, 80, 83, 87
temporally distributive predicate, *see* predicate
temporally distributive reading, *see* reading
temporally heterogeneous event description, 4
temporally homogeneous event description, 4
temporally simultaneous event description, 103
temporally simultaneous predicate, *see* predicate
temporally simultaneous reading, *see* reading
test for downward monotonicity, 197
test for upward monotonicity, 198
thematic role, 55–57, 59, 63, 64, 72, 74, 80, 82–87, 93–96, 98, 101–104, 108, 109
    additive role, 80, 81, *see also* additivity
    agent role, 59, 91, 94, 98
    characteristic role, 81, 82, 84, 86, 90
    constant role, 81, 82, 84, 86, 87, 90, 93
    cumulative role, 80, *see also* cumulativity
    goal role, 83, 95
    gradual role, 81, 82, 84, 86
    object role, 59, 71, 81–83, 94, 98
    summative role, 84, *see also* summativity

theme role, 59, 81, 83, 94
top element, 142
truth-value gap, 126
type, 292, 315
    coercion, 79, 104, 105, 108
    extensional, 239, 243, 246
    lifting, 9, 130
    shifting, 130
    type logic, 285
    type theory, 246
    weak, 162

ultrafilter, 192, 212, 213
undecidability, 129
unification, 91–93, 101, 102
unification-based grammar formalism, 108, *see also* categorial unification grammar

V-Raising, 191
verb modification, 280
verb phrase strategy, 240–243, 252, 254, 256, 257, 266, 276, 277, 279

INDEX OF NAMES

Aczel, P., 6, 17, 115, 126, 130, 166, 173
Allan, K., 44
Allgayer, J., 27, 44
Altham, J., 45
Aone, C., 27, 45
Aristotle, 44, 123
Atlas, J., 235

Bach, E., 24, 45, 107, 109, 235, 352, 364
Bäuerle, R., 45, 64, 69, 109
Balbes, R., 45
Ball, R., 170
Barker, C., 129, 163, 171, 173
Bartsch, R., 20, 45, 239, 246, 280
Barwise, J., 20, 37, 38, 45, 236, 237, 252, 280, 285, 288, 318, 348, 358, 364
Bealer, G., 45
Bell, J., 237
Bennett, M., 20, 45, 55, 109, 114, 173, 239, 246, 260, 261, 281, 339, 357, 364
van Benthem, J., 45, 235, 237, 246, 255, 265, 278, 281, 292, 315, 317, 318, 358, 363, 364
Berwick, R., 46
Beswick, C., 170
Biedermann, R., 236, 237
Biermann, A., 23, 45
Birkhoff, G., 237
Bläsius, K., 45
Blau, U., 45, 126, 173
Bonomi, A., 235
Boolos, G., 25, 27, 45, 46
Bouma, G., 108, 109
Brady, M., 46

Bunt, H., 24, 46, 119, 122, 123, 129, 152, 156–158, 173, 315, 318
Burge, T., 46, 123, 173
Buszkowski, W., 235

Caenepeel, M., 108, 109
Calder, J., 108, 111
Carlson, G., 43, 46, 57, 109, 304, 317, 318
Carlson, L., 46
Cartwright, H., 46, 123, 173
Casalegno, P., 235
Chang, C., 237
Chellas, B., 46, 236, 237
Chierchia, G., 130, 170, 172–174
Choe, J., 24, 46
Chomsky, N., 284, 309, 310, 318
Clark, H., 301, 318
Clarke, B., 46
Clarke, D., 46
Clay, R., 46
Cook, C., 46
Cooper, R., 20, 45, 236, 237, 348, 352, 358, 364
Cresswell, M., 46, 168, 174

van Dalen, D., 236, 237
Davey, B., 47
Davidson, D., 63, 109
Davies, M., 47
Davila-Perez, R., 164, 174
Davis, S., 47
DeMorgan, A., 7, 8
van der Does, J., 3, 4, 8–11, 16–18, 21, 22, 34–39, 43, 44, 47, 54, 239, 240, 242, 243, 262, 264, 271–275,

277–279, 281–283,
285, 290, 291,
296–299, 302,
306–308, 310–312,
315–319
Dominicy, M., 337
Dougherty, R., 47
Dowty, D., 4, 17, 47, 55, 66,
108, 109, 132, 173,
174, 242, 258, 281
Dummett, M., 236, 238
Dunn, J., 236, 238
Dwinger, P., 45

Eberle, K., 4, 5, 58, 107–109
Eberle, R., 47
van Eijck, J., 47
van Emde Boas, P., 45
Engdahl, E., 235
Erne, M., 47
Etchemendy, J., 288
Evers, A., 191, 238

Faltz, L., 49, 236, 238, 284, 318
Fauconnier, G., 7
Fox, C., 5, 6, 115, 117, 123,
143, 165, 170, 172, 174
van Fraassen, B., 126, 176
Frege, G., 6, 19, 115, 126, 132,
140, 166

Gabbay, D., 47
Gärdenfors, P., 47
Galileo, 44
Galton, A., 107, 109
Gamut, L., 236, 238
Gazdar, G., 191, 238
Gierz, G., 47
Gil, D., 24, 47, 48
Gillon, B., 3, 17, 33, 44, 48,
128, 174, 240, 248,

253, 268–271, 273,
275, 276, 280, 281,
296, 305, 312, 318,
347, 348, 364
Goodman, N., 50, 136, 175
Grätzer, G., 48
Grandy, R., 48
Griffith, J., 16
Groenendijk, J., 48, 278
Gross, M., 337
Gruber, J., 300, 317, 318
Guarino, N., 27, 48
Guenthner, F., 47
Gupta, A., 48, 317, 318

Halmos, P., 48, 168, 174
Hamm, F., 235
Hauenschild, C., 235
Hausser, R., 20, 48
Hazen, A., 236, 238
Hedtstück, U., 45
Heim, I., 48, 118, 174
Hendry, H., 48
Henkin, L., 25
Herzog, O., 48
Higginbotham, J., 48, 128, 174,
347, 364
Hindley, R., 133, 174
Hinrichs, E., 24, 48
Hintikka, J., 48, 130, 174, 285,
318
Hobbs, J., 51, 108, 110
Hoeksema, J., 29, 31, 48, 128,
174, 235–238, 252,
273, 281, 358, 359, 364
Hoepelman, J., 108, 110, 151,
156, 157, 171, 173, 174
de Hoop, H., 236–238
Hoppenbrouwers, G., 186, 187,
238
Hughes, G., 168, 174

Jackendoff, R., 300, 317, 318
Janssen, T., 48

Kadmon, N., 48
Kamp, H., 4, 17, 20, 24, 25, 39,
    49, 58, 95, 107, 108,
    110, 115, 118, 147,
    170–172, 175, 235,
    340, 358, 364
Kanazawa, M., 49
Kas, M., 235, 236, 238
Keenan, E., 7, 17, 49, 235, 236,
    238, 284, 318
Keisler, H., 237
Kimball, J., 49
Klein, E., 108, 111
Kolb, H., 16
Kracht, M., 315
Krifka, M., 4, 17, 24, 26, 30, 31,
    49, 65, 66, 80, 83, 96,
    108, 110, 235, 236,
    238, 315, 317, 318
Kripke, S., 130, 175
Kürschner, W., 236, 238

Ladusaw, W., 7, 235, 236, 238,
    364
Landman, F., 2, 3, 5, 17, 24,
    28–30, 43, 49, 107,
    110, 120–122, 126,
    128, 129, 151, 156,
    162, 171, 175, 278,
    281, 284, 318
Langendoen, T., 49
Lasersohn, P., 24, 49, 50, 146,
    147, 172, 175, 242,
    268, 269, 271, 273,
    275, 281, 316, 318
Lasnik, H., 48
Laycock, H., 50
Lehmann, C., 53

Lejewski, C., 50
Leonard, H., 50, 136, 175
Leśniewski, S., 50
Lewis, D., 26, 27, 50, 119, 175
Lightfoot, D., 354, 364
Link, G., 1–4, 8, 9, 14–17, 20,
    22–25, 27, 29, 32, 34,
    36, 40, 44, 50, 51, 96,
    107, 110, 114, 115,
    126, 128, 130, 135,
    137, 142, 165, 173,
    175, 240, 243–254,
    259, 261, 262, 264,
    266–268, 276, 277,
    279–281, 290, 299,
    312, 314, 315, 318,
    339, 340, 345–348,
    351, 353, 355, 358,
    363–365
Löbner, S., 51, 107, 110
Lønning, J., 2, 3, 17, 20, 22, 24,
    25, 28, 32–34, 43, 44,
    51, 121, 125, 129, 130,
    137, 142, 165, 171,
    173, 175, 240, 251,
    264, 265, 267, 268,
    273, 275, 278–282,
    298, 316, 319
Lorimer, D., 24, 51
Luschei, E., 51

Martin, R., 51
Martin-Löf, P., 164, 175
Massey, G., 20, 51
May, R., 48
ter Meulen, A., 45, 53, 54, 281
Michaux, C., 12–14, 321, 333,
    337
Milner, J., 323, 325, 337
Milsark, G., 236, 238
Mithun, M., 47

Moens, M., 108–110
Moerdijk, I., 284, 318
Moltmann, F., 51
Montague, R., 20, 32, 51, 118,
      125, 132, 143, 146,
      160, 172, 175, 283, 284
Moore, R., 51
Moravcsik, J., 47, 48, 51, 122,
      123, 175

Oehrle, R., 235
Ogihara, T., 108, 110
Ojeda, A., 51, 316, 319
Orey, S., 24, 51, 137, 175
van Os, C., 236, 238

Parsons, T., 51, 52, 121, 122,
      126, 163, 176
Partee, B., 52, 55, 109, 130, 176
Pelletier, F., 16, 43, 46, 52
Peres, J., 14, 15, 364, 365
Peters, S., 132, 174
Piñón, C., 49
Platzack, C., 56, 110
Poli, R., 27, 48
Pollard, S., 52
Priestley, H., 47
Pullum, G., 191, 238

Quine, W., 19, 20, 52, 121, 171,
      176, 236, 239

Ranta, A., 164, 176
Reddig–Siekmann, C., 27, 44
Reinhart, T., 284, 319
Rescher, N., 52
Resnik, M., 52
Reyle, U., 4, 17, 20, 24, 25, 39,
      49, 56, 58, 95, 105,
      107, 108, 110, 111,
      118, 175, 340, 364

Roberts, C., 36, 52, 128, 176,
      240, 251, 260, 279,
      280, 282, 304, 319,
      357, 365
Rodman, R., 52
Roeper, P., 24, 52, 121, 129,
      156, 158, 171, 176
Rollinger, C., 45, 48
Rooth, M., 26, 52, 130, 176,
      236, 239
Russell, B., 6, 52, 126, 172

Sánchez Valencia, v., 235
Scha, R., 8, 9, 12, 17, 20, 32,
      33, 36, 52, 103, 108,
      111, 239, 240, 243,
      246–252, 257, 261,
      266, 268, 274–278,
      282, 285, 290, 299,
      310–312, 315, 319,
      347, 358, 362, 363, 365
Schein, B., 2, 17, 27, 53, 310,
      315
Schubert, L., 52
Schütze, H., 27, 51, 53, 107,
      110, 111
Schwarz, S., 16
Schwarze, C., 45
Schwarzschild, R., 2, 17, 30, 31,
      53, 128, 162, 164, 165,
      176, 239, 282
Scott, D., 165, 176
Seiler, H., 53
Seldin, J., 133, 174
Seuren, P., 235–237, 239
Shapiro, S., 53
Sharvy, R., 53
Sher, G., 252, 282
Shoham, Y., 108, 111
Sikorski, R., 53, 236, 239
Simons, P., 53

INDEX OF NAMES

Slomson, A., 237
Smith, B., 53
Smith-Stark, C., 53
Smolka, G., 107, 111
Spaan, M., 252, 282
Stallard, D., 52, 111
Stavi, Y., 49
von Stechow, A., 45, 53
Steedman, M., 108, 110
Steinitz, R., 55, 111
Sternefeld, W., 16
Stokhof, M., 48, 53, 278
Stoll, R., 236, 237, 239
Stone, M., 236, 239
Strawson, P., 146, 147, 172, 176
Sundholm, G., 164, 176
Suppes, P., 48
Szabolcsi, A., 235

Torenvliet, L., 53
Turner, R., 115, 126, 130, 143, 146, 149, 164, 170, 172, 174, 176

Veltman, F., 48, 49, 278
Vendler, Z., 4, 17, 55, 57, 111
Verkuyl, H., 4, 10–12, 16–18, 35, 54, 56, 108, 111, 239, 243, 272–274, 278, 280, 282, 283, 285, 290, 291, 296, 299, 300, 302, 303, 306, 308, 310–312, 314–317, 319

Wald, J., 54
Wall, R., 132, 174
Ware, R., 54
Webber, B., 54
Wesche, B., 235
Westerståhl, D., 7, 17, 54, 317, 319

van der Wouden, T., 235, 236, 239
Wunderlich, D., 53

Zaefferer, D., 23, 43, 54, 235
Zaenen, A., 235
Zeevat, H., 108, 111
Zemach, E., 54
Zwarts, F., 7, 8, 235–237, 239
Zwarts, J., 315

Studies in Linguistics and Philosophy

1. H. Hiż (ed.): *Questions.* 1978   ISBN 90-277-0813-4; Pb: 90-277-1035-X
2. W. S. Cooper: *Foundations of Logico-Linguistics.* A Unified Theory of Information, Language, and Logic. 1978   ISBN 90-277-0864-9; Pb: 90-277-0876-2
3. A. Margalit (ed.): *Meaning and Use.* 1979   ISBN 90-277-0888-6
4. F. Guenthner and S.J. Schmidt (eds.): *Formal Semantics and Pragmatics for Natural Languages.* 1979   ISBN 90-277-0778-2; Pb: 90-277-0930-0
5. E. Saarinen (ed.): *Game-Theoretical Semantics.* Essays on Semantics by Hintikka, Carlson, Peacocke, Rantala, and Saarinen. 1979   ISBN 90-277-0918-1
6. F.J. Pelletier (ed.): *Mass Terms: Some Philosophical Problems.* 1979   ISBN 90-277-0931-9
7. D. R. Dowty: *Word Meaning and Montague Grammar.* The Semantics of Verbs and Times in Generative Semantics and in Montague's PTQ. 1979   ISBN 90-277-1008-2; Pb: 90-277-1009-0
8. A. F. Freed: *The Semantics of English Aspectual Complementation.* 1979   ISBN 90-277-1010-4; Pb: 90-277-1011-2
9. J. McCloskey: *Transformational Syntax and Model Theoretic Semantics.* A Case Study in Modern Irish. 1979   ISBN 90-277-1025-2; Pb: 90-277-1026-0
10. J. R. Searle, F. Kiefer and M. Bierwisch (eds.): *Speech Act Theory and Pragmatics.* 1980   ISBN 90-277-1043-0; Pb: 90-277-1045-7
11. D. R. Dowty, R. E. Wall and S. Peters: *Introduction to Montague Semantics.* 1981; 5th printing 1987   ISBN 90-277-1141-0; Pb: 90-277-1142-9
12. F. Heny (ed.): *Ambiguities in Intensional Contexts.* 1981   ISBN 90-277-1167-4; Pb: 90-277-1168-2
13. W. Klein and W. Levelt (eds.): *Crossing the Boundaries in Linguistics.* Studies Presented to Manfred Bierwisch. 1981   ISBN 90-277-1259-X
14. Z. S. Harris: *Papers on Syntax.* Edited by H. Hiż. 1981   ISBN 90-277-1266-0; Pb: 90-277-1267-0
15. P. Jacobson and G. K. Pullum (eds.): *The Nature of Syntactic Representation.* 1982   ISBN 90-277-1289-1; Pb: 90-277-1290-5
16. S. Peters and E. Saarinen (eds.): *Processes, Beliefs, and Questions.* Essays on Formal Semantics of Natural Language and Natural Language Processing. 1982   ISBN 90-277-1314-6
17. L. Carlson: *Dialogue Games.* An Approach to Discourse Analysis. 1983; 2nd printing 1985   ISBN 90-277-1455-X; Pb: 90-277-1951-9
18. L. Vaina and J. Hintikka (eds.): *Cognitive Constraints on Communication.* Representation and Processes. 1984; 2nd printing 1985   ISBN 90-277-1456-8; Pb: 90-277-1949-7
19. F. Heny and B. Richards (eds.): *Linguistic Categories: Auxiliaries and Related Puzzles.* Volume I: Categories. 1983   ISBN 90-277-1478-9
20. F. Heny and B. Richards (eds.): *Linguistic Categories: Auxiliaries and Related Puzzles.* Volume II: The Scope, Order, and Distribution of English Auxiliary Verbs. 1983   ISBN 90-277-1479-7
21. R. Cooper: *Quantification and Syntactic Theory.* 1983   ISBN 90-277-1484-3

Volumes 1–26 formerly published under the Series Title: Synthese Language Library.

Studies in Linguistics and Philosophy

22. J. Hintikka (in collaboration with J. Kulas): *The Game of Language*. Studies in Game-Theoretical Semantics and Its Applications. 1983; 2nd printing 1985
ISBN 90-277-1687-0; Pb: 90-277-1950-0
23. E. L. Keenan and L. M. Faltz: *Boolean Semantics for Natural Language*. 1985
ISBN 90-277-1768-0; Pb: 90-277-1842-3
24. V. Raskin: *Semantic Mechanisms of Humor*. 1985
ISBN 90-277-1821-0; Pb: 90-277-1891-1
25. G. T. Stump: *The Semantic Variability of Absolute Constructions*. 1985
ISBN 90-277-1895-4; Pb: 90-277-1896-2
26. J. Hintikka and J. Kulas: *Anaphora and Definite Descriptions*. Two Applications of Game-Theoretical Semantics. 1985   ISBN 90-277-2055-X; Pb: 90-277-2056-8
27. E. Engdahl: *Constituent Questions*. The Syntax and Semantics of Questions with Special Reference to Swedish. 1986   ISBN 90-277-1954-3; Pb: 90-277-1955-1
28. M. J. Cresswell: *Adverbial Modification*. Interval Semantics and Its Rivals. 1985
ISBN 90-277-2059-2; Pb: 90-277-2060-6
29. J. van Benthem: *Essays in Logical Semantics* 1986
ISBN 90-277-2091-6; Pb: 90-277-2092-4
30. B. H. Partee, A. ter Meulen and R. E. Wall: *Mathematical Methods in Linguistics*. 1990; Corrected second printing of the first edition 1993
ISBN 90-277-2244-7; Pb: 90-277-2245-5
31. P. Gärdenfors (ed.): *Generalized Quantifiers*. Linguistic and Logical Approaches. 1987
ISBN 1-55608-017-4
32. R. T. Oehrle, E. Bach and D. Wheeler (eds.): *Categorial Grammars and Natural Language Structures*. 1988   ISBN 1-55608-030-1; Pb: 1-55608-031-X
33. W. J. Savitch, E. Bach, W. Marsh and G. Safran-Naveh (eds.): *The Formal Complexity of Natural Language*. 1987   ISBN 1-55608-046-8; Pb: 1-55608-047-6
34. J. E. Fenstad, P.-K. Halvorsen, T. Langholm and J. van Benthem: *Situations, Language and Logic*. 1987   ISBN 1-55608-048-4; Pb: 1-55608-049-2
35. U. Reyle and C. Rohrer (eds.): *Natural Language Parsing and Linguistic Theories*. 1988   ISBN 1-55608-055-7; Pb: 1-55608-056-5
36. M. J. Cresswell: *Semantical Essays*. Possible Worlds and Their Rivals. 1988
ISBN 1-55608-061-1
37. T. Nishigauchi: *Quantification in the Theory of Grammar*. 1990
ISBN 0-7923-0643-0; Pb: 0-7923-0644-9
38. G. Chierchia, B.H. Partee and R. Turner (eds.): *Properties, Types and Meaning*. Volume I: Foundational Issues. 1989   ISBN 1-55608-067-0; Pb: 1-55608-068-9
39. G. Chierchia, B.H. Partee and R. Turner (eds.): *Properties, Types and Meaning*. Volume II: Semantic Issues. 1989   ISBN 1-55608-069-7; Pb: 1-55608-070-0
Set ISBN (Vol. I + II) 1-55608-088-3; Pb: 1-55608-089-1
40. C.T.J. Huang and R. May (eds.): *Logical Structure and Linguistic Structure*. Cross-Linguistic Perspectives. 1991   ISBN 0-7923-0914-6; Pb: 0-7923-1636-3
41. M.J. Cresswell: *Entities and Indices*. 1990   ISBN 0-7923-0966-9; Pb: 0-7923-0967-7
42. H. Kamp and U. Reyle: *From Discourse to Logic*. Introduction to Modeltheoretic Semantics of Natural Language, Formal Logic and Discourse Representation Theory. 1993   ISBN 0-7923-2403-X; Student edition: 0-7923-1028-4

Studies in Linguistics and Philosophy

43. C.S. Smith: *The Parameter of Aspect.* (Second Edition). 1997
    ISBN 0-7923-4657-2; Pb 0-7923-4659-9
44. R.C. Berwick (ed.): *Principle-Based Parsing.* Computation and Psycholinguistics. 1991
    ISBN 0-7923-1173-6; Pb: 0-7923-1637-1
45. F. Landman: *Structures for Semantics.* 1991   ISBN 0-7923-1239-2; Pb: 0-7923-1240-6
46. M. Siderits: *Indian Philosophy of Language.* 1991   ISBN 0-7923-1262-7
47. C. Jones: *Purpose Clauses.* 1991   ISBN 0-7923-1400-X
48. R.K. Larson, S. Iatridou, U. Lahiri and J. Higginbotham (eds.): *Control and Grammar.* 1992   ISBN 0-7923-1692-4
49. J. Pustejovsky (ed.): *Semantics and the Lexicon.* 1993
    ISBN 0-7923-1963-X; Pb: 0-7923-2386-6
50. N. Asher: *Reference to Abstract Objects in Discourse.* 1993   ISBN 0-7923-2242-8
51. A. Zucchi: *The Language of Propositions and Events.* Issues in the Syntax and the Semantics of Nominalization. 1993   ISBN 0-7923-2437-4
52. C.L. Tenny: *Aspectual Roles and the Syntax-Semantics Interface.* 1994
    ISBN 0-7923-2863-9; Pb: 0-7923-2907-4
53. W.G. Lycan: *Modality and Meaning.* 1994   ISBN 0-7923-3006-4; Pb: 0-7923-3007-2
54. E. Bach, E. Jelinek, A. Kratzer and B.H. Partee (eds.): *Quantification in Natural Languages.* 1995
    ISBN Vol. I: 0-7923-3128-1; Vol. II: 0-7923-3351-9; set: 0-7923-3352-7;
    Student edition: 0-7923-3129-X
55. P. Lasersohn: *Plurality, Conjunction and Events.* 1995   ISBN 0-7923-3238-5
56. M. Pinkal: *Logic and Lexicon.* The Semantics of the Indefinite. 1995
    ISBN 0-7923-3387-X
57. P. Øhrstrøm and P.F.V. Hasle: *Temporal Logic.* From Ancient Ideas to Artificial Intelligence. 1995   ISBN 0-7923-3586-4
58. T. Ogihara: *Tense, Attitudes, and Scope.* 1996   ISBN 0-7923-3801-4
59. I. Comorovski: *Interrogative Phrases and the Syntax-Semantics Interface.* 1996
    ISBN 0-7923-3804-9
60. M.J. Cresswell: *Semantic Indexicality.* 1996   ISBN 0-7923-3914-2
61. R. Schwarzschild: *Pluralities.* 1996   ISBN 0-7923-4007-8
62. V. Dayal: *Locality in WH Quantification.* Questions and Relative Clauses in Hindi. 1996   ISBN 0-7923-4099-X
63. P. Merlo: *Parsing with Principles and Classes of Information.* 1996
    ISBN 0-7923-4103-1
64. J. Ross: *The Semantics of Media.* 1997   ISBN 0-7923-4389-1
65. A. Szabolcsi (ed.): *Ways of Scope Taking.* 1997
    ISBN 0-7923-4446-4; Pb: 0-7923-4451-0
66. P.L. Peterson: *Fact Proposition Event.* 1997   ISBN 0-7923-4568-1
67. G. Păun: *Marcus Contextual Grammars.* 1997   ISBN 0-7923-4783-8
68. T. Gunji and K. Hasida (eds.): *Topics in Constraint-Based Grammar of Japanese.* 1998
    ISBN 0-7923-4836-2
69. F. Hamm and E. Hinrichs (eds.): *Plurality and Quantification.* 1998
    ISBN 0-7923-4841-9

Further information about our publications on *Linguistics* is available on request.

Kluwer Academic Publishers – Dordrecht / Boston / London